TOWARD A CRITICAL SOCIOLOGY

TOWARD A
CRITICAL SOCIOLOGY

NORMAN BIRNBAUM

NEW YORK
Oxford University Press
LONDON   OXFORD   NEW YORK

FOR HENRI LEFEBVRE

OXFORD UNIVERSITY PRESS

London   Oxford   New York
Glasgow   Toronto   Melbourne   Wellington
Cape Town   Ibadan   Nairobi   Dar es Salaam   Lusaka   Addis Ababa
Delhi   Bombay   Calcutta   Madras   Karachi   Lahore   Dacca
Kuala Lumpur   Singapore   Hong Kong   Tokyo

PREFACE

An author publishing a set of essays written for different publics, in different countries, over the past fifteen years has awk-
ward choices to make. He may claim a profound inner unity,
nay, progression in his work—and devise a preface to sustain
the claim, whether or not the texts in question can do so.
Struck by the diversity and datedness of the pieces, he may
prefer to revise them. I was greatly tempted, upon reviewing
the collection, to re-write much of it. Had I done so, no doubt
I would have spent the better part of two years at the task. In
offering these essays substantially unaltered, I ask for something other than indulgence for perfectionism resisted. The
very unevenness of the book's parts, the obvious marks the
passage of time has inflicted upon some of these, may be
thought of as records of the intellectual situation between
1954, when the first was written, and 1970, when the last were
prepared.

I have employed the term "intellectual situation" and not
something like, "development of sociology" to describe the
context of these writings. Most were addressed to a public
broader than my colleagues in sociology proper. An academic
discipline (and sociology is one with exceedingly ill-defined
boundaries) is but one mode of apprehending reality. We hear
much of a contemporary knowledge explosion, of an expanding intellectual universe. It is more accurate to think of a
knowledge implosion. Our struggles to depict and master
reality erode the distinctions between areas and types of inquiry. Shifts of emphasis and perspective in the social sciences
have made ambiguous the notion of fact itself. An irreducible

philosophical component, and political judgments, have once again become prominent in social inquiry. The title, *Toward a Critical Sociology,* bespeaks an open avowal of a critical intention with respect to society, an element at least as prominent in these essays as description. The most severely technical of the essays, perhaps, are those in the initial section on *Social Theory.* While these focus on the critical component in social thought, the contributions in the section on *The Sociology of Sociology* extend the discussion to sociology's function in society. The themes are related but, for better or for worse, distinct.

The essays are arranged thematically, but of course they were written in particular cultural and political settings. Perhaps a word on these contexts is in order. Some originated in England, where I taught at the London School of Economics and Political Science and later at Nuffield College of Oxford University. The essay on "Monarchs and Sociologists" [1] is so polemical that I hesitated to reprint it. I decided to do so, not least to show that the critique of functionalism did not quite begin yesterday. The early debate on functionalism was, however, part of a larger controversy. The decade 1950–1960 was dominated, in the English-speaking world, by a variety of conservative schools of thought. Michael Oakeshott and Karl Popper were my respected senior colleagues at the London School of Economics. Each, if in very different ways, challenged the view that critical reason could assume an emancipatory function. The longish essay on British culture and politics, "Great Britain: The Reactive Revolt," is amongst other things a series of reflections on that decade in Britain. The essay also shows the influence of my immersion, from 1957 onward, in the original new left. The historical study of sixteenth century Zurich seems quite remote from these con-

---

1. The essay is a reply to Edward Shils and M. Michael Young, "The Meaning of the Coronation," *The Sociological Review,* Volume 1, No. 2, 1953. The essay by Messrs. Shils and Young was also reproduced in S. M. Lipset and N. Smelser (editors), *Sociology: The Progress of a Decade,* Englewood Cliffs: Prentice-Hall, 1961.

cerns, but it was written when I had the good fortune to be associated with the historians of the *Past and Present* group. The controversy over the role of Protestantism in the origins of capitalism was not entirely without political undertones. If Protestantism had no very profound connections with capitalism, then history was indeed one damned thing after another. In that case, no interpretation of society which insisted on its fundamental structural elements was likely to be possible. If, on the other hand, Protestantism could be shown to have had a causal role in the genesis of capitalism, the Marxist interpretation of society could be dealt a severe—if not necessarily fatal—blow. My own essay, which argues for the capitalist origins of early Protestantism in Zurich, owed much to the methodological inspiration of historians like Eric Hobsbawm, who combined large interpretation with painstaking attention to detail.

The treatment of the Amsterdam Sociological Congress of 1956 (which preceded the Suez crisis and the Soviet invasion of Hungary but followed Khrushchev's famous speech on Stalin) points to yet another context. England was but one hour, by air, from a very different world. From England, I continued and deepened that apprenticeship in French and German thought I had begun, to be sure, before ever leaving America for Europe. Sociology on the continent had two characteristics not impressed upon it in the English-speaking world. Firstly, it was conceived as part of a larger philosophical enterprise, the critique of historical existence. Secondly, it was not disassociated from the larger society's struggles for power. Many of my continental friends were politically engaged—or, at any rate, exceedingly aware of the political implications of their thought. My effort to escape the restrictions of an arbitrarily circumscribed empiricism, in America and England, heightened the attractions of the continent: I developed a concern with Marxism which has pervaded my ventures in social theory ever since. "Science, Ideology, and Dialogue," on the Amsterdam congress of 1956, begins a section which ends with a description of the scholarly gathering at Varna, in Bulgaria, in 1970. A dogmatized Marxism, four-teen years after the state socialist regimes re-entered interna-tional scholarly discussion, still confronted an open one. The document which shows how much I assimilated in Europe was written after my return to the United States (if actually put to paper appropriately enough, in the sixth *arrondissement* of Paris): "The Crisis in Marxist Sociology" bespeaks the influ-ence of Paris, of Frankfurt, and of Zagreb. I have found it diffi-cult to think of Marxism exclusively as an attempt to construct a rigorous theory of history. The account of a journey to East-ern Europe in 1965 and the report on the Prague conference on religion in 1966 ask if Marxism has not served as a secular heir of religion. These were themes tackled systematically in 1962 in the essay on "The Sociological Study of Ideology, 1940–1960," which, in the form of a review of the literature, attempted an assessment of the utility of the concept of ideol-ogy.[2]

I returned to full-time academic work in the United States in 1966. The American political consensus had broken down, and in the academy, the domination of a consensual social sci-ence (poorly disguised as "behavioristic" or "empirical") was at an end. I had kept in close touch with America during my long period of European residence: it was still a surprise to experience the transformation of the *avant-garde* thought of the 1950's into the commonplaces of the 1960's. The negative critique of American society and of an apologetic social sci-ence hardly required reiteration (although it received it). What was needed was the development of a new social theory which could provide the conceptual elements of a new poli-tics. I did not conceive of the relationship between the two as unmediated: there is a difference between the eradication of the boundaries between thought and action—a project futile,

2. The lengthy treatment of ideology in essay form was followed, in the origi-nal, by a substantial annotated bibliography and the whole was published in 1962 as Volume 9, No. 2, 1960, of *Current Sociology*.

because impossible—and the effort to deepen thought. That effort, ostensibly remote from the daily stuff of politics, may in the end have profound political consequences. Necessity, meanwhile, generated its own virtue: after fourteen years in Europe, I found that the only mode in which I could work was the attempt to synthesize European thought and American realities. Western European Marxism was at its most penetrating where it had become part of a national intellectual patrimony: the tasks of a critical social theory in America had to begin with the adumbration of our historical peculiarities.[3]

The four final essays in the section entitled *Politics* were written in 1970, as was the report on the Varna congress. "On the Sociology of Current Social Research" and "Conservative Sociology" were written in 1969 and 1968, respectively. These seven essays represent an effort to move from the promulgation of new assumptions for a critical social theory to the practical task of refining (and amending) these assumptions in work concrete and historical. Reflecting on the entire collection of essays, I do see a series of progressions in them. From the initial attack on a consensual sociology, through the analysis of ideology, the collection concludes with an examination of the contemporary relationship between knowledge and power. From a theoretic consideration of the role of religion

3. The present volume is, of course, part of a larger discussion. See, in particular, Robert W. Friedrichs, *A Sociology of Sociology*, New York: Free Press, 1970, and Alvin W. Gouldner, *The Coming Crisis of Western Sociology*, New York: Basic Books, 1970. I also note with pleasure a translation of a recent work by Juergen Habermas (*Erkentniss und Interesse*, Frankfurt: Suhrkamp, 1968), *Knowledge and Human Interests*, Boston: Beacon Press, 1971. A recent contribution from Great Britain—if with a rather different perspective—is W. G. Runciman, *Sociology in Its Place*, New York: Cambridge University Press, 1970. From France, see René Lourau, *L'Analyse Institutionnelle*, Paris: Minuit, 1970. It would require an essay on the sociology of knowledge to explain why English-speaking, and especially American, sociologists have virtually ignored Georges Gurvitch's important body of work. He raised many of these issues in profound form in 1950 with his *La Vocation actuelle de la sociologie* (Volume I, 3rd edition, Paris: Presses Universitaires de France, 1963; Volume II, 2nd Edition, Paris: Presses Universitaires de France, 1963.)

(and conceptions of transcendence, generally) in history, the essays move on to take up the religious status of socialism. Beginning with the injunction to study society as a totality, the book concludes by turning to some specific components of the movement of contemporary history: new classes and new modes of domination.

These essays, then, reflect the author's rather diverse experience. I note that six of the seventeen were written at Amherst College, whose faculty I joined in 1968 after completing my last book, *The Crisis of Industrial Society*. Amherst has provided a setting at once stimulating and supportive. Its physician President, Calvin Hastings Plimpton, will read these lines in his retirement from the leadership of the College. I trust he knows how much his scholar-teachers owe to the College.

Every scholar is indebted to the institutions which provided him with the means to pursue his inquiries, and it is my pleasant duty to record my own thanks in this respect. The essays collected in the volume derive from research supported at various times by The Social Science Research Council; The Central Research Fund of the University of London; The Rockefeller Foundation; Nuffield College of Oxford University; The Rabinowitz Foundation; The Ford Foundation; the U.S. Office of Education of the Department of Health, Education, and Welfare; the American Council of Learned Societies.

Finally I have dedicated the volume to my friend Henri Lefebvre. We were neighbors and colleagues for but one year at Strasbourg, and he contributed to making it a full one. His humorous appreciation of the human situation, his intellectual venturesomeness, his mastery of the western tradition, make of Henri Lefebvre a presence of an unforgettable kind. May he think these pages not entirely unworthy of our common enterprise.

N. B.

AMHERST, MAY 1971

ACKNOWLEDGMENTS

The author and publishers wish to thank the following for permission to reprint essays originally published under their auspices.

Basil Blackwell, Publisher, for "The Sociological Analysis of Ideology (1940–1960)," published as part of *Current Sociology*, Volume 9, No. 2, 1960 (in 1962).

The Sociological Review, for "Monarchs and Sociologists: A Reply to Professor Shils and Mr. Young," *The Sociological Review*, Volume 3, (N.S.), No. 1, 1955.

The Berkeley Journal of Sociology, for "Conservative Sociology," *Berkeley Journal of Sociology*, Volume 13, 1968.

Social Research, for "The Crisis in Marxist Sociology," *Social Research*, Volume 35, No. 2, 1968.

Archives de Sociologie des Religions, for "The Zwinglian Reformation in Zurich," *Archives de Sociologie des Religions*, No. 2, 1959.

Commentary, for "Eastern Europe and the Death of God," *Commentary*, Volume 44, No. 1, 1967, and "Science, Ideology and Dialogue: The Amsterdam Sociological Congress," *Commentary*, Volume 22, No. 6, 1956.

The Twentieth Century, for "Friends and Enemies," *Twentieth Century*, No. 999, 1960.

Nymphenburger Verlagshandlung for "On the Sociology of Current Social Research," originally published as "Kunftige Grundlagen," in Willy Hochkeppel, Theodor W. Adorno *et al.*, *Soziologie Zwischen Theorie und Empire*, Munich, 1970.

Partisan Review, for "A Socio-Theater of the Absurd: A World Congress of Sociology," published as "Circus at Varna," *Partisan Review*, Volume 38, No. 1, 1971.

Acknowledgments

Crowell-Collier Incorporated for "Riesman's Image of Politics," published in S. M. Lipset and L. Loewenthal (editors), *Culture and Social Character,* Copyright The Free Press of Glencoe, 1962.

John Wiley and Sons for "Great Britain: the Reactive Revolt," published in Morton Kaplan (editor), *The Revolution in World Politics,* New York, Copyright John Wiley and Sons, Inc., 1962.

Dissent, for "A Journey to Eastern Europe, 1965," published as "Journey to Eastern Europe," *Dissent,* May–June 1967.

The Massachusetts Review for "The Making of a Counter-Culture," *The Massachusetts Review,* Volume 11, No. 1, 1970.

International Arts and Sciences Press Inc., for "Is There a Post-Industrial Revolution?," *Social Policy,* Volume 1, No. 2, 1970.

Basic Books Incorporated, for "The Problem of a Knowledge Elite," a chapter appearing in *Social Development, Critical Perspectives* edited by Manfred Stanley, Copyright 1971 by Basic Books, Inc. Publishers, New York, and The Massachusetts Review, for the same essay, published in *The Massachusetts Review,* Volume 12, No. 3, Summer 1971.

Author's Notes

The author wishes to thank June McCartney for her indispensable secretarial assistance, Ralphael Johnson for his work on the index, and Edith Kurzweil Birnbaum for sharing with the author the labors of proofreading. Sheldon Meyer and his colleagues at Oxford University Press, as always, lightened his burdens as the book neared completion.

CONTENTS

I. SOCIAL THEORY

The Sociological Study

of Ideology, 1940–1960

I. Introduction

The sociological study of ideology raises, in acute form, some of the most pressing problems of contemporary sociology. It entails a confrontation of Marxism, in its several versions, and "bourgeois" sociology. ("Bourgeois" sociology may be defined, of course, as sociology done by those "bourgeois" sociologists who do not happen to be Marxists.) The study of ideology, moreover, is at the intersection of the empirical and philosophical components of our discipline; it draws upon the resources of history, psychology, politics, and a number of cultural sciences, including linguistics.

The literature cited in the attached bibliography is diffuse. The range and number of the selections could have been extended with profit, but their representative character may enable us to draw a net balance for the development of the field since 1940. No neat calculation of gains and losses is possible, but certain salient tendencies do require discussion.

The very diffuseness of the literature points to the continuing problem of an adequate definition of the notion of ideology. For this essay, it suffices to assume that ideologies appear wherever systematic factual assertions about society contain (usually by implication) evaluations of the distribution of power in the societies in which these assertions are developed and propagated. We may suppose that a group generally accepts a view of society consonant with its interests; we need not think that ideologies are consciously fashioned to serve these interests or that groups are incapable of acting upon beliefs which appear to contradict these interests. Ideological elements, following this definition, are also found in aesthetic and moral statements about the human situation. It will be seen that this *aperçu* leaves open a number of questions to which no answers of a conclusive sort have yet been found: in particular, the question of the precise relationship (and inter-relationship) of ideas and social structure, and the vexed concept of interests. Just these questions, of course, are pre-occupations of the researches discussed in this text.

The sociological study of ideology, since 1940, may be described as follows. (1) Empirical and theoretical work have developed in disjointed fashion. However, some theories advanced one or two generations ago—particularly, but not exclusively, psychological theories—have been applied empirically. But, despite the important (if programmatic) work of Goldmann and Lévi-Strauss, there have been no definitive theoretical advances to compare with the work of Karl Mannheim. (2) A revival of Marxist analysis has occurred, after a long period of sterility not entirely explained by that convenient *mot,* Stalinism. The revival of Marxism has been most marked and productive in countries not under Marxist regimes, but has not been entirely absent—since 1953—in Communist countries. (In Yugoslavia, of course, the movement began much earlier.) Although there has been some new and valuable Marxist empirical work, it has as yet not precipitated fundamental changes in the received structure of Marxist analysis, although these may now follow. The renewal of Marxism is, in any case, little more than a decade old. (3) The enormous increase in our detailed knowledge of contemporary social structures which has accompanied the widespread utilization of the standard techniques of sociological research has not produced a concomitant enrichment of theory. Rather, some attempts have been made to adjust the scope of the theory of ideology to the limits set by these techniques. The resultant gain in precision is not entirely a compensation for this distortion of theoretical focus. Some recent work, however (that of Chinoy and Popitz, for instance), suggests that these techniques are not intrinsically atheoretical and that they will be used—increasingly—to deepen and not to restrict theoretical inquiry. (4) The techniques of analysis of the inner structure of ideology originally derived from neo-positivism have become less prominent. Recent contributions in this field have come from psychoanalysis, from the history of religions (the work on chiliasm begun by Troeltsch has been deepened by the anthropologists and historians) and from structural linguistics (as transmuted by Lévi-Strauss). (5) The notion of ideology, far from being confined to the writings of sociologists, has been utilized—increasingly—by historians, political scientists, and philosophers themselves. It has, indeed, become an element in political discourse. Thus, the recent announcement—which appears on many counts to be premature—of "the end of ideology" may be viewed as an attempt by a number of thinkers to present their own ideology as a factual version of the world.

An examination of the field since 1940 suggests that the discrepancy between empirical and theoretical developments in the study of ideology is an unusual one. It would be absurd to contrast the theoretical richness of the field (or, at any rate, its rich theoretical legacy as of 1940) with an alleged empirical barrenness. Rather, the difficulty is that theoretical and empirical riches have found no common denominator. This essay begins, perforce, with an account of the theoretical legacy as of 1940.

II. The Legacy

The beginning point of modern discussions of ideology remains the work of Karl Marx. A systematic treatment of his theory of ideology is not to be found in the past decade's extensive exegetical literature. Rubel's discussion of the problem, for instance, has a highly summary character. The last such attempt was made by Barth in 1945. It is true that Marx's references to the problem of ideology are distributed throughout his work, and that some of his general views have been absorbed into modern sociology to a greater rather than a lesser degree. But further discussion of his work on ideology is by no means superfluous. At different times Marx held different views of the problem, and at no point was his theory of ideology free of at least a tendency to self-contradiction. Many of the obscurities in the modern discussion of ideology may be due, in part, to an insufficient appreciation of the problematical nature of Marx's position (Barth has, quite correctly, emphasized this point).

Marx's concept of ideology is not, in the first instance, an empirical concept; it is a philosophical one. The Marxist notion of ideology can be understood only in terms of the connected notions of *alienation, mystification* and *reification.* Ideology is part of that general process of *alienation* by which the products of human activity assume a life of their own, and rule over the men who produce them. For Marx, the insistence on the autonomy of the state, in German bourgeois political theory, was a case of *mystification*—akin, precisely, to the thought processes of religion. *Mystification,* then, occurs when imaginary entities obscure the real relationships of human activity; this has its roots in turn in *reification*. The idea of *reification* is a generalization which finds concrete application in the more familiar notion of the fetichism of commodities. The world of things produced by men not only dominates them in an external fashion. It actually shapes their conscious and unconscious spiritual activity (a point developed much later in a remarkable piece of exegesis by Lukács). Men regard themselves and the relationships in which they are immersed (in itself, in Marxist terms, a reified image) as things.

These notions are far more metaphysical than the familiar assertion of a connection between base and superstructure—between productive forces, production relationships and the social structure which develops in their context (including, of course, ideology). The metaphysical categories of the Marxist analysis fuse with historical ones of the same sort, when it is asked: how can men be freed of their socially-induced spiritual blindness and distortion? The answer is that men cannot repossess their world until they recognize, in it, their own labours. Before this can occur, specific historical conditions have to be met. A specific human group, a class, must so develop that the conditions of its liberation from ideology are identical with the conditions of human liberation generally. This coincidence is possible for the proletariat because its attainment of vision coincides with its termination of its existence as a class. This historical conjuncture also gives us the assurance that Marxism itself escapes ideological distortion. Marxism encompasses and reflects the movement of history to the point where distortion becomes superfluous. Marxism is not simply the ideology of class, but a view of class relations in their entirety—possible only to a class ready to transcend the limitations of existence as a class. (This Marxist account of itself is not a substitute for a sociological analysis of the origin and development of Marxism, which has yet to be attempted on a major scale.) Of course, Marx was aware that the first Marxists were not proletarians—although he insisted upon how much he had learned from working-class socialism. He did hold that his system was made possible by changes in class relationships.

Marx, therefore, did not see history simply as a succession of ideologies. His doctrine of truth was a doctrine of historical movement, in which the anticipation or realization of change was produced by historical processes themselves. It is only in this framework that the empirical components of the Marxist theory of ideology make sense. These components may now be sketched as follows.

The division of manual and intellectual labour originally produces ideology, since it removes thought from its direct and visible connection with the process of production. The general division of labour in that process in time leads to the historical sequence of class societies. In these, the class which controls the means of production also generally controls the means of ideological production. The objective antagonism of classes may well be compatible, for shorter or longer periods, with a high degree of subjective consensus. In this, exploited classes accept the ideology of their exploiters, or at any rate fail to develop an ideological rejection of it in direct terms. The conception of base and superstructure generalizes these and other relationships. The forces of production constitute the base; these forces determine the relationships of production, and these in turn determine superstructure proper. Superstructure includes not only ideology but the state, law, status systems and a number of other phenomena—all of which react to changes in the base.

Upon any reading, the Marxist texts on ideology give rise to a host of questions. Barth has traced the inner evolution of Marxism in the lifetime of its founders—to the point where Engels approached what can be termed either a vulgar Marxist or a revisionist position (depending upon one's viewpoint).

Marx was influenced by the interest theory of the philosophical materialists of the French enlightenment, but the theory of interests remains one of the unspecified components in his system. Engels, and indeed Marx in some of his writings, made this theory far more empirical. The emphasis was on the production of ideology by social position and a doctrine of "false consciousness" was evolved to explain the inability of the working class to comprehend its objective interests; a distinction between long-term and short-term interests was introduced. The metaphysical or epistemological components of the doctrine of ideology receded—to be repressed, indeed, in later Social Democratic revisionism. The historical studies of Bernstein and Kautsky were directly derived from Engels' own empirical tendency—and this tendency was pronounced despite Engels' venture into the philosophy of natural science.

Two modern thinkers, in fact, continued the epistemological analysis of ideology begun by Marx. Lukács has often been termed the most original Marxist of our century. His *Geschichte und Klassenbewusstsein* (1923) is, in effect, a brilliant gloss on Marxism. The author utilizes the idea of totality for a critique of both bourgeois thought and Marxist revisionism. He declared flatly that the empirical analysis of class consciousness, or more accurately its absence, in capitalist societies was not the method of Marxism. If a leap forword into revolution was to be made, proletarian class consciousness would have to be volitional—not simply a reflecton of its situation but the will to change it. Lukács here, of course, repeated Lenin's dictum that class consciousness had, if necessary, to be brought to the proletariat from without. The empirical analysis of bourgeois society, in so far as it renounced the question of a total transformation of that society, practically constituted an ideological capitulation before it. The task of Marxist analysis was to keep the proletariat from accepting bourgeois thought, to show that the proletariat must intend a total revolution and could not therefore think in terms borrowed from the society it was to overthrow. To his credit, Lukács did not hesitate to depict Marxism itself as historically conditioned, its categories as derived from nineteenth-century capitalism. Marxism would of necessity be transformed, he held, by historical development— not least, the coming revolution.

This last, historical, strand in Lukács' thought was taken up by Mannheim and denuded of its specifically Marxist content. Mannheim's conception of a total ideology is, in fact, a sociological formulation of the familiar notion of the *Zeitgeist*. His distinction between ideologies and utopias, the latter opposing new ideas to existing systems of society and thought, the former justifying these systems, contains many difficulties. It does insert the problem of historical movement in the analysis of ideology. Mannheim's epistemological "relationism" is surely questionable, but it does have the merit of drawing one of the possible consequences of a sociology of knowledge; it faces up to the problem of a standard of truth by which ideologies may be judged. Mannheim's analyses of conservative and chiliastic thought, and his approach to the problem of generations, are but instances of the empirical work he did. His conception of "functional rationality" depicted the ideological concomitants of late capitalist social organization by combining Marx's method with Max Weber's historical categories. The first French translation of Mannheim's *Ideologie und Utopie* was done after the war; the English one dates from 1937. With Mannheim, however, systematic theoretical attempts to extend Marxism came to a stop. The recent work of Kolakowski and Lefebvre is to a large extent programmatic; Goldmann's valuable contribution remains to be generalized; Bloch's extraordinary *Prinzip Hoffnung* fits no category.

No discussion of modern Marxism can overlook, however, the singular contribution made by Gramsci. A refutation of mechanical interpretations of Marxism, a description of the incidence of various sorts of Marxism and systems of social thought generally, and an insistence on the importance of the internal properties of ideologies in social conflicts, are but some of the aspects of an *oeuvre* only now gaining attention outside Italy. Gramsci's *Prince,* besides containing a remarkable interpretation of Machiavelli, is an interesting formulation of the ideological pre-conditions of mass political action.

Marxism, despite its dominant position, is not alone in contributing to the modern analysis of ideology. An entire stream of thought, which we may term irrationalist, must also be considered. Marxism may be held the ultimate development of a "progressive" critique of bourgeois society; with not quite equal justification, irrationalism may be associated with conservativism. Its origins lie in the Restoration's attack on the doctrines of the French Revolution, in an insistence on the organic, traditional and essentially unreasoning components of consensus. By the end of the nineteenth century, of course, irrationalism had become a critique of bourgeois rationality; it would be inaccurate to characterize Nietzsche, Sorel or even Pareto as conservatives. They did not—explicitly—defend any particular social order. Rather, they insisted on the permanent role of unconscious and unreasoning elements in society and derided both schemes for rational social reconstruction and liberal apologetics. The doctrines of "the will to power" and "the slave morality"; the analysis of "myth"; the incredibly spirited and cynical conceptions of "residues" and "derivations," have entered the sociological tradition. They have done so, however, compressed and simplified into an heuristic precept: that the analysis of ideology which ignores elements of this sort must fail. These ideas, then, have hardly inspired any direct empirical work. (Crane Brinton did apply Paretian notions in his studies of the French Revolution, but these did not add much to a skilled historian's approach.) The *via regis* for the entry of the unconscious into this area of sociology was provided by psycho-analysis, to which we may now turn.

Three sorts of contribution to the analysis of ideology have been made by psycho-analysis. (1) Freudian social theory, typified in *Totem and Taboo*, was psycho-analysis as applied by its creator and his colleagues to social phenomena. (2) Psycho-analytic revisionism, which united such disparate figures as Fromm, Horney and Reich, attempted to modify certain classical Freudian postulates. In particular, the revisionists insisted on greater systematic emphasis upon the social context of psychological function. (3) Finally, a number of scholars from without psycho-analysis—from positions as diverse as academic cultural anthropology and Marxism—extracted what they found most relevant from psycho-analysis. They applied it not to the study of personality formation alone but to inquiries into cultural values and political phenomena. Their results, it should be added, did not invariably support revisionist hypotheses.

Indeed, the revisionist critique of the alleged biologicism of Freud has not been entirely tenable. *Totem and Taboo*, frequently disparaged, is susceptible of a contemporary reading as a "functional" analysis of authority, ritual and the symbolic components of social systems. The analysis of dreams, with its distinction between primary and secondary processes, is a model for the analysis of the internal structure of ideologies. Later developments in classical psycho-analysis, in particular its emphasis on the ego and the mechanisms of defence, equally provide models for the psychological processes involved in the formation and modification of ideologies.

The revisionist emphasis on the importance of cultural and social factors in the development of character structure, upon examination, entails a quantitative and not a qualitative modification of psycho-analysis. The usual Freudian account of personality can be articulated with a sociological analysis without much difficulty—as the works of thinkers as divergent as Marcuse, Mills, Parsons and Sartre seem to suggest. Much of revisionism has concentrated on neurosis in modern industrial society, on the disorders held implied by its standardization of social roles and their consequences for personality. The revisionists, in effect, have specified the types of social conflict which impinge on the classically described mechanisms of personality formation and function. The major revisionist attempt to deal with ideology, Fromm's work on early Christianity, the Reformation and totalitarianism, tended to rely on explanations which, far from positing variability in psychological mechanisms, assumed that these were stable and attributed primacy to the variable historical factors working upon them.

Those social scientists who have used psycho-analysis eclectically, because they were not concerned with matters of doctrine, have had a certain freedom of intellectual experimentation. They have increased our knowledge of the psychological bases of ideology. In particular, the connection between total institutional context, socialization and ideology has been explored. Erikson's studies of personal identity, meanwhile, have brought the discussion full circle. Personal identity, or the dangers to it, is now a recurrent theme in the clinical literature of psycho-analysis. Erikson has used this notion to study the role of value and ideology in the integration of the personality, in a number of societies. (Meanwhile, our knowledge of the unconscious meaning of witchcraft and other rituals, and the belief systems accompanying them, has deepened our understanding of ideology.)

It should not be thought that, whilst Marxism and irrationalism had philosophical components, Freudianism derives from a purely clinical science. Freud was greatly influenced by the philosophical materialism and evolutionary doctrine so important during his formative years. This great destroyer of bourgeois self-confidence maintained to the last his devotion to the ideal of an objective science. His examination of the unconscious continued and deepened the anthropological analysis of religion, custom, and myth, begun in England—notably by Spencer and Tylor.

It is interesting that the most self-confident of all the European middle classes should have produced scholars who insisted on the importance of the study of primitive, or exotic, forms of consciousness. These were often depicted as premature, confused, and inadequate anticipations of science. The early British anthropologists were by no means as uncritically intellectualist in their views of the human psyche as is sometimes made out (the mention of Frazer alone forbids that simplification), but the major tendency is unmistakable. They were not primarily concerned with political ideologies—although Spencer's picture of social and intellectual evolution did place liberalism at the climax of the process. Despite the intellectualist tendencies of early anthropology, it did develop the evolutionary concept of adaptation. Later, as we shall see, behaviourism put this notion to a variety of uses which, by drawing upon hypotheses suggested by some of their work, transcended the framework used by the early anthropologists.

At this point, we may turn to neo-positivism. Like behaviourism, it was a movement which developed only when the cultured elite of late capitalist society lost faith in the received values of liberalism. Neo-positivism in metaphysics and morals may be deemed the extension, into the late nineteenth and early twentieth centuries, of that faith in science which was originally characteristic of Enlightenment thought. But neo-positivism constituted a neo-enlightenment. The analysis of metaphysics and evaluation in terms of syntax, the view that hypotheses on reality could be verified only in operational terms, tended to reduce the permissible area of ideological discourse—indeed, practically to eliminate it.

The limits set by a rigorous neo-positivism were so narrow that the problems of interpreting society actually faced by men were often denied intellectual legitimacy. Neo-positivism had, in one sense, a liberating aspect: it was a sustained rejection of much that was inflated, irrelevant, and obscure in social discourse. Yet the simple insistence of the neo-positivists on asking precise and limited questions, transferred to the social sciences (who, what, where, when, how?), has contributed much that is valuable to our contemporary technical resources. This has been especially marked in study design, content analysis, and in the identification of channels for the transmission of ideology for special inquiry. Indeed, the work of both Lasswell and Lazarsfeld would be inconceivable without this philosophical influence, exerted directly on both.

Behaviourism, it has been said, utilized the evolutionary doctrine of the adaptation of psychic structures to historical conditions. In the nineteenth century, a unitary human intellectual evolution was argued: science had overcome the earlier obscurity of convention and religion. By the twentieth century it was acknowledged that adaptation did not invariably entail the extirpation of pre-scientific or non-scientific ideologies. The work of James and Veblen in America certainly entailed this position, while the instrumentalism of Dewey clearly provided for the analysis of ideologies as modes of adaption to changing environments, and did not make an abstract conception of science the culmination of intellectual evolution. It was a short step from these views to Mead's description of mind, self and society as components of a whole. The contribution of behaviourism, in its different forms, to the hard temper of American sociology has been immense. Surprisingly, however, it has not led to the analysis of ideas in their social context but to a certain disinclination to take ideas seriously. (This distortion of the original philosophic import of a distinctively American contribution to social thought requires further investigation.)

Once, then, the evolution of ideology into science had been urged, it became possible to describe the ambiguities of science and the omnipresence of (indeed, in pragmatic terms, the necessity for) ideology. The pure sociological positivism of the turn of the century, represented by Durkheim and his school, underwent a similar inner development. Durkheim's search for a scientific fundament of morality, for a real and identifiable sub-stratum of religion, did not simply "reduce" these ideological phenomena to other social processes. Rather, society and its processes were virtually identified with the *conscience collective* and its manifestations. A pure positivism, in other words, seemed to relapse into a pure idealism. The introduction by Mauss of the notion, insufficiently elaborated to this day, of the *phénomène social total,* and the work of Meillet, Granet, Halbwachs, Davy and others saved the legacy of Durkheim from the consequences of at least one logical interpretation of his writings. These writings, however, are rich in formulations of the greatest value for the study of ideology. The view that a society's ideas express the rhythms and spatial distributions of its social life provided a number of interesting empirical hypotheses. The derivation of the categories of philosophy, and thought in general, from the generalized experience of society was an attempt to resolve the Kantian antithesis of *a priori* and *a posteriori*—the individual's experience constituting the latter. This interplay of empirical and philosophical hypothesis was marked in the work of Durkheim's students and successors. It also created a climate which ultimately proved responsive to Gurvitch; despite a philosophical background which was vastly different, he was able to effect in France his own highly original synthesis of Marxism, phenomenology, and empirical sociology.

Difficult to incorporate in a history of sociological thought, the contribution of linguistics must be mentioned, none the less. Meillet, the great French linguist of his generation, was a student of Durkheim. Like him, many linguists were concerned with the influence of social structure upon linguistic development. The work of the structuralists at first glance seems not alone highly technical but not of direct relevance to the study of ideology. The analysis of language advanced by De Saussure, Trubetzkoy, and later Jakobson, concentrated on underlying regularities of linguistic form as a means of deducing regularities of content. Joined to the work of some anthropologists and the study of culture, structural linguistics was a new tool for the explication of the internal structure of systems of meaning. The full consequences for social science, and for the problems that interest us, were to be drawn later by Lévi-Strauss.

Between a Marxism unable to advance beyond its own initial philosophical limitations, and a positivism the net effect of which was often to block the development of what was still empirically valid in Marxism, were there no other approaches to the study of ideology in its social context? As we might expect, it was in Germany that such an attempt was made. Max Weber advanced a modified positivistic method which acknowledged the historical and total nature of social phenomena. His work on religion dealt directly with the Marxist hypotheses on ideology. Master of a thousand historical particulars, Weber ventured generalizations —with the qualification that the plurality of historical experiences as well as the plurality of historical perspectives made generalization tenuous. On ideology, however, he did (particularly in the posthumously published *Wirtschaft und Gesellschaft*) venture generalizations far more complex and much closer to Marxism than the simpler views of his early work on Protestantism. Amongst the ideological problems he studied were: the life style and social organization of the intelligentsia, the uses to which ideas were put once they were propagated, the function of ideas in forcing choices upon men. Weber's notions on ideology are distributed throughout his writings, and his presentation of them is by no means simple; it is only with Bendix's admirable treatise that we have at last a full view of these aspects of his work in all their ramifications. Perhaps we may assert that whereas Mannheim (who was influenced by Weber) generalized the Marxist view of ideology, abandoning class as the sole source of ideologies and replacing it by the total social structure, Weber decomposed the Marxist conception. Not alone did Weber treat of classes, but of a plurality of historical systems in which class was but one (and a highly variable) component. Weber's influence, of course, has been marked through the modern period—although upon reflection it seems to consist of an emphasis on the historical study of large-scale structural problems, rather than of any particular hypotheses.

No account of the study of ideology in the recent past would be complete without some remarks, at least, on Scheler. His efforts to distinguish between an autonomous sphere of immanent spiritual values and a social sphere which affected their realization constituted an interesting attempt to save metaphysics from sociology whilst reconciling the disciplines. Of more empirical interest were his hypotheses on the class origins of styles and systems of thought; these merited—but never received—a systematic elaboration and investigation.

As of 1940, then, the intellectual legacy available to sociologists interested in ideology was complex, even contradictory. The selection of any one method of interpretation did not exclude all others, but it did exclude much that was valuable. Moreover, sociologists at this time were burdened with theoretical problems. With the resumption of formal academic activity in 1945, two decades of depression, fascism, Stalinism and war had this effect: academic sociology became resolutely empirical. (Even so redoubtable a theorist as Gurvitch chose to term his sociology an *hyper-empiricisme dialectique* and Parsons insisted that his system was intended for empirical work.) The philosophies of existence and phenomenology, influential in Europe, and of analysis in the English-speaking countries, emphasized the actual and the concrete. In Communist society, the economic and military reconstruction of the U.S.S.R. and the consolidation of new gains in eastern Europe and Asia were the primary considerations. The tendencies that were to give new accents to the Marxist theory of ideology, in the Communist movement, were there *in nuce*. In their initial form, Zhdanovism, they were extremely negative and repressive. Fifteen years have passed: we shall have to see whether in the meantime theoretical issues once abandoned have acquired a new urgency —or whether old questions are being asked in new ways, appropriate both to the changed social situation and the inner movement of social science.

III. The Empirical Contribution

No agreed conventions have been developed, in the social sciences, to demarcate empirical from theoretical work. We may say that the distinction is connected with the scholar's self-consciousness about his assumptions and intentions. Empirical work, therefore, may be defined as the examination of data within the limits of a given theoretical system. In the past two decades, there has been a marked shift in work on ideology. Theoretical questions have been put aside, or bracketed in consciousness; certain assumptions have been pushed to their limits. Empirical work, in this period, has therefore had a retrospective theoretical aspect: it has drawn on the legacy sketched above, but has not sought to add to it.

The study of ideology has concentrated on the following areas. (1) Studies, chiefly psycho-analytic, of psychological processes. (2) Studies of the structure and effects of mass communications. (3) Studies of the internal structure of ideological systems (including art, myth and religion). (4) Studies of class consciousness. (5) Studies of the ideological biases of social science. (6) Studies of the intellectuals. I propose to deal with these studies in so far as they promise some reappraisal of the theoretical ideas which—sometimes only implicitly—inspired them.

1. A serious deficiency of the Marxist theory of ideology (and not only the Marxist one) has been that it employed an *ad hoc* psychology not derived from a direct examination of psychological processes. The work of Freud now enables us to synthesize psychological and sociological explanation. The synthesis achieved to date is, of course, incomplete and often fragile. Adorno and Lefebvre, amongst others, have suggested that certain ideological difficulties attach to the attempt to synthesize—"psychologization," it is held, entails either a flight from objective social processes or the interpretation of certain psychological by-products of these variable processes as enduring components of human nature. No position in the social sciences, of course, is free of ideological suspicion; these particular suspicions may constitute the price we have to pay for the insight given us by Freud.

A host of studies, in a variety of societies, have established connections between regularities in character formation and the adult acceptance of certain kinds of ideological form and content. Uniformities in character formation, of course, are also produced by the social structure—which includes ideologies. A number of scholars (Child, Kardiner, Kluckhohn, Mead, Whiting *et al.*), however, have sustained their point: it is possible to correlate childhood disciplines with those sectors of adult life in which symbolic systems legitimate moral and political directives. It is true that it has been easier to establish these connections for simple societies than for complex ones. In particular, a body of research on German "authoritarianism" has not been entirely satisfactory; the complexities and historical development of German social structure have been treated summarily. Yet even for complex societies the approach to ideology formation *via* character has some singular triumphs to its credit. Riesman's work on *The Lonely Crowd,* and William Whyte's study—in effect— of adult socialization (*The Organization Man*), each constitute applications of the method. More recently, Miller and Swanson have related character formation in the context of the occupational system, to the very real differences of aspiration and ideology between the American social strata.

Studies of the connection between a relatively constant character and ideology do tend to de-emphasize the radical discontinuities of life in society: rapid, even brutal, changes; disappointed expectations; tasks the personality finds difficult or impossible to manage. Studies of crisis have shown the role of ideology in maintaining personal integration. Erikson's studies of personal identity have been mentioned; these fuse the analysis of personality in crisis with a more longitudinal approach. Erikson's study of Luther's personal development in its historical setting is a model of its kind. Bettelheim and Janowitz, in their studies of prejudice, depicted ideologies as compensation for the ill-favoured (and provided a psychological counterpart to Merton's analysis of "Social Structure and Anomie"). Bettelheim's study of personality in concentration camps, and recent American studies of "brainwashing," provide interesting data on the ideological components in the response of personality to crisis. Work remains to be done, apparently, on the choice of ideological response in crisis—in so far as this is not predetermined by the immediate ideological pressures of the environment.

Yet a third category of psychological studies may be mentioned: those which explore the influence of psychological mechanisms on ideology formation. The remarkably influential and much-discussed inquiry recorded in *The Authoritarian Personality* contributed much in this respect, by concentrating on the mechanisms of displacement and projection. (The implications of the entire work, of course, are much wider: they include a pessimistic analysis of the possibilities of a democratic political system in the social and psychological setting of late capitalist society.) The burden of the work is that the formal conditions of democracy are ineffective by contrast with the social constraints which encourage the development of personality types incompatible with democratic institutions. Not surprisingly, an ideological as well as a methodological critique of the study has followed —although Shils' objection that there is an authoritarianism of the left as well as of the right, whilst true, does not seem particularly relevant in the American setting. Kluckhohn's study of Navaho witchcraft described similar mechanisms at work, and emphasized the role of economic and kinship structures (closely related in a primitive society) in canalizing psychological processes. It may be said that work is still required on the types of psychological mechanism consonant with variations in ideological systems; the inquiries just discussed do not necessarily prove that there is a unique psychological constellation underlying every ideology. (Leites' work on Bolshevism is an interesting instance of the uses of this last hypothesis.)

Much of this work is North American. It is, however, not remote from the theoretical influences generated in Europe. *The Authoritarian Personality* imported the approach of the Frankfurt Institute of Social Research to America. A surprising if indirect influence has been exercised on American sociology by Marxism, much of it by way of the (politically impeccable) work of Max Weber. The Michigan studies of class conditioning for occupational roles may be thought of as (not entirely unintended) footnotes to the problem of alienation. Finally, Shils' interesting inquiries on the strength of primary group ties, relative to ideological commitment, owe much to Simmel.

Not all the relevant work is North American. *Gestalt* psychology's philosophical and technical origins are European. The most recent theoretical advances in psychology of interest to us have been accomplished by Piaget, whose work has culminated in a genetic epistemology. In America, meanwhile, *Gestalt* work on perception has been joined to a psycho-analytic analysis by a number of experimentalists, of whom Bruner is the most interesting. Their work suggests that perceptions cannot be isolated from needs and from cultural standards. For the analysis of ideology, however, studies of the psychology of complex systems of symbols would be of great value; the problem of fitting these systems to the usual procedures of experimental psychology seems, for the moment, difficult of solution.

Piaget's genetic epistemology has important analogies, drawn by Piaget himself, with the analysis of ideology. Piaget has indeed compared what he terms egocentric thought to sociocentric thought, or ideology—characterizing both by the interpretation of the world in terms of the subject's (or the social group's) autisms. Studies of ideology might profit from the work done by Piaget and others on abstract and concrete thought processes. The application of concrete images and thought processes where only abstract ones are relevant is a frequent mechanism of distortion in ideologies; a psychological contribution on this point would be very useful, the more so as much preliminary work has been done in clinical settings.

No discussion of psychological work on ideology, finally, would be complete without mention of the brilliant philosophical contribution of the late Merleau-Ponty. In his treatise of 1945, *Phénoménologie de la Perception,* he discussed the role of intention and of the total personality in the analysis of perception. The experimental work accomplished since 1945 appears to confirm much of what he developed in strictly theoretical terms. His later work alternated between an historical-political approach to the problem and —some of the essays published in *Signes* reflect this tendency —a more metaphysical discussion. His premature death, alas, deprived us of a final synthesis which might well have constituted a new philosophy of human culture.

2. But fifteen years in North America, a decade in Europe, have elapsed since the emergence of television as a major medium of communication. Radio itself is, as a means of mass communication, only twenty years older. The modern, mass circulation newspaper is at least as old as the century. Studies of the mass media, therefore, are relatively new; changes in their structure, further, have imposed changing tasks on those who would study them. Inquiries into the mass media have utilized three techniques of inquiry: a tradition of content analysis derived from the history and criticism of literature; the social survey; a formalized analysis of content derived from the philosophy of neo-positivism and modern statistics.

Sociological studies of the ownership and control of the mass media are, interestingly enough, not as common as studies of what they produce. Where radio and television are public monopolies, studies of the groups and pressures influencing the public officials who control these monopolies are equally rare. Enough research has been done, however, to suggest that for the parliamentary democracies, the familiar liberal image of a society of free consumers choosing amongst and between competing sources of information, is not entirely accurate. In many other societies (some of them in the Communist bloc and some of them in the Western bloc), the media of communication are openly and explicitly controlled for political ends. Both sorts of public, then, hear and see not what they wish to hear and see, but what is given to them in such a way as to shape their subsequent preferences.

One of the results of recent studies has been to demonstrate the existence of an intellectual and ideological stratification of modern industrial populations. Differences of education, associated with differences of occupation, in turn produce differences of experience and taste which are reflected in, and maintained by, the distribution of communications. Yet another result casts some doubt on the suggestion that the mass media exercise an independent effect on opinion. Communications are received, interpreted and utilized—it is argued—in terms of the group's existing ideological predisposition. These may be traced to the group's conditions of existence, independently of the communications to which it is exposed. Certainly, a number of studies have shown that the interpretation and utilization of mass communications cannot be inferred directly from an analysis of their contents. This sort of analysis, none the less, continues to serve as a source of important information about the social structure. *Vide* Loewenthal's oft cited inquiry on shifts in the nature of the heroes in American popular literature and entertainment, from heroes of production to heroes of consumption. Merton's analysis of the content and technique of an American wartime bonds appeal, combined with interview data, allowed him to advance hypotheses on the prevalence and dynamics of an ideology of "pseudo-gemeinschaft" in America. It is much to be regretted that he did not continue these researches.

One of the limitations of much of the work on mass communications is that it has concentrated on the United States —the peculiarities of whose social structure are not duplicated elsewhere. Western Europe, with its mass working-class political parties, presents different structural traits. Studies done on non-western populations suggest that the mass media have had distinctive effects in communities hitherto psychologically remote from the outside world, and even somewhat autonomous of their national societies. The isolation of these communities has been ended, and new perspectives for ideological development (and manipulation) have been opened in the non-industrial societies.

It is here that we may mention the study of informal communication channels. The distinction between "locals" and "cosmopolitans" drawn by Merton for an American city, and the work by Shils and Janowitz on the German Army in the Second World War, each emphasize the primary group context in which communications about larger and more remote social structures are received. In his foreword to the studies of German public opinion published by the Frankfurt Institute of Social Research as *Gruppendynamik,* a distinguished German economist and social philosopher expressed his astonishment that these had revealed the existence, in addition to the public opinion of liberal political theory, of a second or underground public opinion. Balandier, in his valuable study of Central African political movements, showed how African groups reinterpreted propaganda from the colonialists (particularly but not exclusively religious propaganda) in their own terms. It will be seen that, in this discussion, the notion of communication has been given an extremely broad—and increasingly imprecise—meaning. This will have served some purpose if it makes clear the artificiality of isolating studies of mass communications from other social phenomena and, especially, from the problems of ideology. Precisely this sort of isolation also characterizes the recent discussion of "reference groups"—a discussion which has the additional disadvantage, despite its potential value for our purpose, of reducing social processes to their psychological components.

In conclusion, two critical analyses of mass communications may be mentioned. Riesman has insisted not alone that there is more popular resistance to mass media than we imagine, but that the phenomenon of privatization is a defence against this sort of stimulus from outside. Privatization, of course, is worthy of independent investigation as an expression of political—and ideological—impotence. A good deal of the work of Adorno begins, in its turn, with that impotence. Adorno has described Nazi ideology in terms which bear repeating: "A wink reminded the public of power—try to use your reason against us, and you'll see where you end. Many times, the very absurdity of the (Nazi) theses seemed an attempt to see what could be imposed upon human beings, as long as they understood the threat behind the phrases or the promise of crumbs from the table." Adorno denies that the contemporary problem of ideology rests on the opaqueness of social structure; he attributes it, rather, to the excessive transparency of modern society. The spirit has lost that apparent independence which originally provoked the critique of ideology: there is, to-day, no distinction between ideology and the objective condition of spiritual existence in mass culture. The fabrication of goods for mass cultural consumption simply reproduces the profane and tiresome surface of daily life, blinds men to its inner possibilities of improvement, and reinforces a fatalistic and despairing acceptance of existence as incapable of becoming anything else. With Adorno's work, of course, the analysis of ideology again becomes its critique; this expresses Adorno's own disdain for that sort of sociological description which legitimates what it describes, by refusing to acknowledge that things could be otherwise.

3. Before 1940, studies of the inner structure of ideologies were relatively few in number. Lukács' complaint (1923) will be recalled—that historical materialism had failed to take sufficient account of the internal complexities of ideologies. Weber's profound critique of (vulgar) Marxist notions of ideology consisted precisely in demonstrating that each

ideology contained a number of possibilities for development and, therewith, for influencing action. A number of Marxist scholars between the wars, of whom Borkenau and Wittfogel may be mentioned, took these strictures seriously; Groethuysen in his work on the religious origins of the French bourgeois ethic, used Weber's own methods. The contributions of Mannheim and Scheler have been mentioned, and there is, in fact, not much more to discuss under this rubric.

Recent years, however, have given us a number of advances within the Marxist framework on precisely this point. Goldmann's remarkable studies of Pascal and Racine merit the closest attention. Not alone does Goldmann relate their work to the social and political structure of seventeenth-century France; he attempts an interpretation of the possibilities of development in Western thought. (It is striking that Goldmann's more abstract and programmatic essays are much less valuable—because less acute and original—than his empirical contribution, and this precisely on the plane of theory. The implications of this curious situation for our present position are obvious.) Goldmann distinguishes two tendencies in Western thought on the relationship of existence, essence and value: a romantic doctrine of transcendence and a classical view of immanence. Pascal, he argues, began that movement of classicism in modern thought which culminated in Marx. Moving on from that theme, he portrays both Pascal and Racine as expressing the spiritual desperation of the Jansenist *noblesse de la robe,* at the end of its power. Goldmann insists that there were several types of Jansenism. Extreme Jansenism developed into Pascal's and Racine's "intramondane refusal of the world" and their gamble on the existence of a hidden God, which resolved the extreme tension induced by the social situation of its bearers. Quite apart from the other aspects of Goldmann's inquiry, its methodological by-products require further development. His conception of a meaningful cultural structure and his use of the notion of totality, at first sight, promise to connect the static analysis of the inner structure of ideology with the dynamic analysis of its development.

Goldmann's right to term himself a Marxist has been challenged, of course, by the somewhat battered defenders of "orthodoxy." In France, they have yet another important neo-Marxist to contend with: Desroche, the student of nineteenth-century communitarian movements and of the transition from late Christianity to primitive socialism. Desroche's major contribution has been to cast systematic doubt on the utility of the common formula: socialism is a secularized Christianity. Precisely by examining the beliefs and practices of the early communitarians and socialists, Desroche has been able to show that the inter-penetration of "Christian" and "secularized" components of their ideology voids the conception of a linear process of secularization. Desroche, a close student of Marxism, is now engaged in some work on "religion" and "non-religion" which will interest the student of ideology at least as much as the sociologist of religion. Indeed, one of the merits of his thought is that it makes much of the distinction between the two sorts of inquiry superfluous.

Finally, Werner's work on medieval religious movements may be noted. This historian has given us a body of work which suggests that Marxist method applied to the history of ideologies need not be overly-schematized, indeed, that it can synthesize data already obtained and guide research towards data in turn productive of new hypotheses. This is, perhaps, an appropriate place for the author of the Trend Report to express his regrets at his inability to utilize the work of Soviet historians. My impression, from occasional translations and summaries of their work, is that an appreciable amount of it may be far more subtle and penetrating —in the analysis of ideology—than one would infer from Soviet work on Marxist theory alone.

(I have previously said that Bloch's *Prinzip Hoffnung* fits no category; perhaps this is as good a place as any to mention his contribution. Bloch depicts hope as an intrinsic component of human vision and action, and insists that it is false to separate the subjective selves of men from the objects they desire. Hope, in his view, is a means of self-realization through object-relationship. A philosophy which describes the world as it is denies hope, which is not alone a reflection of knowledge of what the world may become, but a constituent of the process of becoming. Bloch's treatise is rich in references to art, myth, philosophy, and religion; the description of the author as "a Marxist Schelling" is not entirely unfounded. A work of this sort can contribute little of a precisely defined kind to the analysis of ideology; however, it has contributed to that revitalization of Marxism which may well precede new work of a precise type.)

The traditions of anthropology appear rather remote from the concerns of Marxism. In fact the possibilities of a new synthesis (*rapprochement* would not be an accurate term) are to be found in the work of Lévi-Strauss. No summary can do justice to the acuity and fecundity of his thought; I content myself with some remarks on his work on myth. He has sought to identify the recurrent social problems expressed in myth. These may be described as irreconcilable conflicts in the society producing myth, presented in a transposed language. Language is, indeed, a key to Lévi-Strauss' analysis, and he borrows from the structuralists a technique for that analysis. Myths have synchronic components: stories, in brief, told in an irreversible order. They also have diachronic ones: structural relationships, antitheses and syntheses. For each myth, a collation of a sufficient number of its versions will give the inner logic of the basic type. This collation entails the application of a technique of structural analysis which separates the abstract pattern of the myth's inner movement from its limited historical content.

The inner movement or logic of the myth, however, can be expressed only in terms of certain constant human psychological tendencies; these are produced by the conflicts referred to above, or rather by the attempt to resolve them. The resolutions can be described as follows. The notion of reciprocity reconciles the fundamental antithesis of self and other; the synthetic character of the gift creates a relationship of solidarity as distinct from one of exchange; the notion of rule makes stable relationships possible. It will be seen that these elements may be viewed as either psychic components of the social structure or social components of the psyche. The analysis of myth, then, seeks to identify what is essential in social structure.

Not surprisingly, Lévi-Strauss when dealing with myth invariably arrives at problems of economics, power, and sexuality (kinship). His analysis is not ahistoric; it leads us, indeed, to a universalized history—in which myth and psychic structure may be understood as ideological depictions of what Marxism knows as the forces and relationships of production.

Lévi-Strauss has, thus far, presented his analysis in a highly technical work on kinship, a series of papers, and in that brilliant *tour de force* entitled *Tristes Tropiques*. Many aspects of his work are instructive: the alternation between and tentative fusion of diachronic and synchronic analyses; the transposition into kinship relation ships and myth (or ideology) of the relationships of production; a consistent refusal to rely on categories derived exclusively from one historical epoch. It is much to be hoped that Lévi-Strauss will soon expand the typology of religions given in *Tristes Tropiques,* as a means of testing his view that both Marxism and Freudianism are susceptible of generalization into a new system of sociological analysis. For the moment, it can be said that he has given us the most formidable of all recent contributions to the study of ideology.

Lévi-Strauss is not the only anthropologist to have taught us something in this period. The entire literature warns us that the Marxist conception of ideology may rest on one limited set of historical generalizations. This lesson is particularly explicit in those works derived from Mauss and, ultimately, from Durkheim. Leach, for instance, in his valuable book on Burma, describes one society living in effect with two ideologies and alternating between them. The (necessary) fragmentation of African and Asiatic civilization complexes in recent field studies has given us a wealth of local documentation on the ways in which non-Western ideologies are related to social structure. The narrow concept of reflection appears inadequate to deal with these relationships. Sometimes, metaphor may be the beginning point of new formulations: the ideologies in question seem to have served as envelopes for the social structure—envelopes which are now being torn off. Needham's massive study of Chinese science and its social origins, however, reminds us that Marxism, suitably used, can indeed illuminate the peculiarities of non-Western civilizations.

The more orthodox sort of work on the history of ideas, of which there has been a good deal in many countries, has not made possible any demonstrable theoretical advance in the analysis of ideology. These texts, of course, do contain much of value in their own terms, and often present material that is sociologically relevant. Hofstadter's distinguished work on American political ideas may be cited in this connection, because the author deals explicitly with ideas as responses to the political and social situation of definite groups and classes. Indeed, Hofstadter was concerned to modify certain crude interpretations of American history; in doing so, he illuminated the ways in which ideologies can serve a variety of functions and impelled us to consider anew categories like "progressive" or "conservative" ideologies. Much, additionally, can be learned from work in theology. Bultmann's

Entmythologisierung of the New Testament distinguishes between the historically-conditioned beliefs of the early Christians and an "existential" interpretation of Scripture not alone more acceptable to twentieth-century men, but allegedly more consonant with Christ's understanding of himself. Bultmann's attack on an entire tradition of theological interpretation (which has provoked an instructive theological controversy) has shown that the possibilities of adaptation open to systems of thought *in extremis* are many. By incorporating what was the critique of theology in theology itself, Bultmann has given both an example of ideological defence—and has acknowledged the pervasive influence of the critique of ideology in modern thought in its entirety.

This account of studies of the internal structure of ideologies has been rather far-ranging. It may conclude by mentioning two attempts to study that structure with more familiar techniques. An entire body of work, in part accomplished by Lasswell and in part inspired by him, emphasizes the quantitative analysis of political discourse—and joins it, at times, to interpretations derived from psycho-analysis. Naess and his associates, finally, undertook a rigorous inquiry into the uses of political terminology; they were able to confirm the existence, with respect to variations in the definition of terms like "democracy," of an ideological Tower of Babel.

(4) Lukács, it will be recalled, criticized empirical studies of class consciousness on two counts. He held that isolated studies of attitude and reaction, conducted ahistorically, were likely to give partial or even false results, and that the correct interpretation of the historical process was a scientific goal superior to the mere establishment of the facts. Many recent studies of class consciousness have taken the first point and made of it a methodological postulate; a certain scepticism appears to have developed, however, as to whether a "correct" interpretation of the historical process can be found.

Recent studies of class consciousness have tended to join this phenomenon to others studied by political sociology: electoral preference, trade union or pressure group activity, more diffuse indices like attitudes towards occupational and other standardized values, have been used to measure ideological commitment and consistency. A valuable Trend Report on Political Sociology has already been published; there is little point in repeating here what has already been said. A few observations may be useful.

The study of correlations between ideology and political behaviour, or their absence, does not necessarily afford conclusive evidence on the depth or potential efficacy of ideologies apparently inconsonant with behaviour as observed at any one moment. These ideologies may be activated under different circumstances, or they may show that a group has been induced to support policies which it neither understands nor intends—a situation neither impossible nor unfamiliar. Further, much contemporary data on ideology comes from questionnaire type inquiries on large samples. In these, responses to a series of specific questions constitute the basis on which a subsequent analysis identifies one or another ideological pattern in the data. Considerable recent advances have been made in the techniques of index construction and scaling. It may be doubted, however, that inquiries of this type provide results which are as valuable as the more intensive and qualitative studies of ideology recently undertaken, for instance, by Chinoy and Popitz.

It may be interesting, at this point, to consider the recently announced "end of ideology." In Aron's interpretation, the area of ideological discussion—in fact, of innovation—in both western and Communist societies has narrowed to the point where ideology is almost irrelevant. Adorno, no doubt, might say that ideological discussion is at one level a *jeu d'esprit,* at another a deception—whether consciously imposed or not. For sociologists interested in the problem, Aron's assertion requires examination. The modern sense of political impotence may well colour ideological development in ways we have as yet to elucidate, on account of our own vested interest in the contention that ideologies are still important.

To turn to the literature itself, it is clear that much recent work on class consciousness in western society has been an inquiry into the fate of the Marxist expectation of revolutionary proletarian sentiment. (Despite the claims of some vulgar Marxist critics, no serious sociologist in the western societies denies the existence of class structures and class conflicts. The points at issue among sociologists are the importance of these conflicts and the explanation for the fact that they do not invariably dominate the politics of the western societies. Frequently, these differences of theoretical opinion reflect political differences.) These studies have included rather simple ones on the class-identification of differing strata (Centers), and complex inquiries into the structure of working-class consciousness (Popitz and Touraine). Within a constant socio-economic position, much variation in this structure has been established. Other variations have been attributed to changes in industrial organization, or in the politics of the larger society. Economic betterment alone, it appears, need not alter the *direction* of class consciousness and may leave intact a sense of exclusion from the national community, or hostility to certain groups; it may, however, alter the *intensity* of class consciousness. Trade union militancy on wages, hours and conditions of work is not necessarily connected with a larger political militancy (*vide* the U.S.A.). Further references to recent research results will show their somewhat disparate character: revolutionary proletarian sentiment has indeed not been found in western Europe and the U.S.A.—and a good many different things have been found in its place.

Some recent studies have made much of generational differences. The older workers have been depicted as ideologically militant, the younger ones as privatized—integrated only into the national society of consumers. Experience and new political crises may influence the younger generation of European workers, however, and it is not certain that these results will continue to be found. It has been suggested that they may be influenced in the direction of a right authoritarianism. Some inquiries, utilized to interesting effect by Lipset, have shown the discrepancy between the humanitarian socialism of the leadership of the social democratic parties and the attitudes of their members and voters.

These studies have, perhaps, over-emphasized temporary fluctuations in working-class attitudes and beliefs. The relative passivity of the French workers during the crisis that ended the Fourth Republic, 1958, occasioned a number of analyses of the end of working-class consciousness. By April, 1961, that passivity had ended. The debate on rearmament and later, on the question of nuclear weapons, for a time ended the passivity of the working class in the Federal German Republic. In sum, recent inquiries have given us an extremely differentiated account of working-class consciousness, and of the factors influencing its components. What we lack, in general, are attempts to find new interpretations of a historical kind. Although there have been a number of references to the effects of prosperity on the working class, there have been no major efforts to study the effect on the European (or, indeed, American) working class of the conflict between western and Communist blocs, nor of the painful process of de-colonization.

Middle-class consciousness, of course, has also been studied. Particular attention has been given (by Croner, Crozier, Lockwood and Mills, amongst others) to the new middle class—to the clerical and technical salariat, strange to bourgeois culture and neither as powerful nor as wealthy as the upper levels of the old middle class. Retrospective studies have suggested that the new middle class was particularly

prone to fascism; many inquiries have insisted upon its resistance to ideological "proletarianization." Crozier, in particular, has found age differences important in determining
the subjective class identifications of members of the salariat.
Lockwood, however, has isolated the specific conditions under which sectors of the British salariat entered trade unions.
Work on the new middle class, then, is no longer limited to
the global analyses with which it began; the problem of its
ideological ambiguity has been resolved into its components.
Similar procedures, it will be recalled, mark present inquiries
on working-class consciousness. The absence of efforts at synthetic interpretations of the latter has been remarked; it may
well be that these await conjoint attacks on the general problem of class consciousness in industrial society. (Dahrendorf's
work is the most interesting of recent attempts to deal with
this subject, in the context of a general discussion of class
structure; Aron's valuable Sorbonne *cours* on the same theme
will no doubt in time appear in a final version.)

Studies of elites are few, meanwhile, and of their ideologies
fewer. Elites seem to talk through authorized or semi-author-
ized spokesmen (not infrequently to be found in the universities) and rather seldom for themselves. The Harvard inquiry
on the ideology of American businessmen is of value; Mitrani's studies of the French bureaucratic-technical elite are
no less so. There have been occasional studies of the views
of elites on any number of specific questions. Full studies of
the ideologies of elites, however, are as rare as studies of
their political operations—and possibly for the same reasons.

These studies of class consciousness deal mainly with western industrial societies, precisely those upon which certain
Marxist hypotheses may be easily tested. There are, clearly,
other forms of class consciousness in different settings. Historical studies of the societies of the non-western world, from
this point of view, are few. Wittfogel's *Oriental Despotism*
—despite its own political biases—is a stimulating study in

what may be termed bureaucratic ideology. Studies of anti-colonial movements, of the type accomplished by Balandier and Worsley, deal with ideological responses to special relationships of exploitation. Werner's work on medieval protest movements has been mentioned. The studies of Rude and Soboul on the French Revolution depict western class conflict at the beginning of the industrial revolution. Hobsbawm's studies of protest movements in the non-industrial interstices of European society illuminate the continuities and discontinuities between class conflict in pre-industrial and industrial societies.

Studies of anti-colonial movements have been cited; these are instances, perhaps, of a type of ideology whose relationships to class consciousness have as yet to be fully clarified: nationalism. Studies of western nationalism have recently tended to draw upon sociological hypotheses, occasionally deepening these by psychological ones. These studies have shared in that general devaluation of human rationality which characterizes so much intellectual work in the past two decades; they have also (with some exceptions) treated nationalism as an ideology superimposed on class-consciousness and have not dealt with the connection between them in more adequate terms. But western nationalism having been studied in so much detail, the way is now open for comparative studies of new nationalisms elsewhere—or of old nationalisms, reborn. The complexities, the many possibilities of political orientation and social development entailed by any one nationalism, indicate that a certain ideological ambiguity may attach to each. The tasks of research, in this sphere, are many.

Finally, it must be said that an important addition to our knowledge of class consciousness and ideology has as yet not been given us: empirical studies of these phenomena in the societies of the Communist bloc are conspicuous by their absence. It is, clearly, insufficient to assert that the transformation of class relationships in these societies has altered consciousness; this has to be demonstrated. Certain Polish inquiries, already published, indicate that new forms of stratification in post-war Poland have evoked new forms of consciousness: specifically, the offspring of peasants and workers who have been educated as members of the intelligentsia experience some difficulty in identifying themselves with the peasants and workers. No doubt, the Communist régimes are working towards the solution of these difficulties. Perhaps they will, in the near future, find it advantageous to utilize sociological research as part of these efforts. For the moment, their failure to do so constitutes, objectively, a contribution to the maintenance of a condition of *mystification* in their own societies.

(5) Studies of the ideological component in social science itself simply continue that epistemological critique which has always been part of social thought. Much of the sociological critique of sociology has been extremely general: suggestions of interest-induced *lacunae* in the work of the discipline, critiques of certain tendencies in research, demands for new beginnings. Specific studies of groups of sociologists and their work have been very rare. C. Wright Mills, to be sure, did attempt such a study for contemporary American sociology in his recent *The Sociological Imagination*; the reception accorded his work will not encourage many to follow him. His book has simply not been followed by the serious discussion it merits. (It is instructive to recall that *The Sociological Imagination* follows, by some two decades, Robert Lynd's earlier *Knowledge for What?* By contrast with Lynd's essay, Mills' seems to bespeak European influences on American radical social thought. Mills, indeed, was a student of Hans Gerth.)

The ideological critique of the dead has proved somewhat easier. The origins of sociology itself have been discussed as part of the growth of a "scientistic" outlook. This outlook is held to entail: an extreme and naïve faith in scientific method as a generator of values, an implicit messianism, a demand that the world be regulated in every detail—a spiritual totalitarianism which must eventually have a political counterpart. Much of this literature deals with Saint-Simon and Comte in their more extreme phases. Some of it extends this critique to contemporary sociologists who are by no means Saint-Simonians or Comteans. This sort of deformation cannot be held against Weber; it is irrelevant when applied to Marx. A different analysis of the growth of sociology, however, attributes it to the organicism of the social thought of the Restoration. Maus, indeed, has shown that Comte's "scientism" is inseparable from his ideological commitment to the Restoration. (Maus' history of sociology, which contains a number of *aperçus* on the ideological components of the discipline, is about to appear in an English translation.)

The primary ideological difficulty of many contemporary sociologists is that they are unwilling to face up to the implications of the problem of ideology for their own work. The promise of the achievement of a science (with an articulated body of concepts, verified hypotheses, and standardized techniques) has been taken for the achievement itself. From this perspective, questions of ideological bias appear to be not wrong, but irrelevant—vestiges of a primitive stage of sociology now (happily) behind us. Some of the insensitivity of sociologists is due to the scholarly division of labour. The argument has been left to philosophers, some of whom share this last view of sociology's potential, some of whom do not. This kind of intellectual warfare, however, is too important for the inner development of sociology to be left to such abstracted generals.

Discussions of the ideological problems of sociology do show considerable national variation. The debates evoked by Schelsky's *Ortsbestimmung der deutschen Soziologie* in Germany, by Mills in the U.S.A., and by Gurvitch and Sartre in France, have been conducted in different conceptual languages—despite all latent similarities of theme. Finally, it is worth remarking that the intensive empirical research which has been conducted since 1945 in a number of countries (much of it on theses as germane to ideological divergences as class structure and class consciousness, the sociology of power, and mass culture) has not stilled ideological debate either amongst those engaged in the research or those simply cognisant of its results. The belief that sociology can end ideological debate by some sort of empirical adjudication requires correction. Empirical sociology, indeed, has been drawn into the debate.

(6) Studies of the intelligentsia should be distinguished from studies of the intellectuals. The former are those in possession of a higher educational qualification, who use their education for specific occupational tasks in administration, the professions, and science. The latter are that ill-defined group who interest themselves in general questions of society and culture. We possess rather more studies of the intellectuals than of the intelligentsia (the two categories, of course, are not mutually exclusive). These studies, moreover, are on the whole less precise than those dealing with the intelligentsia; usually, the social composition and function of the intellectuals are discussed in very general terms, and their attitudes and ideas discussed at greater length but schematically.

We have one major work on the intelligentsia as a whole —Geiger's valuable essay of 1949—complemented by a detailed statistical and historical study of the Danish intelligentsia. The inquiries directed by Plessner, of course, cover some of this ground for Germany. Bendix and Kelsall have studied the American and British civil service, respectively. Previous Trend Reports in this series (in particular, those on Bureaucracy and Education) have referred to much relevant material.

On intellectuals, Aron's witty and penetrating text is the most interesting single study in years. The discrepancy between the formal acknowledgement of the primacy of the spirit and its factual denial, in western society, may well be a source of the intellectual's discontent—as Aron suggests. More rigorous studies of the intellectuals may indeed serve as a corrective to a certain amount of self-pity on their part; but perhaps this hope is too optimistic. In general, we may say that sociological inquiries dealing with those who produce and distribute ideologies have been too few, and that those we do have are mainly historical. Perhaps one reason for the reluctance of contemporary sociologists to study intellectuals is the notion—and, indeed the practice—of "professional" specialization in our field. In so far as sociologists hope to become social research technicians, they seem to think it necessary to avoid problems which can be dismissed as belonging to the *littérateur*. In so far as they have in fact become social research technicians, their ability to comprehend the intellectuals has diminished.

IV. The Situation of Soviet Social Theory

The Soviet contribution to the theory of ideology requires separate treatment. The organization of intellectual life in the Soviet Union differs from that in non-Communist countries—even if the differences, owing to the exigencies of the conflict between the two power blocs, have recently diminished somewhat. Social theory in the Soviet Union is subject to continuous political control, and is not left to the quasi-autonomous judgement of-specialists. This account is far less comprehensive than it should be, owing to my inability to read Russian, but it does deal with: (*a*) the Leninist tradition in the theory of ideology; (*b*) Stalin's contribution (Stalin's estimate of his own abilities as a Marxist thinker was absurdly high, but his pronouncements were influential); (*c*) some recent developments in the Soviet Union, as reflected in two texts, the new version of the *History of the Communist Party of the Soviet Union* and the *Principles of Marxist Philosophy*, published in 1959 under Konstantinov's editorship. The explicitly political nature of Soviet social theory makes a recourse to these authorized sources advisable.

It will be seen that there are a number of omissions. I do not deal with work originating in other countries of the Communist bloc. In all cases but two, little is lost by this omission: the center still exerts decisive influence on the periphery. Two countries do present special problems. The conditions under which the discipline is organized in Poland seem to justify treating Poland under the previous rubrics (under which I also place work by Communist colleagues living in non-Communist countries.) Chinese sociologists, unfortunately, have practically no contacts with their colleagues in non-Communist countries—a situation not entirely of China's making, whose end would be very welcome. It is my impression that recent sociological research in China has concentrated on matters like agrarian social structure, and has not treated of problems of ideology. The original contributions of Chinese thinkers (Mao, for instance) to Marxist theory appear to lie in other areas.

Additionally, the view of Soviet theory presented here is clearly too limited. Works in ethnology and history have been ignored, and I have been unable to take account of very recent, and tentative, moves towards the development of an empirical sociology in the Soviet Union. It can be said that these have as yet to influence Soviet social theory.

(a) Lenin's philosophical work has recently been the subject of much discussion. His view that true conceptions of reality reproduce the external world, in the minds of observers, is a continuing assumption of Soviet social theory. The notion does prevent the depiction of mind, and ideology, as independent of their material basis. (Recent Soviet philosophy, it must be added, conceives of material reality not in the exclusive sense of an organization of particles—but as a reality external to and independent of the observer.) This endorsement of Lenin's assumption has not precluded considerable variation in assertions about the precise relationship of ideas to social contexts.

Interestingly enough, the Soviet Union has never developed what we might term a historical epistemology. Discussions of the relationship between mind and the world, and of the social determination of ideas, have been conducted separately. Pavlovian psychology's doctrine of mind as a "second signalling system" would appear to be a convenient link between the two. Pavlov held that signals coming from the external world (perceptions, in another philosophical language) activated the nervous system; learning consisted of the recognition of the relationship between changes in the external world and these internal stimuli. That recognition, systematized, constituted the "second signalling system." Pavlovian psychology itself appears to be subject to considerable internal tension: it cannot reduce thought to mere cerebral activity, yet it cannot portray thought as independent of that activity. For our purpose, it remains only to observe that Pavlovian psychology does not appear to have been utilized in the Soviet analysis of ideology.

Perhaps this discrepancy between the philosophical-psychological components of the Leninist tradition and the study of ideology can be attributed to the political importance of Lenin's theory of class consciousness. Lenin supposed that, left to itself, the working class would never develop an adequate consciousness; its ideology would be shaped by the bourgeois society of which it was a part. Although he acknowledged the importance of the Russian revolutionary tradition in Russian popular consciousness, he insisted that revolutionary consciousness had to be brought to the working class from without—by a party aware of the latent historical mission of the class. This element of voluntarism entails a certain discontinuity with the Marxist theory of ideology. It may well account for the apparent inhibition in

Soviet social theory—observable throughout all the political vicissitudes of Soviet Marxism—on the elaboration of a theory of ideology.

(*b*) The Stalinist conception of ideology (and the use made of it by Zhdanov) descends lineally from the Leninist one. In his *On Dialectical and Historical Materialism* (1938), Stalin attributed to new ideas "tremendous organizing, mobilizing and transforming value." These ideas "force their way through, become the possession of the masses, mobilize them against the moribund forces of society." These direct quotations with their characteristic emphasis on the manipulation and direction of society illustrate, perhaps, the extent to which Stalin's conception of ideology was subordinated to his theory (and practice) of party leadership.

Zhdanov's campaign, begun in 1947, to maximize Bolshevik partisanship in art, philosophy, science and culture can be understood as an acknowledgement of the "organizing, mobilizing and transforming value" of ideas. Their full mobilization by Party and State in the Zhdanov period, of course, was part of the prosecution of the Cold War: thus the campaign against "cosmopolitanism" and the extreme repressiveness and punitiveness of ideological discipline in this period. It is striking that no formal and explicit change in Soviet theory on this point has occurred. The doctrine of the importance of ideas in the functioning and development of Soviet society has recently been emphasized—in a period when repression has decreased markedly. As we shall see, this decrease in repression has been accompanied by a rather more sophisticated approach to Marxist theory in general, and the theory of ideology in particular. *The Principles of Marxist Philosophy*, indeed, even attacks "vulgar Marxism"—it is not difficult to see that what is meant, *inter alia,* is the constricted and dogmatic Marxism of the period of Zhdanov and the late Stalin. (The possibility of these variations on a basically unchanged ideological theme suggests that even in Soviet society, ideology is labile. Unfortunately, Soviet social theory has yet to consider the full implications of this for the analysis of Soviet society.)

Stalin's intervention in the Soviet linguistics controversy (1951) is, perhaps, of more theoretical interest. The linguist Marr had not alone proposed to analyse language and its history in terms of a simple conception of superstructure; he advanced a number of dubious propositions, amongst them the prediction that in a future classless language formal logic would be superseded by dialectical thought. Stalin held that language was neither base nor superstructure, but part of the relationships of production (because used for communication) and the product of the national society as a whole rather than a class phenomenon. In the classless society of the future, language would develop—like the society itself—gradually. Grammatical laws were valid, additionally, for all classes. Stalin's notions, on balance, constituted an endorsement of the view that consciousness was relatively independent of its social basis; in other words, he emphasized the role of superstructure.

A similar emphasis appeared in his last work, *On the Economic Problems of Socialism* (1952), although he did—having himself previously emphasized the voluntarist factors in socialist society—take the opportunity to rebuke those who held that there were no objective laws in that society. He predicted the increasing diminution of the antitheses of mental and physical labour. Education would enable the members of socialist society to begin the transition to communism. Moral and political unity was the driving force of socialist society in which change occurred as a "revolution from above." This was the theoretical legacy with which the era of Khrushchev began.

(c) Recent political developments in the Soviet Union have been much discussed; this is not the place to review them. Suffice it to say that these do appear to have had positive effects on the development of Soviet social theory; by contrast with the situation a decade ago, it seems to exhibit greater flexibility and depth—a certain number of taboos have been dropped, and the eventual analysis of the contradictions of Soviet society itself from within no longer appears to be a practical impossibility.

The recent *History of the Communist Party of the Soviet Union* is an interesting result of these political developments. The work refers to "distortions," errors," and "negative phenomena" in the execution of the Zhdanov decrees—including an "administrative attitude" to the arts and an approach to science in which "in some cases . . . the conflict of opinions was narrowed." The "cult of personality" is explained as a development in a backward and encircled country; constructing socialism in these special circumstances led to "temporary" restrictions on democracy. It is noteworthy that this analysis denies that the policy of the CPSU at the time was in error. In effect, it continues the "cult of personality" by attributing much of it solely to Stalin's personal defects rather than to the structure of Soviet society.

After the Twentieth Congress, the *History* remarks, "Individual writers who had not understood the essence of the Party's critique of the cult of personality began to see only the errors and dark sides of socialist construction; they denied the necessity of a leading role for the party in the ideological sphere." (Some of the titles cited in the bibliography either exemplify or discuss this problem.) The *History* does contain a programmatic statement on the necessity for including the lower echelons of the CPSU, as well as other groups like trade unions, in the making as well as the execution of decisions; the new *Programme* of the CPSU is quite specific on this point. But, to judge from the *History,* those who have assessed the development of the CPSU find satisfactory its present arrangements for dealing (internally and externally) with ideological problems.

47

The sociological sections of the new *Principles of Marxist Philosophy* assign a considerable role to superstructure and especially to ideology. Contradictions and the absence of correspondence often characterize the relationship of base to superstructure; this cannot be conceived "metaphysically as absolute and unchangeable." Changes in the relationships of productive forces do, indeed, ultimately determine all other social changes. We cannot, however, understand a phenomenon like eighteenth-century French philosophy by reference to production and its technique alone; we must consider the class structure, feudal law and the State, the Church, and the influence of art, morals and science upon the new doctrine.

The analysis of social classes in industrial societies suggests that the authors (*The Principles of Marxist Philosophy* is a collective work) feel obliged to deal with the views of their "bourgeois" colleagues. They acknowledge the existence of status grouping of a sort different from classes in industrial society, e.g. castes. Their response to the recent analysis of the new middle class in western Europe and America, unfortunately, leaves much to be desired: they assimilate this discussion to their own category of *petite bourgeoisie*. They depict the intelligentsia as an "ideal" (their meaning, to judge from context, seems to be "ideological") parliament in which all classes are represented. In a critique of André Philip (a "bourgeois" sociologist, incidentally, whose "bourgeois" ideology did not prevent his expulsion from the SFIO, the social democratic party of France, and his adherence to the PSU, the new French socialist party), it is argued that the interests of a whole class are permanent and decisive, those of its sections temporary. Those sociologists who, with Aron, think that the working class has lost its sense of historical mission and undergone *embourgeoisement* are answered in the following terms. The single proletarian may be confused; but his objective position interests him in the end of capitalism—although only the fusion of the working class movement with theoretical Marxism, in the custody of a Marxist party, can bring these interests to consciousness. It is clear that this argument contains very little that is new.

Social consciousness is not exhausted by ideology (specified here as social theories, legal and political ideology, art, morality, philosophy, science and religion). It also includes a social psychology distinct from ideology. National psychological characteristics (especially apparent in aesthetic apprehension) are of extraordinary duration. The product of history, and of a national class structure, these characteristics in turn affect ideology. We must understand the social psychology of a class in order to understand its ideology. Certain psychological traits are associated with a specific class situation (for instance, a rising class is optimistic but the psychology of a declining one may exhibit a flight into the aesthetic and intimate sphere). The ideology of a class, however, cannot be derived directly from its psychology; equally, it is not a systematic elaboration of processes in the minds of the individuals constituting the class. Ideology is, rather, the assimilation in thought of real social relationships. The proletariat had its own psychology and tended "instinctively" to socialism when it developed; before that, however, it moved within a bourgeois ideology. Classes are divided into different strata with different experiences; moreover, individuals have different educations and experiences. Variations in individual consciousness, therefore, which do not affect our theoretical generalizations may be historically important: in history, certain personalities can affect the course of events.

"Vulgar Marxists" who insist on a "direct and immediate reflection of economic relationships" in consciousness are wrong. These relationships are reflected in ideology only indirectly. Ideas may change independently of social structure due to the influence of intellectual tradition and the fact that some thinkers can anticipate the direction of social development. The attempt to derive either a social theory or a work of art in all of its detail directly from the economic basis without taking account of intervening processes constitutes, in fact, a "vulgar Marxist" error.

These formulations, it is clear, attain a level of complexity and sophistication not to be found in Soviet social theory at the beginning of the period covered by this survey. Their empirical application, in the *Principles of Marxist Philosophy,* gives ambiguous results: some of the empirical conclusions are equally advanced, others not.

The analysis of art, for instance, depicts it as an independent sphere of activity in complex societies. Art can attain a high point of development, as in Antiquity or Russia in the nineteenth century, when productive forces are low. Natural science is excluded—a more lengthy and elaborate statement would have been welcome—from the category of ideology. Religion originally expressed a relationship to mysterious natural powers and developed into the expression of a relationship to mysterious social powers. The persistence of religion in capitalist society can be explained not alone by its utilization by the exploiting classes, but because of the persistence of fear. Not only habit and tradition explain religious survivals in the Soviet Union itself, but the persistence of fear—provoked by the human struggle with nature and the fear of war.

Two empirical areas, in particular, are treated in rather summary fashion. The authors deal with "bourgeois" social thought and philosophy so schematically that they distort it. It may well be true that a positivistic morality, based on the analysis of statements of preference, is "subjectivistic." But the positivistic analysis of morality originated in the effort to enlarge the scope of knowledge in human action. That existentialism isolates the individual from his social setting may be true of Heidegger; it is certainly not true of Sartre. It is shrewd of the authors to observe that both positivism and existentialism eliminate the objective world, the one by reducing it to signs, the other by reducing knowledge to suffering; but these *aperçus* are no substitute for an analysis of these movements in their ideological context. The account of "bourgeois" sociology given in this text is a curious medley of distortion, ignorance, and (somewhat blunt) insight. It is difficult to deal with the assertion that "subjective method" rules "bourgeois" sociology—if those who make it refuse to recognize the internal conflicts of the discipline or the extent to which many non-Communist sociologists consider themselves (with ample justification) to be heirs of Marxism, if not in fact Marxists.

The analysis of Soviet ideological problems is no less schematic. The assertion that political and economic transformations, under socialism, require less time than ideological ones is unaccompanied by concrete evidence. It is observed that with the development of socialism, the importance of the subjective factor in Soviet society has increased. The contradictions and difficulties of socialism, it is held, reactivate residues of bourgeois individualism in the Soviet Union— even including the psychology of private property. It is clear from the text that Soviet social theory now attaches great importance to popular education and popular consciousness as factors in Soviet social development—without having examined that consciousness, empirically, in a manner that could provide new theoretical advances. It is this deficiency, no doubt, which accounts for the cursory quality of a discussion from which much more might have been expected, particularly had it dealt with what the CPSU regards as "negative" aspects of Soviet popular consciousness.

The authors of the *Principles of Marxist Philosophy*, finally, accuse the "vulgar Marxists" of failing to understand human activity and the possibility of subordinating social laws to human decision. The "vulgar Marxists," further, do not understand the reciprocal nature of dialectical relationships (as in the case of ideology) and hold a mechanical view of causation. In their programmatic rejection of "vulgar Marxism," the authors make common cause with a considerable number of Marxists outside the Soviet Union and the Communist bloc; it is much to be hoped that this abstract agreement will be followed by a concrete intellectual *rapprochement*.

V. Conclusion

Much that ordinarily would have been said here has already appeared in the text; brevity, therefore, is in order. The literature on the sociological study of ideology between 1940 and 1960 contains two apparently antithetical tendencies—an empirical and a theoretical one. The dominant empirical one entails the analysis in fact not of ideology but of ideologies. A multiplicity of ideologies have been studied in the most varied historical contexts and have been treated in terms of a number of hypothetical determining factors. These have sometimes been taken together, sometimes separately. In nearly all cases, a direct attack on the theoretical problem of ideology has been renounced; the general conditions under which ideology is produced have hardly been considered. These empirical studies do, of course, utilize past attempts to solve the theoretical problem—in order to isolate critical variables for examination.

This tendency no doubt reflects that increasing division of labour in sociology which has made even of social theory a speciality—if one increasingly devoid of content. It also expresses that preoccupation with the concrete which characterizes so much recent intellectual activity in the humanities and social sciences. Surprisingly, it does not seem to follow from those familiar prescriptions for theoretically relevant empirical work of the sort found in so many programmatic essays on sociology. The theoretical legacy available to those pursuing these empirical studies has not been resolved into propositions subjected to precise and limited tests. It is exceedingly implausible to suppose that this failure to follow what might be termed the officially endorsed procedures of one version of sociology is due to the ineptitude of a large number of colleagues—or to their lack of discipline or insight. Rather, it seems to come from the nature of the problem itself; the general climate in which these researches have taken place, moreover, appears to have imposed this discrete character upon them. (There are interesting implications to be drawn for the contention that sociology is a cumulative science of a sort not different in principle from the natural sciences; this is not the place, however, to examine them.)

The second major tendency reported here seems to be an entirely different one. Rather than treating of discrete ideologies, it depicts them all as instances of one component in an abstract model of society. The contribution of Lévi-Strauss has been mentioned; this tendency is also evident in the very different works of Parsons and a number of Marxists, whether "vulgar" or not. These theories do *not* all treat ideology, or its equivalent, as the dependent variable in a system. The Marxists clearly do so, but Lévi-Strauss and Parsons do not. The thread common to these theoretical ventures is this: the concept of ideology has been severed from its philosophical bases and discussions of it no longer entail epistemological dispute. Moreover, the historical problem of a developing interpretation of a changing truth has been more or less suppressed. These analyses are not all ahistorical; they do deal with ideology in terms of a static set of categories. The debate provoked in Weimar Germany by Mannheim's work (discussed by Barth and reproduced, in part, in Lenk's anthology) seems to be over. In Marxism itself, the philosophical categories of the early texts have little or no part in Marxist empirical work.

This development is not a repudiation of the theoretical problem of ideology, but it does transpose it onto another plane. In the circumstances, the theorists and those doing empirical work seem to agree implicitly on the limits of their concerns. (It must be said that Gurvitch's treatises constitute an exception, as does Sartre's recent critique of social science; it remains to be seen what resonance their work will find amongst sociologists. Adorno has been making these points for a decade—my debt to his thought is clear—but his influence on the younger German sociologists is limited.)

The curious course of discussions of ideological components in social science, perhaps, confirms this analysis. These discussions seem to have a shock effect on many of our colleagues. Those who respond to the challenge cannot do so dispassionately; the usually complacent tone of scholarly discourse suddenly disappears—to become strident and discordant. The intellectual and moral tensions implicit in these questions seem to inhibit many others from participating in the discussion. The insistence on sociology's status as a "science," so common in the literature, sometimes appears to be an article of faith—or a defensive mechanism.

Elsewhere, the end of ideology has been proclaimed. Upon examination, the assertion seems to entail three propositions. (1) Contemporary populations, everywhere, are tired of and resistant to ideological indoctrination. They prefer, instead, to concentrate on the tasks of daily life—however much these may vary amongst societies. (2) The problems of modern society can be solved only in pragmatic fashion, step by step; ideologies are either irrelevant or hindrances to their solution. (3) Within each of the contending power blocs, the possibility of ideological innovation has been exhausted.

It is clear that these propositions are of different types; they include an empirical assertion about popular attitudes, a statement of preference for one rather than another mode of inducing social change, and political judgements of Communist and western society. The latter two propositions, of course, may be defended by reference to other factual assertions—but these are far from being matters of general agreement.

The announcement of the end of ideology, then, appears to represent what can only be termed an ideological position. It is interesting that the analysis of ideology here has been used (once again) as a method of political persuasion. There may well be a certain consonance between this position and the prevailing disinclination to attack the philosophical problems of ideology; both entail an acceptance of what appears to be empirically given as an appropriate framework for theoretical discussion.

The apparent renunciation of discussion of the question of interests, in recent sociology, may be due to these tendencies as well as to the intrinsic difficulty of the problem. It is assumed that some kind of interests are to be found behind every ideology. Interest, as long as the problem is put aside, can hardly be distinguished from disinterest and the identification of a putative social—as opposed to partial—interest need not be broached. The fact that the conception of interest entails these conceptual and evaluative difficulties, however, would appear to make a renewed effort to deal with it all the more welcome.

Finally, the question of the Marxist revival requires comment. It is instructive that this revival cannot be attributed to the economic and political successes of the Communist movement in any simple sense; the revival is the work of those who seek an interpretation of Marxism different from the prevailing Communist one. There is little evidence, moreover, to suggest that a viable *rapprochement* between the contending versions of Marxism can be developed, however welcome it might be on many grounds. The Marxist revival in the western countries, and elsewhere, has emphasized the significance of the early writings of Marx and Engels. This, too, is ideological: it is striking that socialists interested in the humanization of socialist ethics, and Christians interested in the revision of their own morality, have produced the exegetical literature in question. The fundamental question, however, is whether this sort of Marxism—pushed to its limits —must inevitably become not a neo-Marxism but something radically new. The analysis of late capitalism and imperialism as well as of Communist society, and changes in the social and political structure of other parts of the world, have produced empirical data which place the familiar Marxist categories under a heavy strain.

In particular, it is clear that the new Marxists are not associated with the proletarian vanguard. Many of them, indeed, reject the Leninist theory of socialist organization. An "orthodox" material basis for their own Marxism, in other words, cannot be found—with this difficulty, a reconsideration of the Marxist conception of ideology (called for, in any case, by other sorts of data) becomes urgent. The controversy provoked by Goldmann's insistence that Marxism itself entails a "religious" conviction is symptomatic. It follows that, once more, an ideological problem may result in a new development in the general analysis of ideology.

Monarchs and Sociologists:

A Reply to Professor Shils

and Mr. Young

In the course of an analysis of the Coronation in this publication, Professor Shils and Mr. Young have suggested some sociological generalizations of universal scope, ventured a characterization of modern Britain, and taken issue with some of us (variously designated as "intellectuals" or adherents of "secular utilitarianism") for blindness, if not hostility, to truths which they find practically self-evident.

A brief and, I hope, an accurate summary of their views is made easy by the explicitness with which they advance many of their central assumptions. Their most critical assumption is, perhaps, the following: "A society is held together by its internal agreement about the sacredness of certain fundamental moral standards." (Page 80). These moral standards are something more than means for regulating social relationships. They are objects of stubborn and unquestioning commitment, which functions even in secular societies in ways exactly analogous to religious belief. It is this commitment which endows the ultimate moral directives of a society with a "sacred" character. These directives arrange themselves in a single and coherent value hierarchy. The result is a basic unanimity of moral belief and action which renders most societies "generally peaceful and coherent" (Page 65) despite all conflicts which may and do occur.

The sacredness of a society's value hierarchy somehow infuses the authority structure of the society with a similar status. Professor Shils and Mr. Young declare that this process takes place "in an inchoate, dimly perceived, and seldom explicit manner." (Page 80). Authority becomes more than functional. A channel of communication with "the realm of the sacred values" (Page 80) and indeed, the custodian of these values, authority itself becomes sacred.

It is in this framework that Professor Shils and Mr. Young analyse the function of the British monarchy. The Crown symbolizes the authority system of British society in two respects. It represents, or is in close touch with, the value hierarchy constitutive of British society. It also stands for the benign aspects of elites actually governing the society. To this second component of its symbolic role, the very helplessness and powerlessness of the Crown is a critical contribution. The divorce of the Crown from politics enables it to mobilize the positive feelings of the populace. It also refracts these feelings, as it were, onto the effective authorities of the society. And the process of refraction is extremely effective in countering those negative impulses towards authority which might otherwise break down the social structure.

The Coronation ritual was a demonstration of the way in which the Crown keeps British society intact. Joint participation in the ritual induced in the members of British society a sense of unity with one another. The ritual called forth those positive sentiments toward the Crown which are so effective in stabilizing the authority system generally. It was the occasion for the re-affirmation of those moral standards binding the community together. In a very real sense, we may say that the ritual re-constituted British society itself.

Such are the propositions advanced by our colleagues as indispensable aids to the understanding of "the meaning of the Coronation." But meaning, it may be recalled, is an ambiguous word. We may understand the meaning of an event in a factual sense and analyse its antecedents, its accompaniments, its consequences. In discourse of this sort, statement is in principle referable to fact. Professor Shils and Mr. Young present their essay as an exercise of this kind. They do advance propositions both general and abstract. But they are quite obviously aware that such propositions are, ultimately, dependent upon fact.

A closer examination of their text, however, suggests that they have not entirely escaped the ambiguity implied by the term, meaning. The meaning of an event may also refer to its relationship to our subjective preferences. This critique contends that Professor Shils and Mr. Young, in discussing the Coronation, have confused two types of discourse. Their view of objective fact has been distorted by their subjective preferences. They have reconstructed reality to suit their own biases. For reasons other than scientific error their interpretation of "the meaning of the Coronation," then, may well differ from the interpretation other observers would make. But before we pursue this argument further, the authors' claim to have presented the event in scientific terms deserves a close analysis.

I

The authors' central proposition seems to be the following: "In all societies, most of the adult members possess some moral standards and beliefs about which there is agreement. There is an ordering and assessment of actions and qualities according to a definite, although usually unspoken, conception of virtue. The general acceptance of this scale of values, even though vague and inarticulate, constitutes the general moral consensus of society." (Page 65).

The authors advance no evidence in support of this proposition. Nor could they do so. The existence of consensus has served sociology as an operating assumption for so long that its heuristic status has been forgotten. Treating a proposition as proven does not in fact prove it. On the face of it, this proposition violates the evidence we do have, which suggests that complex and rationalized societies like our own are arenas for conflicts of beliefs and moral standards unmatched in comparative and historical perspective. It would be useful to know what sort of consensus does exist in any modern society, what its objects are, and who participates in it. But the existence of unitary value hierarchies of so unequivocal a kind has yet to be demonstrated.

Professor Shils and Mr. Young do attempt to specify their proposition: "What are the moral values which restrain men's egotism and enable society to hold itself together? A few can be listed illustratively: generosity, charity, loyalty, justice in the distribution of opportunities and rewards, reasonable respect for authority, the dignity of the individual and his right to freedom." (Page 65). These values, of course, are specific only to one type of society. Other societies have institutionalized antithetical values but have been successful in the restraint of egotism and the maintenance of their coherence. Even for this society, the specified values are extremely vague. When, for instance, does respect for authority cease to be "reasonable"? Almost any of the values cited could generate mutually exclusive directives for action in a number of easily imaginable moral dilemmas.

When the authors try to show that a single scheme of values unites different components of the social structure, they are not very convincing. Relating the family system to the

Coronation ritual, they claim that this was an occasion "for re-asserting its solidarity and for re-emphasizing the values of the family—generosity, loyalty, love—which are at the same time the fundamental values necessary for the well being of the larger society." (Page 73). The larger society, however, includes very many large-scale and impersonal organizational structures, where "generosity, loyalty, love" are positive hindrances to effective organizational function. Indeed, the antithesis between familial values and those of the occupational system is a familiar theme in much literature on the social background of psychiatric disorder.

Perhaps some of the authors' difficulty in this matter is a consequence of their failure to distinguish complex societies of the modern, industrial type from other social systems. They use the terms, "polis or community," (Page 66) in this analysis of modern Britain as if the familiar problem of *Gemeinschaft* and *Gesellschaft* could be dismissed out of hand. Sociological hypotheses applicable to small primitive village communities or to ancient and medieval city-states may require radical qualification in other situations.

In any case, generalizations about the integration of society around a unitary value hierarchy may not always apply even in pre-industrial systems. Our view of social integration depends upon our view of the authors' contention that in social organization, order prevails over conflict. Professor Shils and Mr. Young do not deny the existence of conflict. They simply assert that "intertwined with all these conflicts are agreements strong enough to keep society generally peaceful and coherent." (Page 65). They phrase their proposition in a manner so inexplicit that it is difficult to see what sorts of evidence might test it. But even on this exceedingly general plane, we may say that most readings of social history do not support the authors' view. Conflict seems to be as prevalent a component of social life as order. One or the other may prevail in a society at any given time, yet history records ceaseless alternation between these two modes. Sociology would be guilty of a peculiarly flagrant over-simplification were it to insist on the predominance of either one. (The insistence on the existence of integration in the essay of Professor Shils and Mr. Young may represent one of the "disfunctional" consequences of their reliance on functional analysis. Functional analysis does emphasize social integration, but the emphasis is a heuristic device and ought not to prejudice our view of social reality).

Some further difficulties emerge with scrutiny of the authors' argument on the function of the value system in the social structure. They hold that "A society is held together by its internal agreement about the sacredness of certain fundamental moral standards." (Page 80). This "agreement" is said to be "unspoken" or "vague and inarticulate." (Page 65). The alleged inarticulateness of the agreement seems to contradict a part, at least, of the authors' subsequent analysis of the ritual itself, which assumes considerable consciousness of values in the populace. If the agreement, however, is inarticulate and not reasoned out, it may well be a sort of enforced agreement, the result of some form of psychological manipulation. Psychological analysis can, of course, involve us in endless regress in the search for some entity like *real assent*. But we may remind ourselves that effectiveness at one level does not constitute authenticity at another. Professor Shils and Mr. Young are not very specific as to what they mean by agreement, and their definition opens problems as well as suggesting solutions to them.

Another difficulty is, perhaps, more disturbing. Despite their definitiveness of style, Professor Shils and Mr. Young are not quite clear that moral standards and beliefs are so important after all. Their discussion tends to veer between two propositions. The first holds that the standards themselves are sacred. The second treats their sacredness as a derivative of submission to some or other authority held sacred. For instance, they write: "The sacredness of society is at bottom the sacredness of its moral rules, which itself derives from the presumed relationship between these rules in their deepest significance and the forces and agents which men regard as having the power to influence their destiny for better or for worse." (Page 66). And, further on, they tell us: "The reaffirmation of the moral rules of society serves to quell their own (the populace's) hostility towards these rules and also reinstates them in the appropriate relations with the greater values and powers behind the moral rules." In these passages, and in the analysis elsewhere in the text, "forces and agents" and "powers" seem more important than the rules themselves.

In the summary of their argument, Professor Shils and Mr. Young declare: ". . . that authority which is charged with obligations to provide for and to protect the community in its fundamental constitution is always rooted in the sacred." (Page 75). We have previously noted their remark that the connection between the sacredness of the rules and that of the authorities administering them is "inchoate." (Page 80). Certainly, the use of terms like "rooted in" does little to improve our understanding of the connection. But it does point, not only to a certain contradiction in the argument, but to one of the authors' most important biases: the extremely high value they themselves place upon authority. We shall have ample occasion to deal with this matter in the final section of this critique. For the moment, it suffices to note it, and to pass on to some more difficulties in the text.

Not only do the authors assume that unitary value hierarchies exist in all societies; they seem unable to treat situations of value conflict systematically. They write of the ordinary man: "He too is a moral being, and even when he evades standards and dishonours obligations, he almost always concedes their validity. The revivalist reassertion of moral standards in highly individualistic frontier groups, or among detribalized primitive societies in the process of yielding before the pressure of a modern economy, are instances of the respect vice pays to virtue. The recourse to the priestly confessor and the psychoanalyst testify to the power of moral standards even in situations where they are powerless to prevent actual wrongdoing," (Page 65):

This statement assumes that in the social situations it describes, only one set of standards can be called "moral." Yet Professor Shils and Mr. Young define as "actual wrongdoing" what seems to be in fact the exercise of choice in a situation of opposing moral standards. They are, of course, quite right to suggest that moral conflicts mount in situations of decreasing social cohesion. But to talk of the revival of "moral standards" (rather than some specific set of standards) in individualized groups is to come very near to the suggestion that morality is that which maximizes group cohesion.

What both priestly confessors and psychoanalysts frequently do, moreover, is to affirm the impossibility of unambiguous moral decision. People turn to these agencies when their situation is overwhelmingly complex, when conflicting pressures for moral decision are nearly intolerable. In these circumstances, the very affirmation of the impossibility of unambiguous decision is a definite social service.

A similar note colours the authors' discussion of the family's place in society: The family tie is regarded as sacred, even by those who would or do shirk the diffuse obligations it imposes." (Page 72). Surely, it is unusual for sociologists to employ the term, "shirk." One would expect scientific students of society to take great care to avoid treating phenomena like divorce and family tension in moralistic terms. In any case, it is difficult to demonstrate that people do in fact regard the family tie as "sacred" in our own society.

The difficulties discussed throughout this section may be artifacts of an unfortunate choice of language. More probably, they may stem from too literal a utilization of the familiar sociological theories of moral integration. Alternatively, they may reflect distortions produced by the authors' value preferences. The next step in this critique is an examination of the authors' views of modern British society.

II

Professor Shils and Mr. Young begin their essay with an indictment of contemporary political science in Great Britain. They tax political scientists with tending to "speak as if Britain is now an odd kind of republic." (Page 63). Most political scientists, however, do more than speak this way; they understand British political institutions to function in just these terms. The authors resuscitate Bagehot's nineteenth century interpretation of the psychological role of the monarchy. Quite correctly, they add that the great editor of *The Economist* supported the Crown for the "precise reason that the republicans opposed it: because it enabled the educated ten thousand to go on governing as before." (Page 64). Professor Shils and Mr. Young argue that the nineteenth century saw the establishment of the stability of the British monarchy and they note that "whereas a century ago republicanism had numerous proponents in England, it is now a narrow and eccentric sect." (Page 76).

But most astonishing is the authors' studied avoidance of any reference to the basic changes in the functions and limits of the British monarchy since Bagehot's day. Its stability has in fact been purchased by a successive series of capitulations to republican demands. Professor Shils and Mr. Young refer to none of the constitutional crises of the recent past, and it must be said that their criticism of scholars like the late Professor Laski and Professor Jennings is a bit gratuitous. Neither would have written, as the authors do, of Lord Melbourne, Lord Beaconsfield and Mr. Gladstone as "the glittering host whose lives are the constitutional history of the realm." (Page 64).

We have already noted the authors' view of the current function of the monarchy. Professor Shils and Mr. Young hold that the very powerlessness of the Crown enables it "to bask in the sunshine of an affection unadulterated by its opposite." (Page 77). The concentration of affection on the Crown is, further, a great contribution to the stability of British political life. Those negative and destructive impulses toward authority present in any society, in their turn, concentrate on the leaders of the actual political parties, while the positive popular attitude toward the Crown keeps the entire authority system intact.

But this argument about the diffusion of positive and negative political impulses is not altogether plausible. It is difficult to see why the negative impulses, released in the ordinary sphere of politics, should not make British political life a shambles. Professor Shils and Mr. Young, apparently aware of this difficulty, interpose the proposition that "An effective segregation of love and hatred, when the love is directed towards a genuinely loveworthy object, reduces the intensity of the hatred as well." (Page 78). Most of us can recall a political segregation of love and hatred which resulted in extreme adulation for the late German Führer, and in extreme bestiality toward the opposition. The last proposition cited, further, does not seem to find a place in psychoanalytic literature. And the question of the loveworthiness of the object, with all respect for the Royal House, is not one which sociologists can answer in their scientific capacities.

The point of these critical remarks is not a denial of the undoubted relative political stability of Great Britain. The point is, rather, that Professor Shils and Mr. Young have given no internally consistent explanation of the Crown's contribution to this stability. What we really have to deal with seems to be a balance of psychological forces within the British population, such that positive impulses towards the political community outweigh negative ones. If so, the Crown as one focus of these sentiments may play a quite secondary and dependent role in the entire process. At times, Professor Shils and Mr. Young come very near to this viewpoint. They argue, in effect, that the British monarchy is so stable because of the high level of social integration attained by British society.

The authors assert that "Over the past century, British society, despite distinctions of nationality and social status, has achieved a degree of moral unity equalled by no other large national state." (Page 76). Again, we must note a considerable vagueness of definition. What exactly is "moral unity"? How are we to distinguish it from that sort of imposed unity found in totalitarian societies, or from the extreme standardization and conformity of a culture like that of the contemporary United States?

Some indication of what the authors mean comes from the immediately following remark: "The assimilation of the working class into the moral consensus of British society, though certainly far from complete, has gone further in Great Britain than anywhere else, and its transformation from one of the most unruly and violent into one of the most orderly and law-abiding is one of the great collective achievements of modern times." (Page 76). This is an extraordinary statement by any criterion. Most visitors to this country from the U.S. are struck by the difference between the *embourgeoisement* of the American worker and the by now traditionalized and self-conscious class consciousness of his British counterpart. In any case, to speak of the assimilation of the working class into the consensus of British society is to define that consensus by exclusive reference to middle and upper class groups. This is at least as much a reference to the presumed extension of the morality and ideology of one class to another as it is to consensus in the usual sense of the term.

Professor Shils and Mr. Young do seem to mean an extension of this sort, or we should find inexplicable their remark that "the painstaking probity of Kings George V and

VI in dealing with the Labour Party . . . has helped to weld the Labour Party and its following firmly into the moral framework of the national life." (Page 77). This statement defines national moral community in terms of the propertied classes and their servitors. It is at least as plausible to assert that the social changes instituted by Labour, and won only as the climax of over a century of bitter struggle, brought the propertied into the national moral life for the first time. Royal probity is beside the point: the Monarchs in question had to choose between accepting socialism or unemployment for their House.

The authors at times write as if conflict, and especially class conflict, were in Great Britain a thing presently unknown. "The universities, the municipalities, the professional bodies, the trade unions, the business corporations . . . co-exist and co-operate in a remarkable atmosphere of mutual respect and relative freedom from acrimony." (Page 79). This is quite true relative to Italy, for instance, but would our authors say so if asked to compare Britain to Yugoslavia? Exceedingly general comparative statements of this kind are useful as rough impressions, but they contribute little to systematic analysis of a social system. Professor Shils and Mr. Young persist in treating Britain as unified without much further specification, which allows them to say that, "The monarchy is the one pervasive institution, standing above all others, which plays a part in a vital way comparable to the function of the medieval Church as seen by Professor Tawney—the function of integrating diverse elements into a whole by protecting and defining their autonomy." (Page 79). The imputed protecting and defining powers of the Crown contradict that portion of the authors' analysis which emphasizes the powerlessness of the Monarchy. And the analogy with medieval society simply distorts historical fact: the Church in that society was the centre of extreme conflict.

Despite their general silence on the problem of class conflicts in modern Britain, the authors do acknowledge that the First World War, the General Strike and the Depression discredited the British "ruling class." (Page 76). (It is difficult to see why a perfectly legitimate sociological concept, that of the ruling class, alone of all the concepts used by the authors merits isolation by quotation marks. Perhaps we are supposed to infer that the idea of a ruling class is some kind of fiction, or that it is hazier than notions like consensus).

The authors note immediately after remarking on the decline in prestige of the ruling elite, that "Consensus on fundamental values remained." (Page 76). It is unclear what these fundamental values could have been, since consensus by the authors' own admission did not quite extend to the legitimacy and efficacy of the society's ruling elite or of its economic institutions. Agreements on "justice" and "charity" do not seem to have precluded the social conflicts of the past decades. It is a question whether they alone set the limits, undoubtedly present, which kept Britain from civil war. The authors' emphasis on the integration of society about a single value system precludes alternative explanations of the phenomena of social cohesion, or, more accurately put, of compliance. And Professor Shils and Mr. Young make very little effort to relate value integration to other dynamic aspects of the social system.

We have previously noted the authors' silence on the question of the Monarch's change in status and function in modern times. Much of their analysis suffers, as already suggested, from a curious attribution to the Crown of powers it does not in fact possess. "The crowds who turn out to see the Queen, who waited in the rain in quiet happiness to see the Queen and her soldiers, were waiting to enter into contact with the mighty powers who are symbolically and to some extent really responsible for the care and protection of their basic values." (Page 75). Some of the language may remind us of a political bed-time story rather than a serious analysis, but the main point is the authors' foreshortened perspective. Professor Shils and Mr. Young do not discuss the prosaic questions of popular sovereignty, representation, parliamentary process and the problem of control of bureaucracy. But surely these are more relevant to the "care and protection" of the basic values of the populace than the Monarchy, whose real responsibilities are so few. The officials who work at National Insurance, from this point of view, deserved a place in the Coronation procession before the fighting services. (And if the authors employ the analysis of the unconscious, they ought to acknowledge that popular adulation for the Queen's soldiers may have its sources in phenomena of social mal-integration, rather than the reverse).

We have noted the authors' views of the society in which the Coronation ritual took place. It now remains to examine their account of the ritual itself.

III

The authors describe the coronation service as itself "a series of ritual affirmations of the moral values necessary to a well-governed and good society." (Page 67). It is unclear whether the authors assert that these values are believed to be necessary in British society, or are simply expressing their own preferences. The supposed British values are not universal, and other versions of "well-governed and good" societies, if there be such, are imaginable. "The whole service reiterates their (the values') supremacy above the personality of the Sovereign." (Page 68). We may, then, note an initial discrepancy between the service and popular response to it. The response focussed, by general agreement, on the personality of the Sovereign.

Professor Shils and Mr. Young treat the Coronation service with an astonishing literalness. We may say that their literalness of interpretation seems to match that of the Archbishop of Canterbury, if of nobody else. Thus they write of the Queen's oath to "govern" the people of the United Kingdom and the Dominions in accord with their law and customs, without noting the anachronism evident in the use of the term, "govern." (Page 68). They describe the Bible presented to the Queen in the course of the service as "a source of continuous inspiration in the moral regulation of society." (Page 69). The Gideon Society would be glad to hear this, but the rest of us must doubt that this book has so much influence on contemporary social life. And when they describe the Queen as acknowledging "the transcendent moral standards and their divine source" (Page 68) all that we may say is that the transcendence of moral standards, and their divine origin, are not subject to verification by the usual empirical means.

Professor Shils and Mr. Young are so insistent on the meaningfulness of the ritual that they get into some difficulties. They deny, for instance, that the organization of the service by the Church of England was regarded as an anomaly. But the participation of the Moderator of the Scottish Church followed very considerable public dispute on this score. The claim that the Coronation role of the Church of England "served the vague religiosity of the mass of the British people without raising issues of ecclesiastical jurisdiction or formal representation" (Page 69) is not, therefore, accurate.

The authors go on to assert that "Britain is generally a Christian country, it is certainly a religious country, in the broad sense," (Page 69) but the assertion is so broad as to be nearly empty. It is likely, indeed, to provoke contradiction from those Churchmen who see their task as the reconquest of Britain for Christianity. What, after all, does "Christian" mean? It can refer either to formal religious affiliation, or to actual ethical practice. In the latter case, assertions about the Christianity of Great Britain are open to serious dispute.

Some other comments of the authors are simply perplexing. They cite the words of the anointing ceremony: "And as

Solomon was anointed King by Zadok the priest and Nathan the prophet, so be thou anointed, blessed and consecrated Queen over the peoples," and add: "It is not merely an analogy; it is a symbolization of reality, in conformity with sacred precedent." (Page 69). But just what reality is meant? Unlike the Ethiopian Emperor, British monarchs do not claim descent from the Kings of the Old Testament. Nor does an alleged linear connection between the Kingdoms of ancient Israel and the British Empire play a significant role in British political theory.

But literalness alone is perhaps the least difficulty of the authors' presentation. Far more serious is their attribution to the ritual of meanings not shared by the populace as a whole. Writing of the presentation of the naked sword to the Queen, the authors tell us: "In this way the terrible responsibilities and powers of royal authority are communicated to the Queen and the people. The people are thus made aware of the protection which a good authority can offer them when they themselves adhere to the moral law, and of the wrathful punishment which will follow their deviation." (Page 70). But the constitutional monarchy in Britain is singularly free from responsibilities and powers, terrible or otherwise. And we have no evidence that the British people in fact made this interpretation of the ceremony. Nor is it clear how they could have done so, in view of the vagueness of a general "moral law" in complex societies.

The authors claim that the Coronation had a ritual function in virtue of a ritual meaning shared by millions. Their evidence for the existence of a shared ritual meaning is very scant. They do report that a survey of London street parties (a sample about which they give no further information) showed "the complete inability of people to say why they thought important the occasion they were honouring with such elaborate ritual." (Page 63). This initial bit of evidence, apparently meant to underscore the unconscious component of ritual, seems to contradict the text a little further on (Page 64) in which "ordinary people," on the authority of a Sunday newspaper, are quoted as describing the Coronation as an "inspiration" or a national "rededication." Some subsequent remarks on letters written to the *Manchester Guardian* in protest at a sardonic cartoon by David Low ignore our lack of information as to the composition of this sample. The persons who wrote to denounce Low's attack on Coronation expenditure might have been country parsons, middle-class ladies of more respectability than means, or even sociologists. But we do not know how representative this vocal group was.

The climax of the article is the authors' attempt to give the ritual a theoretical explanation. They draw on Durkheim to support their claim that the Coronation re-integrated British society about a single scale of values. But we have already seen that the existence of a common value system in Great Britain is not easy to demonstrate. The authors' corollary, that the ritual reaffirmed allegiance to the authority system of Great Britain, is equally unconvincing. Their account of the role of the Crown in that system is anachronistic, and in any case, they fail to distinguish between ritual and real behaviour.

They hold that the Coronation overcame the ambivalence of individuals towards the moral rules of British society, by exerting a strengthening influence on their positive attitudes. But it is not clear what is strengthened by contact with the rules "in their most sacred form—as principles, or when symbolized in ritual activities, or when preached in moving sermons or speeches." (Page 67). We may discount this recurrence of a reverentially literal acceptance of the claims of the self-elected custodians of public morality by the authors. But we cannot discount the more basic difficulties of their position. Ritual may well satisfy the outward demands of conformity and allow transgression of the rules to continue unimpeded. Or it may relieve anxiety and, in the end, produce the same external result. In the ceremonial throng that crowded Westminster Abbey there may have been one or two accomplished evaders of income tax. Yet we have no evidence that ritual enthusiasm moved any such person to make remissions to the Chancellor of the Exchequer.

Professor Shils and Mr. Young amplify their argument by comparing the atmosphere of the Coronation to the blitz, the 1947 fuel crisis, the smog of 1952, "even during the Watson-Bailey stand in the Lord's Test or Lock's final overs." (Page 74). They add: "And to some extent the broad reasons were probably the same. There was a vital common subject for people to talk about; whatever the individual's speciality, the same thought was uppermost in his mind as in everybody else's, and that made it easier to overcome the customary barriers. But no less important than the common subject is the common sentiment of the sacredness of communal life and institutions."

Professor Shils and Mr. Young have phrased this passage so loosely that they are in difficulties. They would surely not wish us to infer that the blitz, the fuel crisis, and the smog were sacred institutions. Cricket is very notably a class-specific game and as such, is no more sacred to the rest of Britain than gin and tonic. The examples they give tend to support those supposedly superficial theories of the Coronation response which they deplore.

They claim that the family was the social unit "recognised" (Page 73) as the most appropriate for entry into the Coronation celebration. Since most people were home from work, it is difficult to see what other units they could have formed. But the note on the family contradicts the claim that the Coronation atmosphere overcame the "customary barriers" between people. The customary barriers of social distance are strongest, by general agreement, where the boundaries of the family begin.

74

The authors state their argument in summary form as follows: "In a great national communion like the Coronation, people become more aware of their dependence upon each other, and they sensed some connection between this and their relationship to the Queen. Thereby they became more sensitive to the values which bound them all together." (Page 74).

Another argument might run this way. The very absence of shared values in Great Britain accounts for some of the attention paid to the Coronation. The Coronation provided, for some sections of the populace, some measure of surcease from that condition of conflict which is more or less permanent for complex societies, of an industrial and modified capitalist type. Under this viewpoint, the role of the press in stirring up popular enthusiasm for the Coronation is less inexplicable. In response to the class interests it generally represents, the press continually seeks to minimize awareness of the real conflicts characteristic of British society. But the Coronation was a holiday, and its connections with the daily routine of social relationships was by no means as critical as the authors imagine. In this context, the personality of the Queen and her family functioned as the object of various fantasies and identifications in a way not much more "sacred" than the cult of adulation built up around certain film stars.

The concluding section of this critique seeks to analyse some of the reasons for the extraordinary value placed upon the ritual by Professor Shils and Mr. Young.

IV

We have noted the scientific untenability of some of the authors' central assumptions. It would be easy enough to attribute these difficulties to one or another conventional source of error: faulty reasoning, lack of critical reflection, reliance on insufficient data. But if we did so, we should ignore a considerable body of thought in social science which tells us that the perceptions of men are frequently dictated by their interests. This final section of the critique is an effort to sketch some of the interests Professor Shils and Mr. Young apparently bring to the analysis of the Coronation.

Professor Shils and Mr. Young, it may be recalled, employ a similar approach. They argue that the "intellectualist" biases of the educated classes account for a functional blindness to religious and quasi-religious phenomena. They argue, further, that the bias of the educated, "particularly those of radical or liberal political disposition, is liable to produce abhorrence towards manifestations of popular devotion to any institution which cannot recommend itself to secular utilitarianism." (Page 71).

But the sociological advocates of religiosity seem unable to grasp something essential in our intellectual situation. They ignore the religious thought of a Karl Barth or an Emmanuel Monnier. They seem unable to take Kierkegaard's heirs seriously, or even to acknowledge their existence. This is no accident. Those most concerned with faith in the age of totalitarianism, whether German Lutheran or French Catholic, existentialist or communal in their assumptions, absolutely reject those "friends" of religion who would make it a prop of *this* social order. The secular utilitarians and the surviving Christians surely unite on this point: the tawdry baubles of the Coronation celebration constitute no adequate substitute for the lost faith of millions.

Professor Shils and Mr. Young place an extremely high valuation upon tradition, conformity, and authority. Their conception of religion assigns to it the role of legitimating the existent structure of power. But it need not conceal from us some of the other historical roles taken by religion: in the activities of the medieval sects, in the Reformation, and in the contribution of non-conformism to British culture. In fact, the authors' attack on the critical habits of the "intellectuals" is an attack on the Protestant tradition, even if directed ostensibly against its secularized derivatives.

Scoffing at the "educated detractors" of the ordinary man, they argue that assent by ordinary men to the moral standards of their society renders them moral beings. "Only philosophical intellectuals and prophets demand that conduct be guided by explicit moral standards . . ." while those persons "who derive and justify every action by referring it to a general principle impress most others as intolerable doctrinaires." (Page 71).

A good many of us have always thought that the continual examination of moral standards was in fact more moral than the uncritical acceptance of received tradition. This may make us "intolerable doctrinaires," but it does not seem that the implicit adherence to tradition celebrated by Professor Shils and Mr. Young is much better. The authors' insistence on the desirability of uncritical acceptance of morality combines with their suggestion that morality is the maintenance of group cohesion to account for the vigour of their attack on the intellectuals. But their own work should give them some reassurance that intellectuality does not automatically lead to dissent.

The intellectuals' desire to elevate the ordinary man from "spiritual slothfulness" (Page 71) is by no means born of that contempt for him imputed by the authors. Most intellectuals critical of modern society (and the number seems to be diminishing) feel that it cheapens and violates human dignity, converts reason from a mode of enlightenment to an instrument of oppression, and obliterates the individual. Those who, with Professor Shils and Mr. Young, argue that the tinsel revels of the Coronation holiday in Britain represent an ultimate in gratification are hardly in a position to reproach the rest of us for contempt of our fellow humans.

Professor Shils and Mr. Young take some pains to remind the intellectuals that the "alienated and cantankerous" attitudes of the 1930s are past. But those who have read the recently published memoirs of Dr. Thomas Jones will wonder who, the intellectuals or the men typified by Baldwin, were in fact "alienated." The intellectuals were at least aware that a catastrophe impended. The authors note with some satisfaction that recent years have seen the assimilation of the intellectuals to British society. Their attribution of this process to employment, government patronage, and repugnance for the Soviet Union as well as national pride must qualify the use of the term "moral" to describe the consensus that was the result. (Pages 76 and 77).

Professor Shils and Mr. Young are so insistent on compliance that they distort the most unobjectionable of assumptions. "Life in a community is not only necessary to man for the genetic development of his human qualities. Society is necessary to man as an object of his higher evaluations and attachments, and without it man's human qualities could not find expression." (Page 66). But we all know of societies, or moments in the existence of given societies, in which social circumstances seem to block the expression of what most of us would regard as man's human qualities. Such societies seem undeserving of attachment, higher or otherwise. But Professor Shils and Mr. Young can find no place in their sociological vocabulary for this sort of value conflict. They write as if the rules were there to be obeyed.

Thus, in analysing ambivalence towards the moral rules of a society, they treat this phenomenon in purely intra-psychic terms, as "the struggle against morality being continually enacted in the human mind." (Page 66). The authors see these conflicts as obstacles to be overcome in the interests of maximal integration of the social system, not as perpetual dilemmas of social life. And if such ambivalence is entirely intra-psychic, or psychological, then this constitutes a curious denial of the possibility of objectively justified conflict. But ambivalence towards the moral rules may express ambivalence towards the existing *elite* of a society, as Professor Shils and Mr. Young know. This may or may not be justified in any given case, but it cannot be dismissed as simply subjective. Freud, we recall, traced the son's ambivalence toward the father to the latter's actual superiority over the child.

What seems to emerge in the authors' analysis of the Coronation is their own strong feeling of adherence to the official morality of Great Britain—and their preference for conformity to such moralities wherever they appear. In discussing poular response to the Coronation, they tell us that "antagonism emerged only against the people who did not seem to be joining in the great event or treating with proper respect the important social values—by failing, for instance, to decorate their buildings with proper splendour." (Page 75). They give no evidence for this assertion, nor any indication of how widespread this aversion might have been. We should also expect them, as social scientists, to show some awareness that such aggression might have been displaced from other spheres. Instead we get what from the language employed seems to be enthusiastic concurrence in it—concurrence quite explicit when we recall the authors' strictures on the "intellectuals."

We may make a similar comment on the authors' note that the ritual reinstated the British populace "in the appropriate relations with the greater values and powers behind the moral rules." (Page 66). Just what constitutes an "appropriate" relationship to such values and powers depends, of course, upon one's preferences. The authors derive an answer satisfactory to themselves from their emphasis on the worth of social integration. But they cannot expect the rest of us to share it.

Perhaps typical of the authors' viewpoint is their warning to us, in the final pages of their analysis, that "The British love of processions, of uniforms and ceremonial is not just simple-minded gullibility—it is the love of proximity to greatness and power." (Page 75). But this is also a judgment of value. The question of the role of authority in a democratic state and society is not one which can be solved by implicit recourse to the old Roman motto, *panem et circenses*. And it is a considerable disservice to sociology to present our discipline as a useful handmaiden of the current effort to make a conservative ideology once more orthodox and unquestioned.

Conservative Sociology: Robert Nisbet's "The Sociological Tradition"

Consider the conventional view of the development of sociology promulgated in American graduate schools. Sociology as an independent discipline emerged from the obscurities of political philosophy and historical speculation when men began to apply the methods so successful in the natural sciences—observation, the verification and falsification of hypotheses—to the study of society. In freeing themselves of metaphysical bondage, the great European founders of sociology had the merit of giving to later Yankee technicians the fundamental elements of a method of social enquiry which is now as universal in its diffusion as it is incontrovertible in its assumptions.

This view is, in fact, nonsense. Its canonical status in our graduate schools rests upon the ignorance of some, the vulgar philosophy of science of others. The division of intellectual labor, separating sociology from history and philosophy, has made of the sociological tradition in its contemporary form a caricature of its own origins. The virtue of Robert Nisbet's book is that he traces these origins to their metaphysical foundations, and that he shows that contemporary sociology —the protestations of many of its professors to the contrary— is not independent of them.

Nisbet's argument is simple, perhaps too much so. Sociology was born of the twin revolutions, the destruction of the *ancien régime* in France and the spread from England of machine production for a commodity market as a dominant element in social life. The nineteenth-century and early twentieth-century sociologists seized upon these phenomena as essential components of a new picture of history, but they generally did so from a conservative point of view. They abhorred the new society and its new politics in terms first uttered by Edmund Burke. Indeed, their depictions of the new society were for the most part transmutations into an observational language of a philosophical rhetoric. A historical vision, in other words, preceded the empirical assertions of a sociology which claimed objectivity.

In Nisbet's words, "The paradox of sociology—and it is, as I argue in these pages, a creative paradox—lies in the fact that although it falls, in its objectives and in the political and scientific values of its principal figures, in the mainstream of modernism, its essential concepts and its implicit perspectives place it much closer, generally speaking, to philosophical conservatism. Community, authority, the sacred: these are primary conservative preoccupations in the age, to be seen vividly in the intellectual line that reaches from Bonald to Haller to Burckhardt and Taine. So are the presentiments of alienation, of totalitarian power rising from mass democracy, and of cultural decay. One will look in vain for significant impact of these ideas and presentiments on the serious interests of economists, political scientists, psychologists and ethnologists in the age. But in sociology they are, transfigured of course by rationalist or scientific objectives of the sociologists, at the very core of the discipline."

Nisbet's method for the study of this episode in intellectual history consists in posing five pairs of antithetical concepts, and in examining their use in a series of thinkers. Comte, Marx, DeTocqueville, Tönnies, Weber, Durkheim, and Simmel figure most prominently in the text, but Burke, Rousseau, Hegel, and Mill are also present. There are, however, some surprising omissions—notably Nietzsche and Freud. Nisbet's treatment of history is, moreover, curiously ahistoric: he takes the modern period as a relatively static entity, and ignores its own inner movement. Important distinctions disappear: the state-allied capitalism of Prussia and the market capitalism of America and England seem to be the same, the free thought of Protestantism and the clericalism and anti-clericalism of Catholicism merge, *étatist* and liberal political traditions are joined. Nisbet's schematism is in part a consequence of his method, borrowed from the historian of philosophy Arthur Lovejoy. He conceives of the fundamental notions of modern sociology as "unit-ideas" which encompass historical description, sociological analysis, and moral evaluation. The ideas, then, define the historical period, more, idea and period merge, so that the one comes to stand for the other.

The "unit-ideas" do indeed point to historical transformations, but these are seen as finished, almost immutable processes. The first pair of concepts opposes society to community. Society is impersonal, so large in scale that it dwarfs individuals, so uniform that it eliminates all particularities of persons and places. Community is familiar, segmented into smaller units (family, locality, workplace), and rests on a diversity of men and conditions, joined in specific traditions. The gigantic change which converted Europe from a set of communities into an accretion of societies inevitably entailed a political transformation: power replaced authority. Power is centralized, abstract, often tyrannical. Authority rests on the moral constraints born of a direct human relationship, on traditional assent in a concrete setting. The third distinction refers to the substitution of status for class. In a fragmented mass society neither fixed economic and political divisions nor familial inheritance determine the individual's social location: status, a quantum of social recognition, attaches to an individual career. Class refers to the antecedent form of social organization, in which economic divisions accounted for rigidified social strata, each with its own culture and each participating unequally in a hierarchical system of power. The penultimate distinction is that between secular and sacred sentiments. Most societies have lived intimately with their particular gods, gave to worship a considerable share of their spiritual energy and material activity, and endowed their social institutions with a religious character. The gods died in the secularized world. Men drew such spiritual sustenance as they could from purely profane activity, and denied the existence of any other sphere. The final set of unit-ideas opposed a conception of progress to the idea of alienation. The doctrine of progress depicted human cultural evolution as unilinear, and held that men were not alone theoretically capable of realizing their full stature but that they would in fact do so. The idea of alienation showed men morally and spiritually crippled by circumstances they had never made, overwhelmed by oppressive powers outside themselves and unable to participate in communities which were themselves disintegrating. It denied the possibility of a human triumph over history, since it denied the possibility of a fulfilled humanity.

Sociology, in Nisbet's view, is a history of the decline and fall of the secular aspiration for a liberated mankind. The sociologist's apprehensions about the new industrial society were deeply pessimistic; they portrayed it as arid, oppressive, and tyrannical. Measuring the new social order of the industrial nineteenth century against the old, they found it wanting. With categories derived in some part from historical nostalgia, from their distaste for their own circumstances, they willed to sociology an intellectual legacy it has as yet to transcend. Indeed, in Nisbet's view it cannot transcend it, since the legacy is in large measure an appropriate apprehension of our historical period. Mere enumerative history, assembling the external facts about the new social structure, can hardly seize the period since what is distinctive about it is not its new structure, but the way in which this has issued in a lesser sort of man. The techniques of sociological research, Nisbet says, can of themselves not give us the contours of the epoch: they can be applied only within a setting previously established by thought.

It is important to see that Nisbet is to a considerable extent right. Sociology as a mode of thought, as what he terms a form of art, undoubtedly has many of its origins in the movement he describes. Many sociologists have belonged to the party of order. Indeed, Nisbet places himself squarely in that camp: "It is only too clear that the idea of 'democratic totalitarianism' was born in 1793." What is only too clear from Nisbet's text is that the single quotation marks within the citation are gratuitous: Nisbet does believe that there is something very like "democratic totalitarianism" and that it is inevitably the consequence of the libertarian aspirations of the French Revolution. Those sociologists hostile to, or at the least skeptical about those aspirations strike him as historically acute. The others he thinks of as interesting but somehow insufficiently perceptive. What he presents, inevitably, is a truncated version of the sociological tradition —with its critical elements systematically underplayed. Those elements in Europe and America are difficult enough to characterize in a summary way. For the moment, we may say that a critical sociology has sought the possibilities of human fulfillment in and through technology and urbanism, in experimentation and if necessary, revolution, rather than in the mobilization of the pathos of nostalgia in the interests of order.

Nisbet's reading of sociological tradition, then, is askew. One of the consequences of his insistence on the conservative character of sociology is a curious brevity (verging on evasiveness) with respect to the encounter of sociological and natural scientific thought. The general confluence of philosophy with models of enquiry based on the natural sciences took different forms in sociology. Their inner structures are as yet historically unclear to us. Nisbet's reluctance to deal analytically with this problem is convenient for him—it allows him to assert, at once, the essential conservatism of sociological tradition and the objective validity of that tradition's view of society. It is distressing to witness as sensitive a thinker as Nisbet resort to formulations like the following comment on Durkheim. "At the time *The Rules of Sociological Method* was published, it must have appeared—in the ultra-individualistic age of social science—as hardly more than a vision of the absolute social mind, a scholastic exercise in reification. As one looks back on that age, it it clear that there were then as few sociologists capable of assimilating Durkheim's central argument into the individualistic categories of their minds as there were, a decade or two later, physicists capable of assimilating Einstein's theory of relativity into the classical categories of their lectures on mechanics." Now, Durkheim was not as original (many of his ideas having been stated by Comte) and the age not as individualistic as Nisbet says. The comparison with Einstein is gratuitous: by Nisbet's own account, the development of the social sciences proceeded in a fashion other than the relatively unilinear progression of the natural sciences. Finally, with all respect for Durkheim's achievements, the intimation that he was an Einstein in sociology is absurd.

Nisbet's general thesis is so compelling, on the face of it, that a hard look at some of the specific modes of his thought is in order. His own endorsement of historical and spiritual conservatism is quite open. He depicts the epoch before the French Revolution in terms which exaggerate its positive aspects. Community in fact brought with it a quite intolerable moral constriction, authority in its traditional form entailed quite an intolerable quantum of domination, the sentiment of sacredness was allied to a blind obscurantism. Class relations under the *ancien régime* were not nearly as fixed as Nisbet thinks, but having a fixed place in the social order meant for most men having an abominably minimal share of social product. If the progress envisaged by the *Philosophes* has not been realized, nothing much will be gained by insisting on alienation as a permanent human condition when (even on the analysis of some thinkers of whom Nisbet patently approves) it is a historical one.

Nisbet does allow himself to take positions which are not entirely true to the texts on which he claims they are based. This difficulty is nowhere more evident than in his treatment of the vexed questions of class relations and their consequences for society's hierarchical arrangements in general. Here is Nisbet's view. "Status becomes a tool of analysis, an explicit framework of observation, through which matters as diverse as religion, economy, education and political behavior are illuminated. From Weber more than any other sociologist has come contemporary sociology's varied use of status and status group in the analysis of human behavior. Down until the 1930s Marx's monolithic and unwieldly vision of class tended to dominate the study of stratification. No doubt what proved necessary to end the spell of Marx in modern sociology was not so much the accumulation of new data, as the political spectacle of Stalin's Russia and the consequent ideological disaffection. But the result, however gained, was the same: the gradual supersession of 'class' by 'status' as the key concept in sociological studies of stratification."

In Nisbet's terms, status has two meanings. The first (which he attributed largely to DeTocqueville) describes an atomized society, riven by anxiety and ambition, unregulated by mechanisms of fixed social placement. In these circumstances, status was the quantum of recognition and honor attained by individuals in their careers. A second meaning used by Nisbet, which he attributes to Weber, rests on the notion of "status groups," of ensembles and strata sharing a common and distictive "style of life." We may note that these two usages, which Nisbet confounds, are in fact exceedingly disparate if not contradictory. An atomized society of individuals pursuing their fortune is not one in which fixed groupings with exclusive cultures can readily develop. Worse yet, the attribution of so sweeping a usage of the notion of "status groups" to Weber is quite untrue to Weber's intentions. Indeed, it rests on an apparent mistranslation of Weber's German term "Stände," for which the equivalent in the English tradition of historical and political theory is *Estates*. Contrary to Nisbet's interpretation, Weber did not for modern societies oppose an estate type of hierarchy to one based on market relations, or class in the Marxist sense. He showed that estates frequently arose through the exploitation of market advantages, and that estate closure under modern conditions was possible only by domination of the market. Nisbet makes much of Weber's theory of bureaucracy as a counterweight to Marxism, but Weber himself spoke of the appropriation of the means of administration, and these are in industrial societies inextricably fused with the means of production. Where Weber did differ from Marx was in his emphasis on the organization of power. With respect to the existence and importance of classes in modern society, Weber was for many practical purposes quite Marxist.

Finally, it is impossible to accept Nisbet's contention that class, as an issue in academic sociology, is dead. It is a curious contention to make in an America which (without much help from most academic sociologists, to be sure) has discovered its own underclass. Moreover, in sociology in the western and eastern European countries, the issue of class is very much alive. Nisbet deals with a European sociological tradition and then allows his readers to suppose that Berkeley and Harvard are its only heirs. The tradition lives at Belgrade, Frankfurt, London, Paris, and Warsaw. Perhaps sociologists ought not to discuss class in Marxist terms; Nisbet himself thinks that this is a waste of time. Many of us, however, persist in doing so and no purpose will be served by calling us academic un-persons.

Nisbet's very considerable efforts at carrying his thesis some-times cause him to take liberties in interpretation. "All of the essential elements of Weber's analysis of the history of political power have their prototype in DeTocqueville's treat-ment of the affinity between social egalitarianism and centraliz-ation of political power. In each instance a single dominating aspect of modernism is endowed with dynamic, even causal, historical significance. What for Tocqueville is epitomized by 'aristocratic' is epitomized for Weber by 'traditional.' " Weber's belief in the omnipotence of bureaucracy is in fact antithetical to a belief in the factual existence of egalitarian-ism. Bureaucracy entails the formation of elites and sub-elites by pervasive means of social selection. Nisbet is so insistent on the continuity between DeTocqueville and Weber that he ignores some obvious discontinuities. "Aristocratic" in DeTocqueville and "traditional" in Weber do not mean the same. The aristocratic society DeTocqueville spoke of existed in the context of the modern European state; Weber did not find very much traditionalism in modern Europe since the Reformation. Weber, incidentally, did not share DeTocque-ville's view that America anticipated Europe's future; he had grave doubts—in the end, utterly justified—as to whether America was in any historical sense a nation. DeTocqueville and Weber both saw something which Nisbet has not dwelt upon: a major element in the modern obsession with status is the market organization of society, and the omnipresence of money and monetary judgments. Nisbet's interpretations point to his own aversion to the analysis of the market as the central institution of an industrial society which is, after all, capitalist.

Another aspect of Marxism causes Nisbet difficulties which verge on embarrassment. He very much wants to depict Marx as old-fashioned, but he seems to admire Marx's faith in the possibility of spiritual autonomy and wholeness for man. Nisbet sees that some of the thinkers he discusses treated the human personality, unto the very core of the self, as entirely a precipitate of society. Whereas Marx held that capitalist commodity production prevented the realization of a given human potential, Durkheim denied that there was any such potential: every society or stage of social existence totally defined human personality. The sociological tradition, in this sense, represents a renunciation of doctrines of human fulfillment, and their replacement by a deterministic pessimism. It is surprising that Nisbet ignores the contribution of Nietzsche and Freud to this tradition. Nietzsche extracted from the legacy of biblical and classical studies an anti-theology, a historical account of the rise of conscience and consciousness. His *Genealogy of Morals* was a historical psychology of unprecedented moral ruthlessness, which contained many of the categories (identification, sublimation, repression) later to be derived from clinical evidence by Freud. Freud himself, despite his tireless detractors, was a sociological thinker of great profundity. His depiction of the antagonism between human nature and the demands of society, of the super-ego as the repository of historical experience and social conscience, his exquisite analyses of authority and religion, constitute contributions to our sociological understanding which require integration with the work of the thinkers Nisbet discusses. The doctrine of alienation is at least as susceptible of psychoanalytic treatment as it is of depiction in terms of the consequences of humanly destructive social institutions. Indeed, we do not understand how institutions affect men until we understand the psychological processes they engender, and psychoanalysis is in this respect our best recourse. Perhaps Nisbet's reluctance to deal with psychoanalysis is part of his singular disinclination to deal with repression—whether political or psychological.

When we turn to Nisbet's consideration of method in sociology, different questions become troublesome. Nisbet is quite right to insist that a sterile positivism has little or nothing to offer sociology. He might well have said that most contemporary research technicians are unconscious Comteans, utilizing his method but not his total philosophy, whilst ignorant of both. (Some do share Comte's manipulative aims.) There is, however, another aspect to the history of social research: its origins in the ameliorative moralism of middle-class social reform. Both the Chicago School in America and the British tradition of social enquiry associated with the London School of Economics had this character. Early modern social research was not intended to devise a timeless science of society (whose achievement is usually predicated on the renewal of the researcher's current grant). Those who concentrate on the collection of politically relevant data may simply be administrative technologists, or may be pursuing reformist or even radical political ends. In no case has Nisbet done justice to this strand of sociological tradition, whose connection with the metahistorical and visionary elements in sociological thought requires a clarification it has as yet to receive (at any rate, in English).

Equally disturbing is Nisbet's version of totalizing method in sociology. His praise for Tönnies is revealing; he approves of Tönnies for having found "a sociological explanation of the rise of capitalism, the modern state, and the whole modernist temper of mind. What others found in economic or technological or military areas of causality, Tönnies found in the strictly social area: the area of community and its sociological displacement by non-communal modes of organization, law and polity." It is difficult to see the advantages of a method which refrains from analyzing the different sectors of society, for the sake of an analysis of the whole. It can be said that the analysis of the whole entails the determination of the unifying principle which infuses the separate sectors. This, however, presupposes a degree of social integration which may well be attained but which is not necessarily present at any given historical moment. Moreover, insofar as societies are integrated, the mere determination of this fact is a feat of description and not explanation. Tönnies, so praised by Nisbet, did bring a certain amount of Marxism into the academy—chiefly by inventing a large number of circumlocutions for the phrase, capitalist commodity production. Marxism itself requires severe emendation, even radical transformation, but there is no point to ignoring its methodological distinctiveness, its effort to apprehend totality by fixing the relationships between the elements of a society. The mere enunciation of the distinctiveness of something called "the social" will not do: Weber, for whom Nisbet reserves so much praise, was far more precise and analytical.

In the end, we come to reflect again on Nisbet's fixation on the conservative tradition in sociology. Perhaps there is an organic connection, more in the nature of an intellectual fatality than an explicit one, between a conservative view of history and the administrative aspects of modern social research. If there are no possibilities for liberation in contemporary society, no hopes for the development of a true community, no chance for the growth of authentic human selfhood, then perhaps the only course is the manipulation of men as they are. The search for laws of behavior (disguised as universal laws of human function) serves the ends of political domination. A deep philosophical despair, disguised as realism, leads to the renunciation of the ancient task of philosophy—to find the good and wise life. Instead, adherence to a philosophy which is a set of commentaries on data-gathering operations becomes a substitute for wisdom. If mankind's historical substance, aesthetic and sensual gratification, and highest moral development do indeed lie in an irrecoverable past, if the present is indeed an iron cage from which there is no escape, then the utilization of a positivistic method follows from a conservative philosophy of history. The aristocratic (or pseudo-aristocratic) nostalgia of the one generates the philistine renunciation of hope of the other. That Nisbet has not seen this is regrettable. Had he seen it, he would have written another book, one which would have given much more weight to Marxism and liberalism. In the event, the book is not an accidental and learned intrusion into the otherwise dull philosophical landscape of American sociology by an especially reflective spirit. Nisbet is reflective (and learned), and the spirit which infuses his text is far more profound than that of the positivism he scores. His work is nevertheless a retroactive justification for the triumph of positivism in American sociology. What Nisbet has done is to give us a conservative version of the sociological tradition. Another interpretation, other interpretations, would write intellectual history in a radically different manner.

The Crisis in

Marxist Sociology*

INTRODUCTION

We confront a paradox. Never before has Marxism been so influential upon bourgeois sociology (which we may define as sociology as practised by bourgeois professors who are not Marxists, in contradistinction to their—no less bourgeois— colleagues who are Marxists), never before has it been analyzed, criticized, and discussed so extensively. The utterly indefensible political restrictions which inhibited the development of a Marxist sociology (or, indeed, of critical Marxist thought in general) in the state socialist societies are beginning to weaken. An international Marxist discussion, ranging from London, Paris, Frankfurt and Milan to Zagreb, Budapest, Prague and Warsaw (with interesting accompani-

---

* AUTHOR'S NOTE—I have established a number of limitations in this essay. In particular, I have made rather free use of shorthand expressions like "Marxist sociology" and "bourgeois sociology." I understand quite well that these are in fact shorthand, that the systems of thought at issue are complex and varied, that the two types of sociology interpenetrate, and that there are serious conflicts and great differences within each grouping as well as between them. A rather full bibliography will be found in my *The Crisis of Industrial Society*, New York, Oxford University Press, 1969.

ments in New York and Moscow) is in progress. Nevertheless, there is a crisis in Marxism and particularly in Marxist sociology: it is the crisis itself which renders the current discussion at once so agitated and so fruitful.

The notion of a crisis requires, in this case, explication. A doctrinal or theoretic crisis in a system of thought occurs when either of two sets of abstract conditions obtains. In one case the possibilities of internal development of a system exhaust themselves; the system's categories become incapable of transformation; the discussion generated by the system becomes scholastic, in the pejorative sense of the term. In the other case the realities apprehended by the system in its original form change, so much so that the categories are inapplicable to new conditions. It is clear that these two sets of conditions often obtain simultaneously; particularly for systems dealing with the historical movement of society, the two sets of conditions of crisis are often quite inseparable. In the case of Marxism, a further complication is introduced by its claims to represent a total system, not alone a description of society but a prescription for human action within it. I propose to deal with the crisis of Marxist sociology, but to do so I shall be obliged to touch upon the political and philosophical elements in Marxism.

The outlines of the crisis in Marxism generally are as follows: The movement of the advanced capitalist societies has not entirely followed the concrete anticipations derived by the first generation of Marxists from their theoretical work. In particular, the (admittedly cyclical) productivity of the capitalist economy has relativized the notion of pauperization. It is true that disparities in wealth, income and access to facilities between the social classes continue to be very great. Nevertheless, an absolute increase in the social product and the political efforts of the working class movement have combined to assure the working class a standard of living which by no means constitutes absolute pauperization. Meanwhile, the class structure itself has been transformed: a new intermediate stratum of administrative, technical and service personnel, often possessing a considerable degree of education, has emerged. Objectively dependent upon those who command great concentrations of property, including state property, this stratum nonetheless has in general refused to align itself politically with the working class. Increasing concentration of property, therefore, has intensified the class conflict in a quite unexpected way, by complicating and differentiating it. Further, the bourgeois state has become so embedded in the economy proper, to the point of assuming coordinating and even command functions in some societies, that we are entitled to speak of a "neo-capitalist" society type which has largely replaced the older type of capitalism, in which state and economy were quite distinct. The persistence of an absurd ideology of free enterprise in the United States need not blind us to the actual interpenetration of state and economy visible in our own society. Under these conditions, the notion of property, of capital itself, has become diffuse: the classical Marxist theorems on the relationship of base and super-structure require emendation.

That emendation is all the more pressing in view of developments in state socialist societies. It is only now that we are beginning to obtain the first elements of a Marxist analysis of these societies from within, in contradistinction to a Marxist analysis practised either in opposition or from without. The analysis will have to deal with the fact that state property and the monopoly of its control exercised by the Communist parties in these societies have developed in such a way as to engender new class structures. Equally, new structures of political and cultural domination have accompanied the growth of state property in the socialist states.

A third historical development has constituted a challenge to the received canons of Marxist analysis. It is true that the third world constitutes a global proletariat, and that relationships of domination and exploitation characterize the ties between the industrial and non-industrial societies; nevertheless, the populations of the third world are a pre-industrial proletariat in whose exploitation the industrial working classes of the advanced societies are accomplices. Moreover (a phenomenon by no means restricted to the third world), the struggles of these populations for economic liberation usually assume nationalist and often extreme nationalist forms. Themselves German in their most profound national identifications, Marx and Engels never achieved a theoretic integration of the problem of the national community with the other dimensions of their theory. Indeed, their own work on imperialism as a socio-economic phenomenon remained fragmentary; their successors and even our Marxist contemporaries have had to amplify and extend it. The precise role played by imperialist economic relations in the advanced economies remains a matter for debate, the larger political and social consequences of imperialism even more so.

To these substantive difficulties of Marxist theory, occasioned by the movement of history and, in some cases, by the propagation of Marxism itself, we have to add the problems posed by the encounter of Marxism with bourgeois thought. At the outset, of course, Marxism was part of a critical movement in bourgeois thought which had its first historical point of crystallization in the work of the *Philosophes;* Marxism, with the left Hegelianism which gave rise to it, may be thought of as the late German counterpart of the work of the French Encyclopedists. Marx and Engels were insistent on the "scientific" character of Marxism in one essential respect: a critical social and historical theory had to subsume the findings and where necessary the methods of the advanced spheres of bourgeois thought—even where this last was not critical in intention, if extremely so in implication. Put in another way, Marxism at its origins was a *chef d'oeuvre* of bourgeois thought: the subsequent distinction between it and the development of thought outside the socialist movement is both cause and result of a movement in intellectual self-definition which has had many negative consequences. Psychoanalysis, the structural analysis of language, entire areas in the development of the natural sciences, important philosophic movements like phenomenology, have been related to Marxism in one of two ways, each deplorable. In the one sort of discourse, a facile translation or transformation of meaning has usually produced the conclusion that the structure and findings of the other systems were gratuitous: the phenomena they encompassed were apprehended best by an intact Marxism. In the other mode of response, an equally facile transformation has been used to show that other methods were in the last analysis truer to the spirit of Marxism than Marxism itself: the specificity of Marxism has often been ignored, or de-emphasized, in the effort to remain with the movement of modern Western thought or its surrogates.

This general problem has been particularly acute in sociology. The sources of Marxism and of bourgeois sociology were in large part identical. Hegel influenced Lorenz von Stein as well as Marx, Saint-Simon's work was continued by Comte, the British political economists' thought is reflected in the writings of John Stuart Mill (in whose *System of Logic* may be found the methodological postulates of a sociology on the model of the natural sciences). As sociology developed as an academic discipline, however, its relevance for Marxism was often enough ignored by Marxist thinkers. The most penetrating and original of the bourgeois sociologists, Weber, challenged Marxism most effectively where he accepted the premise of the radical historicity of social structures; it is difficult to imagine Lukacs' work, or Mannheim's academicization of it, as possible without Weber's critique of positivism. Tentative rapprochements of Marxism with sociology have occurred in Weimar Germany and in France after 1945.

It is striking that in the state socialist societies, sociology today is often identified with the development and utilization of certain technical means of inquiry into contemporary social phenomena, rather than with theoretical work as such. In this connection it is instructive to remind ourselves that sociological empiricism in bourgeois sociology was in its origins closely associated with movements of social reform (the Protestant origins of the Chicago School in the United States, the Fabians and early twentieth century research in Britain, the *Verein für Sozialpolitik* and similar developments, including a project by Weber, in Germany). Empirical technique later became detached from this moral-political basis and was conceived of as an extension of the methods of the natural sciences to social affairs. The recent revival of certain kinds of empirical inquiry in the state socialist societies appears to have compressed these stages into one decade rather than several. At any rate, both the multiple theoretic traditions and the techniques of inquiry developed in bourgeois sociology pose grave problems for a Marxist sociology, problems which are far from resolved and often enough hardly acknowledged.

In the general movement of ideas which has resulted in the crisis in Marxist sociology, we witness not the direct and primitive expression of conflicts of interest among social and political groupings, but rather an effort to apprehend long-term developmental tendencies in society—as concretized in the problems which attach to the understanding of those conflicts. Unintended, often half-conscious, representations of historical process cannot be as effective as fully articulated representations; where, however, our intellectual resources make the utilization of the latter a *desideratum* rather than a real possibility, fragmentary depictions of historical process are often the best we can do. It should be clear that the crisis in Marxist sociology presents the aspects of an intellectual crisis, which has roots in the social position and political engagements of the groups to which sociologists belong (or with which they identify themselves) but which has a definite, if limited, independence of these factors.

One considerable element in the crisis bespeaks both the intellectual fragmentation to which I have referred and the historical circumstances underlying it. We confront not a uniform set of Marxist ideas but a number of Marxist traditions, differing from country to country and indeed sometimes from group to group within the same country. This process of differentiation indicates the authenticity of the crisis: the efforts undertaken to overcome it are in fact responses to real historical problems experienced in concrete forms. Having referred to the relative autonomy of Marxist thought, I have now called attention to a dimension of action (or contemplation before and about action) in Marxist discussion. Movement, reflective movement, between these two aspects of Marxism seems to me to constitute one of the most valuable possibilities of Marxism as a system; it allows a qualitatively different test of thought than that provided for in a model of social discourse fashioned after the natural sciences. It also recognizes antinomies and discontinuities in the human situation; in particular it denies both the total independence of thought and the notion that thought somehow "reflects" realities outside it. The former entails a complacent isolation of thought from reality, and in fact renders thinkers more and not less likely to succumb to extrinsic pressures; the latter denies the value of the intellectual enterprise itself, and at the same time denigrates the capacity of thought to change the world. These, however, are considerations best reserved for the final discussion of the crisis in Marxism as it affects questions of method. I propose to proceed, now, by considering in turn a number of specific areas of sociology in which the crisis is apparent.

THE THEORY OF SOCIAL CLASSES

The original Marxist theory of social classes has a general and a specific component; the general component refers to the internal differentiation of societies resulting from the relationships of production, and the specific one refers to bourgeois and capitalist society under conditions of machine production. Clearly, the weight of the original Marxist discussion falls upon the latter; Marx himself announced his intention of establishing the "laws of motion" of capitalist society, and acknowledged that the concept of classes as such had already been elaborated by bourgeois historians and social philosophers. Two sets of problems must concern us: the question of the utility of the notion of classes in their relationship to property in industrial societies, and the interpretation of the class structure of other social types.

It is clear that for Marx the fact of social domination in capitalist society rested upon the possession of property by a distinct social group, the bourgeoisie. It is equally clear that for a long period in the history of the nineteenth and early twentieth centuries the relationships among the possession of property, the control of the state, privileged access to higher culture, and the promulgation of a central ideology which purported to legitimate these conditions, were unequivocal. The cases which have been advanced as exceptions do not seem upon closer examination to serve as such. The early characteristics of the United States as described by De-Tocqueville, which resulted in an egalitarianism based on free competition for property by a population whose members were placed in conditions of approximate equality at the beginning of the struggle, were erased soon enough with the advent of industrial capital. It must be said, also, that a war for independence had displaced some of the original property owners of the country. The many complexities attendant upon the survival in Europe of pre-industrial elites (early bourgeois and aristocratic groups) were real enough. These elites did manage, however, to attach themselves to industrial property and have in the long run merged with the proprietors of the latter; the length of the historical process in question cannot obscure its finality. As industrial property and industrial proprietors came to dominate their societies, however, certain other transformations intervened.

In the first instance, as property became ever more concentrated it became ever more impersonal. The development of late capitalist structures of production and market exploitation required, in due course, the well known separation of ownership and management. Phrased in extremely simple terms, the control of property has become more important than its ownership. In itself, this development would appear to pose no great challenge to Marxism. Concentrated property remains property, and concentration was foreseen, of course, by Marx. Moreover, a number of inquiries in different societies, undertaken at different periods, shows a definite conjunction between propertied and managerial elites. The concentration of property, however, and the emergence of managerial groups have rendered the former (by way of political pressures upon the latter) peculiarly susceptible to controls exercised by the state upon the economy. Concentration has also, to be sure, permitted those in command of property to act more effectively upon the state. I shall deal shortly with some of the problems this entails; for the moment, let it be said that the loci of class conflict, and the strengths of the conflicting parties, have become extremely variable. While bourgeois sociology has manifested a certain tendency to mistake the dispersion and differentiation of class conflict for its elimination, Marxist sociology has paid insufficient attention to the complexities of the new situation. Indeed, a considerable opportunity for a new application of Marxist thought has been largely ignored. The concentration of property in new corporate forms, and the increasing role of the state in the economic process, have resulted in the penetration of an entire spectrum of social institutions by a variant of economic rationality. The attenuation of certain relationships of direct exploitation, particularly the partial integration of the working class in a system it was supposed to destroy, do not exhaust entirely the consequences of the development of capitalism. The obscurity and at times latency of class conflict have combined with its fragmentation to blind Marxists and non-Marxists alike to newer forms of class conflict.

A new approach to this set of problems, perhaps, waits upon the assimilation of the problem of the new middle class or technical intelligentsia. The growing complexity of the productive process, the increasing embeddedness of the state in society, the development of large systems of administration, distribution and services, have resulted in the growth of a new labor force, characterized by educational qualifications, organization in bureaucratic hierarchies, and a somewhat labile political disposition. In general, this technical intelligentsia has identified itself with those in command of the property and the state; expropriated, with respect to access to the means of administration, it has nonetheless behaved as if it possessed a vested interest in the maintenance of existing structures of power. In a real sense it has precisely that interest: its own material and psychic income depend upon the conventional functioning of the social apparatus.

The existence of this group suggests a new possibility for Marxist analysis. Expropriated from control of administration, it nonetheless possesses the skills without which administration (in a large sense of the term) would be impossible. Often enough, groupings within the technical intelligentsia experience a contradiction between their capacities and insights, and the imperatives visited upon them from above. Some Marxists have even extrapolated from this to the hypothesis that a considerable revolutionary potential resides in the intelligentsia. This may well be so, but before it can be realized certain problems of consciousness will have to be solved. For the moment, the analysis of the integration into capitalist society of the working class itself is defective with respect to these problems. It is easy enough to observe that recent changes in social atmosphere visible in a number of societies are due to the increasing quantitative importance of the technical intelligentsia: the boom in education, the spread of a certain privatization in consumption, the impression of levelling. Working class prosperity, under present political conditions, has contributed as well to this situation. It is much more difficult to apprehend the social and ideological mechanisms by which the technical intelligentsia is attached to current elite structures; it is useless to suppose that anything is gained by viewing the group as successors of the old *petite bourgeoisie* with respect to anything but a certain submissiveness.

Meanwhile, the analysis of the manual working class itself presents its own problems. At its upper limits, this class begins to merge with the technical intelligentsia; at its lower limits, it joins an underclass (particularly evident in the United States) without skill qualifications or chances of steady employment. The simple establishment of the limits of these groups is easy enough; conclusions about phenomena of consciousness are much more difficult to attain. The constriction of revolutionary perspectives in working class ideology requires no new demonstration, but it must be said that this constriction is not simply the product of developments since 1945 but represents the working out of an historical tendency visible in the second half of the nineteenth century. It is at this point that a Marxist sociology requires assistance from Marxist historiography, if indeed the two can be distinguished. The processes of internal differentiation in the working class, its modes of affiliation to national communities and the state, variations in the scope and intensity of its self-consciousness, particularities in its utilization of the possibilities of union and party organization, give us greater quantities of material from which to reconstruct traditions and continuities in working class consciousness. A somewhat mechanical application of both Marxist and non-Marxist sociologies of class conflict has until recently ignored the culmination of these factors in traditional or preformed responses by the various working classes to specific historical situations. The political responses of the working classes to the recent prosperity have been sufficiently varied, and are still sufficiently open, for us to be cautious of stereotyped sociological observations. A number of facts, indeed, appear to have escaped the attention of certain of our colleagues. These are: that working class access to the general facilities and advantages of the superior social classes remains extremely restricted; that access to mass culture is not the same as access to high culture; that the acquisition of certain economic advantages does not constitute a reversal of the total position of subordination of the working class in the society; and that incorporation in a bureaucratized trade union movement willing and able to negotiate with the elites in command of property does not constitute a realization of the historical goals of trade unionism—even in the United States. Automation may, in certain industries, restore (in a vastly changed historical context) a reserve army of the unemployed, indeed an army that may be unlikely to be mobilized again. Both bourgeois and Marxist sociologies of the working class, in sum, have been curiously defective: the one has welcomed evidence of integration, the other has deplored it, but both have failed to depict the fate of the working class as a component of the larger development of the social structure. A renewed appreciation of the potential social role of this class may indeed signify a consolidation of historical insight in Marxist sociology; at the moment, insight and analysis both remain fragmentary.

The analysis of the social structure of the state socialist societies, and in particular the Soviet Union, presents an especial challenge to Marxist sociology. One simple solution to the difficulty has been the observation that large-scale capitalist property does not exist in these societies; it follows (for some) that class analysis is inapplicable. A good deal of this is, of course, a sterile play of words. Large-scale property does exist, and control over it is exercised by an elite. This elite acts in the name of the total society, and with a certain conception of the general welfare; nevertheless, the elites in the state socialist regimes have managed to derive considerable advantages from their positions of power. Domination exercised in the name of a higher ideal remains domination, and it cannot be said that the working classes in these societies enjoy trade unions conspicuous for their resolute independence of the political elites. Interesting possibilities for analysis concern conflicts among political and technical elites with respect to economic priorities, the institutionalization of facilities for social mobility and the consequences of this process, and the modes by which in the absence of direct political representation a public opinion is formed and becomes effective. In this last connection, it may be said that the explicit coalescence of state and economy in the state socialist regimes makes of occupational discipline a political phenomenon. Our colleagues in these societies have now begun to investigate certain of these problems: their work constitutes at once a welcome demystification with respect to schematic depictions of the "triumph" of socialism and a refutation of facile views as to the similarity of all industrial regimes. Even a casual visitor to these countries is struck by the social atmosphere apparently generated by the absence of the sort of institutionalized privatization which is a psychological accompaniment of market structures.

An amplification and extension of current inquiries into the structure of state socialist societies will necessarily touch some of the critical issues in contemporary sociological theory, not least the question of the inevitability of one or another form of alienation. These putative theoretic gains, however, can be derived only from a Marxist sociology true to the critical traditions of Marxism—that is to say, a sociology which refuses the function of an administrative technology. The refusal of function, however, presupposes a refusal of a certain form: the view that purely empirical procedures can totally displace the critical elements in a Marxist sociology is incompatible with the tasks of viewing the state socialist societies in their historical specificity.

I now turn to the other element of difficulty in the Marxist theory of social classes: the problems presented by class systems in non-industrial societies. These occur today in a particularly acute form as questions of development. The discussion of development, however, often enough is ahistoric (in both Marxist and bourgeois sociologies). The ahistoricism of each is rather like a distorted image of the other. Bourgeois sociology tends to a certain reification of cultural traditions, emphasizes the incentives and disincentives to "modernization" (in itself an extremely dubious concept) intrinsic in those traditions, and is often enough curiously silent about the intrusion upon the historical development of the societies under examination of colonialist and imperialist forces from without. A good deal of Marxist analysis concentrates on this last element, while ignoring the weight of history except for these factors. It is particularly insensitive to the specific cultural traditions and social institutions which often enough combine in historically specific structures for which we have as yet to find adequate concepts.

107

In particular, the varieties of class conflict in the non-industrial societies merit systematic attention. Phenomena like the existence of "compradores" in symbiotic dependence upon imperialist forces, or of a "national bourgeoisie" aligned with the veritable proletariat in these societies, are familiar enough. What is required is a mode of dealing with the genesis of cultural traditions radically different from the Western one in class structures which were no less different, and the specification of the ways in which these traditions have combined with new historical accretions to give us the societies of Asia, Africa, and Latin America in their present forms. Something can be learned from the theoretic justifications developed for the political practise of neo-Marxist regimes like that of Castro's Cuba.

Much can be gained by referring to the classical Marxist discussion, recently revived, of an "Asiatic mode of production." Wittfogel's extension of the idea was terribly exaggerated, but the notion of the state as in itself proprietor and exploiting agent has the virtue of reminding us that the forms of class conflict are historically extremely variable. This was, if I have read him correctly, the burden of Max Weber's comparative sociology. His intention was not to show that Marxism was false (the Marxism he dealt with was often enough the evolutionary positivism of German Social Democracy), nor yet that stratification rested on status rather than market considerations, but that the predominance of the market in capitalism was but one historical variant of class conflict.

The present phase of world history, the emergence of civilizations and peoples long held in subjugation, renders peculiarly acute the emendation of Marxism to cover the structures peculiar to these societies and to the struggles in which they are now engaged. The depiction of the latter of course entails a refinement of the political sociology of the advanced societies to include the colonial and imperialist phenomena which may well now constitute important elements in the internal functioning of the advanced states (in this connection, the period 1945–1956 in eastern Europe and 1948–1961 in Asia cannot be ignored if we wish to understand the Soviet Union). It also demands that considerable attention be paid to the specific historical traditions of the societies termed underdeveloped, and not least to their religious traditions. We shall see, subsequently, that the rediscovery of the historical role of religion is an important element in the current Marxist discussion. It remains now to turn our attention to the political sociology of the advanced societies.

THE THEORY OF THE STATE

Among the defects of a Marxism which has become rigidified has been its failure to follow Marx and Engels themselves in focusing analysis on the state. A misconceived Marxism has sought to reduce state power immediately to its supposed bases in the action of the social classes, without taking account of the manner in which the state subsumes these influences and transforms them. Bourgeois sociology, on the other hand (although here again Max Weber and to a certain extent the post-liberal Italians are important exceptions), has at the same time insisted on the autonomy of the state and, often enough, denied the role of brute force in recent history. No easy solution to these contradictions can be expected, but at least some of the elements in question can be identified.

Until the present, the role of state power in socialist societies has constituted a source of great embarrassment for Marxist scholars working under, or in political sympathy with, the state socialist regimes. The maximization of the power of the state was, after all, a central characteristic of Stalinism. Moreover, the fusion of the state with the total society meant that any critical analysis of a sector of the society would inevitably touch upon the role of the state. The utilization of entirely schematic notions of the continuation of class conflict under socialist regimes, through the vehicle of the state (deemed, by fiat, "historically progressive") was one solution to this difficulty. Another, more recent one adopted apparently in imitation of the political evasiveness of bourgeois sociology, has been to fragment discussion by concentrating on the several sectors of society without reference to the integrating and command functions of the socialist state. It may be said that a certain "official" bourgeois sociology, often difficult to distinguish from political intelligence and/or political propaganda, has committed the opposite error: the role of the social classes in political decision in the socialist states has been systematically ignored, and the state has been depicted as an irresistible force, sovereign in the society. The elucidation of these relationships in socialist society awaits a new forward thrust by a Marxist sociology free of political tutelage.

For the Western societies, a similar range of problems awaits solution. One answer to a simplified Marxism has been the curious doctrine of the total autonomy of the sectors of society: the role of the state as an integrating factor has been underemphasized, and political conceptions of a pluralism more ideal than real have been allowed to preform or, rather, deform analysis. It is here that we can take note of some of the few positive contributions of Western European Marxism. The integration of the capitalist societies, particularly in their recent, or neo-capitalist, phase has been the object of a good deal of work. The analysis of the functioning of systems of education and mass communications, of the encapsulation of class conflict in formalized relationships among unions, employers and the state, of the development of welfare institutions, of a partial but definite control of the market, has shown how modern Western states are able to institutionalize and control class conflicts. The analysis of the role of consciousness remains defective, and, in particular, the analysis of identifications with national communities or pseudo-communities on the part of the different social classes has not progressed very far. Two major problems require consideration.

The recent modifications in the nature of capitalism as an economic system mean that market analysis alone cannot give us the structure of the system: the state is indispensable to the functioning of the economy, and in a sense, the society as a whole has been converted into an economic apparatus. This I referred to earlier, when insisting upon the penetration of the most diverse sectors of society by an economic rationality. Under these conditions, a specific political autonomy is difficult to attribute to the state, but a specifically economic autonomy is impossible to attribute to the market. Indeed, the classical market has disappeared and has been replaced not simply by structures of a monopolistic or oligopolistic sort but by a complicated apparatus of controlled, interlocking processes. The original notion of base and superstructure has little meaning in the face of this concrete totality. We do, however, confront the question as to whether an autonomous sociological analysis, which leaves to other disciplines and other perspectives the tasks of the analysis of the economy, of the state, and of culture, is not in some danger of falling into either formalism or an artificial restrictiveness which is self-defeating. Marxist sociology has, traditionally, concentrated upon the social classes. As long as these were, in capitalist society, relatively stable and easily identifiable there was considerable justification for this focus. The experience of totalitarian integration in the state socialist regimes and what may be termed "consensual integration" in the neo-capitalist societies renders the limitation increasingly arbitrary.

The case of the debate over imperialism makes this somewhat clearer. The emergence of a world market and a world polity, in effect of a world society, is no longer arcane; it is, quite simply, obvious. Our understanding of the history of capitalist and other societies in the nineteenth and early twentieth centuries would appear to require substantial revision. Our understanding of the internal movement of the separate societies of the Western world requires enlargement to include the role of imperialist relationships. In the late nineteenth century, Marx raised the possibility that Britain's imperial position had converted the British working class into a privileged group. In the wars for European hegemony fought since 1866, the European working classes have generally sided with their national elites against other nation states. Indeed, part of the rationale for the development of national welfare institutions by Bismarck and David Lloyd George was the necessity of increasing national cohesion in the interest of the more efficacious conduct of imperialist rivalry. There is some evidence that the contemporary American working class is not at all averse to repressive adventures against foreign "communism," particularly insofar as these are accompanied by high employment levels. These facts, however, require a systematic interpretation which for the present is lacking.

I do not refer only to the difficulties, from the viewpoint of a purely economic analysis, of estimating the component of imperialistic economic relations in the separate domestic economies of the West (and, let it be said, of the Soviet Union). I refer to the difficulties attendant upon identifying a stratum of the elite particularly charged with the management of imperialist political-economic relations. An exception is the case of Great Britain in the classical epoch of the imperial magnates, who were quite distinct from, for instance, the Midlands industrialists. The identification of this stratum once accomplished, it will remain to examine its mode of domestic operation, the mechanisms of cooptation it employs to integrate other elites in the imperialist enter-

prise, the ideological resources at its disposal for the attainment of "consensus" or its *simulacrum*.

In attending to these problems, a Marxist sociology must
inevitably avow its critical and interpretative character; it
must do so in the absence of "positive" evidence on the inter-
connections between imperialism abroad and domestic social
structures, precisely because the normal canons of "positive"
social science do not encourage synthetic ventures of this
sort. Perhaps this accounts for the very fragmentary beginnings of this sort of Marxism in the world's major imperialist
power, the United States: there is little in the tradition of
American social science, even critical social science, to support and encourage the use of the scientific imagination in
this way. The same may be true for England, where we may
say that even the Marxists are "empiricists." But empiricism
directed to imperialism in Great Britain can hardly ignore
that country's historical legacy. It does seem that French
sociology has progressed farthest with these analyses, not
alone because of the French political tradition but because
French social thought iş in its structure far more synthetic.
But I have moved, unintentionally, from consideration of a
substantive problem to consideration of method. Before continuing, it will be necessary to consider two areas of Marxist
analysis in which the consciousness of crisis is, perhaps, most
developed.

THE ANALYSIS OF CULTURE

I have chosen the term, the *analysis of culture,* in preference
to the *analysis of consciousness* or the *analysis of ideology.*
Culture does not seem to me to be entirely a matter of consciousness, since human consciousness in culture responds
to the unconscious communicaton of meaning through symbols, and conscious reflection or analysis often rests on a

deeper stratum of experience not always immediately accessible to consciousness itself. Ideology, in turn, refers to formalized systems of social discourse which are equally subject to accumulated cultural experience as well as immediate social pressures or interests. The analysis of culture, at any rate, is of peculiar interest to Marxism precisely because Marxism is in no vulgar sense a materialist doctrine. It is, rather, a doctrine of the human genesis of forms for the satisfaction and containment of need, in the actual and necessary shape of crystallized labor-power, and in the future and possible institutions of a realm of freedom.

One of the major recent advances in Marxism has taken the paradoxical form of a return to the Marxist sources. In place of a mechanical derivation of "super-structure" from "basis," in place of the reductive interest-psychology found in the Marxism of Bernstein and Kautsky (and to some extent of Lenin as well), a conception of the totality of human culture has marked recent Marxist work on culture. In this development, extrapolations have been made from the early writings of Marx and Engels themselves. This has entailed treating the materialism of the early writings as a polemical emphasis occasioned by the attack on the Hegelian system, although this materialism has also been redefined as an existential humanism. At any rate, the Marxist theory of culture now understands symbolic or ideological representations of a given historical situation as an integral and defining part of the situation. These representations do not simply "reflect" material constraints; indeed they can anticipate, some would say, create, new material possibilities in historical situations. Further, the notion of contradiction has been employed to nullify the view that culture (as "super-structure") must absolutely "reflect" material constraints: culture may in some measure constitute a spiritual denial of these constraints and, again, an anticipation of their eventual disappearance. This last point has been the occasion of a systematic reconsideration of the Marxist theory of religion, which has led some Marxists, and, admittedly, there are some theologians among them, to take a much more refined and favorable view of religion as a human phenomenon than heretofore.

Is this simply a manner of repeating Engels' familiar warning, made late in his life, against over-emphasizing material factors, his insistence on the process of interaction between "basis" and "super-structure"? I think not. Rather, it represents the influence on Marxism—or the discovery within Marxism—of three distinctive, if often confounded, components. (1) By recourse to the early texts, and in particular to their anthropological components, a Marxist existentialism has been established. This depicts man as the maker of history, its subject rather than its object. Of course, the entire point of the Marxist anthropology has been to show that man could not make his history under conditions of capitalist commodity production and the attendant situation of alienation from his own potential nature. The newer Marxist interpretations of culture certainly do not deny this proposition, but they modify it by insisting on the universality of the struggle against alienation expressed in all cultural history. This does constitute a greater or lesser modification of the Marxist temporal schema, by inserting the struggle against alienation in a variety of contexts and not simply a revolutionary one. (2) Again, by recourse to the early texts (and also, as is the case with Lukacs, to Hegel's writings) the dialectic as a method of thought has been re-emphasized. Its application to the theory of culture presents peculiar difficulties of specification. With respect to the action of real men, it entails among other things the utilization of notions of ambivalence, whereas Marxist psychology, heretofore, has been conspicuous neither for its plausibility nor its subtlety. With respect to temporal sequence in the development of cultural structures, the notion of dialectic

115

has been most effectively employed when confined to the interior of one structure, a movement of thought or style, a period in the history of a given group, rather than when applied to changes in structure. With respect to cultural meanings, the use of dialectic has required concentration on the condition of ambiguity. Its most convincing expressions to date have been concretized in yet another notion, that of totality. (3) The systematic explication of cultural totalities by dialectical methods in recent Marxism owes much to the incorporation of ideas derived from Gestalt psychology and philosophical phenomenology. One aspect of a situation has been treated as reflecting in a specific mode of organization all other aspects—a procedure which at times has come close to the denial of the determining role of the relationships of production. In the case of one Marxist thinker, Goldmann, the analysis of cultural totalities proceeds after the establishment of a basic socio-economic relationship. That is to say, the dialectic is effective within a previously defined historical totality, and the processes of change—from one total structure to another—do not enter into the analysis itself.

These developments in Marxist thought are certainly challenging, and they have resulted in some of the most interesting of recent essays in the field. Nonetheless, it is legitimate to assert that these too partake of the crisis in Marxist sociology. These innovations in the Marxist theory of culture incorporate a good many assumptions and methods derived from other philosophical systems and methodologies. An open Marxism has proved exceedingly fecund in an area in which the original texts promised much, but delivered little. The question is, how much further can Marxism be opened without itself undergoing a radical transformation? The insistence that a new procedure is consonant with the critical spirit of early Marxism is no doubt reassuring, but changes of substance cannot be dismissed in this way.

Two further sets of problems affecting the theory of culture must concern us. The first has to do with the vexed idea of "rationalization" in advanced industrial cultures. The most profound treatment we possess of the process of "rationalization" is found in Max Weber; its similarities to the Marxist analysis have been noted by Löwith and more recently by Marcuse. Marx began with the notion of the alienation of man in the process of commodity production, went on to analyze the immanent structure of capitalist production itself, and to predict its eventual self-destruction on account of a higher historical rationality which would overcome the short-term and superficial rationalities of bourgeois culture. From the early Marxist writings and from Weber as well, Lukacs derived the notion of "reification" as an essential component of Marxist sociology. Mannheim incorporated an analysis derived from Weber (without subjecting himself to the rigors of a Marxist analysis) in his distinction between "functional" and "substantive" rationality. A certain process has been ineluctable: the rationality of capitalism has been transformed, partly by an extension of Weber's idea of bureaucratization, into an industrial rationality. Insofar as Marxist elements remain in the discussion (as with the idea of "reification") these have become isolated, separated from a total account of historical process and historical possibility. Tacitly or overtly, contemporary Marxism accepts the inevitability of an industrial rationality, which it sees little or no chance of overcoming. Its analysis of that rationality has become ever more refined, its awareness of its intrinsic irrationalities ever more acute, precisely as the Marxist concept of a higher historical rationality has receded. One of the consequences of this elimination of the original Marxist conceptions of historical progression from contemporary Marxist analysis has been not unlike the fate of the theory of ideology freed of the notion of an ultimate truth. Specific ideologies can be analyzed in their historical contexts, but history is viewed as a sequence of ideologies and not as a progression through conflict from ideology to truth.

For this last situation, the Marxists attached to the Communist movement bear as much responsibility as those who, in bourgeois sociology, relativized the notion of ideology. For both groupings, ideology has been treated as the expression of the interests and perspectives of discrete groups. The Communist Marxists generally restricted the term to overt expressions having, ultimately, a socio-political reference. Bourgeois sociology could justify its own methods by referring to the richness of material presented by ethnology and social anthropology, and by the history of ideas (disciplines which of course were in turn influenced by Marxism). In the one case, we have a certain political vulgarization; in the other, a philosophically barren immersion in empiricism, or rather, the implicit enunciation of the highly debatable philosophical position that the world is precisely as it seems to be. Briefly, a striking aspect of the crisis in Marxist sociology is the failure of development of the original notion of ideology—and this despite the reality of a deepening of our appreciation of the structure and function of a multiplicity of concrete historical ideologies.

The Marxist Anthropology

Some of the difficulties sketched with respect to the theory of culture can be found, transposed on to another plane, with respect to the Marxist anthropology. The original Marxist texts are definite, but exceedingly general. Man is a sensual and active being who can fulfill himself only in the right Praxis. That Praxis, in turn, would constitute a medium through which man could re-constitute himself. Under conditions of capitalist commodity production, the right Praxis was impossible: labor-power invested in work, which should express man in his wholeness, served only to consolidate his impotence. The products of work, commodities, ruled over men in a sovereignty which rendered them alienated. Only revolutionary Praxis, then, could restore—or institute—a truly human condition.

The profundity of this historical vision has, alas, so impressed many Marxists that they have been by and large unable to enlarge it or even render it more precise. One tendency follows from the work of Marx and Engels subsequent to the early writings on alienation: attention has been re-directed to the social institutions and historical processes which function to maintain a condition of alienation. This has led, imperceptibly, to a theory (more implicit than explicit) of infinite human psychological malleability. In the absence of revolutionary Praxis, and in light of the evidence of the corruption of much of the revolutionary Praxis undertaken hitherto, a despairing conviction has possessed Marxist sociologists: men are capable of assimilating any injury, and any insult. The more profound the analysis (*vide* Adorno's remarkable essays on high and mass culture) the more despairing the conclusion.

In this setting, the assimilation of Freudian psychoanalysis to Marxism has been most penetrating where most negative in its conclusions, where the analysis of instinctual repression, of the self-abasement entailed in the internalization of authority, has supplied an account of the psychological dimensions of alienation. Again, this has been accomplished largely through separation from an analysis of the possibilities of liberation. Marcuse, who did attempt that analysis in his own work on Freud, thereafter returned to the study of institutional process, of the institutional repression of freedom.

One possibility has been overlooked by many Marxists: suppose that we do take seriously the notion of malleability. We confront not one historical universe, but several, given to us in the variety of human cultures and historical societies, each separate historical configuration producing a distinctive human type. According to this view, no single sort of human liberation can be postulated. There may exist, indeed, diverse possibilities and types of liberation. Recent Marxist work on religion, with its acceptance of a liberating component in the religious experience, its skepticism about the simple or unilinear sketch of secularization found in nineteenth century thought, reflects this doubt about the immediacy and finality of the earlier Marxist treatment of the historical course of human nature.

It is true that a proper attention to historical variability is the necessary preliminary to a general view of human possibility. Thus, the Marxist analysis of historical variability cannot limit itself to the variability of institutional forms, but must follow ethnology and comparative psychology in studies of the variety of psychic structure. Here, clearly, Marxist sociology has failed to profit very much from a considerable body of work accomplished on other assumptions. Perhaps, however, certain early Marxist assumptions are at fault. Influenced to some extent by romanticism, as well as by Hegel and Feuerbach, Marx and Engels supposed that work was the privileged form of human self-expression and self-constitution. They saw machine work as, however, deforming, and envisaged an eventual liberation from deformation (insofar as they envisaged it concretely at all) in something like the assumption by every man of the totality of work functions fragmented in the division of labor.

Modern production processes appear to move in two quite contradictory directions. Some functions require more and more comprehension on the part of the worker, and expand the scope of his control of the process. Others limit the worker's operations to a minimum, and deprive him of a vision of the sense of his work. In fact, there are two quite distinct components in the Marxist theory of the human potential for liberation from the bondage imposed by work under conditions of capitalism. One entails a direct transformation of work itself; the other entails a transformation of the context of work, particularly with respect to the structure of authority and control of the disposition of the social product. The recent development, in the Marxist theory of imperialism, of the notion of the "nation-class," with respect to the "third" world, points in the latter direction. The peasants in underdeveloped countries certainly do not directly experience the fragmentation caused by the capitalist division of labor. But they are not really masters of their historical circumstances, since the latter are determined by forces distant from them socially as well as geographically. (The same may be said, on a rather different scale, of course, for large parts of the advanced industrial labor force in the developed societies, including the intelligentsia.)

A new view of the problem of work is essential to further progress in Marxist sociology. I do not refer alone to the immense discussion of leisure (which often enough is conducted in curious separation from the discussion of work). I refer to the possibility that the development of the productive forces in industrial society is changing the nature of work, less in the sense of its real or imputed significance than in the more precise sense of its inner structure. Marx may well have predicated his anthropology on the basis of an image of *homo faber;* it remains to ask what revisions in this image are made necessary by the computer, and by the possibilities of large-scale social control implicit in bureaucratic organization. To some extent, of course, these problems bring us again to the problem of domination.

It would appear, then, that a Marxist anthropology must confront anew the problem of domination. Max Weber once observed that psychoanalysis would prove an invaluable means of analyzing relationships of authority. A few Marxists, associated with the Frankfurt Institut für Sozialforschung, have worked on these problems, but a renewed attack on them is imperative. In particular, we shall have to ask to what extent men can transcend the universality of structures of authority, liberate themselves from authority internally, and accept authentic, but as yet quite unrealized, conditions of equality. Alternatively, we may inquire into the possibilities of what in the recent American literature, mainly as developed by younger thinkers, has been termed "participatory democracy." Upon examination, then, a paradoxical methodological conclusion emerges: even with respect to so abstract a consideration as its anthropology, the Marxist system requires certain answers in Praxis. I now turn to the last section of the essay, and deal with questions of method.

METHODOLOGICAL PROBLEMS

A distinction between method and substance, with reference to Marxism, is difficult to establish. Unlike positivist doctrines, Marxism in its classical form has supposed that the historical world could be understood as it was, that is to say, that our theoretic understanding of it was not simply a matter of agreement among observers on conventions concerning observations and on protocols about observed data, but a construction which apprehended the movement of history itself. A good many of the unresolved difficulties of Marxism are consequences of its denial of a total separation between subject and object in the process of historical knowledge: the knower is immersed in the substance he seeks to elucidate.

The recent expansion of sociology as an academic discipline and as an ancillary administrative service has been accompanied by a considerable expansion of those inquiries termed "empirical." Obviously, a settlement of Marxism's accounts with this sort of inquiry is in order. A number of preliminary points may be made: (1) There is nothing in principle or in fact truly new about the collection of sociological data of a quantitative sort, although of course the development and refinement of statistical method has increased the precision of certain of the techniques in question. Quantitative inquiry descends from the eighteenth century; in the nineteenth, Marx himself designed a questionaire. (2) There is no epistemological or practical warrant for assigning a privileged place to inquiries entailing interviews or direct observations rather than the utilization of other types of data. In particular, historical inquiries are neither less nor more "empirical" than other kinds. The insistence of some that the term "empirical" be restricted to quantitative work on contemporary populations is easy enough to explain, but difficult to excuse. (3) Inquiries on contemporary populations are generally conducted, as Mills among others has shown, in considerable abstraction from total or even partial historical contexts. This abstraction, or isolation, implies a possibility of systematic distortion in the interpretation of data.

These points stated, a number of problems remain. Whatever limitations attach to their use, the inquiries now typical of sociological research can be valuable modes of acquiring knowledge. Marxist sociologists have for too long contented themselves with negative critiques of the deformations possible in these inquiries, and only recently has it been thought necessary to develop new modes of interpretation. These might consist of either employing a different contextual analysis to interpret data or a redefinition of the categories according to which data are constituted. At this point, questions of method fuse with questions of substance: interpretation and reconstitution entail substantive assumptions. At any rate, a more serious and systematic approach to these questions is indicated; perhaps our colleagues from the state socialist countries will be able to contribute to our enlightenment. It is difficult to believe, however, that inquiries undertaken to serve the purposes of administrative clients will be more critical of the clients in state socialist society than elsewhere.

One area in which method and substance, in Marxist sociology, are inextricably fused is that of "basis," "super-structure," and ultimate determination. In one sense, a solution to questions in this area can be nothing but theoretical: the concepts with which reality is analyzed dictate our views of its structure. A dogmatic insistence on the purely theoretical nature of these questions, even in circumstances in which the content of the theoretical discussion allows a new view of the relationships involved, would in fact constitute a denial of the capacity of Marxism to depict the real movement of society, and thus result in an assimilation of Marxism to a conventionalist epistemology. A new, or, more accurately, a revised view of the relationships in question has been developed by Althusser, but I find it difficult to situate his contribution. He allows for considerable variation in the relationship of "basis" and "super-structure," denies an inevitable, mechanical, or universal set of determining relationships, but is exceedingly general in his conclusions. His work represents an academization of Marxism, an energetic, and at times inspired, elucidation of concepts, but one which rarely, if ever, leaves the conceptual level to deal, as did Marx himself, with historical structures. In this light, Althusser's insistence on the importance of an "epistemological disjunction" ("coupure epistemologique") in Marx is curious. If Marx proceeded from philosophy to the empirical study of society, Althusser's explication of that movement is entirely philosophical and quite remote from any consideration induced by the empirical study of society. If revisions of Marxism like Althusser's are to bear fruit, they will have to be combined with systematic attention to the content of generalization from historical evidence.

It is necessary to say something on the discussion of the importance of "structuralism." I do so with reluctance. The theme has been treated at great, indeed exhaustive, length elsewhere; there are a good many competing and confused versions of structuralism; the claims advanced for the doctine (or method) seem to be considerably greater than its concrete achievements. Let us consider, very briefly, the work of Lévi-Strauss, who has himself insisted on the consonance between his ideas and some aspects of Marxism. It is easy enough to enumerate the contradictions between his theory of society and Marxism. From the point of view of method, the extrapolation from concrete historical relationships to hypothesized systems of code destroys the historical specificity of social structures. These are "de-coded," the relationships of exchange and production treated metaphorically as communications, history in short is reduced to a message or a set of messages. The elements remain the same, and the fundamental historical processes also; the world of structuralism is a world of infinite variation on the surface, of terrible sameness in its depths. It is a world, moreover, in which historical transcendence is impossible—in which men construct their societies with a limited set of elements susceptible of combination in a limited number of ways. The determinism structuralism promulgates, then, is different in kind from the determinism enunciated by Marxism. The former is irrevocable, the latter capable of transformation. Philosophically, structuralism and Marxism are incapable of reconciliation.

The negative humanism of structuralism, its tendency to eliminate men from history in favor of systems of signs and symbols, is disturbing only when we take structuralism not as a method, but as a privileged method with total philosophical implications. If, however, we treat structuralism as strictly a method for the analysis of communications, it is impossible to deny its very great utility for Marxism. Much of the agitation in the current discussion appears to be connected with a certain confusion on these points. The capacity of structuralism in the forms developed by Lévi-Strauss himself to explicate hidden consonances between symbolic systems and other sectors of society, a notion of the interpenetration of symbolic and other series of behaviors, in short an analytical idea of totality, renders Lévi-Strauss' work exceedingly important. It is no less important, however, to recognize its limits; these are particularly acute in connection with the problem of Praxis.

The original Marxist idea of Praxis, which had deep roots in Western philosophical tradition, is in some danger of degenerating into a slogan as tawdry as the term "empirical" in bourgeois sociology. Praxis is a concept with several connotations; let us examine them. In the first instance, the idea clearly implies that a totally detached or objective science of society is impossible. The truth for human beings is not simply constituted by a set of propositions about reality but, since man is a political (which is to say moral) animal, the truth about society is ultimately a true condition, a manner of organization consonant with man's potential. It does not follow from this that all social science has to be "engaged" in any direct sense, and assertions to this effect have contributed largely to the doctrine of *Partinost* (fidelity to party spirit) which has vulgarized Marxism and reduced it to the status of a propagandistic ancillary of the working class movement or, more precisely, of those who claimed to speak for this movement. It does follow from the idea of Praxis, however, that the moral and political implications of an assertion as to the organization of society and its movement be examined, that the possible consequences of a given historical situation be explored in their relevance for the future direction of human activity.

Scientific Praxis, in other words, is itself a form of human activity which affects and increasingly shapes the future. This brings us to the second connotation of Praxis: its directional content. The Marxist anthropology, for all its defects and *lacunae,* implies that the historicity of man consists not least in his capacity to make or re-make his history. Sociology and social science as Praxis, then, have the task of anticipating and apprehending the future. Finally, the idea of Praxis contains an intention which remains programmatic (indeed, utopian): the abolition of the division of labor, the achievement of human nature through activity. This, along with the other connotations of Praxis, poses serious, and as yet unsurmountable, difficulties for Marxist sociology; clearly, the practise of sociology entails the division of labor, and the triumphs of modern science, including social science, would have been unthinkable without it.

It will be seen that the notion of Praxis is as much of an embarrassment for Marxist sociology as for its bourgeois counterpart. The precise relationship between propositions about reality and a philosophical conception of humanity remains to be established. Equally, the Marxist critique of the "objectivist" pretensions of a "positive" or "empirical" sociology does not constitute a solution of the difficulties entailed in integrating the empirical or positive components of a Marxist sociology with other aspects of Marxism. Neither does the assertion of the directionality of history make for an easy resolution of the problem of historical extrapolation. Finally, the view that a Marxist sociology is also an aspect of a Praxis affords no guarantees against its subservience to the wrong Praxis. I have no solution to these multiple difficulties, but one line of development may prove not without promise.

Earlier in the essay, I insisted on the relative autonomy of Marxist sociological thought, its relative detachment from immediate political considerations. There are, of course, occasions when a social science and specifically a sociology are directly subordinated to political purposes—usually as an ancillary technique of domination rather than as a mode of facilitating liberation. In general, however, we would do well to understand sociology as a part of a larger scientific Praxis, as an effort, often unconscious, caused by the extreme division of labor implicit in intellectual activity, to master history. The preliminary methodological task of a Marxist sociology, then, is to make explicit the difficulties and contradictions in its own version of this general Praxis. This can lead to a critical view of the totality of our historical situation, not by the imposition upon it of pre-formed schema for depicting history but by the examination of the difficulties of apprehending history. It is not by total detachment that a Marxist or any sociology can attain a view of history, but by critical reflection on its own specific historical location. For the indefinite future, this entails an acceptance of those aspects of the division of labor which have produced modern science. It also entails, however, systematic reflection on possible modes of overcoming that division—that is to say, it entails conscious acceptance of the dissensual status of a sociology which does not view itself as the culmination of human spiritual evolution but rather as a potential step in an evolution far from completed.

The crisis of Marxist sociology in its methodological aspects, then, partakes of the general crisis of the social sciences. Originally intended to apprehend human history so as to fulfill the history of mankind, the social sciences and in particular sociology have broken down in two ways. The intention of apprehending history has been renounced in favor of a total capitulation to the scientific division of labor: abstractly recognized, the historicity of mankind is denied in scientific practice. This last contents itself with a fragmented description of a fragmented reality. In the second place, social science has become another instrument of domination, rather than a mode of liberation. Not the least contribution of those who sense themselves to be in the Marxist tradition is the insistence that the original humanist intent of sociology be incorporated in contemporary sociological practice; not the least of ironies is the fact that Marxist sociologists are often as incapable as any others of realizing that intent.

There seems to be no immediate way out of the many contradictions, dilemmas and difficulties which I have adduced as constituting a crisis in Marxist sociology. Originally conceived as a depiction of the totality of human history, Marxism's very fruitfulness has made us conscious of its limitations. We now see industrial society, in its capitalist form, as one variant of historical development among several. History, in other words, may in the end be understood not as having one structure but a succession of structures. The notion that meaningfulness can be found in history, if necessary, by invention and innovation, is a Marxist legacy to sociology which can be dispensed with only by acceptance of the pseudo-rationality of a sociology so in bondage to the present that it ignores past and future. It may be, however, that those sociologists most aware of their debt to the Marxist tradition will have to transform and transcend it; if so, the crisis in Marxist sociology may mark the beginning of the end of Marxism. Those Marxists who fear this eventuality would do well to re-read the original texts: a revolution in Praxis which cannot begin with its own theoretic presuppositions is in fact not a revolution at all.

II. RELIGION

The Zwinglian
Reformation in Zurich[1]

THE PROBLEM

Although the theological and ecclesiastical distinctiveness of the Zwinglian Reformation in Zurich (1519–31) has been recognised,[2] its historical significance has often been overlooked or minimised.[3] Zwingli developed his own conception of the

1. I am indebted to the American Philosophical Society and the Central Research Fund of the University of London for grants in aid of those researches. I have reported on some of them in my doctoral dissertation, "Social Structure and the German Reformation," Harvard University, 1958 (prepared with the support of a Pre-doctoral Fellowship of the Social Science Research Council). I also wish to thank Professor Joseph Lortz for introducing me to Reformation studies, and Dr. Paul Guyer for placing at my disposal his list of members of the Zurich Council, 1515–40. I am also indebted to Professor L. van Muralt (Zurich) for valuable advice. I am also grateful to Dr. Werner Schnyder for correcting a number of mistakes in an earlier version of this paper.
2. There has been something of a renaissance in Zwingli studies, recently: see R. Pfister, "Die Zwingli Forschung seit 1945," Archiv fur Reformationsgeschichte, xlvii (1957), pp. 230–40.
3. Ernst Troeltsch, (Die Soziallehren der christlichen Kirchen u. Gruppen, Ges. Schriften, I, Tübingen, 1919) hardly mentions it; Max Weber dismissed it as of but transitory historical importance (Die protestantische Ethik u. d. Geist des Kapitalismus, Ges. Aufsätze z. Religions-Soziologie, I, Tübin-

Reformed faith and church in partial opposition to Luther, and in conflict with the extremely articulate and active Zurich Anabaptists, who claimed legitimation from Zwingli's early teachings. The influence of the Zurich church by the middle of the 1520s extended to all of south German Protestantism;[4] Calvin's Geneva was profoundly affected by it;[5] Anglicanism and Puritanism (through Bullinger, Zwingli's successor in Zurich) bore some of its traces.[6] But for our understanding of the Reformation, Zwinglianism has a rather special importance, independent of the question of the direct influences it exerted and of the indirect lines of ecclesiastical descent from it. The Zwinglian Reformation poses, in small but critical compass, a sociological problem touched upon by much of the modern historiography of the Reformation: the question of the relationship between capitalism and early Protestantism.

Zwinglianism, with its radically anti-sacramental doctrines, its initial emphasis on popular participation in Church government (however modified by Zwingli under political pressures), and above all its ethical attitude to the profane world

---

gen 1920, p. 84). With his usual perspicacity, Professor Tawney has seen that it cannot be dismissed so lightly); Religion and the Rise of Capitalism (Pelican Edition), London, 1938, pp. 104 and 114–15. The brilliant essay by Franz Borkenau, "On Lutheranism," Horizon, III (1944), pp. 162–76 ought also to be mentioned in this connection.

4. W. Kohler, Zwingli u. Luther, I (Quellen u. Forschungen z. Reformationsgeschichte, VI), Leipzig, 1924 and II (QFBG, VII), Gütersloh, 1953, deals with the political and ecclesiastical ramifications in this area of the sacramental controversy. His Zürcher Ehegericht u. Genfer Konsistorium, I–II (Quellen u. Abhandlungen z. Schweizerischen Reformationsgeschichte VII, X), Leipzig, 1924–42, depicts the influence of the Zurich Church on the organisation of the neighboring ones.

5. Kohler, Zürcher Ehegericht etc. and J. McNeil, The History and Character of Calvinism, N.Y., 1954.

6. H. Kressner, Schweizer Ursprünge des anglikanischen Staatskirchtentums, Schriften des Vereins f. Reformationsgeschichte, CLXX, Gütersloh, 1953; C. H. Garret, The Marian Exiles, Cambridge, 1938.

of work anticipated, in important respects, those Calvinist doctrines described by Max Weber as indispensable to the emergence of that complex of ideas, aspirations, and anxieties he designated as the capitalist spirit.[7] This is not the place to rehearse, yet once again, the controversy over Weber's thesis. Weber himself said that he had not proposed to substitute, in his words, a one-sided idealistic interpretation of history for an equally one-sided materialistic one. And, it will be recalled, Weber dealt primarily with the seventeenth century variants of Calvinism. But if the Zurich Reformation enables us to see some of the components of Calvinism in statu nascendi, an investigation of its social context may allow us to consider anew the connection between capitalism and Protestantism.

The view that the special characteristics of Swiss Protestantism in general, and of the Zurich Reformation in particular, were shaped by the republicanism of the Swiss cities is familiar. We find it in Ranke,[8] in the latest survey of the subject[9] (by an authority on Zurich) and in the recent volume of the CMH.[10] But this view clearly raises questions rather than answering them. The constitutions of the Swiss cities in fact differed; some were more, others less, oligarchic.[11] And the formal political institutions of the republics, as well as the factual balance of power within them, were legacies of centuries of social conflict. Zurich had, throughout the latter half of the fifteenth century, experienced violent political struggles: these were produced largely by the opposition of

7. Weber, op. cit.
8. L. v. Ranke, Deutsche Geschichte im Zeitalter d. Reformation, (edited by P. Joachimsen), III, München, 1925, pp. 43 ff.
9. L. v. Muralt, "Die Reformation," Historia Mundi, III, Bern, 1957, p. 69.
10. G. Rupp, "The Reformation in Zürich, Strassburg and Geneva," C.M.H., III, 1957, pp. 96–7. (Rupp does suggest that the cities differed from one another, socially).
11. L. v. Muralt, "Stadtgemeinde u. Reformation i.d. Schweiz," Zschr. f. Schweizerische Geschichte, X (1930), pp. 349–84.

artisanry to patriciate.[12] The Reformation, too, was accompanied by the conflict of social strata—but we cannot, here, speak of a simple opposition between artisanry and patriciate; each was rent by internal divisions of various kinds. And to this complex and changing system of alignments was added the complication of the relationship between town and countryside. Rather than considering the general characteristics of the society in which the Zwinglian Reformation occurred, therefore, we should do well to relate it to the specific pattern of social conflict of which it was, at once, the expression and the partial resolution.

ZURICH'S SOCIAL STRUCTURE ON THE EVE OF THE REFORMATION[13]

By 1519, Zurich had had a generation of relative political stability after the violent conflicts of the late fifteenth century. In these, a group of newly wealthy guild masters had challenged the previous ruling elite. They sought, further, to limit the autonomy of the countryside. Peasant and patrician had joined the artisanry in a counter-attack on the new elite, whose wealth had been won in trade. In the ensuing struggles, these last two eventually made common cause to the permanent disadvantage of the patriciate. And the peasantry was soon opposed, in turn, by all the urban strata.

The constitution of 1498, the outcome of these conflicts, enabled the artisan guilds to dominate the state. It did not follow that the artisans did so. Rather, the politically important guildsmen were often those wealthy masters whose bid for a near monopoly of power had been unsuccessful, but who

---

12. K. Dandliker, Geschichte d. Stadt u. d. Kantons Zürich, I, 1908; P. Guyer, Die soziale Schichtung d. Burgerschaft Zürichs v. Ausgang des Mittelalters bis 1798, Zurich, 1952.

13. This section rests on a number of sources, which are cited in connection with specific points in the text.

were able to manipulate the constitution to their own advantage. Indeed, they effected a partial rapprochement with the remaining patricians, whom they joined in the state service and as officers in Zurich's army. The artisanry now saw itself governed by a unified political elite, despite all the fissures within the latter. The process of rapprochement between burgher and patrician in fact could not be completed. The Reformation was to divide all these strata (and the omnipresent peasantry) and to recombine them in a series of transient camps; the period of relative political stability ended in 1519.

The total population of the state of Zurich in 1519 was some 60,000.[14] Of these, 50,000 lived in the countryside; 5,000 in the two towns of Winterthur and Stein am Rhein; 5,000 in Zurich itself. (The great German cities of the era were five or six times the size of urban Zurich). The number of male citizens in 1529 was, according to the military rolls of the city, 923. There were some 200 places in both the Great and Small Council of the government; theoretically, every citizen had a high chance of holding office.[15] Participation in government no doubt involved a higher proportion of the citizenry than elsewhere, but it was nonetheless limited. This discrepancy between theoretical possibility and factual restriction may very well have acted as a political irritant, the more so because in a small city politics were of necessity far more visible than in a large one. For the moment, we need only note that a system which in the city was at least formally representative exercised authority of a far more arbitrary sort in the countryside: the government of the city was identical with the government of the state, despite a certain rural local autonomy.

14. W. Schnyder, Die Bevoelkerung d. Stadt u. Landschaft Zürich vom 14 bis 17. Jahrh., (Schweizer Studien z. Geschichtswissenschaft, XIV, I), Zurich, 1925.

15. P. Guyer, Verfassungszustände der Stadt Zurich im 16, 17, 18. Jahr., Zürich, 1943. I have found both of Guyer's works invaluable in preparing this essay.

Since the middle of the fifteenth century, the economy of Zurich had undergone some striking vicissitudes.[16] Decisively defeated by the Confederates, in 1446 the city lost much of its population and wealth. The silk weaving industry disappeared. In 1440 the depleted guilds of woollen weavers and linen weavers merged into one. This was a radical caesura in Zurich's development; by 1500 the economy had been set upon another basis. Zurich was now a city whose wealth derived primarily from trade; it took iron ore from the northeast of Switzerland and exchanged this for salt, grain and manufactured goods obtained via Basel—and for wine, imported and home-grown. One of the most important local industries of the new period was that of the Smiths: weapons were in demand. Further, cotton wool was being produced in the city for export. And we obtain a hint of some sort of industrial development when we note that of 435 foreigners naturalised by the city between 1500 and 1530, 232 at least, were artisans.[17] The publicans, meanwhile, were favoured by Zurich's position as a crossroads and by the constant Confederate political gatherings within it.

Our understanding of Zurich's economy in 1519, however, would be incomplete did we not consider two factors absent in the German cities of the time: the direct exploitation of the countryside by the city, and the revenues from mercenary service. All the urban strata profited from the former: the political strength of the city depended largely upon the military uses of the peasantry, and direct control of its sources of agricultural supply was an advantage to any city. In the latter

16. H. Amman, "Untersuchungen u. d. Wirtschaftsstellung Zürichs im ausgehenden Mittelalter," Zschr. f. Schweizerische Geschichte, XXIX (1949), pp. 305–56; P. Keller, "Grundzüge einer Zürcher Wirtschaftsgeschichte," Zürcher Volkswirtschaftliche Gesellschaft, Zürichs Volks—und Staatswirtschaft, Zürich, 1928, pp. 113–151; J. Maliniak, Die Entstehung d. Export-industrie u. des Unternehmerstandes i. Zürich i, XVI. u. XVII. Jahr., (Zürcher Volkswirtschaftliche Studien, II) Zurich, 1913.

17. Guyer, op. cit., p. 77.

half of the fifteenth century, peasant resistance forced relaxation of urban efforts to restrict the rural expansion of the crafts; significantly, rural mercantile activity was successfully limited. We see, then, that the chief beneficiaries of this relationship to the countryside were certain urban social groups. These were not landlords. Most of Zurich's peasants were holders of hereditary feudal tenure in their land, but they had considerable autonomy with respect to the disposal of it. They were those urban notables who administered monastic lands, who represented the state in its rural jurisdictions, and who held mortgages on peasant holdings or who had bought the rights to specific Church tithes.

The revenues from mercenary service, again, were of more importance to some urban groups than to others, namely to the patricians whose rural incomes were insufficient for a patrician style of life and to those offspring of artisans and merchants who, schooled as officers in the state forces, found mercenary life congenial. The city's casual labour force and the surplus rural male population enlisted under these Swiss condottieri for obvious reasons.[18] This sort of private military entrepreneurship must be distinguished, of course, from those state treaties which sent Zurich contingents into foreign wars to benefit the public treasury, although these funds too were eventually redistributed. (State office holders must have profited considerably; they, with the army officers, of course belonged to the city's political elite). It is clear that the foreign payments made to Zurich notables not alone for services rendered but for services anticipated constituted both an important source of income for the urban elite and a political issue of the first order.

At first sight, therefore, Zurich does not look like a center

---

18. G. Gerig, Reisläufer u. Pensionsherren in Zürich, 1519–32 (Schweizer Studien z. Geschichtswissenschaft, N.F. XII), Zürich, 1947, p. 32. Gerig's monograph is a most useful discussion of the entire mercenary problem in the period of the Reformation.

of the new capitalism. There were no great local money houses, manufactures were not of the scope of Augsburg's textiles (there was little sign of a local industrial proletariat), the merchants (who did not even have their own guild) hardly operated on the scale of those in southern Germany. Rural revenues, income from state and mercenary service met the economic requirement of many whose energy and advantages, elsewhere, might have led them into mercantile and entrepreneurial activity. Yet we cannot describe Zurich as either backward or provincial. The ore trade and the smithies, with textiles, brought some important aspects of early modern trade and manufacture to the city. More important still, it had an intangible but perhaps inestimable advantage with respect to the possibilities for economic development: the radical discontinuities in its economic history just prior to 1500 meant that fixed and traditional economic values could not develop among important sections of the populace. Augsburg, too, it will be recalled, had a rapid and discontinuous development from the fifteenth century onwards; possibly the two cities were not as dissimilar as appearances might initially suggest.

The changes in the economy had visible effects on the entire social structure. The patriciate, composed of rentiers—some of them of mercantile origin—had to share its elite social status with new men, often still active in trade, and frequently of artisan origins, who remained in the artisan guilds. This was the great period of Zurich Junkertum, when parvenus adopted patrician manners and promptly pushed the old families from their previous monopoly of state office and military leadership. The city's new elite, then, was a fusion of old and new elements—these differed not alone in past family origins but in their present economic activities. Despite their temporary mutual accommodation, a certain conflict of interest and value persisted between them, and this was not without influence in the Reformation. Meanwhile the ordinary artisanry was confined to routine economic tasks. It, too, was divided: there were traditional trades and crafts (barrelmakers and bakers, for instance) and newer or technically developed occupations (smiths and printers), native Zurichers, immigrants from other cities, and recruits from the countryside. And although the average opportunities for accumulation were low, some were better placed in this respect—though not, apparently, journeymen in the newer and more capitalised crafts. To the artisanry's almost instinctive distaste for the patriciate was added its resentment of new wealth. But it retained enough in common with the bearers of the latter, who were much more closely connected with their workaday world, to join them, initially, in the struggle over the Church.

This was fought out within the City Council, which consisted of a Large Council, its members elected for life by the guilds, and a Small Council, half designated by the Large Council from its own ranks, and half named by the guilds.[19] (The patricians in the Konstaffel were, in both places, allocated a special if limited number of seats). The Small Council served for a year; when the Large Council met, as it did to decide important questions, it sat with the former. Finally, there was a Secret Council, which consisted of the two majors (life councillors who led the Small Council), four guild representatives with watching briefs, two treasurers and the administrator of the city's cloister estates. Life memberships in the Large Council, the frequent renewal of membership in the Small Council, the reservation of election rights within the guilds to officers, appointments to state offices from a limited circle, all suggest that the government of Zurich was oligarchic. The Small Council, indeed, met four times weekly —no ordinary artisan could devote that much time to the state. When the citizens of Zurich referred to their council-

19. Guyer, op. cit.

141

lors as "My Lords," it is clear that they did so with good reason.

By 1519, the state was agitated by the one issue which reflected its basic political tensions: foreign pensions and mercenary service.[20] Not only did the artisanry resent the inequitable distribution of official foreign subsidies paid into the treasury, it had good reason to suspect the notables of enriching themselves secretly by accepting foreign favours. We may suppose that the city's merchants supported those foreign alliances which kept open (or extended) their trade routes; the artisanry's interests were more local, and it had no sympathy for the Junkers who lived off war. Habsburg, Pope and France contended for the city's aid: the French party was decisively defeated in 1521; the oligarchs sought to counter Habsburg by supporting the Pope, but the dominant popular sentiment was Confederate. Zwingli was summoned to the city as a bitter public opponent of mercenary service in general and of the French in particular; from its beginning, then, the Reformation was politically coloured.

THE REFORMATION IN ZURICH[21]

The Zurich Reformation was politically coloured; the city's social conflicts were reflected in its religious divisions. But, equally, religious conceptions shaped the angle of vision with which contemporaries grasped their situation—the inner dissolution of late medieval Catholicism, far from producing a secularised indifference, had heightened religious aspirations and tension.

Zwingli's own position, when he arrived as preacher to the

---

20. Gerig, op. cit.
21. O. Farner, H. Zwingli, I–II–III, Zürich, 1943–46–54; W. Kohler, H. Zwingli, Leipzig 1943; and (by far the most valuable recent brief sketch of Zwingli's work) J. V. M. Pollett, "Zwinglianisme," Dictonnaire de Théologie catholique, XV (1950), pp. 3745–3927.

city cathedral at the age of thirty-five, may be briefly summarised. The son of a rural headman in North-eastern Switzerland, he had learned to hate mercenary service: he had accompanied his parishioners to Marignano. His antidote was the moral regeneration of Swiss society in the Erasmian terms he had learned while a student at Vienna and Basel. When he was called to Zurich in 1519[22] he was not yet an opponent of the Papacy, but still deemed a Christian renaissance possible within a purified but not revolutionized Church. Though he had developed a "social theology" on humanist foundations,[23] he did not arrive at a properly Protestant position until 1520–1. Thenceforth he held that reliance on man's unaided moral will was blasphemous and only faith in God's mercy could constitute justification for sin. The embodiment of that mercy was Christ, and its sole record Holy Scripture. Only the Word had moral authority, and it did not mention Pope or Catholic Hierarchy. Though Zwingli clearly took some impetus from Wittenberg, the consensus of recent scholarly opinion is that he was a good deal more independent of Luther than was once supposed.

Zwingli was brought to Zurich by the notables; his sermons, however, found immediate resonance amongst the common folk. In plastic and vivid imagery, he denounced abuse in Church and society; he broke precedent by preaching directly from the Bible. For the moment, he crystallised a variety of social and religious discontents and demands: the city, already stirred by the events in Germany, was swept by a wave of enthusiasm for the Evangile.

There was, of course, opposition. The Cathedral Clergy and the monks, mercilessly attacked, were quick to raise the cry of

22. A. Rich, Die Anfänge der Theologie Huldrych Zwinglis, (Quellen u. Abhandlungen z. Geschichte d. schweizerischen Protestantismus, VI), Zürich, 1949.

23. E. Wolf. "Die Sozialtheologie Zwinglis," Festschrift Guido Kisch, Stuttgart, 1955, 167–188.

heresy; Zwingli's political opponents were not much slower. The city's Erasmian episcopal Lord, the Bishop of Constance, at first conciliatory, became ever more insistent on suppression of the new doctrines. Most of the other Confederate states were hostile. Rome kept its peace until, in 1521, it succeeded in hiring Zurich troops (but then embarrassed the local Catholics by refusing to pay for them). These pressures on the City Council were more than balanced by profound popular Evangelical sentiment, often manipulated by Zwingli and his followers to push the government farther.

In the years 1521 through 1523 the state broke, effectively, with episcopal and Roman authority. It had always insisted on certain administrative rights over the local Church, now, however, it proceeded to rule on doctrinal matters. The campaign against Luther convinced Zwingli of the futility of expecting reform within the received structure of the Church. He turned to the City Council to further his work; with some hesitations, it supported him. The climax of this first period of the Zurich Reformation was the first Disputation (1523) when Zwingli argued his Sixty-seven Theses against episcopal representatives: Catholic rituals offended the faith which was alone Christian; Christ was the sole head of the Church; the believers congregated together locally had the right of ecclesiastical self-government and the distinction between priest and layman was null and void; secular authority was legitimate only if based on scripture. The Council endorsed Zwingli's views, an implicit contradiction which was to become the explicit focus of deep conflicts among the Zurich Evangelicals: Zwingli had enunciated a new Christian freedom, and as promptly bound himself to another authority. He had in fact resigned his Episcopal commission in 1522, only to accept a preaching position from the Council.

The break with Rome was practically complete; the inner structure of Zurich Protestantism, and the implications of the Evangile for the larger life of the society had now to be decided. A current of radicalism surged through the state: Zwingli found himself pushed or opposed by Evangelicals who used his own Biblicism against him. There was pressure for the immediate abolition of image and mass, for the recognition of congregational autonomy of the state. Some elements formed conventicles for prayer and study; Anabaptism was shortly to appear. Six rural communes demanded of the Council that tithes be abolished as unscriptural. Zwingli, with and against the Council, had to formulate a positive programme.

In 1523 Zwingli published his major treatise on politics: Of Divine and Human Justice.[24] A direct answer to those who read in the Evangile a legitimation for radical social demands, it insisted that no ideal Christian condition was attainable in the sinful world. The state's Christian duty was to strive for the maximum possible justice (Zwingli was not, of course, as quietist as Luther), but this by no means entailed a repudiation of contractual obligation, as he now described tithes. But Zwingli also utilised the demands of the radicals (possibly, too, he was impelled by their pressure) in his long campaign against the mass—finally abolished in 1525. The net result of his encounter with the more consistent of his followers was, however, the theory and practice of the State Church.

Zwingli took this road with some visible reluctance. He justified it, as against his early insistence on congregational autonomy, in two ways. First, the state was simply doing its Christian duty: removing the hindrances to the promulgation of the Word. Its theological decisions entailed recognition of the truth, not pronouncement of it. Secondly, the state was acting on behalf of the entire local community of Christians in enforcing ecclesiastical discipline within it. More, Zwingli's conflict with the Anabaptists and the other

24. H. Zwingli, Von göttlicher u. menschlicher Gerechtigkeit, in H. Zwinglis sämtliche Werke, II, Corpus Reformatorum, LXXIX.

resistances he met led him to see positive advantages in that discipline: he deplored the "many who claimed their absurd conceits were of the Holy Spirit" [25] and held that the "evil spirited and ignorant" [26] community needed overseers.

The conflict with the Anabaptists, indeed, turned, not so much on the issue of infant baptism as on the doctrine of the Church.[27] Zwingli (unlike Luther) held that infant baptism was simply a symbolic transaction, a pledge from parents and community to raise the child a Christian. What he repudiated in the Anabaptists was their separatist convictions and their literal biblicism: these, he held, were a danger to the unity and integrity of both Christian community and the social order. In 1525, the Council prescribed infant baptism, proscribed adult baptism, and proceeded to terrible punishments for the Anabaptists: exile and in at least one case, death.

The constraints imposed upon the Anabaptists were but part of a larger system of controls developed in the period 1524–28. Confiscated Church and cloister property was administered by the state (not without one or two scandals) for welfare purposes. Schools were established to train new preachers, conceived as incumbents of a *Predigtamt,* a preaching office. The clergy was organised into a Synod, under ultimate state supervision. Most important, however, was the Marriage Court, established in 1525 and reconstructed in 1526 as, in effect, a Morals Court.[28] A model for similar institutions elsewhere, notably in Geneva, this proved

25. Cited by P. Meyer, Zwinglis Soziallehren, Linz, 1921, p. 79.

26. Cited by R. Ley, Kirchenzucht bei Zwingli, (QAGSP, VI), Zürich, 1948, p. 60 from H. Zwinglis Sämtliche Werke, IV, p. 427 (in CR).

27. The significance of this controversy is emphasised by F. Littel, The Anabaptist View of the Church, Philadelphia, 1952, which summarises recent research into the early Anabaptists in a most illuminating way. A second edition has been published (Boston, 1959); my citations are from the first edition.

28. W. Kohler, Zürcher Ehegericht etc.

a remarkable instrument of control—at once ecclesiastical and political.

Its composition and competences indicated the balance of forces in the new Zurich Church: four laymen, two each from the Small and Large Council, and two pastors, could cite miscreants before the Council. Zwingli originally wanted a Church-administered right of excommunication for adulterers, blasphemers, whores and usurers. The Council reserved this right to itself and excluded usurers from the category of sinners. We should be mistaken were we to suppose that the Marriage Court, at least in Zwingli's lifetime, was an Erastian institution: granted the control of the Council won by 1526 by Zwingli and his supporters, it was in effect theocratic. Zwingli used it to terrorise the political opposition (espionage and denunciation were some of its techniques), as well as to punish sinners and encourage, if that is the word, the morally weak. The Marriage Court was an attempt to actualise a vision which Zwingli had not entirely abandoned, despite his retreat from his early biblicism: the idea of a sanctified community, obedient to God's Will, and militantly committed to the Evangile. Aware of the contradiction between a State Church and Evangelical Freedom, Zwingli sought to overcome it in the Evangelical State.

The contrast with the Lutheran Territorial Churches was marked: the formal reorganization of the Church in Saxony did not begin until 1527, and the Lutheran cities were not subjected, apparently, to this sort of inner discipline.[29] Yet the differences between the active and innovating Zwinglian ethic and the more traditionalist Lutheran one were already manifest in the sacramental controversy.[30] The dogmatic foundation of Zwingli's many ritual reforms was his denial of scriptural warrant for the efficacy of the Sacraments: the

29. C. A. H. Burkhardt, Geschichte d. dt. Kirchen-und Schulvisitatione im Zeitalter d. Reformation, I, Leipzig, 1879.
30. W. Kohler, Zwingli u. Luther etc.

Spirit spoke only to the Spirit and the sole aim of Divine Service was the preaching of the Word. He rejected the real presence in the Eucharist; the new order of worship in 1525 introduced a simple service of commemoration but four times a year. Luther's theology of the sacraments was equivocal; he retained Baptism and the Eucharist, but held them objectively efficacious only if faith were present. Zwingli's symbolic interpretation of the Eucharist struck him as unmitigated blasphemy: he asserted the Real Presence.

The sacramental controversy had major political consequences for the Reformation as a whole and for Zurich. The Catholic, inner Swiss, cantons allied themselves with Hapsburg; Zwingli hoped to end this threat, and to carry Protestantism to these cantons, by joining a grand alliance.[31] Bern reformed in 1528, Basel in 1529: these were already Zurich's allies. Strasbourg and the southern German cities, Zwinglian in their sacramental doctrines, were agreed. But the Lutheran cities and princes of northern Germany refused an alliance on account of the sacramental issue. Zwingli was ready for an alliance on purely practical grounds; had he not sought a rapprochement with his old opponent, the Catholic King of France? But the Lutheran proponent of the alliance, Prince Philip of Hesse thought it imperative to summon both Zwingli and Luther to a religious colloquy in Marburg in 1529. The sacramental question proved insoluble (the more so since the Lutherans had not abandoned hope of an eventual agreement with the Catholics); doctrinal agreement on other matters did not overcome Lutheran resistance to joint political action.

Zurich meanwhile had signed a compromise peace after a bloodless war with the Catholic cantons; a sceptical Zwingli redoubled his political efforts. Now, Butzer and Strasbourg attempted to mediate on the sacramental issue, in order to bring the Swiss into the Schmalkaldic League, but this effort,

31. H. v. Schubert, Bekenntnisbildung u. Religionspolitik, Gotha, 1910.

too, failed (1530–1). Zwingli called for war on the Catholic cantons, but Bern urged restraint and the Zurich citizenry was unenthusiastic. In the spring of 1531 Zurich blockaded the food supplies of the inner Swiss, despite the preacher's warning against half-measures. So strong was Zurich's unwillingness to fight that he threatened to resign in July. And in October, the Catholics defeated a remarkably unprepared and demoralised Zurich army on the borders. Zwingli fell in battle, Zurich remained Protestant, but Switzerland remained confessionally divided. Zwingli's refusal to compromise on the sacramental issue had isolated the Protestant Swiss, but the lack of enthusiasm of the populace was not simply a consequence of that isolation nor was military inefficiency entirely due to lack of morale; rather, all three facts reflected the social situation in which the Zurich Reformation was embedded.

SOCIAL CONFLICT AND REFORMATION

The social conflicts of the period were directly reflected in the political controversy over the Reformation. So intense was the controversy that Zwingli in 1522 had to have an armed guard. (Somebody who had stoned his windows was later found hiding in a priest's empty wine barrel in a cloister).[32] This was a period when few defenders of the Church could be found in the city; of these few Bullinger said: "The prominent pensioners and officers, and others who had praised his sermons and practically run to hear them, now cursed Zwingli as a heretic. Many who were never particularly attached to the faith now declared their allegiance to it, saying that they wanted to defend the true old faith against the heretic Zwingli, but what concerned them was not the faith but the money-bag."[33] To these secular op-

32. Farner, op. cit., III, p. 324.
33. J. J. Hottinger and H. H. Vogeli, editors, Heinrich Bullingers Reformationsgeschichte, I–IV, Frauenfeld and Zürich, 1838–1913, I, p. 48.

ponents were joined, of course, many of the clergy. The Catholics of the Cathedral Chapter were, in some cases, members of prominent Zurich families.[34] But the entire oligarchy of the city was not opposed to the new doctrine; indeed, many were among its most ardent supporters.

The Reformation began in Zurich, in fact, with a united front of artisan and merchant behind Zwingli—opposed by a considerable part of the patricians. In 1522 at the famous Friday meat meal at the printer's, Froschauer, merchants and prosperous artisan masters joined simple journeymen (in Zwingli's presence) to defy the Church. Froschauer showed considerable theological eloquence in defending himself before the Council:[35] many were prepared to take seriously the priesthood of all believers. It was a group of laymen who answered, in a pamphlet, the episcopate's attack on the Sixty-seven Theses. These included three members of the important Saffran guild, where many merchants were found, and a patrician—if one from a family later to turn to trade. These were typical of the educated elite's support for Zwingli. The new doctrines were also popular, of course, amongst the more self-taught artisanry and we can read in a Council protocol of an artisan greeting his mates, amidst laughter, "What are you Pharisees doing?"[36]

The leadership of this initially united Evangelical political movement was a new and energetic group of oligarchs, most young, grown prosperous in crafts and trade—particularly, in the new branches of the economy associated with the upturn in the city's fortunes at the beginning of the century. In 1524, with the death of the two mayors, these offices passed to convinced Evangelicals. One, the son of his predecessor

---

34. T. Pestalozzi, Die Gegner Zwinglis am Grossmünsterstift in Zurich (SSG, XI, 1) Zürich, 1918.
35. E. Egli, Actensammlung z. Geschichte d. Zürcher Reformation i. den Jahren 1519–1533, Zürich, 1879, Nr. 234.
36. Ibid., Nr. 238.

(Roist), was from a patrician family recently risen from the artisanry; the other (Walder) belonged to Smith's Guild and was himself the proprietor of a bathhouse. I have made a list of thirty-nine prominent Zwinglians active in politics and the administration of the new Church.[37] There were seven apiece from the Tailor's Guild and the Meise, five from the Saffran and four from the Simth's. The Tailor's Guild, of course, included textile merchants; the Meise, wine dealers, painters and glaziers; the Saffran, merchants; the Smiths', all who worked with metal. The Secret Council at the time it worked most closely with Zwingli included a goldsmith, a blacksmith, a tanner, a merchant, a carpenter, and a glazier. (Two of Zwingli's closest lay associates were, in fact, glaziers: Funk who accompanied him to Marburg, and Lavater, later a mayor). When the opposition, after Zurich's defeat in 1531, expelled five Zwinglians from the Council as warmongers, three were tailors (two cloth cutters), one from the Shoemaker's and one from the Butcher's guild. The results seem reasonably clear; not only did the leading Zwinglians represent the city's mercantile and artisan elite but they were, in striking measure, from those trades and crafts in which economic and technical change was most pronounced.

What may be said about the social characteristics of the

37. I have compiled the list from: the authors of a 1523 pamphlet defending Zwingli against attacks from Constance (Farner, op. cit., III, p. 361); those delegated by the Council to confer with Zwingli on the proposal for the Marriage Court (Egli, op. cit., Nr. 654); 4 those delegated to confer with him on the Pensions question in 1526 (Gerig, op. cit., p. 54); those who replaced Catholic Councillors purged in 1528 (H. Wirz, "Zürcher Familienschicksale im Zeitalter Zwinglis," Zwingliana, VI (1938), p. 558); the Secret Council in 1529 (Wirz, op. cit., p. 566); and those expelled from the Council after the defeat of 1531, as warmongers (Gerig, op. cit., p. 109). I have also included those who served on two of the most important organs of Protestant control and patronage in the early Reformation period: the Marriage Court (Kohler, Zürcher Ehegericht, etc., p. 36) and the administrators of the secularised Grossmünsterstift (J. Figi, Die innere Reorganisation des Grossmünsterstifts in Zurich von 1519 bis 1531, Zürcher Beiträge z. Geschichtswissenschaft, IX, Zürich, 1951, pp. 56–7).

opposition? Again, I have made a list of opposition leaders, numbering twenty-eight.[38] Of these, eleven came from the patrician Konstaffel. The only other noteworthy concentration was in the Kambel Guild, comprising retailers, second-hand dealers, and oil vendors. The patricians, of course, were largely mercenaries and rentiers (although not all mercenaries were patricians) and in general offended by the ecclesiastical and political innovations of the Reformation. But why should the Kambel have provided some of the opposition? Possibly, these rather traditionalised elements were unenthusiastic about the activities of the Zwinglian elite. Finally, it must be said that among those expelled from the Small Council in 1528 as opponents of the Reformation (or Zwingli's politics) were a butcher, a furrier and a hatmaker. The butchers and millers were at this time embittered with Zwingli: their trade had suffered because of strained relations with the Catholic agrarian cantons of inner Switzerland. Perhaps some of the other occupations, too, suffered these local economic pressures and, more fundamentally, were of a character that allowed no new spiritual perspectives to develop. It does seem, then, that the opposition was not entirely the work of the patriciate and the mercenaries; it included, under the leadership of the latter, some of the artisans —apparently those in the more traditional and local trades. Here, as amongst the Zwinglians, there were exceptions; but the general situation is clear. The Reformation in Zurich entailed an alliance of a new mercantile and productive elite with a large group of lesser artisans, against the patricians

38. Here, the list is drawn from those who led the French party in 1521–2 (Gerig, op. cit., p. 29); those accused as recipients of pensions in 1526 (Gerig, op. cit., pp. 53–59); those expelled from the Small Council in 1528 (Wirz, op. cit., p. 558); those who ate fish ostentatiously, New Year's Day, 1529 (Gerig, op. cit., pp. 73–8); those relieved of their military posts in 1529 (Gerig, op. cit., pp. 86–8); and those cited before the Council by the Marriage Court in 1530, allegedly for helping an adulterer to escape, in fact for oppositional behaviour (Egli, op. cit., Nr. 1723).

(mercenaries and rentiers) and certain artisans, very possibly concentrated in the more traditional sectors of the economy.

These conflicts were visible in the proceedings of the Council. Resistance to the Reformation, and the delaying tactics of its more hesitant supporters, was originally concentrated in the oligarchic Small Council. In 1523, an Evangelical cloth cutter, himself of the Large Council, said that there were but fourteen good Evangelicals among the fifty members of the Small Council: "the others are sick of the matter." [39] In 1524 the Large Council itself assumed the right to judge false doctrines; it also reversed a Small Council order to a rural commune demanding the restoration of Church images.

Despite the clear balance of opinion within the city, the Council as a whole often moved more slowly than the Evangelical enthusiasts wished. Zwingli asked for the abolition of mass in 1523; this was voted, and then only by a narrow majority, in 1525. Zwingli had often to intervene from the pulpit to stir the Council; only after he had done so in 1526 were recipients of foreign pensions prosecuted and condemned, and the purge of the Catholics and other opponents from the Council in 1528 was equally due to his intervention.

The purge, ostensibly the high point of his power, actually marked its turning point. Its immediate occasion had been the elections, the results of which displeased him. It was followed by an ostentatious Catholic display during the New Year's Dinners at the gild halls: it was Friday, and some ate fish.[40] The Council chose not to impose punishments, but issued a general warning, instituted compulsory Church attendance, and forbade attendance at mass outside the city. In 1530, a general mandate was issued; it complained that the public houses were full during service, and that the preachers

39. Egli, op. cit., Nr. 434.
40. Gerig, op. cit. pp. 73–8.

had been jeered.[41] The guilds, in the city, were left to impose punishment on those warned by the Marriage Court, for these and other transgressions. But this provision, a concession to democratic theory, pointed to a fatality in the oligarchic practice of the new state.

The purge, followed by a constitutional revision which reduced the Konstaffel to the political status of the other guilds, enabled the new Zwinglian elite to consolidate its hold on the state.[42] In 1529, too, a new military organisation was introduced: this gave reliable Zwinglians command positions and reduced the patrician officers to the status of technical advisers.[43] It also increased the financial burdens of service on the average citizen; and in general, the rise of the new oligarchy was unaccompanied by concrete concessions to the artisans who had originally supported the Reformation. Zwingli's policies met increasing resistance; he had to threaten to resign, in 1529 and 1531, on account of opposition to his war plans. The final defeat in 1531 (and the restoration of the patricians' constitutional advantages) was due to some considerable extent to popular coolness towards the reformer's political works. A contemporary is quoted: "My Lords burned the wooden images, but they took the golden ones and stole away with them in their pockets and many became Evangelical, only to obtain office." [44] The Zwinglian elite had indeed streamed into the state, not least into the administration of secularised Church property; some had been exposed for speculating with funds intended for poor relief.[45] The moral impulses originally mobilised by the

41. Egli, op. cit., Nr. 1656.
42. Guyer, Verfassungszunstände etc., p. 16.
43. The military reorganisation, and its political causes and consequences, are discussed (and the relevant literature reviewed) in R. Braun, "Z. Militärpolitik Zürichs im Zeitalter d. Kappeler Kreige," Zwingliana, X, 1958, pp. 537–73.
44. Quoted by R. Staehlin, H. Zwingli, II, Basel, 1897, p. 480.
45. H. Hussy, "Aus der Finanzgeschichte Zürichs in d. Reformationszeit Zwingliana, VIII (1946), p. 349.

reformer amongst many artisans had not been satisfied; no wonder that they subsided, or turned elsewhere.

But there developed in the city of Zurich no strong movement which seemed to unite theological and social radicalism; social conflict of this sort in the Zurich Reformation seemed to occur mainly in the countryside. It is not easy to find reasons for this missing factor in the city. Most important, perhaps, was the relative absence of an industrial proletariat and the relatively high degree of political participation enjoyed by the artisans—high, that is, by contrast with many contemporary cities. Nor have I found evidence that Zurich had much economic discontent. But we have also to consider the fate of urban Anabaptism in Zurich.[46]

The assumption of an automatic association between theological and social radicalism, in Zurich as elsewhere, has been disproved.[47] Some of the Zurich Anabaptist leaders, indeed, were quietist in their attitude to the state—opposing only its intervention in religious affairs—and by no means the social revolutionaries, specifically the Christian Communists, their opponents so often claimed. The mutual aid the Anabaptists practised was indeed a practical imitation of primitive Christian models and not a political programme. But there is no doubt that in the Reformation, radical social demands were based on the more self-consciously Biblicist of the competing Protestant doctrines of faith and the Church. We have already seen that Zwingli regarded Anabaptist separatism as a threat to the state. In Zurich, the persecution of the Anabaptists led to the elimination of this movement as a possible channel of expression for artisan discontent. Anabaptism in Zurich began, in fact, amongst dissenting and

46. Quellen z. Geschichte d. Täufer i .d. Schweiz, I, Zurich, edited by L. v. Muralt and W. Schmid, Zürich, 1952; P. Peachey, Die soziale Herkunft d. Schweizer Täufer i. d. Reformationszeit, Karlsruhe, 1954.
47. Littel, op. cit., pp. 1–49 and Peachey, op. cit. See also W. Kohler, "Die Zürcher Täufer," Gedenkschrift z. 400 Jährigen Jubiläum der Mennoniten oder Taufgesinnten, Ludwigshafen, 1925, pp. 49–71.

educated laymen—not amongst the artisans. Peachey's careful investigations show that the urban Anabaptists known to us included five priests, nine other educated men (both categories including some of Zwingli's early associates), five nobles and but seven ordinary citizens.[48] Anabaptism in the state of Zurich became a rural movement; it is to the countryside in any case, that we must turn for a fuller understanding of the social context of Zwinglianism.[49]

The peasants (and rural artisans) took as their point of departure Zwingli's own early criticism of tithes and his expressed sympathy for those who lived by their hands and not from exploitation. But when the peasants rejected the tithes, and when interest payments on rural mortgages were threatened, Zwingli quickly drew his distinction between divine and human justice. The voluntary sharing of property was good, but to repudiate contractual obligation was theft: human justice in the condition of the fall required that the division of property be maintained. We may recall that the new as well as the old political elite of the city drew income from rural rents, and that the state itself had rural holdings.

Zwingli by no means reacted to peasant demands as did Luther; he urged negotiation with those of Zurich's rural subjects who rose in 1525, and he proposed a number of reforms. In particular, he held that rural mortgages could be

48. Peachey, op. cit., pp. 107 ff.
49. W. Classen, Schweizer Bauernpolitik i. Zeitalter Zwinglis, (Ergänzungshefte z. Zeitschr. f. Sozial-und Wirtschaftsgeschichte, IV), Weimar, 1899; A. Farner, D. Lehre v. Kirche u. Staat bei Zwingli, Tubingen, 1930; L. v. Muralt, "Jorg Berger," Festgabe Hermann Escher, Zürich, 1927, pp. 98–126; H. Nabholz, "Z. Frage nach d. Ursachen d. Bauernkrieges, 1525," Gedächtnisschrift f. G. v. Below, Stuttgart, 1928, pp. 221–253; P. Meyer, op. cit. See also C. Vasella, "Bauerntum u. Reformation i. d. Eidgenossenschaft," Hist. Jahrbuch, LXXVI (1957), pp. 47–63. Vasella shows that the opposition of the peasants to their political overlords was associated, elsewhere in Switzerland, with an antagonism between Catholic peasants and Protestant city states—above all in Bern. And he notes that many peasant communes insisted on retaining the mass but rejected tithes.

justified only as advances on the future productivity of peasant holdings; interest, therefore, ought to vary with the harvest. He insisted that tithes had to be restored to their original uses (welfare and the support of a purified Church) and he held that the lesser tithes could be cancelled if the greater ones were promptly paid. But the reforms did not materialise; there remained Zwingli's advice to the peasants to leave their uneconomical holdings rather than mortgage themselves anew. But those who sold their farms had to pay the state's representative in their communes one third of the price, as compensation for the loss of a subject: the advice was gratuitous.

These demands cannot be attributed to Anabaptist teaching: indeed, some scholars suggest that Anabaptist successes in the Zurich countryside followed (and were due to) the frustration of the peasants' social protest.[50] Peachey's figures show that some thirty rural artisans and over two hundred peasants were identified as Anabaptists.[51] But if it was more effective in the Zurich countryside than in the city (in one commune, a number of conscripts refused military service on grounds of biblical pacificism),[52] it was in both places, by the end of the decade, without major effect.

Thus the Zurich Reformation mastered—more easily than was done elsewhere—the double challenge of theological and social radicalism. Overt pressure on Zwingli's social ethic developed in the countryside; in reaction to it, he modified his biblical critique of society. In the city, the challenge was far less pressing—and he could, in general terms, denounce "usury" and condemn the trading companies; the Zurich merchants were also against them. Zwingli's disdain for a biblical social radicalism (he recommended to authority that

50. L. v. Muralt, "Jorg Berger," etc. and Peachey, op. cit., pp. 50 ff.
51. Peachey, op. cit., pp. 107 ff.
52. P. Schweizer, "Die Schlacht bei Kappel," Jahrbuch f. Schweizerische Geschichte, XVI (1916), p. 12.

"those who are so well informed that they know that all things shall be held in common . . . should be fixed to the gallows as a common example for us all," [53] and his anger with the Anabaptists, were understandable. Taken separately, each was a threat to his version of the Christian polity in Zurich; together, they might well have overwhelmed it. But his work produced a state and a state church which excited the hatred of those who claimed to be more faithful to his early teachings than the preacher himself.

It is clear that the Zurich Reformation was the occasion, indeed, the vehicle for the replacement of one political elite by another: the merchants and master artisans, some of them veritable entrepreneurs, displaced the old patriciate. In doing so, they alienated the peasants and at the very least did nothing to maintain much journeymen artisan enthusiasm. These, however, were the external uses of the new doctrine in Zurich, once it appeared. Was there something intrinsic to it, however, that bespoke its origins? Zwinglianism's most pronounced characteristics were three: its anti-hierarchical view of the Church, its symbolic theology of the sacraments, and its strongly activist social ethic. These general positions were not surrendered, whatever concrete interpretations were placed upon them under the pressure of social circumstance.

The Zwinglian view of the Church reflected the self-respect of an urban citizenry, educated burghers and a literate artisanry, already disgusted with a Church corrupt and profane and ruled by an alien system which combined the arrogant remoteness of impersonality with the gratuitous insolence of nepotism. The self-confidence of social groups unbeholden to the traditional powers of late medieval society, and possessing their own independent and vivid political traditions, rendered a hierarchical theory of Church government ever more difficult of acceptance. The clear demonstra-

53. Cited by Meyer, op. cit., p. 50.

tion of its want of scriptural legitimation effected the break: the recourse to scriptural authority (and, of course, the theology of salvation through faith) gave every man direct access to the path of salvation. The peasantry, for reasons not dissimilar but accentuated by their frequent encounter with churchmen as rural exploiters, found it very easy to accept the new view.

The symbolic theology of the sacraments was a blow at the pretensions of the priestly estate and as such, welcome to nearly all the discontented in late medieval society. But the Evangelicals in Zurich came largely from those sectors of the economy in which they dealt in new technical processes, mastering material, or in which they commanded relatively abstract economic forces. They were more or less easily brought, therefore, to distrust an earthly presentation of divine processes. This does not mean that they were forerunners of theological liberalism: the ultimate mystery remained, in the form of an inscrutable God, but it was banished from ordinary sense experience.

The social ethic of Zwinglianism insisted that Christian theory could not be satisfied by Christian ritual practice alone; developed in the highly visible political and social circumstances of the city state, it appealed to the many who sought new standards which would both justify themselves and control their neighbours. But the general Zwinglian imperative to the Christian life, capable of uniting a number of groups in either latent or active conflict with one another in opposition to those aspects of the existing order they all opposed, proved incapable of specific application to any of these conflicts—or was applied to the advantage of the most powerful elements in the Zwinglian Church.

The embodiment of this new version of the Word in a Church, then, called into play the balance of forces in Zurich society and, to some extent, altered it. The divisions within the society and the explosive potentialities of religiously legitimated dissent were too great: a disciplined State Church had to be constructed. Its masters were the new men engaged in a struggle for control of the state: they used the Marriage Court, devised as an institution of moral discipline, as an instrument of political rule. The Biblical promise of Zwingli's early teachings was unfulfilled, and Evangelical freedom remained a vision pursued, in despair, by the persecuted Anabaptist conventicles. Meanwhile, more sacrifices were demanded of the ordinary artisan and peasant than rewards offered to them: an outer discipline was imposed. In later generations this was to result in the modern Protestant personality.

Finally, we have to consider the light thrown by the Zurich Reformation on the problem of the relationship of capitalism to Protestantism. Weber asserted that the "typical bearers of the capitalistic ethic and the Calvinistic Church" were those petty and middle bourgeois rising up into entrepreneurial roles.[54] Weber's interest was mainly in the seventeenth century, but the sixteenth century antecedents of this type were surely the dominant element amongst the Zwinglians in Zurich. Weber also asserted that Calvinistic Protestantism was an indispensable precondition of the development of a capitalistic work ethic. We have seen that Zurich in the early sixteenth century was by no means a center of the developing capitalism of the period; we know that later, its Protestant population (admittedly, swelled by Protestant refugeees from the Ticino) was conspicuous for its ingenuity at technical innovation and its success in accumulation. We

54. Weber, op. cit., p. 50. For another attempt at a sociological interpretation of some aspects of Zwinglianism see H. Koditz, "Die gesellschaftlichen Ursachen d. Scheiterns d. Marburger Religionsgespräche v. I bis f. October 1529, Zeitschrift f. Geschichtswissenschaft, II (1954), pp. 37–70. See also the very good article by G. Fuchs, "Karlstadts radikal-reformistisches Wirken u. Stellung zwischen Müntzer u. Luther," Wiss. Zeitschrift d. Martin Luther Universität Halle-Wittenberg, III (1954), pp. 523–551.

know, too, that the typical career of members of the Zurich elite, at the beginning of the sixteenth century, took them out of the economy into the service of the state and eventually into a late medieval patrician style of life. At first glance, then, it would seem that the Reformation in Zurich did break into an historically indeterminate situation and induce capitalist attitudes in part of the population.

But no such simple formulation is legitimate. The very indeterminacy of the historical situation in Reformation Zurich allows another interpretation. Many of the elements of capitalism were already there: mercantile accumulation and technically advanced production. The fact that Zurich was not a capitalist metropolis like the Augsburg of the Fugger may have been an advantage: the great monopolies were missing, and the newer economic forms could crystallise there free of the restraints and encrustations of the transitional patterns of the late medieval urban economy. Urban Zurich's relatively small size and its difficulties as an autonomous state amidst political and economic convulsions of late medieval European society may also have been advantages: like litmus paper, Zurich society was especially responsive to the changes around it. Most basically, it was a society which had experienced a very rapid rate of social change; many of its members had participated in the making of their own traditions, and the vested values and ideologies which elsewhere hindered change were missing or weak. The breakthrough of a radically new religious system was more possible in these circumstances than elsewhere: the potentialities for the development of both capitalism and Zwinglianism were simultaneously given in the city. If Zwinglianism was the road towards capitalism for Zurich, it was taken because the route in any case led in that direction.

161

Eastern Europe

and the Death of God

In his book on the German Peasants' War, Friedrich Engels observed that in a religious epoch, even revolutionary ideas have to be expressed in a religious rhetoric: the very thoughts which anticipate the future assume old forms. I was reminded of Engels's remark when, last December (1966), I attended a conference of Marxist sociologists of religion in Prague. The participants, nearly all of them from Eastern Europe, were troubled by the persistence of religion among the populations of the Communist countries. A few reacted dogmatically: as the case was put by one scholar from the German Democratic Republic who held to a rather narrow version of Marxism, if religion did not decline under socialism, then the Marxist theory would have to be considered false. Other participants who took a much more subtle, comprehensive, and comprehending view of religion in history (including their own recent history) did so in different Marxist terms. I believe that their utilization of Marxism to explore the social and spiritual realities around them may anticipate new developments in Eastern Europe.

Engels was writing, in fact, about the great Reformation theologian and Christian Communist, Thomas Münzer, who

162

died a horrible death at the hands of vengeful German (Protestant) princes for having taken seriously the doctrine of the
Imminence of the Kingdom in early Protestant theology.
My colleagues at Prague were sociologists and philosophers,
not theologians, and none spoke directly against his own
princes. Yet some of the things they said in the course of the
meeting reflected deep changes in Eastern Europe, and these
may very well portend new developments in other spheres—
not least in politics.

Ever since the end of Stalinism, the Communist parties of
Eastern Europe have been seeking a *modus vivendi* with the
populations they rule. Janos Kadar's *bon mot,* "all who are
not against us are with us," typifies one prevalent attitude.
The peoples of Eastern Europe cannot yet be described as
enthusiastic about socialism in its Eastern European version.
A less hostile and more sophisticated view of the religious
beliefs and communities to which these peoples remain attached is a consequence of the new Communist awareness of
this fact. It is true that the Communists (or some of them)
remain most hostile to religion where the churches have been
strongest: above all, in Poland, where the Primate is about
as stubborn as the General Secretary of the Communist party,
both being old men who grew up in a different world; and
in Germany, where the Protestant Church has been the one
functioning all-German institution. In general, however,
Eastern European regimes have now learned to distinguish
between the political views of certain ecclesiastical leaders
and the religious convictions of their peoples—if only the
better to split the two. Indeed, the regimes have found some
politically compliant churchmen, and there are groups of
theologians (the most distinguished of whom are at the
Comenius Faculty of Protestant Theology at Prague) who
see no scriptural warrant for depicting Communism as the
work of the devil.

In addition to setting off a general attempt at discussion between Christians and Marxists, the demise of Stalinism has also entailed the development of empirical social research in the Eastern European Communist countries. Instead of deducing the contours of reality from a few exceedingly primitive political postulates, Communist parties and governments have begun to rely on social inquiries and occasionally on broader sociological analyses. In some countries, such inquiries and analyses were first undertaken by politically courageous thinkers (like Djilas and others) who had a clear revisionist intent—to demonstrate that the official picture of reality was grotesquely untrue. There seems, however, to be a law at work in both East and West by which ideas and techniques originally meant to create new social possibilities serve only to consolidate old ones. Empirical social inquiry in our own societies was devised as an instrument of social reform; it has become very largely another piece of administrative technology. The same thing seems to be happening, in a much more compressed period of time, in Eastern Europe. Ten years ago, "sociology" was a politically dubious term in much of Eastern Europe: it evoked fears of the penetration of "bourgeois science." (We may define "bourgeois science" as science done by bourgeois professors who are *not* Marxists.) Today, Communist parties and governments alike look with great favor on sociology. As for "bourgeois science" —speaking of the intense interest shown by his colleagues in sociology in the work of Talcott Parsons, a "revisionist" Czech philosopher told me with some feeling that "if this goes on, Marxism in eighteen months will become a revolutionary doctrine again."

At any rate, the scholars who met in Prague were interested in developing an empirically grounded sociology of religion from a Marxist point of view. They had met together once before, at Jena in Germany, the university which gave Karl Marx his doctorate. I have termed them scholars, and the description is exact: most were teachers at universities or research workers at the Academies of Science in their respective countries. There was a professor of the sociology of religion from the German Democratic Republic, Olaf Klohr, even if his chair was designated as the *"Lehrstuhl für wissenschaftlicher Atheismus"* (Chair of Scientific Atheism). There were also two or three publicists from party institutes for the struggle against religion; even they acknowledged the necessity for an empirically founded approach to religion, and indeed the institute attached to the Central Committee of the Soviet Communist party has actually conducted sociological research on a large scale. My own presence was accounted for by my position as secretary of the International Sociological Association's Committee on the Sociology of Religion. Actually, there had been certain hesitations about inviting me, but these probably had less to do with my status as a "bourgeois" scholar than with the fact that I was known in some Eastern European countries as a "neo-Marxist." What, precisely, this may mean, and whether or not it is true, in parts of Eastern Europe the accusation is a grave one.

The conference, and particularly the lively spontaneous discussions of the prepared papers, made national differences among the participants very evident—differences which resulted from local intellectual traditions, the particular shape of the problem of religion in the various countries, and the degree of intellectual freedom permitted by the individual regimes.

The Bulgarians, for example, were quite rigid intellectually, and I must confess that I did not always sense that they followed the contributions of some of the others with sympathy, or even with total comprehension. The Czechs, our hosts, were there in large numbers (some fifteen, whereas there were only three or four from each of the other countries). Czechoslovakia at the moment enjoys a considerable amount of intellectual freedom, and the Czech contributions showed this: they were direct, even blunt, and did not circumvent real problems with empty formulations. The East Germans were solid and thorough, precisely like scholars from the other German state. They came, however, from working-class families in a society in which workers' children had rarely gone to the universities in ages past. Not surprisingly, their Marxism coincided almost exactly with the Marxism of the German Social Democratic party in the Wilhelminian Empire. It was a doctrine of the sovereignty of applied science, in which socialism was reason triumphant. By contrast, the Hungarians evinced great imagination and subtlety: their group included Ivan Varga, who is a pupil of Georg Lukacs and has inherited the critical humanism which is the best side of his teacher. The Polish group was divided between scholars from the Academy of Sciences and anti-religious publicists.

The Soviet participants were extraordinary. Fully in possession of their own intellectual tradition, they seemed also to have recaptured the long Russian tradition of mastery of Western thought. About the Yugoslavs, finally, little need be said. In that country, Marxism is not obligatory in the universities: one of the Yugoslavs present struck me as a positivist and rationalist. When the Yugoslavs do work with Marxism, they often make something interesting of it.

The conference went on for three days, in what was once the chapel of a Franciscan cloister, now converted into the headquarters of the municipal Communist party. (The building is next to the old Opera House, where Mozart himself conducted the premiere of *Don Giovanni*.) There were Baroque religious paintings on the ceiling, and stern busts of Marx, Engels, Lenin, and Gottwald stared fixedly at us from the front of the room. The discussion returned to a number of central themes which were systematically—I am inclined to say dialectically—interrelated. The findings of a number of research projects pointed to the difficulties of a Marxist interpretation of religion under Marxist regimes. Discussion of such difficulties soon enough turned into a reexamination of the moral experience of these societies.

The sessions began, straightforwardly enough, with a lucid exposition by our chairwoman, Dr. Kadlecova of the Czechoslovak Academy of Sciences. She had studied the religious consciousness of a group of her compatriots, in a locality in which religious affiliation was still rather strong. Among those who said that they were religious, nominal adherence to the Church and traditional ritual participation far outweighed deep inner conviction; the belief in immortality, or in the divinity of Jesus, was conspicuously absent from their affirmations. Seventy-five per cent of her sample, however, said that religion was a means to master life. They consciously saw religion, in other words, as an instrument of adaptation and were therefore outside the religious experience or historically past it. These results, of course, correspond almost exactly to those found in many Western countries.

Professor Ugrinovtisch of the Lomonosov University in Moscow was the next speaker. A humorous and sympathetic scholar who had impressed many of the Western scholars at the World Congress of Sociology in France in September by the suppleness and sharpness of his mind, Ugrinovtisch suggested that studies in the Soviet Union yielded much the same findings as those of Dr. Kadlecova. I was reminded that at the World Congress of Sociology, Ugrinovtisch had insisted that religion was strongest in the Soviet Union among those least integrated into Soviet society: older persons, rural communities relatively untouched by urban currents. At Prague, however, he added some new dimensions to his argument. He held that there were secular or non-religious, indeed even anti-religious, cultic and ritual observances in socialist society; ritual alone, therefore, was not necessarily connected with religion. What he intended was to support his contention that studies of religious comportment by itself were meaningless—we had to study the psychological and spiriutal content of religious beliefs. What in fact he did was to raise the vexed question of the spiritual status of civic belief in the socialist societies. For the moment, this passed unremarked; the participants argued about other matters.

Dr. Kadlecova pointed out that an ideal community had not yet been constructed under socialism. In the circumstances, she felt it justified to ask if there were social grounds for the continuance of religion, in some form, in socialist society. Ugrinovtisch carried this argument further. He described as "an old dualism" the view that men controlled their own destinies under socialism but did not do so under other social systems. We required concrete inquiries into the precise degree of control over the social process exercised by specific individuals and groups. To begin with, we already knew that in socialism some individuals could exert far more influence on the social process than others. These remarks seemed to be unexceptionable, yet they quickly led to controversy. Professor Klohr, from Germany, strenuously denied that religion and what he called a high degree of educated consciousness could coexist. Klohr and his colleagues proceeded to present statistics which showed, to their satisfaction at least, that religion declined as socialism advanced.

The East German researches rested on the assumption that there is nothing universal about religion, or about human consciousness in general. Indeed, neither religion nor atheism was a primary form of consciousness: both, rather, were derivatives of more fundamental modes of thought. The sources of these, in turn, were in class relationships and the relationships of production. Atheism arose when a materialistic view developed, quite spontaneously, as a result of social changes which increased society's conscious power over social and natural processes. It followed, the East Germans insisted, that there had to be a sociology of religion specific to socialist societies: the identical categories could hardly deal with religion in different social systems.

The evidence they introduced to support these contentions did not entirely convince many of their colleagues. Klohr and his group found, to be sure, that many with religious convictions had a "progressive" (by which they meant positive) attitude to the East German state. But they also insisted that those who were most engaged in "constructive" social activity were most remote from religion. I found their mode of inference curiously devoid of psychological penetration: they seemed to care little about what people thought, and even less about what they felt, and to concentrate on what they said. "Socialist" science in this case was rather like the more backward sectors of "bourgeois" research. In one respect, however, it was true to old traditions in classical sociology. August Comte enjoined the European elites after the convulsions of the French Revolution to use sociology as an instrument of domination. Klohr and his colleagues made their own aims quite clear: "The analysis of this entire complex . . . gives a further basis for a differentiated educational and pedagogic activity."

The response to the German presentation was vigorous. Dr. Kadlecova declared that different categories were not needed for the same religious systems in the same cultural areas, despite political differences. This was an interesting way of insisting on the unity of European culture, an idea more Gaullist than "orthodox" Marxist. Varga of Hungary doubted that the actual content of religious beliefs was different in the different types of society. The East German categories, he continued, referred to the sociology of politics and not of religion: he doubted that it was useful to make the strengthening of socialism the direct aim of study. In any case, Hungarian inquiry had shown that young Catholics and young Communists were quite identical with respect to social engagement. Moreover, Varga observed, a materialist world-view did not always lead to positive social action. He did not elaborate on this point.

Klohr defended himself against his critics rather well. He noted that "bourgeois" sociology also dealt with the political correlates of religious conviction, that it too had shown that the same Christian convictions gave different results in different political contexts. I myself took the floor at this point, to say that the interpretation of Marxism as a doctrine of man's mastery of nature and society with the aid of science and technology was not absolutely true to Marx's philosophic intentions. We in America also had a doctrine of the use of science and technology for mastery of the human environment. Perhaps its most conspicuous current proponent was our secretary of defense, Mr. McNamara, himself a former professor of economics. (Many at the conference, if not our German colleagues, appreciated the point.) I also said that those who had the most radical and revolutionary ideas about society in the West were often theologians. "Theologians, perhaps, but the churches not. Socialism is always the doctrine of the working class," objected Klohr. "In America," I responded, "socialism is more likely to be found in seminaries of Protestant theology or in the universities generally than in trade unions."

The argument about the fate of religion in Eastern Europe quickly touched upon a critical theme: the persistence of an alienated human condition under socialism. Alienation, in the early writings of Marx, was the stunted and unfulfilled human condition which resulted from the subjugation of men to powers outside themselves. These powers were in fact the products of their own labor, but in the class society men could not enjoy the fruits of their labor. Rather, they were ruled over by them in the form of the laws of the market, and the coercive might of the state. In the sphere of consciousness, men were hauted by the phantasmagoria of their own minds: they made an eschatology of their unrealized yearning for fulfillment, and the idea of God expressed at once their desperate hope in the beneficence of a world become strange and their awful submission to it. Religion was therefore also a product of alienation.

The participants were aware that the term alienation has come in the West to cover practically every spiritual disease known to man. They were also fully conversant with the early Marxist texts, and they knew that until very recently, discussion of these as anything but youthful aberrations had been officially discouraged in Eastern Europe. The elimination of market relationships, or so the official doctrine went, rendered all talk of alienation gratuitous. This attitude, along with much else, has changed. Dr. Kadlecova declared directly that the future ought not to be confused with the present—alienation had not yet been eliminated from socialist society. Varga remarked that other forms of alienation besides the "fetishism of commodities," perhaps political ones, could also account for the persistence of religion. "There are also in socialist society phenomena of alienated consciousness capable of evoking the so-called substitute religions." He mentioned the mythologizing of technique as a religious substitute—which provoked an immediate protest from Klohr, who found the notion of substitute religion extremely dubious. Klohr went on to say that the class roots of religion had been eliminated in socialist society, and to deny that there was any religious continuity between capitalist and socialist society. Finally, an Austrian Marxist, Walter Hollitscher, objected that the present and future difficulties of life under socialism need not engender a recourse to religion.

In the end, historical developments may prove Hollitscher right. For the moment, he received little support from those at Prague who reported on psychological researches into religion in Eastern Europe. A Czech scholar said that despite

171

the general decline in religious belief and feeling, sentiments of passive dependence and of homelessness in the universe persisted. His studies have shown that among students, those who sought a harmony unobtainable in their daily lives turned to religion. Another participant from Czechoslovakia, but this time a Russian lady who worked at the Slovak Academy of Sciences in Bratislava, noted that religion could be derived from hope as well as from anxiety. Ugrinovtisch concluded this part of the discussion by observing that there was no specifically religious psychology, only a general human one.

The entire discussion was moved onto another plane by a second Soviet participant, Dr. Levada of the Academy of Sciences. Levada began by noting that Marx and Lenin had treated the economic roots of religion as fundamental, but not as the only ones. Religion was not simply a matter of social classes, and socialism was not just a global negation of the previous class system. Socialist society was undergoing a process of secularization which had to be compared to the same process in capitalist society. An entire culture was being secularized, certain values had become desacralized. Meanwhile, those affected by religious influences in the secularized culture were not always aware of the fact. Perhaps this was because the distinction between religious and non-religious rituals was not always clear. Sometimes, non-religious rituals had the same social function as the religious ones they replaced, even if the values attached to them were different. Levada found the entire discussion of alienation too general and abstract: we required studies of new forms of consciousness in socialist society before we could say whether these were religious or not. He himself did not think of the mythologizing of technique mentioned by Varga as religious, but simply as an illusory solution to social and psychological problems.

If I understood Levada correctly, he took the view that the antithesis of socialist society and capitalist society was too ahistoric to be of very much use. Rather, he proposed that the antithesis should be translated into specific terms for each social type before we generalized further about it. And he did insist on the common element in the religious situation across ideological frontiers.

Levada's contribution did not quite evoke the discussion it merited, possibly because it moved in historical and spiritual dimensions otherwise touched at the conference only by his immediate colleague, Ugrinovtisch, and by Varga. I was genuinely surprised, however, that an excellent historical contribution by a Hungarian, Jozef Lukacs, produced almost no discussion at all. Lukacs presented a panoramic view of the difference between oriental and occidental religion, the one fatalistic and resigned, the other activistic and world-changing. "It would be an error, of the sort that occurs not only in propagandistic activity but also in scholarly work, to ignore this active element in Christianity and to exaggerate the quietistic-contemplative element which is always present in religion, and it would be particularly an error to do so for the Western forms of Christianity." Lukacs did not directly raise the possibility that Marxism might be thought of as descended, spiritually, from the more activistic elements in the Judaeo-Christian tradition. The suggestion, however, was not very far from the surface of his paper. Indeed, many of the most interesting things about the Prague conference were not quite on the surface—but they were not very far below it either.

What was said at the conference was important enough, and I have tried to give a sense of it. There were no visible constraints on our colleagues, and the discussion was quite free. The things which were not quite said bespoke an underlying movement of thought which has not yet been completed: a search for new general ideas, their outlines barely discernible but their substance still obscure. The constraints under which the participants labored, in other words, were inner ones: the difficulty of altering a set of assumptions, a fixed structure of thought. The contradictions, differences, and disputes at Prague, the schematism of some and the tentativeness of others, point to a new spiritual future in Eastern Europe. In trying to explain how, let me take four major areas of discussion.

The continuity of European culture, across all political boundaries, was very much emphasized at Prague. Our Czech chairwoman said quite explicitly that we lived in a common culture, and the Soviet participants touched upon similar themes. The participants were familiar with religious tradition, and their familiarity was not the familiarity associated with contempt or the deep hostility born of fear. It would be vulgar (and, above all, wrong) to suppose that the dispute with China has suddenly brought Eastern Europe to the realization of its common heritage with Western Europe. Rather, the historical force of that heritage itself, the population's stubborn attachment to it, the equally strong attachment of the intellectuals, have made another view of religion inevitable—following the removal of these questions from control by the police. A sense of the concrete, of national particularity, of the value of tradition: these are now emphasized by the Communist regimes as part of a new political strategy. (I would also say that these are values congenial to new Communist leaders well aware of the perversion of "internationalism" under Stalinism.)

The Jewish participants no less than the others seemed to share in this temper—although Jewishness, Judaism, and Jewish communal life in Eastern Europe were not discussed at the Prague conference. I have the impression, from other experiences in Eastern Europe, that a number of Jewish intellectuals in the Communist movement now identify themselves with things Jewish. It will be recalled that Professor Adam Schaff, member of the Central Committee of the Polish party, recently published a book which among other matters dealt with the problem of the continuation of anti-Semitism in Poland.* At any rate, the situation of Judaism and the Jews in Eastern Europe is perhaps best understood in the light of newer developments in these countries.

The rather more explicit discussion of alienation under socialism entailed more delicate questions. If fifty years of socialism in the Soviet Union, and twenty years elsewhere, had not brought appreciable progress toward the end of alienation, then clearly second thoughts were in order. The possibility was broached at Prague that there may be forms of alienation peculiar to socialist society, but this possibility was not thoroughly explored. The participants tended to insist on the general human problems which socialism had not yet eliminated (and which it might not eliminate in the foreseeable future), rather than on oppressive elements in Eastern European socialism. They did, however, prepare for a thorough critique of the quality of life in socialist society —by showing that the persistence of religion, in some cases at least, had real roots in human distress.

The discussion of alienation was rather general, but the exploration of the question of secular derivatives of religion was somewhat more specific. The participants from the Soviet Union were quite prominent in this discussion: they came, after all, from a country which has a religious tradition rich in ritual and litany. I was glad to see that the Eastern European states were depicted as resting on psychological forces somewhat more subliminal than the insight of their citizens into the high degree of political perfection they had attained. The participants did *not* say that there were civic or state religions prevailing in Eastern Europe (religions which used the Marxist rhetoric without having much connection with

* See pages 351–359 below.

Marxism in its original form). I myself find the notion of Marxism as a substitute religion very debatable: Marx intended to end a transcendental form of human thought in favor of a humanism immanent in the world. I do think that the Communist sociologists of religion are beginning to approach the terrain on which this debate has been conducted elsewhere. They will have to cross it before they can find convincing answers.

Finally, I was struck by the repeated references at the conference to secularization as a universal process in Western culture. Some of the participants shared that nostalgia for the religious past of mankind which is so curious a part of the current discussion of the death of God, among the religious and non-religious alike. I wonder whether this aspect of the exchanges at Prague may refer, if obliquely, to Marxism as much as to Christianity. In the Constantine epoch, Christianity became a fixed part of the social order—and lost its prophetic qualities as a result. In due course, the social order itself began to dispense with Christianity. What of a Constantine epoch in Marxism? Having become a state doctrine, it has legitimated a system which seems no less problematical than those it has replaced—and in which the universal reign of justice and fraternity, reason and human sovereignty, seems remote. These are familiar enough ideas outside Eastern Europe, and familiar enough experiences inside it. The persistence of religion must strike many Marxists as not unlike the persistence of Marxism: a stubborn perseverance of a belief in a better world, despite the experience of a worse one.

This places the discussion of alienation at Prague in a somewhat different light. Talking about unfulfilled human needs under socialism, some of the participants may have been attempting to say that religion was but one historical solution to the absence of human fulfillment. Marxism may offer another—but not in its present, its own Constantine form. A rediscovery of other elements and possibilities in Marxism, perhaps related to the chiliastic tendencies in Christianity noted by one of the speakers, might offer an alternative to that official Marxism which has become a state doctrine. From a consideration of the fate of religion under state socialism, the Marxist sociologists at Prague were edged by the nature of the theme itself toward critical reflection on the fate of Marxism under their regimes. The process of reflection has begun, and although it is as yet tentative and usually covert, its continuation and enlargement is a certainty for the future.

III. THE SOCIOLOGY
OF SOCIOLOGY

Science, Ideology, and Dialogue: The Amsterdam Sociological Congress

The World Congress of Sociology, which met late in August of this year (1956) in Amsterdam, if it did nothing else, may have shocked some of the participating sociologists into practicing their discipline on themselves. The Congress began as a venture in science. It developed into a conflict of ideology. The presence of forty representatives from the Communist countries made possible an informal encounter between East and West which absorbed and fascinated the sociologists. By contrast, the formal scholarly discussions on the program seemed somewhat tedious and remote—except when illuminated by flashes of political conflict, occasionally conflict within the West itself. All this implied the question of what sociology was: a science objective and neutral or one affected by social conflict.

The Congress provided the setting for more than an encounter: its theme, "Social Change in the 20th Century," and the claims of sociology to depict society entire, allowed a dialogue between Communist social thinkers and their Western colleagues to open. The conversation started in a faltering and partial way, and the Soviet Russians, as distinct from some of their satellites, had no part in it. A generation of Stalinism had done its work: the Russians at Amsterdam could only be described, in one observer's words, as Neanderthalers. But the Czechs, East Germans, and Poles were quite capable of talking to the rest of us, and were obviously delighted at the opportunity to do so. They belonged, culturally, to the West—as did indeed the old Russian intelligentsia and the Bolsheviks before Stalinism.

Why did we fail to establish contact with the Russians? Sociology as such is proscribed in the Soviet Union. The mixed bunch of official philosophers, philosopher-officials, economists, and publicists who came to the Congress had no acquaintance with the discipline. But they would have been equally lost in their own fields. Social science can develop on a Marxist basis and Marxists have done and are doing useful work in a number of countries, if generally not under Marxist dictatorships. The Russians have no social science, Marxist or otherwise. They have, instead, an ideology which they reiterate upon every occasion.

The encounter with the Russians mostly took the form of collision. But the Czechs, East Germans, and Poles sought out the Westerners and ignored, almost ostentatiously, the Russians. And the whole process was both complicated and facilitated by the fact that some of the Western sociologists present, most notably a number of French and Italians, were themselves Communists, fellow-travelers, or left socialists. Also, a strong Yugoslav delegation was present, and the Yugoslavs are exceedingly experienced in dialogues of all kinds with all camps. The lines were fluid, so fluid at times that many of the participants had to acknowledge, in one way or another, contradictions within their own camps and often found themselves more in agreement with their nominal opponents than with their allies.

Whether polemic or sympathetic exchange, all this dialogue was highly stimulating. But it also carried a lesson. The Amsterdam meetings showed, in a way that the more abstract discussions of the Congress for Cultural Freedom cannot, what the consequences are of political limitations on social inquiry. It dramatized the intellectual utility of freedom.

But the meetings may also have shown that Western sociologists do not invariably make the best use of their freedom. They were divided, at Amsterdam as elsewhere, by a number of conflicts over approach and value. Such conflicts are not necessarily bad; social science, in fact, may thrive on them. But they ought to be faced and explored, and many of the Westerners at Amsterdam seemed unready to do so. We heard the usual arguments, of course, about the scope and methods of sociology. (Henri Poincaré, the mathematician and philosopher of science, once remarked that sociologists were always writing treatises on methods they were scrupulously careful never to apply.) But the disputants, by and large, ignored a fact under their very eyes: the fact that a good many of the Westerners at Amsterdam were, *as sociologists*, relatively uninterested in the dialogue with the East and in the central political experience of our time. As citizens, of course, they were glad to listen. But as social scientists, they remained curiously uninvolved.

Those in the West who took the initiative in the conversations with the East were, philosophically, highly assorted. There were Catholics, existentialists, liberals; and in great numbers, Marxists, neo-Marxists, ex-Marxists. Politically, the divergences were fewer: the "democratic left" of a number of countries was much in evidence. And all those eager for conversation with the East seemed to share the view that sociology's scientific work begins, as paradoxical as it sounds, only in historical urgency and political commitment. Before you can describe history objectively, they held, you had to live in it. Many of their colleagues took the opposite view: that sociology was a science like any other, and that their own involvement in its subject matter was of small account. Perhaps my own sympathies mislead me, but I have the impression that the pallid papers at Amsterdam came from this latter group. Faced with the theme "Social Change in the 20th Century," they dropped an iron curtain of their own across their desks, and separated their political concerns from their scientific interests.

Even the locale of the Congress had political implications for those who looked about them. Not only is Amsterdam a charming city: its history reminds us of the historical effectiveness of bourgeois democracy. The Netherlands today is a free society which has obtained a welfare state while learning to live amid considerable political and social tension. During the Congress, in fact, the country was undergoing a cabinet crisis. The building in which the Congress met had its own historical associations; now called the Royal Institute for the Tropics, it was still known to streetcar conductors and hotel porters as the "Colonial Institute."

The formal organization of the Congress was not entirely conducive to conversation, whether between East and West or anyone else. There were too many plenary sessions: a conversation among six hundred scholars is—perhaps luckily —impossible. And the smaller working groups into which the plenary sessions dissolved were often preempted by professors suffering from a common occupational ailment: an over estimation of the importance of their own words. But Dutch hospitality was immense and there was a large number of receptions. And the sidewalk cafés and Oriental restaurants in which Amsterdam abounds provided other opportunities for talk.

And it was talk that interested most of the delegates. Unlike scholarly gatherings in the United States, European and international meetings are not academic track meets with

184

jobs and research grants as the prizes. The hunt for prestige, of course, is not absent from international congresses, and scholars outside the United States are no less eager than their American colleagues for its tangible benefits. But academic entrepreneurship abroad is more subtly done, more disguised, while the younger men have little to occupy them beside their immediate tasks, since jobs and grants are so few anyhow.

Talk, however, requires language. French and English were the official Congress languages, but German was more useful in dealing with most of the East Europeans. The worst linguists at the Congress were not the Americans, British, or French (most of whom seemed to assume that God had spoken to Adam in their own tongue) but the Russians. The old Russian intelligentsia was at home in French and German; their Stalinist successors overworked their interpreters.

Conversation began over the formal papers. These were uneven in quality and the arrangements for discussion were cumbersome, but they were the first things the delegates had to talk about. The papers covered an astonishing variety of topics. Opening my program at random, I found "Changes in Family Structure in the Baltic Islands," "The Working Class in the British Social Structure," "Some Problems of Rural Collective Settlements in Indonesia." Economic organization, the distribution of property, class structure, family systems, education, agricultural tenure—these were the main themes on the program. Politics as such was surprisingly absent, despite the recent revival of interest in political sociology. But as we shall see, it intruded itself quickly enough.

It was in the formal sessions that the delegates first encountered the Communists. The Russian contributions precluded real conversation. Propagandistic tracts, they were written in a tone defiant of contradiction or even question. We were told of the Soviet Union's democratic electoral law, of wide popular participation in political decision, of the equality of individuals before Soviet law—claims not requiring comment. The Soviet speakers referred rarely to problems in their own society, and then usually as "survivals" of the bourgeois era. They hardly cited statistics, and their discussions were so diffuse that they scarcely touched on those spheres in which many were less skeptical of Soviet claims of progress, like education and medicine.

But the Soviet delegation did have some notion of the kind of questions that would really interest their Western colleagues: those dealing with a class system in the "classless" society. This is the kind of thing they prepared: "The equality of citizens, firmly established in the norms of socialist law, does not however mean equalization either of the amount of payment for work or in the fields of needs and everyday capacities, as sometimes ill-informed people imagine. Equality under socialism means equal relation of everyone to the means of production and equal duty on the part of everyone to work according to his or her abilities, and an equal right of all the working people to receive compensation in accordance with their labor. Such a proposition does not exclude any property differences among the citizens of the socialist state or considerable differences in the organization of everyday life and the character of the requirements that are to be met. These property differences result, however, not from the fact that the sources of the citizens' incomes are different, but exclusively and wholly from the fact that the compensation paid is fixed according to quantity and quality of work performed. It is individual work that is the source of income in every case."

It is, of course, nonsense to suppose that a member of the Soviet cabinet, making a decision about the economy, and an ordinary worker—bound to do as told—enjoy "equal relations to the means of production." And if commissar and peasant both live by their work, and not off inherited capital, what may we say of the different advantages they can bestow upon their children? The statement quoted admits the existence of class differences in income and culture in all but name. But it ignores their implications. Yet the paper in which it was contained was about the most honest of all the Soviet contributions, formal and informal, at Amsterdam. The Soviet delegates could not allow themselves to see their society as it was—or at any rate they could not talk about their real perceptions. They did not even have any very advanced techniques for gaining information about their society: their statistics were minimal and fragmentary and they seemed to have done little empirical research.

Soviet ideological fervor provoked some unfortunate reactions from the West. One American professor announced that his researches demonstrated that successful businessmen in America were self-made men, that the American myth of success was substantially correct. This did not attract quite the attention it deserved in view of the fact that everybody else's researches showed quite the opposite. Another American declared that we no longer had a working class, only a "labor force." This attempt to match Soviet skill in altering facts by renaming them was resisted by no less a figure than Talcott Parsons of Harvard.

The satellite delegates were much less bound by ideological straitjackets than the Russians. The Poles' entire appearance foreshadowed, on an intellectual plane, the political explosion in Warsaw in October. They issued reports on research into the structure of their society; they brought along non-Marxist professors, who quarreled publicly and privately with their colleagues; they invited Western sociologists to teach and do research in Poland. The Czechs, who were not sociologists, collected bibliographies and books on recent inquiries into Western society. Their questions showed them to be well informed and critical. Even the then Hungarian Minister of Justice, Molnar, who was largely circumspect and silent (and, as if he anticipated the imminent revolution, depressed), said that he had come to renew contacts with "bourgeois science." The East Germans insisted on their pleasure at being in Amsterdam. One of them said that, until recently, Karl Mannheim's books had been *verboten* in his university. Mannheim was, of course, the most brilliant of Weimar Germany's neo-Marxist sociologists. Any Marxist regime but a Stalinist one might have encouraged the study of his work.

The informal contacts at the Congress were, therefore, most illuminating for the Westerners, and possibly for the Communists as well. The Russians were very sociable, an improvement on their reported behavior at congresses even two years ago, but it was difficult to exchange more than pleasantries with them. One of them expressed sheer bewilderment at the frequent references to the "middle classes" in Western papers. "Why aren't the categories 'bourgeoisie' and 'proletariat' good enough?" he asked. "Where do the 'middle classes' come in?" Others answered questions, not hostile or pointed but sheerly factual ones about Soviet society, in highly general, almost formula-like terms. They seemed on the defensive and ill at ease. The French sociologists, however, were reasonably satisfied after a private meeting with the Russians. But I gather that the French did most of the talking.

The Poles, on the other hand, were remarkably frank. Even the Marxists among them (and two of the professors present were members of the Central Committee of the United Workers party, the Polish version of the Communist party) seemed to prefer associating with the Westerners rather than the Russians. And the non-Marxists made no secret of their differences with their colleagues: at a private meeting with an American-British group the Poles argued violently among themselves on the methodology of the social sciences. One of the Polish Communists, and not the least of them, when asked to explain the difference between the behavior of his delegation and the immobility of the Russians, exclaimed: "It's simple. They've had thirty years of it and we only ten."

The Poles were anxious to import Western sociological research techniques—the Marxists simply because of their value as techniques, and the non-Marxists because they see them as an opening for a more critical general sociology. One Marxist professor, who deplored "anecdotal empirical sociology," hoped to combine the measurement of social phenomena with a "reformulated and completed" Marxist theory. The Poles planned to send students to America and Britain (a number are already in France) and they began arranging for academic visits to Poland by Western professors. It would be unfortunate if the only Western visitors they got were social research technicians. However skilled the technicians, they are unlikely to infuse Polish students and professors with a new vision of society to replace the Marxist one.

The Poles were the most active and interesting of the satellites at Amsterdam precisely because they were so free of satellite intellectual characteristics. The Czechs and East Germans were as reasonable and receptive as the Poles in private, but they read no public papers. (One Polish paper, by Professor Ossowski, was the initial sensation of the Congress. Its author, a non-Marxist, analyzed the class structure of the present Communist societies in unadorned terms.) The Bulgarians and Rumanians went around talking about peace and international cooperation. The vice president of the Hungarian Academy of Sciences, who accompanied the Minister of Justice, was sufficiently unimpressed by the official company he kept to explain that he was not personally a Marxist.

Of all the Communist delegations, the Yugoslavs were the freest. Unlike many of the Russians, all the Yugoslavs were genuine scholars, at home in sociology even if primarily economists or lawyers. They were Marxists, but they put observed facts into the Marxist vocabulary rather than insisting on the vocabulary and ignoring the facts. And they seemed more varied, more distinctive as personalities than the Russians—although perhaps this impression is the result of a political judgment. They distinguished themselves in the two special sessions on Marxism and the interpretation of social change in the 20th century, sessions that were, in many respects, the highlights of the Congress.

These sessions developed because a group of younger French and Italian sociologists wanted to discuss Marxism with their colleagues in general, and with the East Europeans in particular. Their motives were political as well as intellectual. One of the Italians was a Communist (although he publicly told a Russian that in his opinion Stalinism was the work of a social stratum and not of one man), and others were Nenni Socialists. The French intelligentsia, and not least the social scientists, are fascinated with Marxism; this reflects their ambivalence toward the French Communist party. It also reflects the persistence of an indigenously French socialist tradition on which Marx himself drew. (Many French intellectuals can simultaneously debate supporting the Communists and speculate as to how many days they personally could survive a Communist seizure of power.)

This group was joined by another, which held that Marxism was a set of hypotheses like any other, even if a remarkably useful one; therefore, if the meeting were not to degenerate into scholasticism, it ought to provide opportunities for a critique of Marxism. This initial divergence of purpose led to some misunderstanding, but it also opened the way for a more stimulating and penetrating discussion than would have been possible had either group monopolized these sessions.

The first meeting, lasting four hours in the most smoke-filled of rooms, was egalitarian, even comradely. Some twenty-five speakers took the floor, unannounced and largely unprepared, for five minutes each. There was confusion and repetition at first, though enlivened by pronounced national differences in rhetoric and style. The French made even the most banal of observations sound like something from Pascal. The Americans clothed logic in casualness. The Southern Europeans were uniformly intense. The Germans, although well represented, were surprisingly silent. Most of the speakers were Westerners, although three Yugoslavs made a great impression. By midnight the discussion had begun to converge on a number of points. At the beginning it was a series of monologues. Later, however, the participants began to talk to each other. What did they say?

Marx had predicted that society would split into two completely antagonistic classes, that an impoverished and humiliated working class would unite to overthrow the exploiting class. But industrial society had developed a new middle class not identical with the exploiting one. The working class was itself internally differentiated and, in the advanced industrial countries, demonstrably richer. Extreme economic differences between the working and middle classes were now gone in these countries. In some, the workers had either become "bourgeois" or accepted bourgeois leadership. The revolution, in other words, had either failed to occur, or had taken forms not foreseen by Marx.

Marx had, further, viewed political power as a simple function of economic power. The state, he claimed, was an executive committee for the bourgeoisie. Yet in our time the state had frequently altered the balance of economic power between the classes to the workers' advantage. And in Soviet Russia, the state itself had become a massive exploiting agency. Also, Marx had written of "alienation," of men's estrangement from the vital and healthy potentialities of their own nature. Alienation, Marx implied, would supply the psychological dynamic for the revolutionary overthrow of capitalist society. But alienation has, in our time, produced horrible political movements and not that brotherly commonwealth envisaged by the early socialists and—despite his professed scientific amorality—Marx himself. Finally, both Asiatic and Western speakers asserted that the problem of exploitation had shifted largely to the colonial sphere, where new forms of imperialism required new ways of analysis.

These things were said in a Marxist temper, in the conviction that much in the Marxist method was still viable, and that even Marx's mistakes had been fruitful. Even an anti-Marxist could agree with this last. But some critical voices were raised to ask why, if Marx had made so many concrete mistakes, it was still necessary to take him as anything but a historic figure. No clear answer was really attempted. There was, to be sure, some discussion as to whether Marxism as a method of sociological analysis necessarily entailed acceptance of dialectical materialism as a philosophy. There was also much talk about removing the mythological elements from Marxism. But unfortunately, no one could say why some intellectuals should have made a myth of what was something else in Marx's hands.

All of this was on a fairly general plane—until more immediate problems made an insistent appearance. A Pole spoke of revising Marxist—by which he meant Stalinist—analyses of contemporary society. All that he could propose was that we should now attribute Nazism to the "petty bourgeoisie" rather than to the "monopoly capitalists." He added that the Polish Communists were now willing to accept the "honorable capitulation" of the Polish "kulaks," and sat down. (The more "flexible" of the Polish Marxists had avoided these sessions, intimating that they did not want to come into direct conflict with the Russians. But the speaker showed that not all Poles were flexible.) The Yugoslavs caused a stir by insisting that even nominally socialistic states could behave imperialistically toward other socialist states, and they argued that it was the task of Marxists to prevent the development of new forms of domination imposed in the name of socialism. Their references were clear—yet the Russian speaker referred later to the "valuable" comments of the Yugoslavs.

An American, Professor S. M. Lipset, described Stalinism as simply a mode of enforced industrialization. Lipset recalled the controversy over industrialization in the Soviet Union in the 1920's and he cited the views of both Bukharin and Trotsky, important participants in that controversy. The Russian speaker later declared that his delegation "did not find it necessary" to enter into discussion with anyone who quoted Bukharin and Trotsky.

Perhaps the Russian—he was editor of the Soviet trade union newspaper *Trud*—really believed that these two old Bolsheviks had been imperialist agents. His reaction was, in any case, a striking reminder of the survival of many of the most repugnant features of Stalinism. He drew a laugh from the audience, involuntarily, by assuring them that he was pleased to see knowledge of Marxism growing outside the Communist countries! He made a gesture, at least, towards real conversation with the West by declaring that there was much "merit" in a question by Professor Georges Friedmann, the distinguished French scholar who was elected President of the International Sociological Association. Friedmann had declared that workers in Russia did subordinate and laborious work, like workers everywhere; did this not affect their attitudes even in a "socialist" society? The Russian speaker, despite his cordiality, did not answer the question.

The delegates left the session exhausted but satisfied. The Yugoslavs were nearly everybody's heroes. They seemed to be those Marxists without myth demanded by the speakers. And they talked the language of democratic and utopian socialism. Nobody mentioned Djilas and Dedijer, who had been persecuted for trying to persuade the Yugoslav Communist party to pursue those goals. In general, that evening, people spoke softly.

A second meeting provided much more open conflict. There were four speakers: Professor Raymond Aron of Paris, S. M. Lipset, the Hungarian Justice Minister, Molnar, and a Yugoslav law professor, Rudolph Legradic. Lipset made a reference to the view that industrial development might have taken place in Russia even if the Czarist regime had continued. This infuriated the Russian spokesman, who had returned for more, and he ignored Lipset's real points. One of them, on the Stalinist bureaucracy, was made later by an Italian Communist and found at least nominal acceptance by the Russian. The Yugoslav had, indeed, opened the evening with a discourse on the dangers of bureaucracy and an astonishingly utopian demand for the elimination of the state.

Aron began by remarking that a dialogue between East and West was desirable, and that it might be easier if the East were to stop jailing and executing opponents. He declared that Western Europe and America were now welfare societies and had surpassed Soviet Russia in providing for their members—at infinitely less human and moral cost. The Russian, in his reply, rightly recalled his country's late start and wartime losses. The rest of Aron's points escaped him.

Molnar's manner was singular. His very brief statement fell into two distinct parts. He began by saying that a superficial look at Communist countries might lead us to suppose that they were characterized by unequal control of the means of production, by a dictatorship not of but over the proletariat. That would be a mistake, he declared, and in the second half of his talk he told us that behind this deceptive and depressing mask lay the true and just face of social revolution. Some people had the impression that he himself nevertheless inclined privately towards the first view. Or perhaps he was simply looking at things dialectically: he did tell Aron to read Hegel.

Thus the second session on Marxism left the sphere of abstractions and dealt in hard and disputed realities. It was not alone ideas that were argued about, but the actual structure of human society. And the arguments were political, about the uses to which power was being put. This underscored the remoteness of a good deal of the Congress program. In the last analysis, knowledge about society—or the refusal of such knowledge—is something we need in order to attain political aims. And, quite apart from our aims, politics is frequently a decisive category of change in social structure.

What began, then, as detached intellectual analysis became a political controversy. And the sociologists, despite their theoretical structures and research techniques, found themselves arguing in the same terms as everybody else, even if they had an acuter sense of the social limitations on political decision. It is now, perhaps, a bit clearer why many Western sociologists retain an interest in Marxism despite Marx's mistakes. For Marxism treats society in terms historical in conception and political in application. And it was a political contact with history that they were seeking, a search which led them into the dialogue with the East.

The Amsterdam Congress, then, gave rise to a number of reflections—many of them bearing on the political relevance of social science both in the West and in the Communist countries. Our conversations with our Communist colleagues have now been overshadowed by the dramatic and moving events in Poland and Hungary (and by the time this appears, perhaps elsewhere as well). We thought we were glimpsing a world in motion. Actually, it was a world about to explode. The mixed despair and hope with which our colleagues talked showed us that to them, de-Stalinization was a matter of spiritual life and death. The reactions of an official like Molnar, or of the restive delegates from countries not openly defiant of Stalinism (the Czechs and East Germans), were as instructive—in their own way—as the outspokenness of a man like Professor Hochfeld of Warsaw, who came to Amsterdam in the midst of his parliamentary struggle for socialist democracy.

Our experience at Amsterdam, and the things it foreshadowed, confirmed David Riesman's criticism of the Orwellian exaggeration of the omnipotence of totalitarian rule. Through the blackest period of Stalinism many East European intellectuals, whether Marxist or not, persisted in thinking. The difference between the satellite intellectuals and the Russians, however, was disheartening. It is sobering to recall the Pole's remark on the effects of thirty, as opposed to ten, years of Stalinism.

The immediate evidence available to us at Amsterdam, of course, concerned the fate of social inquiry in the intermediate phase of de-Stalinization. Looking back, we can now see how the forces mobilized about this issue reflected underlying political conflicts. Social inquiry as such was rejected by Stalinism: had not Marx, Engels, Lenin, and Stalin discovered, once and for all, the laws governing social events? As Stalinist controls loosened, the Communist policy-makers were either confused or at odds on allowing the resumption of social inquiry. Some may have thought that non-Marxist or critical Marxist sociologists could be allowed their say, in the expectation that they would gradually die out. But those we met at Amsterdam were busy reproducing themselves, intellectually, by writing and teaching. Then again, social inquiry may prove an indispensable instrument of government. Public opinion surveys and studies of industrial relations, never undertaken by the Stalinists, may be precisely what a Gomulka needs.

A general turn from dogmatic rigidity in social and economic policy in some of the Soviet bloc countries, then, seems to be leading to a renewal of empirical inquiry. But empirical inquiry itself may encourage some Communists to look anew at their assumptions. A good deal of modern Western sociology originated in the effort to grasp the limits of Marxism. A similar large-scale effort in Eastern Europe is still in the future. But at Amsterdam we witnessed stirrings in this direction, and recent political events (themselves partly the result of intellectual dissent) may open new perspectives. The anxieties of the Stalinist die-hards are easy enough to understand. Once permitted in a limited way, inquiry of this sort can break all bounds.

For the present, we can expect a pronounced increase in concrete research programs in Eastern Europe. The Poles began before Gomulka's return, the Czechs and East Germans are in contact with the Poles, and the Yugoslav experience fits this pattern. (One Yugoslav at Amsterdam asked to meet some Western industrial sociologists. I told him that many of us in the West thought that some of our industrial research was ideologically biased. His answer was: "I know ideology when I see it: it's the techniques and the facts I want.") The Easterners are turning to the West for scientific assistance and collaboration. What attitude ought Western social scientists, and intellectuals generally, adopt to these requests?

It is practically our duty, I think, to accede to them. Technical issues are hard to distinguish from substantive ones. We ought to be clear that such collaboration is a political act. But unless, in the face of all recent evidence, we cling to a demonological image of the Communist regimes, we can proceed with a good conscience. Communist opinion in East Europe is far from monolithic. The recent struggles in these countries began when the Communist intellectuals seized upon the Khrushchev speech to open an attack on totalitarianism on many fronts. Many of the people we help will have taken considerable risks. Many others, in countries that have yet to go as far, are prepared to do so. Scholarly collaboration is, at once, the repayment of a debt of honor to those who have won their first battles and a gesture of encouragement to those who may tomorrow find themselves in desperate struggle.

The most important thing we can do is simple enough. It is to keep talking, to keep open our lines of intellectual communication with the East. And conversation may affect those who listen to it as well as those who participate in it. It was noticeable at Amsterdam that the Western Communists seemed to feel themselves closer to their Western colleagues than to their Soviet comrades—especially after the Soviet speeches.

It would be futile, of course, to expect very much in the way of conversation from Stalin's professors. The "thaw" in Russia has yet to melt any number of icebergs in the social sciences. But conversation with Stalin's professors may be the price for the chance to talk to their students, who have noticed their teachers' discomfiture. (The old Bolshevik intellectuals who came to the Congress from Moscow were a good deal more accessible than their middle-aged colleagues, and the rising generation ought to be more accessible still.) And if a certain amount of tact is the price for talking with the Russians at all, then it may be well to consider paying it. "Tactlessness," of course, may also bring gains and it may be a gain to upset a Soviet ideologue—not least to the ideologue himself.

Totalitarian societies repress their own social conflicts, or their leaders may invent pseudo-conflicts to avoid the real ones. In any case, no social science is possible. In free societies, the fact that conflicts are not forcibly repressed allows them to be expressed in social science itself. But the Western social scientist, in these conditions, may find it difficult to see things as they really are. He may mistake an issue involving the fundamental nature and freedom of social science for a professional difference over methods and approach. Both Eastern and Western sociologists agreed at Amsterdam that there were objective laws governing social life. The Communists claim to have discovered them in Marxism. This claim, in Stalinist hands, became an ideological justification for exploitation and tyranny. The resistance of the Stalinists to empirical inquiry (a resistance which would have been repugnant to Marx himself) is of course due to their fear of disproof of their claim. Social inquiry, under Stalinism, was really something subversive.

But what about Western claims? Many Westerners at Amsterdam were themselves not free of ideology. It took the form of supposing that the laws governing social life lie very near the surface, just awaiting discovery. One more inquiry (and one more grant) and there they'd be—lacking only suitably simplified packaging for freshman courses. Part of this is simply a professional attitude: sociologists need to convince themselves, and university administrators, that they really are entirely distinct from economists, historians, political scientists, and, above philosophers. But something else was at work.

The notion that we can begin our search for the laws of social life just anywhere rejects a good many lessons, of which the Amsterdam Congress was only the latest. A sociology that proceeds from one randomly chosen inquiry to another may be fleeing social conflict. Our task is to see our society as a whole. Inquiries subversive in the East may in the West be simply evasive. Amsterdam, then, may have reminded some of the Westerners of the problem of significance in their work. It may have turned them away from excessive preoccupation with the model of the physical sciences. A nominally free social science that is unaware of its roots in conflict may remain chained. The very measure of the strength of social science may lie in the way it diagnoses specific social conflicts which are the essence of the society in which it functions. Our frank admission of uncertainty may be our strongest weapon in the attempt to enlarge the dialogue with those minds in the East now struggling for their freedom.

Postscript. The tragic and brutal destruction of the Hungarian revolution by the Red Army demands a melancholy postscript. Professors and students alike were conspicuous in the local revolutionary committees. Organized student groups fought alongside the army and the workers' militia in the streets and, according to the last depairing broadcasts from Hungary, fought to the end. Public criticism of Stalinism in Rakosi's Hungary began, we may recall, with pronouncements by the Budapest intellectuals. And the Academy of Sciences used Hungary's few brief days of freedom to appeal to scholarly bodies elsewhere for aid. Molnar, meanwhile, has disappeared: he was a member neither of Nagy's national front government nor of Kadar's pro-Soviet regime.

Friends and Enemies

Discussions of sociology, although usually boring, provide an opportunity too good to be missed by inveterate academic polemicists, by specialists in *Weltanschauungen* (their own *Weltanschauungen*) and by "methodologists" afraid of reality. Sociology is vast and amorphous, disjointed and self-contradictory; anything can be said about it. There is no intellectual foible it does not contain, no *gaucherie* of which some sociologist is incapable, no political ideology which some version of it cannot defend. Sociologists range from educated and cultivated men to leaden-footed philistines; they write about everything from the nature and destiny of man to fallen women. They thus provide any comer with particular excuses for venting general grudges. Sociology is the great intellectual grab-bag of our time: everybody, from the Provost of King's to the Professor of Logic at the London School of Economics, can reach into it, certain to find precisely what he wants. Discussions of it, then, ought to be specific. Personally, I'm more afraid of its friends, particularly its American friends, than its enemies.

I first met its friends upon beginning research at Harvard. A New Yorker, I'd read Marx at an age when most English schoolboys had yet to discover Tennyson. I supposed that sociology was about the struggle for power in societies, their division into social strata, the inter-play of material interests and spiritual values in social change. But my teachers were "building social science" by trivial studies whose very triviality allegedly attested their contribution to some gigantic (future) accumulation of knowledge, by devising systems of categories so top-heavy that they collapsed upon contact with even the surface of social life, and by developing a "methodology"—in effect, the study of nothing in particular, designed to increase our means of understanding everything in general. These were sociology's friends. They insisted that to doubt them was to join its enemies. I was bewildered, the more so since there were men of talent and conviction amongst them. I soon saw that they were obsessed. Like all obsessions, theirs was rationalized by an illusion—that precision and technology exhaustively characterize a science.* The illusion dies hard, but the mistake is not ignoble: a rigorously scientific conception of the world appears to promise intellectual liberation. It becomes pseudo-scientific, however, when it ignores the fatalities of the human sciences.

There are, of course, other voices in American sociology. C. Wright Mills has studied the new middle classes and the power élite. David Riesman has noted changes in the American character. William H. Whyte has shown some of the debilities of large-scale corporate organization. Riesman is a solicitor turned professor of general studies, Whyte a journalist, and only Mills a "professional" sociologist, if one of whom his colleagues are remarkably disapproving. Mills does take risks. He does not produce papers like a recent disquisition on "Status After Death," which showed that, other

---

* I recall an enormous pay-off on a study of "values," which excited much local comment—not least because none of the recipients seemed able to say what precisely "values" were. A Faculty Club wit made some impression on me when he remarked, "Values are what these guys lack." Some years later he went to another university to direct an inquiry—into values. That made an even greater impression on me. In fact, many who in 1948 were most enraged had within five years decided that their fields too, were, "behavioral sciences"—and therewith eligible for large-scale foundation support.

things being equal, rich men had costlier funerals than poor men. Mills's generalizations may be false, but they are not cosmically irrelevant. Then there is a whole group of younger American sociologists (most of them ex-Marxist) who work on similar problems, if with different results.

Recently, Pitirim Sorokin and Mills have each exploded intellectual land-mines under their colleagues' chairs. In Sorokin's *Fads and Foibles in Modern Sociology* (1956) and Mills's *The Sociological Imagination* (1959) they have criticized their colleagues' servile imitation of the (misunderstood) methods of the natural sciences, the pretentious verbiage with which they advance banalities and tautologies, their failure to read anything written before 1950 and not published in a sociological journal, and their want of any historical and moral criteria in the selection of problems. Mills attributes these aberrations to the bureaucratic structure of the American academy, and to the pressures of a society requiring human engineering but resistant to social criticism. These strictures have not been without effect on the educated public as a whole, and those criticized have begun a tacit abandonment of positions they were once committed to defend, down to their last research assistant.

At some point in 1958, *The Times Literary Supplement* appears to have discovered the discussion. In those terms of genteel and tired reproach it reserves for things it does not understand, *The T L S* has constructed an image of sociology derived exclusively from its lugubrious American professors. There is in Britain, however, a far more serious opposition to sociology, far less concerned with sociology's manifest absurdities (which serve it well for propaganda purposes) but with the very real intellectual challenge it poses. If we are to understand this, we had best consider sociology's recent history.

Sociology has, in fact, many traditions. Such unity as it possesses comes chiefly from the difficulty all sociologies share.

Both subject and object of ideological conflict, sociology has a peculiar liability. It usually deals with the core of a society's institutions, the class structure; its depiction of that structure and of the cultural and political conflicts endemic to it is invariably controversial. Sociologists themselves are never outside their societies, and affected as they are by their experience they cannot approach even distant societies with complete detachment. Combined with the intrinsic difficulty of dealing with processes extended through time and society, this means that the sociologist can be objective only within limits. The limits are not fixed, and the border areas between fact and interpretation are unmarked and obscure—an ambiguous balance sheet which has given rise to a large number of philosophic bad cheques.

I am, of course, as aware of the difference between fact and value as any sixth-form reader of *Language, Truth and Logic*. But the facts about the larger aspects of social life are not as clear-cut as those of biology or geology. Smaller, more accessible phenomena are embedded in larger ones. We can employ social survey techniques to ascertain recent shifts in political opinion (if with rather less certainty than Mr. Henry Durant would have us believe). But we cannot use the social survey to analyse those recent changes in the class structure which account for these shifts. Our interest in smaller phenomena, usually, is the light they throw on larger questions. In sociology, then, men shuttle back and forth between the particular and the general. They are men, not machines—influenced by temperament, value, political preference and social milieu. No automatic formula can guarantee the validity of their perceptions, and their inferences and interpretations are subject at a hundred points to error.

Sociology's eighteenth-century origins, indeed, are to be found in the warfare of philosophy with religion. The social thinkers of the Enlightenment held that history, and human activity within it, was not God's immutable work but the result of man's faltering hand. The first great figures of sociology were avowedly philosophical and practical in intention. Comte, Marx, and Spencer sought both to establish an objective science of society and to realize one rather than another set of values. Their legacies, somewhat truncated, still constitute the essential concerns of sociology: despite all differences amongst them, they agreed that sociology had to lay bare the inner structure of the new industrial society and to consider whether men could live in it without God.

Contemporary quantitative research gives effect to Comte's prescription for a positivistic science of society—devoid, however, of the moral certainty he expected to result from social inquiry. Spencer's interest in non-Western society was the beginning of social anthropology and of the comparative study of social institutions generally, although we no longer seek the origins of free enterprise in the devolution of primitive mankind. Marx—after a century of refutations—is the one sociologist who cannot be ignored. His notions on class conflict, on the process of change in society, on the conditions for the emergence of ideology and social awareness, his general and ill-specified view of "alienation" as the human condition in capitalist society, have infused all of sociology.

These thinkers, in the inimitable invective of the currently dominant school in English philosophy, were muddled. They confused fact and value, rearranged data to suit their *a priori* conceptions, and in general showed themselves unworthy of pass degrees in the P P E School at Oxford. The world, however, is perverse. Their muddles were enormously fruitful, and had they lacked the courage of their speculations, they would long since have receded over the intellectual horizon.

Much of modern sociology is the result of the decomposition of the unified systems constructed in the nineteenth century. Sociology since then made two sorts of mistake. Either it attempted synthesis where none was possible, or it stuck to facts when synthesis was required. Not intellectual error alone, but the larger social pressures affecting the field account for the fact that sociologists to-day speak in a babble of tongues. These pressures have often been conveyed through the continuities in a nation's mode of thought, themes derived from its major conflicts of power.

On the Continent, sociology has been largely conservative, engaged in a search for a counter-theory to Marxism. Weber's work was a continuing dialogue with Marxism, and his views on the omnipresence of bureaucracy and the independent role of religion in history were attempted refutations of the Marxist theories of the state and of ideology. Durkheim's interest in the integration of the individual to the group was a reflection of his effort to establish a Republican and secular morality, a counterweight at once to Marxism and the Catholic social theory of the French right. American sociology, by contrast, was mainly reformist. To recall Nietzsche's aphorism about German philosophy, its father was a Protestant pastor. It was the product of the Social Gospel and the movement of middle-class social reform, whose protagonists were horrified by the immigrant slums and determined to ascertain the dimensions of the mess before cleaning it up.

Sociology, then, lives in a plurality of value universes. Despite or because of its habitat, it has been an uncommonly productive discipline amongst the social sciences. Sociologists, under the usual rules of evidence, have accumulated a large amount of data. These concern the social strata and their organization; the modes of recruitment into them; the social élites; the social setting of religion, art, and science; the interaction of institutions in political conflict and in social change generally. The empirical findings of sociology are not controverted by the partisans of any number of differing ideologies. Interpretations, of course, vary.

Where, in all of this, does British sociology stand? Sociology is rather new in the universities, rather ancient in the nation's intellectual life. Millar and Hume did sociological work. The tradition of "political arithmetic" is British; the modern social survey began in eighteenth-century Scotland. The nineteenth-century movement of social reform entailed the careful accumulation of data by the early students of poverty and the working class. These were not subjects thought fit for University education. The young gentlemen of the ruling class, and those being trained to serve them in the Civil Service, were not expected to need knowledge of this sort about their contemporaries. The classical curriculum, with its fantastic image of antiquity, sufficed for apprentice rulers supposed to be sure of their heritage; better that they studied the principles and techniques of rule (with Plato) than the society in which they enjoyed their advantages.

The Fabians took the opposite view. The Webbs initiated and themselves executed an astonishingly comprehensive programme of social investigation. They did so without doing violence to the historical sense: a continuing component of the British sociological tradition—one which distinguishes it from the American one—is its refusal to accept arbitrary distinctions about its subject matter, its insistence on analysing modern society in temporal depth. The Webbs were associated with those enthusiastic and not imperceptive amateur sociologists, Shaw and Wells. At the London School of Economics, which they founded to provide an academic setting for the kinds of inquiry which the British academy had so far refused, they were succeeded by a distinguished group of scholars who worked sociologically, whatever their disciplines: Graham Wallas, Leonard Hobhouse, R. H. Tawney, Harold Laski, Bronislaw Malinowski, Morris Ginsberg, Karl Mannheim. Each of these scholars made a consideration of social structure the centre point of his work; each was interested in the control of social change.

The intellectual descendants of the Webbs are still concentrated at the L S E. The studies of the Welfare State by Titmuss and his associates have already destroyed one carefully propagated myth, that the middle classes somehow lose by it. The investigations directed by David Glass have shown how the nation's élites, by controlling the educational system and the professions, have retained their supremacy inside the social structure altered by the Welfare State. (It is ironical that on the whole, the institution founded by the Webbs has abandoned its reformist past; there are today several company directors on its teaching staff but no members of the National Executive Committee of the Labour Party. The L S E, of course, also houses Professor Popper, whose animadversions on sociology are read with the greatest attention by many British sociologists; they fail to find much evidence that their philosophical colleague is acquainted with the literature of their field.) British sociology, then, seems to retain its early reformist bias. In the younger generation of university teachers, partly as a result of Mannheim's influence, that bias has given way to a more sophisticated and modernized interest in Marxism.

A good deal of sociology is done in this country under another name. Britain's imperial position has stimulated an interest in variations among different types of society. From the elder Mill through the Indian Census, in the Royal Asiatic Society and the researches of the social anthropologists, British scholarship has accumulated an enormous amount of data on institutional variation. Resistances to the sociological study of British institutions appear not to have prevented the Colonial Social Science Research Council from sending teams of anthropologists into the field. Sociology does seem to be more acceptable in Britain if its objects are remote, or foreign, or dead. (The Reverend Montgomery Watt, who lectures in Arabic at Edinburgh, has published an impressive analysis of the class basis of Muhamed's prophecy; none of his colleagues has performed the same service for John Knox.)

Sociology is taught at the newer universities, although not at all of them, and not yet at the older ones. The sources of resistance to sociology in British academic life are complex, and the reasons given by its enemies are often good ones rather than real ones. They point with horror to the American scene, of course, but they might equally well point with admiration to an elegant and flourishing school of sociology at the Sorbonne; their selective perception requires investigation.

Part of the resistance is, of course, due to the association of sociology with the British Left. But the Continental example, where theoretical sociology has largely been Conservative, suggests that the right is rather more anxious than it ought to be. The American example, further, suggests that a certain kind of sociology makes as ideal an instrument of administrative technology as certain kinds of economics. However, sociological generalization about contemporary Britain may well involve the projection of future trends, and perhaps this violates that "empiricism" by which a good many intelligent Britons persuade themselves that what they can read in *The Times* exhausts reality. Part of the resistance, too, comes from a certain type of literary amateur, more honoured in Britain than elsewhere, who finds any hard intellectual work somehow in bad taste. Whatever the reason, thinking about the whole of British society and its conflicts, as well as the identification of material or spiritual poverty within it, seems difficult for influential sections of the British intelligentsia—perhaps most difficult for those who identify themselves most closely with the present distribution of power and advantage in British society.

Within the universities, resistance to sociology seems strongest in the three disciplines to which it is most allied:

history, philosophy and politics. It would be vulgar to suggest that resistance is due to the fear of losing students, but it would be sociologically unrealistic to ignore this ignoble motive entirely. History is the simplest case. The revulsion against sociology amongst certain historians is a continuation of history's own internecine warfare. There are many historians who regard statements more venturesome than the assertion that every Greek coin has two and only two sides as dangerously speculative. What they fear from sociology is what they fear in history itself: the intrusion of general ideas. The controversy on the rise of the Gentry shows that sociological ideas, derived from Marx and Weber, have already entered historical studies. Professor Trevor-Roper and his Marxist opponents are at one on this, that history without sociology is blind.

The case of the philosophers is more difficult. In these pages recently, one of Mr Ernest Gellner's critics dismissed as "gossip" his sociological analysis of Oxford philosophy. The critic is not well informed as to the history of his own field; unless we are to accept that Hobbes and Hegel were nothing but gossipmongers, we must admit that a search for the social psychological origins of belief has been a traditional part of philosophy. Indeed, as philosophy has become detached from the social sciences it has been in some danger of losing philosophical relevance. What is the use, in the era of thermonuclear weapons, of the kind of moral philosophy that still depicts the individual as an ethical Robinson Crusoe? Be that as it may, those who hold that philosophy is now a special technical discipline amongst other disciplines ought not, on the face of it, to be disturbed by sociology's claims. Those who hold that philosophy is some kind of synthetic science, however, might for their part welcome sociology in order to have yet more to synthesise. Philosophers, however, exhibit no very reasoned attitudes on these points; perhaps one of them can tell us why.

Resistance to sociology amongst teachers of politics is rather more interesting. Politics as a field is in itself seriously divided, between the study of political institutions and political philosophy. Its amorphousness, and many of its uncertainties in relation to history, are not dissimilar to problems encountered within sociology. Politics, too, is a *parvenu* discipline; newcomers to the academic hierarchy may feel especially obliged to defend its present arrangements. More important, sociology by its very existence seems to imply that the criteria by which many students of politics define their problems are simply the claims of liberal political ideology, taken at face value. The separation of politics from sociology constitutes an answer to sociological questions: it declares them *a priori* irrelevant. In fact, many teachers of politics do think that they have a good deal to learn from the sociological study of public opinion, of bureaucracy and of class structure.

These resistances will no doubt be overcome in time, although not entirely by argument. Britain's decline as a world power, and the changes now taking place within British society, may make sociology appear more attractive as a university subject; they also make sociology more disturbing. Those outside the universities would find it difficult to comprehend the dogmatism, rigidity, and sloth with which universities generally meet proposals for major alterations in the curriculum. For the moment, there are more teaching posts in philosophy at Oxford than there are teaching posts in sociology in the entire United Kingdom. (This last number is also exceeded by the number of research posts in sociology in Paris.)

The absence of sociology at Oxford and Cambridge has inhibited the development of the subject in the country as a whole. (In so far as sociology has been excluded from the older universities on account of the political tradition associated with it, the exclusion has served to keep sociology left,

by maintaining unchanged the class composition of its recruitment.) Cambridge, however, is now about to begin
undergraduate sociology teaching on a considerable scale. At
my own university, Oxford, many students and no small
number of dons, manifest an intelligent and critical curiosity
about the field. But I should not want to be in the unhappy
position of denying a self-evident proposition: Oxford has
attained such a state of academic perfection that changes
would be superfluous.

Should there be some expansion of sociology in the British
universities, the field may find itself endangered by certain
of its British friends. The social anthropologists, whose usual
objects of inquiry are dissolving under their very eyes, are
beginning to study industrial societies. But the techniques
applicable to primitive village communities have only limited
value when transferred elsewhere. Then, too, there is a school
of strictly practical social research, whose canons of practi-
cality are absurdly narrow. To understand contemporary
society is not easy, and sometimes the long way around may
prove the surest. In any case, it is a service neither to sociology
nor to the left to make of sociology in Britain simply an
instrument for measuring defects in the supply of social
services.

The important point is to see that sociology is neither
monolith, machine, nor party. In the last analysis, the success or failure of sociological work depends upon the intelligence, education, and sensitivity of the individual scholar.
Not the least of the tasks incumbent upon him is an acknowledgement of the ambiguities and uncertainties of his own
field. It would be pleasant to hope that such an acknowledgement would be met, by those who conceive of themselves as
sociology's opponents, with a willingness to re-examine received assumptions. But there are good sociological reasons
why the hope is not likely to be fulfilled. The arguments for
sociology are practical, not theoretical. Since Marx, a socio-

logical mode of analysis has penetrated the study of history and politics; the question of whether it belongs there is academic in the pejorative sense. The study of literature and reflections on the wider questions of contemporary culture are equally influenced by consideration of the social context of spiritual effort; Eliot, Hoggart, and Williams agree on that. Among the claims that can be made for sociology as an academic discipline is that it does what no one else can or will do. For the study of class structure, of the distribution of power and cultural values in contemporary Britain, this claim can most certainly be made for British sociology. Yet another claim is that sociology does what others do, not better, but in a manner that is interestingly different. This claim could be made with respect to the comparative study of institutions, although just on whom the burden should fall is not a serious question.

Sociologists, at their best, insist on a sense of the interconnectedness of the whole; they may help others from isolating and therefore falsifying their reading of its parts. Their experience is beginning to teach them to live with a paradox: ideological interests produce the most objective sort of sociology, provided that the sociologist is reasonably self-conscious about his ideology. The tension between ideology and science, then, remains sociology's fatal and recurrent crux; the effort to overcome it is the source of such intellectual and spiritual dignity as it possesses.

On the Sociology of

Current Social Research[1]

Discussions of the sociology of current social research usually begin with an antithesis. Research, in the form of empirical social inquiry (surveys, interviews, questionnaires, direct observation, and statistical or quantitative analysis) has been opposed to theory. The latter, it is argued, is the philosophically privileged form of social discourse. It is holistic,

1. The literature on the problematical nature of the relationship between social theory and social research is very considerable. C. Wright Mills' *The Sociological Imagination,* New York, 1959, and Georges Gurvitch's *La Vocation Actuelle de la Sociologie,* I, II, Paris, 1963, may be taken as evidence for the international nature of a dispute over method which has recently been quite strenuous in the German Federal Republic. See Jürgen Habermas, "Zur Logik der Sozialwissenschaften," Beiheft 5, *Philosophische Rundschau,* 1967. Further reference to the German discussion is given in the collection of essays by younger German sociologists, Bernhard Schafers (Herausgeber), *Thesen zur Kritik der Soziologie,* Frankfurt, 1969, a collection which would have been more interesting had some systematic effort been made by one of the contributors to develop a concrete sociology of German sociology. A very useful example of this genre is given in the article by Pierre Bourdieu and Jean-Claude Passeron, "Sociology and Philosophy in France Since 1945—Death and Resurrection of a Philosophy Without Subject," *Social Research,* Vol. 34, No. 1, Spring 1967, 162–212. Writing for a foreign public, these two younger representatives of French sociology have analyzed the French post-war equivalent of the current German dispute over positivism in terms both of philosophy and the sociology of knowledge.

in that it deals with the social totality. It entails a view of society's inner movement and of its larger contours, of the inter-relations of its parts, of the co-ordination—either willed or unintended—of its activities. Theory, on this view, may have a critical purpose: to illuminate the present social order (or disorder) to expose its insufficiencies, oppressiveness, or inhumanity. It may therefore serve as the indispensable spiritual pre-condition for reform or even revolution. Equally, theory may have a conservative tendency: to show that what exists can take no other form, that in the worst of all possible worlds, man's social institutions are the best his collective traditions and the capacities of present generations will provide. Critical or conservative, theory in these antithetical terms serves as a supreme mode of historical consciousness: it reproduces, symbolically, our collective and historical condition.

Social research, or more precisely empirical social research, is in the framework of this antithesis incapable of apprehending the social totality. It can deal with partial sectors of social reality, with concrete motivations, with single situations, unique or otherwise. By its very nature, it must ignore the whole: it is technically confined to its parts, and cannot by any means within the repertory of research technique itself ascend to the whole. It may, indeed, have a baleful effect on the making of social theory, by encouraging or generating an additive view of social reality. A notion of social totality constructed exclusively with the aid of the findings of empirical social research must eventuate in systematic distortion: the essence of totality, of the inter-connectedness of society, cannot enter into its empirical basis. Worse yet, by drawing generalizations from the surface appearances of present-day social phenomena, it can give rise to historical fore-shortening in our depiction of society. We can be led to suppose that social phenomena are related, invariably, as they are at present. This, in turn, can entail a compelling conservative bias:

the present structure of society may appear to exhaust all historical possibility.

The antithesis I have sketched is common enough in discussions of our discipline. It is admittedly dramatic, but it has the virtue of providing a convenient and lucid model to which the disparate varieties of theory construction and empirical research in contemporary sociology may be fitted. It does, however, have one major drawback. It is false. The relationships between theory and empirical research, between critical disposition and conservative apologetic, in the conduct of empirical inquiry, are far more complicated—so much more so, that convenient antitheses do in the end obscure far more than they illuminate. A consideration of the intellectual structure of the problem will clarify the sociological analysis of the process of empirical research as in itself an aspect of social activity. If in practice the two, intellectual structure and social activity, are inseparable we can only understand their conjoint appearance by first separating their components.

Another commonplace must engage us. Empirical research has, it is said, a dynamic function with respect to theory, verifying or falsifying hypotheses, breaking the ground for new theoretic constructions. This view in contemporary sociology itself is most prominently associated with the name of Robert Merton, although in fact it derives directly from the tradition of positivism, from August Comte and John Stuart Mill (both of whom presented the view with far more elegance and persuasiveness than most of their twentieth-century *epigones*.) Suppose, however, that theoretical ideas enter into the very definition and circumscription of the empirical social universe we wish to understand? The notion of human beings as seeking a maximization of pleasure or profit, as requiring social legitimation for their conduct, as bound to the good or conventional opinions of their immediate associates and peers, enter into the very categories with which we seek to interpret—for instance—the results of a survey of opinion. Indeed, the very idea of public opinion presupposes a social order in which opinion has an effective function, an attained level of practical democratization which is historically rare. It may also, of course, ignore the extent to which opinion is manipulated and prefabricated. Briefly put, we may say that social theory and empirical research are dialectically inter-related, the categories of the one infusing the other, the findings of empirical inquiry presupposing and even pre-forming theory. On this view, an image of the social totality is given in the analysis of even its parts, and our ideas of totality shape the empirical inquiries we undertake. Schematic conceptions of a correction of theory by research, then, are insufficient because artificial.

What concrete consequences emerge for our understanding of the sociological function of contemporary social research? Let us begin by considering the origins of empirical social inquiry in the nineteenth century. The founders of sociology (the Scottish historians like Millar and Ferguson, the French encyclopedists, the German historicists from Herder and Hegel to Marx and von Stein, Saint-Simon and his disciple Comte) had quite varied relationships to the formal organizations chartered by their societies to perpetuate and cultivate knowledge: academies and learned societies and universities. All, however, worked in a way which expressed their closeness or identification with the classical tradition in philosophy. For these early sociological thinkers, whatever formal prescriptions they might have issued for empirical inquiry, sociology was quite unequivocally a philosophical enterprise,[2] a matter of reflection which could and

2. Did not John Stuart Mill, in praising his contemporary Comte as the author of the first scientific sociology, specifically remark that "if laws of social phenomena, empirically generalised from history, can when once suggested be affiliated to the known laws of human nature; if the direction actually taken by the developments and changes of human society can be seen to be such as the properties of man and of his dwelling place made

217

did employ historical findings but which did not necessarily require special techniques for the apprehension of contemporary social realities. In general, those methods of observation we today identify as distinctively sociological developed in a considerable degree of isolation from the development of sociological thought itself. Moreover, these methods developed outside the universities, in response to the practical requirements of governments and voluntary associations for valid knowledge of immediate social circumstances. Their origins in earlier times remount to Sir William Petty's *Political Arithmetick* in the seventeenth century, their close connection with the German school of *Kameralwissenschaft* has been remarked. Their scientific form was given by the rise of statistical reasoning, their political content was determined by the imperatives which motivated governments and political groupings to examine at first hand the unprecedented conditions of a society which was undergoing urbanization and industrialization.[3]

The entry of these methods into the universities followed and did not precede the recognition of their administrative and political indispensability for those seeking to exercise some control over the new industrial society. Consider the

antecedently probable, the empirical generalisations are raised into positive laws and Sociology becomes a science." J. S. Mill, *August Comte and Positivism*, cited from 1961 edition, Ann Arbor, Michigan, p. 86. We may note that the "known laws of human nature,' if deductions from them make probable sociology's inductively established laws, are in themselves the controlling assumptions of an empirical sociology. At the programmatic beginning of empirical sociology, then we find that it rests on philosophical assumptions which were—in the view of those whose program it was to establish an empirical sociology—irreducible.

3. Two recent historical studies by American sociologists, originally done as doctoral dissertations under Paul Lazarsfeld, make remarkable contributions to our understanding of these aspects of the development of our discipline. See Terry N. Clark, "Emile Durkheim and The Institutionalists of Sociology in the French University System" in the *European Journal of Sociology*, Vol. 9, No. 1, 1968, 37–71, and Anthony Oberschall, *Empirical Social Research in Germany*, New York, Paris, and The Hague, 1965.

origins of academic sociology itself. In America, this grew out of the Social Science Association, founded in the mid-nineteenth century to deal with the problems of immigration, urbanization, and industrialization. The famed Chicago School of Sociology, which at the beginning of our century and for four decades thereafter dominated American sociology, was characterized by empirical inquiry intended to respond to the reformist impulses of the educated middle class—horrified at corporate capitalism but afraid of proletarian socialism. The Chicago School had close connections with Social Protestantism, precisely as did in Germany the Verein für Sozialpolitik. Max Weber's own initial empirical inquiries were conducted under the auspices of this body of higher civil servants, professors, and churchmen ("die Kathedersozialisten") and were addressed to pressing German socio-political problems, like the condition of the agricultural labor force in the east. The prestige of the Verein, the sense of the social utility of its undertakings, transferred itself subsequently to the German Sociological Association (Deutsche Gesellschaft fuer Soziologie) and contributed to the legitimation of sociology in the German universities.[4] It has been argued that Weber became disenchanted with the Verein fuer Sozialpolitik as a vehicle for large-scale sociological inquiry and turned, instead, to the German Sociological Association, of which he was one of the founders, and whose initial program made provision for the conducting of social research by the Association itself. A political motivation for the pursuit of social inquiry need not always be salient in the consciousness of those engaged in inquiry. Indeed, those actively pursuing social inquiry may subjectively believe themselves to be responding to a disinterested curiosity, when in fact political factors in the environment may well have induced them to define their object of inquiry in one way rather than another. Weber himself saw this quite

4. Oberschall, *op. cit.*, p. 142.

clearly (cf. "Wissenschaft als Beruf" and "Die Objektivitaet Sozialwissenschaftlicher und Sozialpolitischer Erkenntnis"), although some who have subsequently pronounced themselves Weberians have not. In any event, it would be a mistake to say that the shift in the locus of German sociology, from the Verein für Sozialpolitik to the German Sociological Association, entailed its radical de-politicization.

In England, the Fabians could find a home in the universities for the newer techniques of social inquiry only by founding their own academic institution at the turn of this century, the London School of Economics and Political Science. In France, Durkheim and his school were the first university sociologists, bringing to the academic study of moral and social problems the methods employed decades previously outside the French universities by social statisticians. The avowed aim of the Durkheim group was not alone to found an incontestable science of society but to employ its methods in the defense of the moral patrimony and moral integration of the Third Republic. In each of these cases—Max Weber's strictures on the ethical neutrality of the procedures of the social sciences to the contrary notwithstanding—the fusion of the tradition of philosophical reflection in theoretic sociology with the techniques of empirical research had definite political ends. Generally, the collection of empirical social data at the beginning of our century served reformist political purposes. Empirical sociology, then, entered the universities simultaneously with theoretical sociology, in response to the educated middle classes' demand for orientation in a society become ever more bureaucratic and complex.[5]

5. The classical text of the early phase of American sociology, R. E. Park and E. W. Burgess, *Introduction to the Science of Sociology*, Chicago, 1921, shows the profound influence upon American sociology of European thought. The text, in effect a collection of readings, had many excerpts from the works of scholars like Durkheim and Simmel. It also showed the ways in which early American social theory was an academic reflection of

We confront a paradox. In the course of the twentieth century, a sociology whose very empirical components were intended to contribute to strengthening the role of an enlightened public in the control of social affairs was turned to quite antithetical goals. The reformist phase of sociology lasted for a generation, more or less (until 1933 in Germany, until 1939 in America, until 1940 in France). Thereafter, empirical sociology became increasingly an ancillary technique of bureaucratic domination. How may we explain this singular transformation? Again, we must have recourse to the inner structure of sociological thought, as it developed in a setting new to it at the beginning of our century, the universities.

The simple fact of its reception in the universities did not at once alter sociology. The conception of theoretic discourse closely tied to empirical research, and in turn united with political ends, was not specific to the universities. We may recall that in 1880 Marx himself devised an "enquête ouvrière," a questionnaire for administration to the French working class. LePlay had concretized and deepened his conceptions of the nature of industrial society by his studies of familial budgets. The universities, however, did seem to offer a highly suitable setting for the development of an empirical sociology in a very positive relationship to theory and larger social purpose. Did not the universities' traditions of scientific activity allow the optimal pursuit of sociological insight? More, did not the academic division of labor, the very principle of scientific specialization, encourage the development of specifically and rigorously sociological methods? Finally, did not the traditions of academic freedom allow the individual scholar to follow the dictates of his political and moral conscience in his work, without having to worry about narrow and immediate political constraints?

---

the concerns of the educated American middle class: immigration, urbanization, and "social control."

At first, to be sure, the development of an empirical sociology seemed to confirm these early promises. A number of general ideas were pursued into hitherto hidden recesses of social reality. Consider the utilization by empirical sociology of the distinction between "Gemeinschaft" and "Gesellschaft" by Tönnies. In America, Cooley extracted from Tönnies' dichotomy the distinction between the intimate and solidary relationships of the primary group and the impersonal and distant relationships of the secondary group. An entire range of sociological and social psychological inquiry was fructified by these notions. In due course, the empirical results of these inquiries came to exert an influence on a new phase of social theory. George Herbert Mead's views of the social self, the revisionist Freudians' ideas about personality, reflected the impulsions transmitted to empirical research by Tönnies, but they also reflected the correctives administered to the original ideas by the process of inquiry itself.

Similarly, in the area of industrial sociology, critical notions extracted from the Marxist tradition produced an entire literature on work. The Paris manuscripts of Marx were not published until 1932, and their utilization in empirical inquiry had to wait some fifteen years after that: the researches of Friedmann, Naville, and Touraine in France, of Bahrdt, Lutz, Pirker, and Popitz in Germany, of Ferrarotti and Pizzorno in Italy, and Mills in the United States testified to the creative energies this publication unloosed in the study of industrial and office work, of manual and white-collar workers. But, previously DeMan, Dreyfus, and Lederer had in the 1920s and early 1930s depicted the workings of the new production system, the differentials between types of work, in empirical terms which took the Marxist theories as points of critical departure. A new idea of the role of new middle class, of the function of work in the psychic economy of the population of industrial society, was the result.

In both instances, an admirable union—or more precisely,

a contrapuntal relationship—between theory and empirical research followed from the academic pursuit of political interests. The notions of the destruction of community in industrial society, of the alienation of the worker in the process of machine production, of the rise of a new inter-mediate stratum with an indeterminate political potential, inspired an entire program of empirical research. If soci-ology, however, had these high points, it also had some rather pronounced low ones.

With the assimilation of empirical research to academic sociology, the university's criteria for academic "neutrality" began to exert a profound influence upon sociology. The effectiveness of this influence depended upon three prior factors. (1) The enormous prestige of the physical sciences convinced an increasing number of academic sociologists in the mid-twentieth century that the fate of their discipline, uncertain of its intellectual and academic status, resided in a close imitation of the natural sciences. (2) The increasing frenzy of social conflict in capitalist society frightened many scholars and discouraged them from taking anything other than a superficial and conventional set of political options. Their sociology, therefore, was increasingly emptied of politi-cal relevance—and, as a result, increasingly remote from the inner conflicts of their societies. (3) These two tendencies in turn gave rise to a third: the techniques of empirical research became detached from their original theoretic and political uses, and took on a life of their own—real or alleged.

It was, in other words, not the use of empirical research technique which encouraged a view of society separated from a view of the movement of the whole. It was, rather, the use of empirical research technique in isolation from the im-peratives of theoretic clarification which accounted for the autonomy and mechanization of technique. In these circum-stances, the process of reflection escaped the conscious control of the sociologist. The categories of empirical research were dictated, not by thought, but by the object (a transitory phase in modern social history having been reified through a total reliance on technique as a means of apprehending reality). Little wonder, then, that the object of inquiry was in itself transformed. Once the inner movement of society, the structure of its conflicts, the contours and mechanisms of its organization, the object of sociological inquiry now became the most visible and superficial aspects of the society's functioning. Quite unnecessarily narrow, the limits to empirical technique set the limits of sociological inquiry; thought itself has disappeared from a certain kind of sociology.[6]

The institutional consequences are of two kinds. For the past twenty-five years (roughly, since the end of the Second World War) there has been an enormous increase in the employment of empirical research technique by sociologists either working directly for or on behalf of governmental agencies, industry, the mass media, the political parties, and a great variety of interest groups. These sponsors of sociological research are, clearly, not interested in knowledge or orientation in an abstract sense; they seek to manipulate, to control, the social environment. It is significant in this con-

6. There does appear to be a "ruse of reason" at work. In the most recent development of applied social research in the United States, a group of social scientists are preparing a set of "Social Indicators" for a proposed "Social Report" to the President of the United States, to provide a counterpart to the annual reports of his Council of Economic Advisors. The rationale for this is that "Social Indicators" can constitute a "qualitative" diagnosis of the deficiencies and ills of American society as opposed to the merely "quantitative" indicators of macro-economics. This, it is argued, will lead the American citizenry to think of its collective problems in terms other than crudely material ones. "Qualitative" indicators of this sort, of course, must entail judgments about social priorities, the construction of categories of deficiency and pathology, and notions of social causation at an extremely general level. Briefly, they call forth an entire process of evaluative and synthetic thinking which is antithetical to a narrowly conceived empiricism. See Bertram M. Gross and Michael Springer, "Developing Social Intelligence," in Bertram M. Gross, editor, *Social Intelligence for America's Future,* Boston, 1969.

nection that the governments and ruling parties of the state socialist countries (including the Soviet Union[7] and the DDR) look with favor upon the introduction of empirical social research, but are conspicuously unenthusiastic about precisely those aspects of modern sociological thought (e.g. the schools of Frankfurt and the work of the Parisians like Gurvitch and Lefebvre) which can legitimately claim descent from Marxism.

The enlargement of the market for sociological research projects and a large number of extra-academic posts for sociologists has also had institutional consequences for the universities. Many teachers of sociology spend most of their time conducting inquiries for one or another agency external to the university. Inevitably, their assistants and students are drawn in. Even where this is not the case, research originated in the universities has come to resemble in method, technique, and aim the sorts of inquiry sponsored by clients external to it. The pronounced separation of sociology from philosophy, a recent development in France and Germany, has been mistakenly attributed by some to an imitation of the philistinism long since institutionalized in American sociology. This is not the case; it is an expression of tendencies immanent in a certain conception of the division of intellectual labor, in the environment of the European universities themselves.[8] The chief result, then, of the recent insti-

7. See George Fischer, *Science and Politics, the New Sociology in the Soviet Union*, Ithaca, 1964, "Current Soviet Work in Sociology" in *The American Sociologist*, American Sociological Association, Vol. 1, No. 3, May 1966.

8. See the remarkable discussion of the organization of French sociological research by Jean Cuisenier, "La Sociologie et Ses Applications," *Révue Française de Sociologie*, Vol. 7, 1966, 361–80. Cuisenier's paper was originally delivered as a talk to the Société Française de Sociologie and the printed comments of his interlocutors are of considerable interest. Cuisenier takes the view that sociological research must be evaluated in terms of the cost of producing its products (research findings). Curiously, this notion of sociology organized in terms of criteria for efficiency on a bureaucratized market for scientific products is joined to a theoretic point of view which suggests that

tutional changes in the setting of sociological inquiry has been intellectual. Technique has dictated a view of human behavior which eternalizes the present constraints to which men are subject. It has also led to intellectual absurdities.

Some sociologists have made preposterously exaggerated claims for their discipline—as if they were in possession of a sociological equivalent of Laplace's celebrated, if hypothetical, formula for the world. A particularly flagrant example may be found in the notorious Project Camelot of 1964.[9] This project, briefly, entailed an investigation sponsored by the United States Department of Defense to study a number of countries to establish their potentials for what was euphemistically termed "internal war"—in other words, social revolution. By expending six or seven million dollars on sociological research, the United States military authorities hoped to obtain clear and infallible prescriptions for averting or, if necessary, defeating social revolution. The project had a premature end when Latin Americans protested at the inclusion of their countries in this scientific enterprise. American generals and politicians were persuaded that sociology could in fact perform miracles for them. Mathematical analysis, computers, systems analysis—a term which upon examination is devoid of intellectual content—were to be employed. The total absence of any but the most primitive, repressive, and banal socio-political conceptions in the pro-

---

findings about concrete aspects of the social universe are less valuable than those which tend toward "une théorie générale de la société qui soit operationnelle." That is, Cuisenier believes that "artisanal" production in sociology has become outmoded, but calls for a bureaucratized research system directed to a "market" to pursue a "pure" science—a reminiscence of August Comte's depection of a "pure" sociology as having great social utility as a doctrine of order. A pronouncedly more pluralistic view of the organization of French sociology is taken by one of its most brilliant "artisans" in Edgar Morin's "Le droit à la Reflexion," *Révue Française de Sociologie,* Vol. 6, 1965, 4–12.

9. See I. L. Horowitz, editor, *The Rise and Fall of Project Camelot,* Cambridge, Massachusetts, and London, 1967.

gram for Project Camelot did not disturb its sponsors. It did show, however, what intellectual degradation can follow from the total technicization of sociology—at a moment in its development when technique and thought have simply separated.

Yet, technique is indispensable to scientific activity. Has any attempt been made to fuse in a new synthesis what has been rent asunder? Here and there, we do find evidence for an effort to re-think the relationship between empirical technique and theory. The utilization of psychoanalytic schema for the interpretation of interview data entails the introduction of a less superficial view of man in the process of data collection. From this perspective, the ambivalence of the individual respondent may be used to establish the dissonances and conflicts induced in his life by society. A less mechanical and more complex sociology may emerge from these efforts. Further, the introduction of a temporal dimension in the collection of certain data may enable sociologists to make more specific the impingement of historical change upon the processes they study. Indeed, in some countries (France, Britain, and the United States are here in the vanguard and Germany rather far behind) we begin to see the emergence of a new group of social historians and historical sociologists, united in a certain critical sophistication with respect to the operations of data collection. Finally—particularly evident in the United States rather recently and in France—empirical inquiries have been undertaken with political purposes which directly and consciously influence the use of empirical technique. Those criticizing the bureaucratic and authoritarian administration of the American welfare state, for instance, have been impelled to develop programs of "action-research." [10] In effect, new social milieux have

10. See Daniel Patrick Moynihan, *Maximum Feasible Misunderstanding*, New York and London, 1969, and Lee Rainwater and William Yancey, *The Moynihan Report and the Politics of Controversy*, Cambridge,

been created to serve as tests for new views of social possibility. It will be seen that the conventional notion of the sociological recording of process in a fixed social reality is incompatible with experiments of this kind. However great the danger they entail of manipulation of others, they also contain the potential for a new approach to the very conceptual content of the discipline.

A summary and a conclusion are in order. Empirical research entered the universities with the academicization of sociology. It became a legitimate (that is to say, effective) instrument of deepening and changing theoretic views of social

Massachusetts and London, 1967. The "Moynihan Report," briefly, was a proposal by Moynihan (who was President Nixon's Advisor on Urban Affairs, 1969–1971 that federal efforts against poverty be directed to rectifying the disintegrated condition of the black family. The report, submitted to the Johnson Administration, aroused strenuous opposition from black leaders and some social scientists—who saw in it evidences of a "paternalistic" view of the blacks, if not worse. Undaunted, Moynihan in his own recent book has traced the history of the participation of local community leaders in the anti-poverty program, the most controversial and conflict-laden aspect of the program. He concludes that social scientists have attempted to manipulate American society on the basis of insufficient knowledge and as a consequence of their own political prejudices. Moynihan's own book, and the account of his report's reception, have the merit of raising in clear and unequivocal form many questions concerning the neutrality of social research and the manipulation by social scientists of social contexts. Moynihan's conclusion is that even with a maximization of knowledge, social scientists cannot make value choices on behalf of the citizenry. A rather different position is taken by Alvin W. Gouldner in "Explorations in Applied Social Science" in A. W. Gouldner and S. M. Miller, editors, *Applied Sociology*, New York and London, 1965, pp. 6 ff. Gouldner distinguishes between "clinical" and "engineering" approaches to applied sociology. In the "clinical" approach, with depth psychotherapy as a model, the sociologist attempts to enable the client group to overcome or at least to make conscious the resistances (often, social interests) impeding attainment of its aims. In the "engineering" attitude, the sociologist simply manipulates the situation to attain a given aim. Gouldner does insist that there is no real and fixed relationship between theoretic and applied sociology in the sense of a body of principles which can be applied more or less directly to social situations. The principles, he asserts, simply do not exist in this form.

reality. Disengaged from these views, separated from any larger social or political purposes, empirical research was taken up by a great many agencies interested in manipulating the world and those who live in it. An entire climate was created in the universities themselves in which sociology as a discipline became identical, in practice, with these techniques. An impoverishment and indeed a falsification of sociological thought resulted from this institutional process.[11]

11. It is generally supposed that American sociology is most advanced in respect of applied sociology, that is to say, in respect of sociological inquiry conducted for agencies of power and contending power groups in society. It is instructive, in this respect, to read Neil Smelser and James Davis, editors, *Sociology,* Englewood Cliffs, N.J., 1970. This is a report on the present position and propects of sociology as a discipline in the United States prepared by a committee of distinguished sociologists for a report to the National Academy of Sciences and the Social Science Research Council. Of those who hold doctorates in sociology, 88 per cent are found in universities, 3 per cent in the federal government, 1 per cent in state and local government, less than 1 per cent in the military, 5 per cent in non-profit organizations (e.g. foundations), and 1 per cent each in private business and industry, working for other employers, or in the group of self-employed. That is to say, those who wish to employ sociologists on research must have recourse to groups of sociologists in the universities. An enumeration of major sources of support for sociological research in 1967, cited by these authors, shows that 17.7 million dollars came from the Department of Health, Education, and Welfare (of which 15.8 million dollars alone from the National Institute of Mental Health), 10.1 million dollars from the Office of Economic Opportunity, 3.2 million dollars from the National Science Foundation, and 2 million dollars from the Department of Defense. It was estimated that 75 per cent of the funds from the Office of Economic Opportunity and 66 per cent of the funds from the Department of Health, Education, and Welfare were for "applied" projects. It is clear from this statistic that the role of the Federal Government, through its agencies, in American sociological research is enormous. (Using a somewhat different basis of computation, Moynihan, *op. cit.,* p. 31, notes that the Federal Government increased its spending on social research from 4 million dollars in 1956 to 44 million in 1966.) That the universities have not been entirely apolitical may be gathered from the remark by Raymond V. Bowers, a sociologist who works for the Department of Defense, in his essay on "The Military Establishment" in Paul Lazarsfeld, William H. Sewell, and Harold Wilensky, *The*

Certain recent experiments with technique show, however, that given different institutional ends, the techniques need not lead to manipulation or intellectual fraudulence.

At the moment, it is true, sociology presents the appearance of chaos, an intellectual tower of Babel. It is noteworthy in this connection that at Berkeley, Berlin, Beograd, Nanterre, and Warsaw the students of sociology have been in the vanguard of the student revolt.[12] The refusal by the students of a technicized discipline which put its technique only at the service of the bureaucratic forces directing their lives is an expression of a valid criticism of the discipline. The criticism is, at once, intellectual, moral, and political. It points the way,

---

Uses of Sociology, New York and London, 1967, p. 265: "The record shows that well over two hundred professional sociologists have contributed to the postwar use of sociology by the military establishment, and the list approximates a Who's Who of current American sociologists." Yet, in fact, the predominant political attitude of American sociologists in the universities may be described as "liberal." In the United States, they support the politics associated with the left and center fractions of the American Democratic Party. Funds for research, and of equal weight, the definition of problems for inquiry, generally come to the universities from without; this has been sufficient to outweigh such intrinsic social judgments as a sociology primarily institutionalized in the universities might have developed if not subject to these influences. The notion of a university free of these influences, however, is absurd: it is at this point that the recent critique of the universities by the radical students has begun.

12. The literature on the student movement is voluminous. An international view is given by A. Cockburn and R. Blackburn, *Student Power*, London, 1969, which has the virtue of giving the text of the manifesto of students at Nanterre originally entitled "Tuez les Sociologues" (pp. 373 ff.). These were students taught *inter alia* by Alain Touraine and Henri Lefebvre: depicting them as agents of oppression is as grotesque as the curious belief manifested by some German students that Jürgen Habermas is reactionary. The response of the radical students to the institutionalization of sociology, however, suggests that the discipline has been unable to assimilate the self-critique administered by radical professors like Habermas, Lefebvre, and Touraine. The conclusion of a fragment of the student movement, that the only solution is the destruction of the universities in their present form, would alas prepare the way for universities more "technocratic" than those we have hitherto experienced.

therefore, to a re-consideration and a re-vivification of the use of empirical technique in sociology. It does so by raising the possibility of new institutional settings for a discipline recently constricted by the circumstances in which it has been practiced.

A Socio-Theater of the Absurd: A World Congress of Sociology in Bulgaria

A southern sea resort, set in olive groves, would normally constitute an attractive setting for a scholarly conference. The resort in question is Varna, on the Bulgarian Black Sea coast, and the gathering was the eighth post-war World Congress of Sociology. To the charms of nature were added the attractions of Bulgaria's condition as a "developing" nation, and the prospect of the first major and public encounter between "bourgeois" sociology and its orthodox Marxist counterpart on the soil of a state socialist society. The whole seemed to promise, at once, esoteric decor and a genuine historical experiment. The result, however, was a mitigated disaster. Both the disaster and its (slight) mitigation merit attention, but had best be understood in the context of the course of sociology since 1945.

The vertiginous post-war expansion of sociology as an academic field (I hesitate to use the term "discipline," for good philosophical cause) is reflected in the attendance figures for successive international gatherings. The first one I attended, at Liege in 1953, had some 300 participants. At Amsterdam in 1956 there were already about 500 sociologists, and at Stresa in 1959 there were over a thousand. At Washington in 1962 the number was higher still, and by the time the Evian conference was held in 1966 there were over 2000 present. The throng at Varna numbered 4000—even if the Bulgarians threw in by official count 501 persons, many of them farcically unqualified. The quantitative growth of sociology in the United States and western Europe over the past twenty-five years had similar sources. Initially, the catastrophes of fascism and war and the problems of reconstruction gave rise to a general political introspection. The constriction of post-war western politics, the consolidation of a consensus about a restored capitalist productive machinery, turned introspection into its antithesis. Instead of asking how society could be made whole and rational, sociologists portrayed its fragmentation and senselessness as inevitable. Those who sought something else were dismissed as "utopians" by those who fancied themselves in possession (or about to come into it) of immutable laws of behavior, of higher and systematic insight into the necessary and beneficial constraints of social structures. Rapidly emptied of critical ideas, sociology soon lost any intellectual content at all: it became a set of techniques for gathering data. The techniques were useful, not least to those in command of the corporate and governmental bureaucracies which set such narrow limits on our political choices. Sociologists became minor ancillaries of the administrative technologists: they presented their instruments of inquiry as aspects of a pure science, if a nascent one, but their work served purposes profane or worse.

Not all of sociology, to be sure, was self-consciously technical. Serious efforts were made in the United States to develop abstract criteria for sociological analysis and general models of society. These, too, were subject to political assumptions. The abstract criteria often dealt with social constraints as "functions," as mechanical necessities imposed on men and not as historical precipitates of social existence which could be criticized and changed. The models frequently presupposed a social consensus which, in fact, they contributed to bringing about. In Europe, a serious and desperate search to derive contemporary relevance from the Marxist tradition began as soon as it was clear that the anti-fascist resistance had not been the prelude to socialist alterations of European institutions. The reluctance of the European working class to assume a revolutionary mission led to studies of new forms of psychic coercion. The process of alienation, briefly, was now seen not alone in the fragmentation of man, citizen and producer, but in the willed servitude of a new generation of consumers. Meanwhile, phenomenologists looked beyond politics for a human essence. They sometimes found it, not alone beyond politics but beyond community, and so reduced social existence to a gigantic charade. Western sociology in its multiplicity had a saving philosophical virtue. Political ideas might infuse sociological notions, but they did so in mediated fashion. The sociologists could and did argue about their assumptions, but they also argued about the social world. Ultimately, what has diminished the appeal of doctrines of consensus and function is the historical evidence that consensus no longer exists, that institutions no longer work.

The state socialist regimes have allowed, by and large, no such public corrections of social thought. A flourishing pre-Bolshevik Russian sociological tradition was eradicated. As Stalinism replaced the frequently adventurous Marxism of the early revolutionary years, a dogmatized and impoverished "Marxism-Leninism" was all that could be heard in the Soviet Union. The promulgation of "laws" of social development of an entirely invented kind had one clear aim: the point was neither to understand the world, nor to change it, but to justify it. The implantation of Stalinism in eastern Europe by the Red Army resulted in similar, if more compressed, consequences in countries like Poland, Czechoslovakia, and Hungary. Only in Yugoslavia did a sociology autonomous of state and party control emerge. Marxist and critical, theoretic in substance but empirical in focus, Yugoslav sociology had to defend itself against inane denigration in the east, and incomprehension in the west.

The decomposition of Stalinism and the growth of productive capacity in the state socialist regimes have altered the situation. In Poland and Czechoslovakia, a suppressed sociological tradition often Social Democratic in inspiration was reborn. In Hungary, while the aging Lukacs labors away at his treatises, his younger disciples do empirical sociology. The cross-currents of Communist politics at times silence a sociology which has refused to become a sloganized exegesis on party programs, but the intellectual territory liberated by the sociologists has not all been lost. The resilience and honesty of sociology in eastern Europe owes much, alas, to the Communist technocrats' need for reliable information as a mode of extending and consolidating their rule. The increasing complexity of problems of administration, distribution, and political manipulation in societies now entering the advanced stages of industrialization, requirements for reliable data on consumer preference, educational choice, occupational discipline, and political opinion, leave the technocrats little choice but to encourage a certain kind of sociology. Once housed in Moscow only in the Institute of Philosophy of the Academy of Sciences (an Institute not so long ago notorious among the learned in the Soviet Union as an assemblage of ideological hacks), sociology now has found other quarters. Moscow now also has an Institute of Concrete Social Research. In Akadamsgorod near Novosibirsk computerized and mathematical models of behavior are advanced with an ardor we experienced in this country two decades ago. The technocratic cultivation of sociology, however, carries danger with it: suppose the sociologists do not confine themselves to the execution of technocratic directives for data collection but begin, instead, to think critically about society? This has happened in Czechoslovakia, Hungary, and Poland, and is a constant internal threat to the Soviet Union's intellectual controllers. The Varna Congress, indeed, was a gigantic mechanism of defense against this possibility.

The first line of defense was left to the Bulgarians. Their organization of the Congress, if it can be dignified by that word, did not seem to have been planned in Moscow (many Soviet colleagues were revulsed by the local arrangements). Among the most retrograde of regimes in Eastern Europe, the Bulgarians probably acted instinctively. The impression of openness had to be given, but the effects of genuine openness had to be minimized, since they could not be entirely eliminated. Masterful only in their disorganization, lack of coherence, and inability to deal with simple matters, our Bulgarian hosts may indeed in large part have acted in good faith. The result was as good as purposeful sabotage.

The combined talents of early Koestler and Waugh could barely do justice to the scene (it was hardly worth the art of a Victor Serge.) The participants from eastern Europe were, largely, lodged in hotels ten kilometers distant from the resort town of Gold Strand, where the rest of us were housed. There was no list of participants with their local addresses, although there was under the counter of a Balkan tourist desk a preliminary list of bookings arranged by hotels—an inaccurate one. Only one hotel had telephones in its rooms, and in any event, receptionists and clerks at the other hotels were usually unable to find the names of their guests on their registers. A bus service did shuttle back and forth between Gold Strand and the Congress meeting sites at the Palace of Culture and Sport and the university in Varna. The eastern Europeans, however, had buses only at the beginning of sessions and meal times. It was not easy for them to get to

Gold Strand for those extracurricular talks which, frequently, constitute the life of a scholarly congress.

The participants had been instructed, in the strictest of terms, to ship their papers in advance to the Bulgarian organizing committee. Those who did quite often never saw their papers again. Some never arrived, others were given out at random, so that none were left for the sessions for which they were intended, and still others were strewn about in such disorder that hours of searching by their authors were required to extricate them from the pile. Four out of every five summaries in the printed volume of abstracts were by authors from eastern Europe. The daily Congress Bulletin, issued in Bulgarian, French, and English, invariably stressed the contributions from eastern Europe. The Bulletin outdid itself, however, on the second day. There was no room, its (anonymous) editors explained, for conveying changes of room, modifications of programs, and other notices—these were too numerous. We were favored, instead, with the full text of the address of greeting delivered the day before by His Excellency, the Prime Minister of the Bulgarian People's Republic. To these difficulties of communication were added others. The Italians who constituted the secretariat of the International Sociological Association took several days of negotiation during the Congress to obtain a bulletin board in the Palace of Culture. Their request had been agreed to by the Bulgarian organizers but the Palace personnel simply removed it. The gallery was crowded during the opening address by the Prime Minister with persons who wore Party membership buttons, but local students and the local populace could not attend the discussions: entrance to the buildings was by Congress badge only. Meanwhile, room allocations were constantly shifted about, two groups were sometimes assigned to one room, and at one point the distinguished Egyptian sociologist (in Parisian exile) Abdel-Malek, had to convene his group on the floor of a corridor.

Large groups were given small rooms and small groups found themselves in large ones.

There were other episodes. The Prime Minister had invited some 300 of the participants (chosen from among session chairmen, rapporteurs, and the like) to a closed reception— but the Organizing Committee had printed the time and place of the event on the program. Bulgarian police and plainclothesmen took the invitations at the foot of a hotel staircase (some were promptly handed over the bannister behind their backs to uninvited sociologists), and pushed back hundreds of others. Professor Roland Robertson was thrown down the staircase and a German teaching assistant who remonstrated with the police was rather thoroughly roughed up. No apologies were tendered, but the Bulgarian sociologists did plead with their foreign colleagues to treat the incident as a "provocation." By this time, however, the irritation and disgust of many of the participants at the course of the Congress were quite audible, and even the least perceptive of our hosts began to wish us gone. The International Hotel, where the reception was held, reverted to its normal status before the sociologists had left. A previous set of guests had been thrown out of their rooms and transferred to other hotels upon our arrival (scheduled, after all, only two years in advance). Now a curious mixture of inelegant German tourists and stocky indigenous bigshots filled its lobby. The latter were well protected: the detectives I'd first seen with the Prime Minister were very visible. Their comportment was such as to suggest the "defense of socialism" was quite consonant with classically Turkish manners: they made themselves conspicuous by shoving aside women at the elevators. The Bulgarian élite enjoyed ostentatious privileges and showed hopelessly provincial and *pétit bourgeois* taste. The bigshots drove about with motorcycle police escorts who compelled all traffic on broad and empty roads to stop while they passed: their limousines had white chintz curtains. Pathetic

Bulgaria! Like many nations once ruled by the Turks, its people seemed broken in culture and spirit. And to Orientalism was added Stalinism.

Was there any scholarly value at all to the conference? A considerable number of sociologists had anticipatory doubts, and stayed away. Aron, Bell, Bendix, Bottomore, Cazeneuve, Dahrendorf, Etzioni, Gellner, Gouldner, Lefebvre, Habermas, Pizzorno, Supek, and Worsley were among the absentees. Adam Schaff, apparently swept aside by the recent Polish campaign against "revisionists" (and Jews), was missing. His Warsaw colleague Zygmunt Bauman had chosen the road of exile—or return—to Tel Aviv and did not travel to Bulgaria. The absences were very regrettable. Some of the missing scholars are neo-Marxists, and their encounter with a dogmatic orthodoxy would have had educational consequences for the younger sociologists from the state socialist regimes, who were present in great numbers. Some are decidedly ex-Marxists, and the sharpness of their positions would have enlivened the Congress. In the event, discussion was befogged, and I had the impression of swimming in a gelatinous substance. Talk was cheap but genuine controversy was rare.

Sociologists in no country are conspicuous for their reluctance to speak, and the relative absence of conflict remains to be explained. Harangues there were aplenty. A pseudo-Marxist aggressivity marked the contributions of many participants from eastern and central Europe, so much so that many seemed quite unable to distinguish between intellectual polemic and a level of discourse which would have stupefied Agitprop cadres at a party school. We also had to bear with those who, in the midst of discussions, read from totally irrelevant prepared texts. Chairmen who had prepared their sessions for months in advance were at the last minute asked to accommodate just another three or five more Soviet or Bulgarian papers. What I have termed pseudo-Marxism is less an ideology than it is a catechism or an incantation.

Pseudo-Marxism is also a sociological phenomenon. The groups from the state socialist regimes were quite profoundly divided, and that division was in itself a mitigating element at the Congress. There were, initially, differences of intelligence: even Stalinism and Brezhnevism in their several varieties have been unable to alter certain variations in human genetic inheritance. I had the impression that the more dogmatic colleagues from these societies were in fact the less gifted ones. Factors of social inheritance also played their part. Among the Bulgarians, the Communist Germans, and some of the elder Russians, recruits to "intellectual" activity from Party organs were quite obviously not from academic or professional families, not offspring of the intelligentsia, but sons and daughters of manual workers. Upward social mobility, in state socialist regimes as well as our own, extracts its own cultural price: the crudity and historical short-sightedness of the pseudo-Marxists expressed a lack of education, an inability to work with the complexities of a tradition—even their own. I recall a moment when Alain Touraine reminded a session that not all revolutions were made by Leninist-type parties: the French one had not been. Cultural and intellectual isolation must also have played their part in engendering vulgarity: the Poles, the Czechs, and some of the Russians have traveled widely, as have the Rumanians. The Communist Germans rarely get to the Sorbonne or Berkeley, and most of them have not been to Frankfurt, Goettingen, or West Berlin. Their more sophisticated spokesmen (Hahn, Steiner, Braunreuter) were interesting. The others should have been told by a regime jealous of its international standing to shut up.

Intellectually, pseudo-Marxism consists of a few elementary propositions, repeated compulsively, and quite wrong. The theme of the Congress was "Contemporary and Future Societies, Prediction and Social Planning." The pseudo-Marxists were insistent on a rigid distinction between state socialist and other societies. The "laws" of development applicable to the one type could not be applied to the others. None gave thought to the possibility that there are no "laws" of social development at all, simply successions of historical structures with different degrees of responsiveness to conscious historical will. This was surprising, since their conception of "law" in their own societies depicted their respective Communist parties as the sole legitimate and effective incarnations of human historical will. To this was linked the assertion that the working class (exceedingly vaguely defined) in fact exercised power and held productive property in these societies. I did ask a Communist German how we could understand this last claim: were there not, as mediating instances, state, party, the division of labor, authority structure in the work process, and differential allocation of the social product? The answer was brief: the question was a "theoretical and not an empirical one." As I heard it, I could not help but think of the German phrase, *auf die Gesinnung kommt es an,* it all depends upon one's attitude.

The "laws" of social development for the state socialist regimes set the context for the interpretation of some of their empirical research. Since these societies were "victoriously" developing their productive and moral capacities, they had no conflicts. Occasional hindrances to development represented insufficient assimilation of the official social morality. Critical studies of bureaucracy were few, although the Vice-Rector of the Komsomol Academy in Moscow did report on a study of popular attitudes to local bureaucracy which suggested something other than perfect satisfaction. The pseudo-Marxists, then, used empirical research to "verify" laws which were nothing else than programmatic exercises in historical voluntarism. The Marxist analysis of production relations, of super-structure, in their own regimes was lacking. The central Marxist idea of contradiction as a category for apprehending history was not in their possession.

In the circumstances, the pseudo-Marxist contribution to administrative technology in their own countries was nil. States and societies cannot be governed by recourse to a few elementary dicta, particularly when the dicta are false. This difficulty constituted an opportunity for the more serious sociologists in these countries. I would divide them into two groupings, although it was sometimes difficult to tell these apart. We did meet no small number of colleagues who were overtly or covertly critical, even oppositional, with respect to the exercise of power in state socialism. One distinguished younger Soviet colleague told me, "Marx died a long while ago; much has happened since then, not least in what some refer to as 'bourgeois' thought." From another country, a participant explained his silence: "Under present political conditions at home, I cannot speak my mind, and I will not say things I do not believe." Criticism, for these sociologists, consists in describing social reality. They cannot, in general, deal with it as a political totality—but they can and often do say enough to illuminate the whole by dealing with its parts. The Poles and the Czechs were, as we might have expected, masters of the art: there is evidence that they are being joined by an increasing number of sociologists from the Soviet Union.

What kind of studies do come from those with a minimally critical attitude? I heard, or read, accounts of social mobility in the socialist societies which left no doubt as to the existence there of a stratified system of social relations—a class system based on state property. There was an intelligent Polish contribution on workers' participation in economic planning as a goal of Polish socialism which left no doubt that the goal was very remote of attainment. An inquiry on religion in the Soviet Union pointed to its decline, but also left open the question of the universality of religious aspiration. Studies of this sort were distinguished from the pseudo-Marxist harangues not alone by their attention to nuance and detail but by an entirely superior intellectual level, a realization of the difficult relationship between theory and fact, a refusal to assimilate reflection to political exhortation. There are, of course, limits which these colleagues cannot as yet force. Moreover, as they succeed in developing a valid sort of sociological inquiry, will they not contribute to the consolidation of the state socialist technocracy, by rendering it more efficient? The answer, unfortunately, is yes. I have written of two groupings among those sociologists in eastern Europe who inhabit our world of discourse. The second is not so much critical as pragmatic. Some, to borrow a term from von Hayek not heard much recently, are "scientistic." The enormous development of the culture of mathematics and the physical sciences in the Soviet Union has induced some sociologists there (the parallels with our own recent academic experience are striking) to experiment with the mathematical and formal descriptions of social process. Lenin's famous dictum, that socialism equals the Soviets plus electrification, has a new Soviet version: socialism equals the Soviet state equipped with computers. In a regime which has not begun to solve its enormous problems of bureaucratic ossification, the reduction of some problems to terms susceptible of theoretic solution by computers is obviously a political priority. The Communist Germans, too, have made much of computerization: the aged Ulbricht himself, some years ago, took a three-day crash course in programming. They, however, cannot yet begin to relinquish the notion of controlling all social processes from the center. The Soviet interest in computerization of social research seems to reflect a political decision—however contested and however uncertain—to allow some areas of society a relative autonomy. It is of a piece with economic decentralization and the conscious development of a socialist market. The appearance, for the first time at a World Congress of Sociology, of Soviet sociologists of this type went largely unremarked. It is a phenomenon which may in the end be more significant than the crudities inflicted upon us by some of their colleagues. The establishment of a framework for the study of these processes presupposes a prior intellectual decision that they are relatively independent. The license to study them implies a political decision to use manipulative rather than coercive means of control. Those regimes which have an intelligentsia closer to contemporary western culture are precisely those which have been persuaded to move toward the cultivation of empirical sociology—and for technocratic reasons.

What about the western sociologists? Many of our stars were there, and they were accompanied by a good many intellectual footmen. The diversity of topics covered by the western papers was immense: family, community, social psychiatry, work and organization, politics, methodology, and much more. Indeed, there was no one western sociology represented at the Congress. A fragmented social world has been reflected in a fragmented social science. Conflicting and contrasting assumptions of social nature, its malleability and manipulability, infused the contributions. Pluralism is a good thing, no doubt, but the absence of much debate as to the essential nature of our society casts doubt on our intellectual seriousness. In that sense, we promulgated distorted antitheses of the absurd simplifications of our state socialist brethren. There a terrifying uniformity, here an intolerable confusion. Perhaps, however, the confusion is willed: a certain kind of categorical pluralism allows every man to take sociology in his own hand. In the final analysis, this is a caricature of a free market—but the market society has long since disappeared in history, to be replaced by its technocratic and bureaucratic successors. Western sociology is indeed confused, but it has redeeming elements. Bureaucracy and technocracy have become the objects of inquiry for some who seek to make contemporary the large ideas of that sociological tradition which had early industrial society as its field. Inquiry of this sort, of course, inevitably becomes political: the pluralism of sociology cannot justify, for any sociologist, a flight from politics.

Political voices from the westerners during the Congress were not entirely silent. Some, like myself and a few allies, attempted to engage the pseudo-Marxists and above all the authentic ones from the state socialist regimes in dialogue. Publicly, this proved almost impossible. Privately, over Slivowitz, we fared better. At the very least, we managed to trade our books and articles for caviar and vodka: the Soviet and general Communist demand for printed matter was very great. A note of political pathos was added by the group of younger sociologists who managed to hold a few meetings on the sociology of sociology. Was international sociology at the service of the international power élite, they asked? The answer is that, in general, it has very little to offer to that élite. Nevertheless, the younger Dutch, Germans, and Americans who organized the meeting struck a responsive chord. Hundreds of colleagues rushed to inscribe themselves on their mailing list. I asked about their co-ordinating committee and learned that of its five initial members, one was a young Bulgarian and one a student from Niger attached to a Bulgarian university. Given the critical tenor of these informal meetings, and the generally rigid attitude of the Bulgarians, it did seem surprising to some of us that the organizers obtained the use of a car and other facilities from our hosts. Perhaps—as they thought—the Bulgarian intellectual opposition was at work. Perhaps there were other, less comforting, explanations. The lists, after being posted in the lobby of the Palace of Culture for all to see, were later removed by the American and Québeçois members of the committee. I would have wished for much more criticism of our technocratic reality—in the neo-capitalist and state socialist regimes—on the Congress program, but it was good to see that the critical element in sociology broke through in the form of this radical group. Their level of rationality contrasted favorably with that of the radical caucus at the September annual meeting of the American Sociological Association. There, radical professors were denounced for writing radical books, for "not doing anything," and one leaflet declared that radical sociologists were henceforth to be considered the main enemies of radicalism. Reminders of the inanities of the American scene were not, however, entirely missing. One younger American described Manson as an exemplar of a new communal way of living, and portrayed as components of an American avant-garde the "fat people's liberation movement" and the "gay people's liberation movement." The chairman of the session did interrupt to ask that the terms be explained: he lived in Paris and knew what they meant, but he doubted that they were current in Bulgaria.

My last image of the Congress was at the airport in Sofia. Sixty of the French had been bumped off an overbooked flight to western Europe and had been told that they would have to spend the night in Sofia while alternative routings were found. They made a terrible fuss, and in the end, Bulgarian Airlines whistled up a special jet to fly them directly to Paris that night. I congratulated them on their success: it was no doubt the first demonstration in Sofia in decades. And probably the last for some decades to come, we agreed.

Our own plane was a Lufthansa Boeing, with drinks and newspapers available before we had crossed the border. An airborne fragment of our own reality, but a perfectly representative one: crowded, hurried, efficient in the small things, and in no small measure tinny. Perhaps, I thought, society has begun to escape even analysis and reflection, much less mastery. The early sociologists were indistinguishable from political philosophers or philosophers of history. They examined society to find possibilities for the fulfillment of human nature, to inquire into the historical chances of a newer and truer *polis*. Our own generation has renounced these aims. Empirical sociology is largely a strained gloss on a reality we do not believe we can change. Max Weber, asked early in this century why he studied society, said that he did it to see how much he could stand. (*"Wieviel ich aushalten kann."*) We lack even this ironic acknowledgment of individual moral purpose, and our search for a new public good has been halting and ineffective where we have indulged it. The word *indulged* is frightening, but I shall let it stay. What was once the highest force behind intellectual activity is now a mere psychological oddity, a matter of personal whim, a moral idiosyncrasy. The most desperate and the least satisfactory aspects of our Congress were, however, perhaps the truest ones: the effort, beyond the depiction of things as they are, to find a moral and political vocabulary to describe a world society irrational and oppressive. The self-designated party of revolution in the state socialist societies, however, has become a party of the institutionalized revolution—apologists for old tyrannies writ new. Its most intelligent and rational subjects are agonizingly aware of their servitude. We do not embrace our own, but we do not seem to be transcending it, either. Our own younger revolutionaries think that they can start history anew, and so fall easy victim to its most trivial ruses. A happier synthesis may await us in the future—but international conferences, upon reflection, are not always conducive to thought's success in its tasks.

IV. POLITICS

David Riesman's Image of

Politics

I do not find it easy to write about any aspect of Riesman's work. Perhaps unfairly, I hold the author responsible: himself a master of ambiguity, he cannot be surprised that his colleagues are ambivalent about his thought. The ambiguity of his writing, and the ambivalence of my reaction, are most pronounced in the sphere of politics. Riesman appears to be developing a new image of the political process; in fact, he has projected his own values into the analysis. The most challenging of the traditions of social science tells us that total objectivity is impossible, whilst enjoining upon us as much of it as we can attain. Riesman meets this challenge no worse than the rest of us, and better than many: he does not pretend to detachment and he is aware that behind the instruments of social research there are human beings. Inevitably, however, a critique of Riesman's view of politics entails a critique of Riesman's values. As critic, I claim no warrant for my questions other than that they seem to me just;[1] it would be ungracious to record them without ac-

1. I hope that my own political values are sufficiently clear from the text. If not, they are set forth in: "Monarchs and Sociologists," *Sociological Review*,

251

knowledging Riesman's patent willingness to be scrutinized in this way.

Riesman does not employ ambiguity as a stylistic device. His style, indeed, is ostensibly clear. It is usually possible to see what he means—in any given sentence. It is the total effect that is ambiguous: his allusions are often irrelevant, his analogies imprecise, his thoughts expressed in a manner apparently informal but actually casual. (The contrast with his earlier published work is striking. There[2] his sequences of thought were most orderly, his evidence more exact, his meaning unequivocal. Perhaps the disarray that is so disturbing, from 1950 onward, is the price of greater flexibility.)

Riesman's work often lack explicit factual reference. Hardly, in *The Lonely Crowd*, does he attempt to identify in any determinate way the strata and groups of which he writes.[3] His historical examples are randomized where they should be selective, and his contemporary examples are selective where they should be randomized. Moreover, the latter usually consist of the received data of American social

---

Vol. 3, No. 1 (1955): "Die Intellektuellen in der Gegenwärtigen Politik der Vereinigten Staaten," *Zeitschrift f. Politik*, Vol. 2, No. 2 (1955); "Science, Ideology and Dialogue," *Commentary*, Vol. 22, No. 6 (1956); "Nothing Land," *Encounter*, Vol. 11, No. 1 (1958); "America: a Partial View," *Commentary*, Vol. 26, No. 1 (1958); "Politics and Abundance," *Dissent*, Vol. 5, No. 3 (1958); "Social Constraints and Academic Freedom," *Universities and Left Review*, Vol. 5 (1958); "Friends and Enemies," *Twentieth Century*, May, 1959; "The Year Zero of British Socialism," *Antioch Review*, Summer, 1960; "'Empiricism' and British Politics," *Commentary*, February, 1961. I also deal systematically with the problem of ideology in a forthcoming UNESCO Trend Report (in the series "Current Sociology").

2. See, for instance, Riesman, "Equality and Social Structure," *Journal of Legal and Political Sociology*, Vol. 1 (1942), 72–95.

3. *The Lonely Crowd* (New Haven: Yale University Press, 1950), pp. 293 ff., contains some very vague suggestions. It is interesting that C. Wright Mills, whose appendixes are full of factual data, has been roundly criticized for being deficient on this account; Riesman—who has no appendixes—has hardly been challenged.

science, and these presuppose the kind of social-psychological analysis they are supposed to corroborate. I find philistine in the extreme the use of the term "impressionistic" or "literary" as opprobrious by social scientists—but surely the point of sociological interpretation is that it does not dissolve the facts but, recognizing their integrity, goes beyond them.

Riesman's ambiguity, the way in which his interpretations press away the data, serves the moral purposes that (quite properly) pervade his entire work. The author has written of his "moral experimentalism," [4] of his belief that values can be understood and effective only in context. He is quite frank: he employs differing moral emphases with different interlocutors. His moral lability can be justified by its instrumental functions for his total moral system. But it is disconcerting that his assertions about reality, no less than his directives for dealing with it, continually shift. His "experimentalism" appears to have been extended to his image of society and he advances, particularly about politics, seemingly contradictory notions of its structure.

All moral philosophies rest on some examination (if only a hasty or unacknowledged one) of factual possibility. A flexible moral philosophy, as Riesman envisages it, must deal with the complexities of an industrial society. Riesman asks two distinct moral questions of society. Does it allow the realization of my values and (if not), what values ought I to develop to meet limiting circumstances? These questions appear, at times, to have fused—and in their fusion, to have affected Riesman's approach to society's factual complexity. He seems to have moved (unconsciously) from the perception that a highly differentiated society requires a highly differentiated morality to the assumption that a highly differentiated morality requires a shifting image of the social structure.

4. Riesman, "Values in Context," *Individualism Reconsidered* (Glencoe: The Free Press, 1954), p. 23.

But if there are factual necessities that impinge on morality it does not follow that moral necessities can legitimately impinge on our view of fact. The political implications of Riesman's philosophical ambiguity, in the end, shape his view of political process.

Ideologies are not simply falsifications of experience; they are, rather, selective interpretations of it. Riesman's image of politics is not without a certain internal logic, but it is the logic of his ideology, which leads him into a number of factual contradictions and inhibits his exploration of the implications of a number of perceptions. An image of politics, meanwhile, contains implicit as well as explicit assumptions: the sorts of thing it emphasizes are often no more important to the total impression it conveys than the things it leaves out. The aim of the analysis that follows is to uncover the internal logic and the implicit assumptions of Riesman's view of politics: these are, indeed, not very far from the surface.

POLITICAL THOUGHT AND POLITICAL REALITY

Riesman has a considerable awareness that thought about politics is itself political. He sees social science in danger of immobilization between the two poles of too much and too little ideological commitment.[5] He praises the disinterestedness of disinterested curiosity; but he warns that curiosity of an uncommitted sort, fixated on the present, may unwittingly serve some very interested parties—if only by omitting to

5. "I don't want us to become any more influential than we are, lest out of piety and politics we might censor our curiosities," in Riesman, "Psychological Types and National Character," *American Quarterly*, Vol. 5 (1953), 326–327. "What we do find is that American scholars, despite our country's tradition of pluralism and foreign study, are for the most part readily enlisted in an era of total war and total loyalty," in Riesman, *Constraint and Variety in American Education* (New York: Doubleday Anchor, 1958), p. 103.

ask critical questions.[6] He holds that knowledge has "long-run healing qualities,"[7] but he cannot see how those who know can establish contact with those who need knowledge most.[8] Briefly, he sees the multiple involvements of knowledge with contemporary American politics—but, for all the good sense and insight of his methodological views,[9] he cannot identify an underlying pattern in these involvements.

Similarly, he is reluctant to assert a firm conclusion on the scientific and political status of survey-type research. He criticizes the ideological assumptions underlying much public opinion polling: this exemplifies the "nineteenth century liberal's approach to the individual as a social atom."[10] He began his work on polling and interviewing by noting that it might well convey an illusion of influence to the powerless[11]—but more recently, he has settled for the therapeutic worth of the interview. Despite the pretensions of all concerned, it may do nothing at all by way of affecting political decision, but it is at least a dialogue between the classes, "in which both parties gain in esteem and understanding and nobody loses."[12] More recently still, he has attempted to convert some of the liabilities arising from the use of a stand-

6. "By and large, the people whose function it is to think, under the division of labor, are over-impressed by what they think about," in Riesman, "Some Observations on Community Plans and Utopia," *Individualism Reconsidered*, p. 77.

7. "Psychological Types and National Character," p. 327.

8. "I speak from the point of view of the individual, for whom the political framework of society has become opaque, bewildering or uncertain. The framework and the individual's own tasks in relation to it are not presently obvious—or, if obvious, are not teachable by those to whom they are obvious," in Riesman, *Faces in the Crowd* (New Haven: Yale University Press, 1952), p. 32.

9. Riesman, "Some Observations on Social Science Research," *Individualism Reconsidered*, pp. 467–483.

10. Riesman, "The Meaning of Opinion," *Individualism Reconsidered*, p. 495.

11. *Ibid.*, pp. 495–496.

12. Riesman, "The Sociology of the Interview," *The Midwest Sociologist*, I (1955), 15.

ardized interview procedure by a semi-skilled field force into assets: by showing that the intellectual and emotional reactions to the instrument were susceptible of meaningful interpretation outside of its formal framework.[13] But it is still not entirely clear how Riesman would balance off the social and scientific liabilities and assets of survey research as a whole.

Riesman's concern with the survey and the interview follows, of course, from his interest in the role of opinion and personality in the political process. Here, again, Riesman is ambiguous: initially we cannot tell whether he considers political psychology the centerpiece, an indispensable component, or simply an appendage of the analysis of politics. Without much difficulty, we can find assertions of all three positions in his work.[14]

Riesman's interest in the way people relate themselves to politics, his assessment of the efficacy of their political "styles" in terms of their own experiences and capacities, shows a

13. See his contribution to Paul Lazarsfeld and Wagner Thielens, Jr., *The Academic Mind* (Glencoe: The Free Press, 1958).

14. ". . . psychologists sometimes show a tendency to overestimate the importance of individual personality, or of the 'field' created by a number of personalities, while overlooking the bearing of a long historical development of a structural and institutional sort, to which these personalities, unless quite crazy, will defer, at least up to a point," in Riesman, "Toward an Anthropological Science of Law and the Legal Profession," *Individualism Reconsidered*, p. 461. See also ". . . many people today flee from the realities of power into psychological interpretations of social behavior in order to avoid the challenge of contemporary political faiths or to restore a wished-for malleability to politics by reliance on a new analytical gadget. Nevertheless, it should be equally obvious that a political realism that ignores the dimensions of character, that ignores how people interpret power configurations on the basis of their psychic needs, will only be useful in short-run interpretations and not always even there," *The Lonely Crowd*, p. 179. And see also, "The struggle of classes and societies may therefore be viewed, to some extent, as a struggle among different characterological adaptations to the situation created by the dominance of a given mode of insuring conformity," *The Lonely Crowd*, p. 31.

sensitive concern for the nuances of individual experience in the mass society. But it is not an image of political process as such; rather, it deals with the psychological forces that can be attached to or detached from politics—for reasons outside the individual's control or awareness. "Politics seems to me increasingly carried on as a *marriage de convenance* between traditional political institutions and irrational psychological pressures." [15] The analogy of the *marriage de convenance* is genteel; but there are times when Riesman suggests that a variety of social constraints and interests exercise a shot-gun function in wedding personality to political decision.[16] In any case, his argument on the accidental and external character of the relations between personality and politics is inconsistent with his larger analysis of the emergence of socially standardized character types in history; here, clearly, politics and political institutions constitute one of the forces acting on the development of personality: he shows, for instance, that the other-directed character is made to order for a bureaucratic career.[17]

The burden of Riesman's analysis, however, is clear: he frequently uses psychology as a mode of apprehending the very essence of the political process. This is not simply a matter of methodological emphasis. It is quite possible to employ psychology to extend our understanding of politics without asserting that explanations of an institutional sort are insufficient; Riesman goes beyond a mere enlargement of our vision. He often sees decisive social conflicts being fought out in the psychological sphere, within and between personalities. (And it can be said, at this point, that he seems to think values constitutive of social institutions, a view that

15. *Faces in the Crowd*, p. 35.
16. See the entire analysis in "The Intellectuals and the Discontented Classes," Daniel Bell (ed.), *The New American Right* (New York: Criterion Books, Inc., 1955), pp. 56–90.
17. *The Lonely Crowd*, pp. 203–204.

opens the way for his psychological analysis.) This is expressed most clearly in his celebrated dictum: the class struggle has been replaced by the characterological struggle.[18]

Of course, Riesman denies exclusive status to his dictum and to the analyses it implies. But it is his beginning point, and carries with it much of what follows. Even when Riesman attributes the characteristics of contemporary political attitudes to the limitations of the situation, to factors given in the social structure, he sometimes does so in a psychological vocabulary—thus the claim that the "crisis mood" of contemporary politics[19] inhibits the development of new political styles. And although he sets these styles in their historical context,[20] he as quickly takes them out of it. His description of the reserve army of the apathetic points to their susceptibility to certain kinds of political appeal,[21] just as he holds that the other-directed characters are sometimes likely to accept the leadership of the political primitives.[22] Riesman does acknowledge, of course, that long-term structural developments will determine the political use to which this psychological raw material is put.[23] But his analysis of long-term structural developments also tends to dissolve these into psychological processes: we read of anxious businessmen, oversensitive politicians, of the eager and the apathetic, the generous and the resentful. Formally, the characterological struggle merges with others; effectively, it is for Riesman the ultimate locus of political decision.

18. *Ibid.*, pp. 31 ff.
19. *Ibid.*, p. 178.
20. *Ibid.*, pp. 178–179: "If politics is a ballet on a stage set by history, style tells us neither whence the dancers come nor whither they move but only in what manner they play their parts and how the audience responds."
21. *Ibid.*, p. 190.
22. *Ibid.*, pp. 231–232.
23. See the analysis of Gibbons, *Faces in the Crowd*, 220: "The social conditions of America in the next years will probably be more important in shaping Gibbons' political role than the compulsions springing from his personal tragedy."

Why Riesman's preoccuption with interview technique, rather than with the problem (which he surely recognizes) of giving contemporary effect to the liberal aspirations for an informed and enlightened citizenry? Why his fascination with the varieties of personal expression within a system of social constraints, rather than with the structure of those constraints? Riesman's choice of problem has an obvious source: it is the old and honorable liberal concern with the fate of the individual in society. It is that concern, however, devoid of the will to alter society—very possibly, as we shall see, because devoid of the capacity to do so. The want of external social focus is unbalancing: the result is an up-to-date and subjective individualism. Unable to consider the maximization of the conditions of individual freedom, Riesman turns to the dimensions of the individual's inner prison. Unwilling, however, to renounce the view that the individual can affect history, Riesman converts history into psychology —but thereby gives the individual only a perverse kind of freedom.

POLITICS IN GENERAL

Riesman's interest is almost exclusively in contemporary America—and he gives it a universal justification by supposing that other societies must inevitably develop the same structure and the same problems. On the face of it, his view of politics is somewhat broader: he draws on America's nineteenth-century past, refers to western Europe, to societies totalitarian and underdeveloped. Unfortunately, the analysis is too familiar; he seems to project, backwards and outwards, the analytical conceptions he has developed to deal with the American present.

He depicts nineteenth-century America as a good deal less complex than our own society. Then, we are told, politics and economics were kept separate: there were limits to the powers of early capitalist enterprise.[24] Individuals had clear notions of their material interests; the familiar notions of "self-help" allowed them to pursue these with all the energies their superegos could mobilize. Conflict between groups and classes was open and direct: few had difficulty locating themselves in the social structure.

The view presents a number of difficulties. The separation of politics from other spheres of social life (in particular, the economy) will not strike many as an accurate characterization of the nineteenth century in America. Did not America, as well as Europe, know politically committed artists in this period? In Europe, of course, there were old elites for the new middle classes to contend with; in America, class structure was constituted by several overlapping strata, one rising after the other. It is unclear why Riesman supposes that the "harmony between character and politics" [25] was closer then than now—particularly since he holds that both character and politics have changed. And he does recognize one of the origins of other-direction in the old acquisitive society, with its own fusion of business and pleasure.[26] The point of Riesman's essay in history is to illuminate his characterological analysis; fair enough, but it does represent a distinct crudification of history.

Of more interest is Riesman's treatment of totalitarianism. In opposition to apocalyptic views of totalitarian systems, he insists that the modes of resistance to them were and are utterly trivial: "apathy, corruption, free enterprise, crime." [27] A good part of his argument is intended, however, to justify the ideological apathy of the American people: this Riesman

24. *The Lonely Crowd,* pp. 191 ff., and "Some Observations on Community Plans and Utopia," p. 92.
25. *Faces in the Crowd,* p. 32.
26. *Ibid.,* p. 381.
27. Riesman, "Some Observations on the Limits of Totalitarian Powers, *Individualism Reconsidered,* p. 416.

sees as a prophylaxis against totalitarian infection. Yet Riesman contradicts himself—on the one hand, he attempts to
cut totalitarianism down to size, picturing it as just another
and more effective naked power system; on the other, he
uses it to exemplify the dangers of ideological commitment.
The Cromwellian Bolsheviks, indeed, he finds more danger-
ous than the Nazis[28]—overlooking the ideological character
of Nazism.

Riesman's difficulties with totalitarianism seem to have
been produced by his own ideological aims in discussing it:
to warn the intellectuals against overinterpretation[29]—in
effect, against taking their own ideologies too seriously. It is
striking that Riesman's remarks on totalitarianism seem to
have rather less connection with the rest of his analytical system than we might expect. His insight into the structural
determinants of totalitarian success[30] is a plausible and unexceptionable sociological hypothesis. I cannot see why this
discrepancy should exist—possibly the massivity of the totalitarian phenomenon precludes explanations that are too exclusively psychological.

Riesman's view of western European society is straightforward enough: that it has been unlike the United States
(chiefly with respect to the political class struggle and the
differentiation of mass and elite in higher culture), but that

28. *Ibid.*, p. 417.

29. *Ibid.*, p. 415.

30. *Ibid.*, pp. 416–417: "Most large-scale societies will offer a spectrum of
people available for the high-minded, middle-minded, and low-minded
aspects of totalitarian politics, though probably a crisis is necessary to
convert their organization into a fighting revolutionary party with a real
hope of capturing power. That is, the fact that totalitarianism has captured
a country doesn't tell us as much as some observers have supposed about
the character of its total population; the mass base necessary can be far
less than a majority and it can include people of profoundly non-totali-
tarian personalities who have been fooled—to whom the appeal has not
been a deep-going one."

it is increasingly coming to resemble America.[31] Riesman does not, as far as I know, try the opposite hypothesis: that America is beginning to resemble Europe, not vice versa. I think neither hypothesis is correct or, where correct, very relevant. But the negative one is worth trying, not least within Riesman's framework: suppose that other-direction means, for instance, that America is developing a new and shared life style of a kind long since rooted in Europe? [32]

Riesman's remarks about the underdeveloped societies are few, but not irrelevant to this discussion. He supposes that the Soviet Union has every chance of influencing these countries, because it is a model of rapid industrialization.[33] But his explanation is curiously nonpsychological. The Soviet Union may also supply—in the eyes of the new elites in these countries—a model of disciplined national effort. It has the inestimable advantage, moreover, of never having occupied any of them. Riesman advises these countries to postpone industrialization and limit their immediate aspirations to improvement of agricultural technique.[34] This is, in my view, effrontery—and fairly unrealistic effrontery at that: Riesman himself supposes that only industrialization of an advanced type can bring about the possibility of human freedom, and, in any case, the non-industrialized countries have good reason to feel at the mercy of the industrialized ones.

Riesman is somewhat patronizing in discussing the "sloganized xenophobia" and "suspiciousness" of middle-class intellectuals in the mid-Eastern countries.[35] His view that they are compensating for their lack of spiritual community with

---

31. *The Lonely Crowd*, pp. 20–25 and 30–31. Riesman does express some doubts about the extent and speed of the development of other-direction in Europe; but his underlying assumption is clear.

32. See Dwight Macdonald, "America! America!" *Dissent*, 5 (1958), 313–323.

33. *Individualism Reconsidered*, p. 295.

34. *Ibid.*, p. 287.

35. In David Lerner, *The Passing of Traditional Society* (Glencoe: The Free Press, 1958), p. 6.

their countrymen might be applied (indeed, Riesman has applied it) to the American intellectuals.[36] Riesman's remarks about these suspicious mid-Easterners were published after the Western interventions in Suez and the Lebanon, events that may suggest to some that the suspicion was not entirely without reason. Finally, Riesman finds the mobs in the mid-Eastern streets engaged in "pseudo participation" [37] in the politics of their countries. But the leaders who can call out the mobs (Nuri could not, for instance) seem to have distinct advantages over their opponents—and the emergence of the mob as a political force has, in recent years, altered mid-Eastern politics. Whether political and social "enlightenment," which Riesman finds so conspicuously missing in the Middle East, is more prevalent elsewhere is a question he ought to consider, perhaps, at more length.[38] Riesman sees that these populations have been torn out of their traditional context; but his adoption of the term "transitional" [39] to describe them suggests that he visualizes their future development in unilinear terms derived from the Western experience. It is at least as possible that the emergence of these newly activated populations in world politics will alter the future course of Western development.

The chief difficulty in Riesman's view of politics in general is his refusal of a consistent structural view of political systems. Sometimes the inconsistencies follow rather closely upon one another. In one essay, for instance, he describes law as social interest in its own right—and proceeds to praise lawyers at the turn of the century for having the "courage" to endow corporations with powers not envisaged in the

36. Riesman, "Some Relationships between Technical Progress and Social Progress," *Individualism Reconsidered,* p. 288 (footnote on the intellectuals from non-Western countries), and Riesman, "Some Observations on Intellectual Freedom," *ibid.,* pp. 137–138 (on American intellectuals).
37. *The Passing of Traditional Society,* p. 5.
38. *Ibid.,* p. 7.
39. *Ibid.,* pp. 1–15.

statutes and common law decisions.[40] More striking, still, is his view that the organization of the economy in an advanced industrial society has rendered a Marxist analysis out of date: he confuses the specific predictions made by Marx (the theory of polarization of class relations, and of pauperization) with the more general aspects of his theory. (In this connection, it would be helpful if his view of Marxism did not tend to caricature.[41]) In fact, the minutiae of cultural and status differentiation observed by Riesman in contemporary America are not, on his evidence, uncorrelated with variations in class position—if with small variations. But he moves back and forth between assertions about the ultimate determinants of behavior within the system (on this level, he is rather closer to Marxism than is commonly supposed) and statements about processes within its fixed limits.[42] These categories are not joined, and the latter are frequently employed to answer

40. "Toward an Anthropological Science of Law and the Legal Profession," *Individualism Reconsidered*, pp. 447–448.

41. See, for instance, in Riesman, "The Themes of Heroism and Weakness in the Structure of Freud's Thought," the remark: "A good many people embrace Marxism, for instance, in order to make sense of the world, or to contribute to it, and not only because of class consciousness." *Ibid.*, p. 366. Marx, of course, never asserted the contrary. See, also, the observation, "Paradoxically, both Marxism and traditional American individualism conspire to produce this powerful ideology—for that is what it is—of 'self-interest.'" *Faces in the Crowd*, p. 37, footnote. The concept of "interest" in Marx's works is a difficult one, but it is clear that Marx did not mean the kinds of vulgar and atomized conceptions of "interest" found in American individualism.

42. An example may be taken from a casual footnote in Riesman, *Thorstein Veblen* (New York: Charles Scribner's Sons, 1953), p. 86: "James Worthy's studies at Sears show that women have almost universally better morale than men, in industry and office work. Is this because they are more, or less, matter-of-fact? This is reversed where men are in a minority among women—there, they have better morale, whereas of course when women are in a minority among men, they have better morale. It would appear that the emotional relationship to the industrial plant itself may be secondary to sexual and cultural factors." But these sexual and cultural factors are, in turn, determined by the organization of an industrial society and the total role of woman within it.

questions of the former sort. All of this contrasts with the sober and unadorned analysis of social constraint in his earlier work: there the problem of equality is examined in terms of the relationships of power and economic advantage controlling the access to facilities formally free.[43]

POLITICS IN CONTEMPORARY AMERICA

It is about America that Riesman cares, in particular about the spiritual problems of a segment of American society: the urbanized (or suburbanized) upper middle class. He assesses other groups and strata in terms of their proximity to this one, and he supposes that they are all inexorably moving toward the other-directed pattern. Riesman has a point; the upper middle class has managed to imprint itself upon a lower-middle-class nation as the embodiment of the standard human type, so much so that the underprivileged in American society, encountered by Riesman in the Bridgeport trade school, "tend to throw up pathetic caricatures of the American cash customer, or the 'man of distinction' in the whiskey ads." [44] But its cultural superordination is not, according to Riesman, accompanied by equivalent political status.

Some part of the reason for the upper middle class's lack of power, on Riesman's analysis, is its psychology. Its members are fundamentally passive in politics, dutiful consumers of inside dope and occasionally manifesting spectators' paroxysms of excitement at a critical moment in the game—but ideologically thoroughly uncommitted. They occupy command or executive positions in a number of bureaucratic hierarchies. In these, they could exercise not alone influence but power; yet on Riesman's account they shrink from the latter—they prefer being liked to being obeyed.

So striking is the deference of this group, in Riesman's

43. See the article referred to in footnote 2, above.
44. *Faces in the Crowd*, p. 191.

view, that its members allow themselves to be pushed around by those who are politically committed: the indignants, who lag behind them in the flow of historical time, and who are on balance in less advantaged positions in the structure. The indignants, Riesman holds, are now the only Americans capable of generalized political emotion, but they lack the technical skills that could guide their overabundant energies to lasting political success. (And, in any case, they are dying out.)

The present American political system, Riesman thinks, is structurally, if not quite shapeless, very indeterminate. The key to his account of it is his insistence on the historical importance of the characterological struggle. But psychological styles do not in fact compete politically, any more than do emotions or persons: the competition is over access to facilities, control of command positions, over concrete decisions—large and small. Riesman has given us some new, even profound, insight into the psychological content of some of the processes by which opinion is formed, mobilized, and manipulated. But the notion that the dynamics of opinion are decisive, that a plurality of wills resolve themselves into a system of political constraints—this is a new version of the liberal political theory. Here, however, the nonrational (or irrational) individual substitutes for the rational one, and a host of affects, ego and superego functions serve as the scheme's constants in place of the simpler conceptions of liberal psychology.

Of course, Riesman makes the necessary qualifications: the characterological struggle adjoins or overlaps with other ones. But his analysis of these suggests that the characterological struggle is their motor. This is not the first time that psychology has entered political analysis, but the usual route of entry has been through the conception of ideology. Ideology, a system of ideas and values particular to some social group or situation, becomes part of the personality's mode of adaptation: social psychology and sociology have, to date, met most usefully in this sort of analysis. Riesman neglects the formal analysis of ideology; he eschews the category, in general, as an explicit mode of organizing data.

The exclusion of ideology would appear to throw him back upon two sorts of analyses. Either politics is a matter of more or less naked power relations, and/or it is a screen on which personalities project needs derived elsewhere. Not alone does Riesman alternate between these two sorts of approach to Amrican politics; he does not in fact dispense with the analysis of ideology—despite his reiterated contention that America's political system is largely without it. Indeed, his description of the role of "personalities" in recent American politics attributes considerable weight to ideological factors—sometimes, Riesman thinks, the personalization of politics is a consequence of the want of ideological coherence in American society.[45]

Riesman is contradictory on the substantive role of ideology in contemporary American politics. At times, he depicts the American party system as pragmatic in its approach. The parties do not ask for agreement on ideological fundamentals; this contributes to a certain political calm, since ordinary folk do not become excited and exercise their rights of veto.[46] (Riesman uses terms reminiscent of what the less critical Britons say of their own system: American politics rests on a procedural consensus and agreement on short-term goals.[47]) At other times, he is less sure that ideology can be dispensed with. In discussing the spiritual impoverishment of many of his contemporaries, he writes of the "vaguely re-

45. *The Lonely Crowd,* pp. 215 and 231.
46. Riesman, "Individualism Reconsidered," *Individualism Reconsidered,* pp. 36–37.
47. Riesman, "Values in Context," *ibid.,* p. 18.

called, half-dreamlike allegiances and prejudices serving most people for ideology." [48] He recalls, not without nostalgia, the 1930's—when the intellectuals provided the economically discontented classes with an egalitarian ideology they now reject. It is here that he asserts that political demands require ideological elaboration to be effective.[49]

Moreover, he occasionally deplores the absence of critical ideologies in America: he makes a plea for more utopian thinking.[50] He notes that the absence of ideology may produce cynicism as well as political tolerance[51]—and he deplores the intellectually debilitating effects of the cult of neutrality in the social sciences.[52] Even his conception of "secret" or "undefined" marginality in the social structure is, by implication, a critique of some of his sanguine views on the absence of ideology.[53] Where no general systems of ideas allow people to relate themselves to the whole, they may well relapse into secret and peevish modes of differentiating themselves from others rather than tackling the total context of their problems. And he does say that "an ideology can be fashioned out of an anti-ideology, as totalitarian parties have been fashioned out of the anti-party program. And a world is certainly ill-omened in which we must fear the enthusiasm of the young, and prefer their apathy, because we have learned (150 years after Burke) to fear ideas in politics." [54]

Riesman's discussion of the social roles of the mass media is, of course, relevant to his view of ideology in American

48. "Intellectuals and the Discontented Classes," *New American Right*, p. 66.
49. *Ibid.*, p. 79.
50. Riesman, "Some Observations on Community Plans and Utopia," *Individualism Reconsidered*, pp. 70–89.
51. *Ibid.*, p. 75.
52. *Ibid.*, p. 77.
53. Riesman, "Some Observations Concerning Marginality," *Individualism Reconsidered*, pp. 153–165.
54. Riesman, "Some Observations on the Limits of Totalitarian Power," *Individualism Reconsidered*, p. 424.

politics. His assertion that the media constitute a conspiracy to conceal the extent of political indifference in America is startling.[55] He does say that they supply "facts" and "attitudes" differently interpreted by those at different levels in the social structure; indeed, the internal differentiation of the media makes this easier.[56] But these processes allow us to suppose that the media are more effective politically than Riesman asserts, either as sources of or reinforcements for (or both) ideologies consonant with different positions in the social structure. It is difficult to see why he can find no more relevant criticism of the media than that they are insufficiently apolitical.[57]

The heterogeneous, often contradictory, elements in Riesman's image of American politics are part of his central contention; that a system of contending veto groups effectively prevents the concentration of power. Riesman find it difficult, if not impossible, to distinguish the leaders from the led. The veto groups are often coalitions of all characterological types, but they generally adopt the style of the other-directeds. There is an implication, here, of political stratification, but Riesman does not do much with it. Riesman's catalogue of those groups with power[58] presupposes that they share equally in it—but on Riesman's account, this supposition requires qualification.

The veto groups are special groups; each has its territory, and they very rarely seek to influence national decisions. Indeed, the larger and more powerful the veto group, the more restrained its politics. "In the big leagues of the veto groups the limits of power are seldom tested by combat, though this restraint, resting, as I think, on psychological grounds, is easily rationalized in terms of power politics and public rela-

55. *The Lonely Crowd,* p. 225.
56. *Ibid.,* p. 209.
57. *Ibid.,* pp. 232–233.
58. *Ibid.,* pp. 254–255.

tions." [59] But what brings these attitudes into being, if not the stabilization of power relations in the system? Riesman's entire analysis of the genesis of the characterological struggle, it will be recalled, tells us that it is possible only *after* the attainment of a high level of productive stability. Riesman does say that "while it may take leadership to start things running, or to stop them, very little leadership is needed once things are under way." [60] What is under way, however, seems to be precisely that hierarchical system the existence of which Riesman formally denies, and informally acknowledges. He does, after all, write of the "intractability of a mature politics" [61]—by which he quite explicitly means the concentration of the power to make critical decisions outside the hands of those most affected by the decisions. It is, therefore, a *non sequitur* for him to jump from the fact of special local power hierarchies (California, Montana, Virginia) to the conclusion that "any discussion of class and power on the national scene can at best be only an approximation." [62]

Does Riesman give sufficient weight to the postwar interaction of internal and foreign politics? There are times when he adopts an astonishingly simple view: the decisive factor in both the economy and the political system is preparation for war.[63] He has also interpreted, albeit reluctantly, the public opinion poll finding that both elite and mass are willing to fight in Asia—by saying that "a national consensus among all classes can be reached where decisive events, remote from both community leaders and followers, can be decisively interpreted from the top." [64] It is clear that the conception of

59. *Ibid.*, pp. 250–251.
60. *Ibid.*, p. 252.
61. *Faces in the Crowd*, p. 41.
62. *The Lonely Crowd*, p. 253.
63. "Intellectuals and the Discontented Classes," *New American Right*, p. 75.
64. "Orbits of Tolerance, Interviewers, and Elites," *Public Opinion Quarterly*, 20 (1956), 53.

an elite, and of "the top," is not entirely consistent with the veto group theory.

Riesman's own view of America's foreign policy has some interesting overtones. He is in favor of the intelligent and rational conduct of the cold war, but he notes with some distress that the question of appeasement "now becomes more insistent intellectually even while it becomes outlawed politically." [65] He is aware that the recent problem of civil liberties is inextricably bound to the reaction of the populace to international tension. He notes that not popular will but institutional guarantees and elite resistance have prevented the total erosion of civil liberties.[66] This, he supposes, has brought about an alliance between the intellectuals and the enlightened conservatives against the newly risen masses. But the enlightened conservatives and the unenlightened masses appear to share many of the same foreign policy goals, however much they disagree on means. Riesman simply does not deal with this dilemma; it is for him one of the facts of political life, within which and not about which analysis proceeds.

Meanwhile, Riesman has promulgated a rather idyllic picture of an American business system devoted to organizational morale, external public relations, and conspicuous production—to nearly everything, that is, but profit. He insists on the inner uncertainty of the businessmen in the face of their intellectual and political critics, but he tends to overlook their real political experiences in the New Deal and the Fair Deal.[67] Riesman argues that the intellectuals have to some considerable extent impressed the businessmen, although few intellectuals these days seem to be at work on a critique of business. In any case, the general improvement

65. "Intellectuals etc.," *New American Right*, p. 79.
66. *Ibid.*, p. 78.
67. *The Lonely Crowd*, p. 250: "If businessmen *feel* weak and dependent, they *are* weak and dependent."

in the manners and finish of the businessmen, the commissions they extend to avant-garde architects, their substitution of psychologists for thugs in dealing with their workers: these —as Riesman at times admits[68]—do not necessarily entail a change in power relations.

Riesman is, in fact, ambivalent about the benign character of American politics.[69] He cannot decide whether Americans, under the stress of change, are crabbed and hateful moralizers lost (and potentially amok) in a world they never made, or pragmatic, competent, and sensitive to others, going about their political business in workman-like fashion. Riesman might well reply that it depends upon which sector of the social structure he is discussing; but even within his framework he gives us no clear view of the balance of these psychological forces in affecting political decision.

Riesman depicts the majority of the American people as "powerless and voiceless," and grasping at "straws of participation." [70] He does not seem to entertain an exaggerated notion of the extent of the devotion to liberal values amongst his countrymen; he is bitter about the new nationalism in America.[71] His occasional optimism about the diffusion down-

---

68. *Ibid.*, p. 250.
69. "The 'Militant' Fight against Anti-Semitism," *Individualism Reconsidered*, p. 151: "Many Americans have lost faith in freedom and have lost hope in the future. Many Americans have imitated the methods of their totalitarian enemies and have swung away from complacency and over-timidity in the direction of paranoia and over-aggression, still others have swung away from tolerance as a public-relations maneuver." But, in "Totalitarianism," *ibid.*, p. 412 ". . . my satire ['The Nylon War'] sought to highlight some of the amiable qualities of the United States—industrial energy and romanticism, imagination, activism, generosity—as well as some of the salient qualities of the Soviets—inflexibility, cupidity, 'projective' interpretation of the enemy, want, and fear."
70. Riesman, "The Meaning of Opinion," *Individualism Reconsidered*, pp. 499–500.
71. "The Saving Remnant," *ibid.*, p. 108: ". . . Americans are not sufficiently aware of the current changes in the quality of their own nationalism. For many people, the program of their lives is determined by the fear of a

wards of the values of the intellectual elite[72] is tempered by his awareness of that elite's spiritual and political frailties.[73] Riesman, indeed, holds that there is considerable psychological fascist potential in the populace:[74] he leaves open the question of what conditions could release and canalize it into politically efficacious forms. Confronted with McCarthyism, Riesman at first seemed more worried about the reaction of the intellectuals than about the dangers to civil liberties; he later altered the balance of his concerns.[75]

There are, then, a number of questions about American politics that Riesman cannot decide: whether prosperity is due to the immanent development of the economy of consumption or preparation for war; whether the conversion of politics into entertainment and its correlate, ideological apathy, is consonant with the values of American democracy or not; whether the political system has no centers of power or is, in matters of life and death, in the control of very few hands.

CONCLUSION

I have said that the sources of Riesman's ambiguity about political process lie in his philosophical difficulties. These are of two sorts: his inability to shape a morality, and therefore an ideal politics, suited to contemporary social realities, and

---

fifth column, and what the Russians or their allies do is an urgent and all-embracing preoccupation. To such persons there is little identification with America in terms of positive aims, but rather a neurotic clinging to a shadow war in which our national Superman is engaged."

72. *Constraint and Variety in American Education*, p. 44.

73. *Ibid.*, p. 43, where he says that many members of the professoriat who would not censor themselves for the sake of their own peace of mind do so because of loyalty to the places at which they teach.

74. *Faces in the Crowd*, p. 220.

75. Riesman, "Some Observations on Intellectual Freedom," *Individualism Reconsidered*, pp. 123–138. He has also manifested some concern with the problem of the legal defense of those accused of "subversion." See Riesman, "Law and Sociology," *Stanford Law Review*, 1957, p. 671.

his refusal to reject contemporary social and political possibilities for the sake of ideals incapable of realization within them.

Riesman is interested in inner and outer freedom, both; he doubts the opportunities for their development in contemporary American society.[76] Theoretically, to be sure, he holds that autonomy can develop out of other-direction; practically, he cannot tell us how this is to be done, still yet give us examples of its attainment. Although in the preliminary essay, "The Saving Remnant," [77] he was very critical of other direction, he seems to have tempered this criticism in *The Lonely Crowd*. But for all the advantages (not least political advantages) he finds in other-direction, by his own criteria its disadvantages appear to outweigh them. In a complex industrial society, the expression of autonomy in politics appears impossible; even his category of competence is, moreover, equivocal: those who are politically competent appear to accept limitations, on their aspirations for political expression, which are dictated by the system and which preclude autonomy. Riesman cannot, therefore, promulgate an ideal politics to serve his moral ends.

This last point is fundamental; neither his negative nor his positive evaluations of the political system can be understood without it. These alternate, but the inner dynamic of that alternation is his unwilling renunciation of a set of ideal political goals. His praise for (other people's) utopias, his disenchantment with ideology; his view that basic political decisions at the top enforce consensus on the bottom, his assertion that nobody has the power—all of these contradictions reflect a basic indecision. Ought one to develop a critical new politics, or ought one to be content with such advantages as one has? In general, Riesman opts for the latter

76. Riesman, "The Saving Remnant," *Individualism Reconsidered,* p. 118.
77. *Ibid.*

course—which accounts for his tendency to invent advantages, if none seem immediately visible.

Given his factual assessment of the world, Riesman seems inclined to accept it: he does not formulate a radical rejection of its version of human possibility. He is, it seems, suspicious of the pretensions of spiritual heroism: Veblen, and even Freud, attract his skepticism, if not his censure. And he reserves an acerbity, uncommon for him, for those who do manifest a critical politics.[78] We may also reverse the direction of this analysis. I have said that Riesman, finding the world inhospitable to his ideal ends, has tended to seek proximate ones attainable within it; this seems to have forced him toward a more positive evaluation of contemporary politics than certain of his perceptions suggest. We can also begin with his positive attitudes toward much in American politics, his conviction that the system requires no structural alternations. This, in turn, has minimized the effect of a number of insights into what he recognizes as structural flaws in the system—and to have produced explicit political values consonant with its continuance. In any case, it is clear that Riesman's ambiguity of moral assertion is bound to his ambiguity of political perception: no simple picture of his image of political process, therefore, is likely to do it justice.

POSTSCRIPT

My essay was written in 1958. Since then, Riesman's view of politics has become a good deal less ambiguous. Political psychology now appears to him less as a motor force and more

78. The politics of Friend and Poster (*Faces in the Crowd*, pp. 441 ff. and pp. 607 ff.) are absurd, if not quite as absurd as Riesman thinks: but why expend so much energy on a fifteen-year-old follower of Henry Wallace and Wilhelm Reich, and on a proto-adolescent graduate student? By contrast, Riesman's treatment of Miss Hawkins, who is spiritually, sexually, and politically disinherited—and thinks nothing wrong—is tender. (*Ibid.*, pp. 682 ff.)

as a result of political structure. The politics of abundance, in its American form, now strike him as less open; he is, in general, critical of America's role in the world. Most of all, he is terribly frightened at the prospect of atomic war. Conventionally, we could say that he has moved to the left—but the conventional terms do not quite apply to American politics at the turn of the decade. Riesman himself sees this: what he proposes, for the moment, is not so much movement toward concrete alternative policies or political alignments as critical reflection on prevalent definitions of the situation. Riesman's change of mind apparently mirrors what is happening amongst increasing numbers of American intellectuals; he is, once again, sensitive to the times.

It would be untrue (and, therefore, unfair) to leave it at the assertion that he has simply changed his mind. Certain themes in his work, under changed conditions, have become salient. Riesman himself suggests that he now tends to emphasize solidarity, while retaining his concern for the quality of individual experience. Solidarity clearly interests him, as in his enthusiasm for the recent campaign for civil rights for Negroes as an instance of new frontiers (or, rather, old frontiers rediscovered) in American politics. More central still is his concern for basic human solidarity, devotion to life itself, which he thinks is threatened by the prospect of atomic warfare. I should hold that the basic change is that he has concluded that present political conditions preclude the development of human autonomy.

His previous willingness to find something good in political apathy has diminished. Instead, we hear a note of despair about the possibility of intelligent popular political participation, not unmixed with apprehension lest the stuff of mass credulity and anxiety explode in our faces. The theory of veto groups has receded somewhat and a certain emphasis on elites, even on power elites, is now discernible; Riesman's work and that of Mills are not now as opposed as they were.

More important, he finds the United States unprepared for the politics of prosperity, to which, previously, he had looked forward with such hope. It is in his analysis of the conflict between the Atlantic and Soviet blocs that the changes in Riesman's view of politics are most pronounced.

Riesman views America as suffering from a psychological *immobilisme* that is in part the consequence of a fixation on the threat of Communism; the fantastic and obsessional dimensions of the fixation have come to disturb him, and it may be said that the events of 1956 in the Communist countries surprised him far less than they did many of the "experts" who had spent so much time assuring us that totalitarianism was irreversible. Riesman portrays that *immobilisme* as a result, not alone of demoniacal images of Communism, but of the lack of alternatives to America's present, extremely limited, internal political goals. Those who should be formulating these alternatives, he fears, are in fact mobilized for the Cold War. Throughout these recent analyses, a new structural tendency is visible: Riesman interprets current political motivation as a result of the current political situation and not vice versa. (Of course, he does say that these psychological attitudes can in turn affect political behavior; it is on this basis that he fears a catastrophe.)

Finally, Riesman has found new political tasks for the intellectuals. America's intellectuals, he has observed, were of much more use to their country when they had less use for it; there is something self-critical in this remark. He has asked his colleagues to be more careful about placing themselves at the disposal of the government, to reconsider their retreat to purely technical preoccupations (one wonders what will become of his own interest in the interview). He has revised his estimate of Veblen, and his insistence on the practical value of utopian thinking has never been so pronounced. He hopes that a critical intelligentsia may one day establish contact with those who need critical reflection most; for the moment, he is exceedingly pessimistic on this score. His pessimism is generalized, and the entire situation, in his new view, is positively ominous. He will not, I hope, think it entirely inappropriate if I suggest that he has, in sum, become more realistic.[79]

79. The new tendencies in Riesman's political thought are evident in: "Abundance for What?" *Bulletin of the Atomic Scientists,* Vol. 14, No. 4 (April, 1958); "Private People and Public Policy," *Shenandoah,* Vol. 10, No. 1 (Autumn, 1958); "The American Crisis," *Commentary,* Vol. 29, No. 6 (June, 1960) (with Michael Maccoby) and in the preface to the 1960 paperback edition of his book on Veblen (with Staughton Lynd), which Riesman was kind enough to let me see in manuscript. Riesman's interest in the conditions favorable to autonomy led him, some years ago, to begin an intensive program of research on American education; his present political views seem connected with his determination to talk less about autonomy in general and to see what it could mean, in particular. It may well lead him to another and more intensive encounter with the legacy of Marxism. It has been suggested, most recently by Riesman's student, Roger Hagan, that his work is in the tradition of Mill and De Tocqueville. But the search for the political conditions of human self-realization must lead him, sooner rather than later, back to Marx.

Great Britain: The Reactive Revolt[1]

PART ONE

I

The face of Great Britain in this fall of 1961 has a paradoxical appearance. The octogenarian Bertrand Russell goes to jail, if only for seven days, after violating police regulations during a campaign against nuclear weapons and NATO. One week later, he is followed in the courts by some thirteen hundred demonstrators—most of them rather younger—from among the ten thousand who sat down in Trafalgar Square to continue the protest. The rest of the country, however, seems quiet and even placid—preoccupied with its own affairs. An economic crisis and labour disputes, even a small race riot in the industrial north, do not erase this impression.

1. Two treatments of the period immediately preceding this one may be mentioned: C. L. Mowat's excellent historical study, *Britain Between the Wars, 1918–40* (London: Methuen, 1955), and Asa Briggs' remarkable essay in H. Clegg and A. Flanders (eds.), *The System of Industrial Relations in Great Britain* (Oxford: B. Blackwell, 1954). Briggs' account of recent social changes in Britain does consider the very pervasive effects of the war, as well as the influence of the Labour governments of 1945–50 and 1950–51.

Britain seems to be a society stable and confident, enjoying what are by contemporary standards an extraordinary amount of freedom and an only slightly less extraordinary quantum of prosperity. The paradox is so striking that many will suppose that it cannot be resolved. The discrepancy between an impassioned minority's gesture of protest at world history and the prosaic insularity of the majority is too great: We have to conclude that, psychologically, minority and majority simply inhabit different worlds.

The paradox can be resolved, but only if we acknowledge that all is not as it seems. The psychological differences at issue ought not to obscure a common characteristic of all contemporary Brritish reactions to politics. *Reactions* is, in fact, the appropriate term. In Britain, conformist and rebel alike are objects and not subjects of history.

The present ineluctable decline of the country's power and influence began but half a generation ago. Many who have experienced it are unwilling to admit that it has occurred— although it affects the consciousness of all Britons, at one or another level. An immediate consequence of this process of decline, of course, is that the scope of meaningful British intervention in world politics has been drastically reduced. This does not imply that British society has been thrown back upon itself. The problem, rather, is that the decisions affecting Britain's future are taken by others.

The compulsive rebellion of some, the cramped local perspectives of others and the yawning apathy of most are all responses to this situation. These particular responses, to be sure, are not inevitable. A decline in power may precipitate political convulsions of a major kind; it need not be accompanied by what is, in Britain, a national sense of shock. (The parallel, and contrasting, case of modern France is instructive.) The exigencies of Britain's postwar position do not, however, affect the British in a vacuum; their capacities (and incapacities) have been preformed by some of the more pervasive aspects of modern British social structure.[2] So pervasive, indeed, are the constraints which shape contemporary British political psychology that their analysis is exceedingly difficult. Many intelligent Britons do not view the pressures to which they are subjected as constraints. They tend, instead, to depict their institutions as uniquely perfected devices for maximizing human gratification.[3] On this view, the sociological analysis of British society itself is, if not impious, irrelevant.[4] In no other major Western country (with the possible exception of the German Federal Republic) is social criticism so obviously confined to a segment of the intellectuals.

The prevailing ideological defensiveness is so strong, indeed, that it takes the form of an attack. A series of positive propositions about British society have been promulgated by articulate politicians, professors, serious journalists, and educators.[5] The argument, reproduced here in crude but not quite caricatured terms, is as follows: British society is in possession of tested modes of meeting and inducing social changes. A broad consensus of political values is the basis of an effective national community in which each section of soci-

2. A sociological analysis of contemporary British society as a whole is still lacking. Much can be learned, however, from the systematic treatments given in: G. D. H. Cole, *The Post-War Condition of Britain* (London: Routledge and K. Paul, 1956) and A. M. Carr-Saunders, D. C. Jones, C. A. Moser, *A Survey of Social Conditions in England and Wales as Illuminated by Statistics* (Oxford: Clarendon Press, 1958). One appreciation of the social atmosphere may be had from T. Harrisson *et al.*, *Britain Revisited* (London: V. Gollancz, 1961).

3. See my essay " 'Empiricism' and British Politics," *Commentary* (February 1961), and "Social Constraints and Academic Freedom," *Universities and Left Review*, No. 5 (1958).

4. See *Twentieth Century* (May 1960), entitled "The Science of Society" which discusses the position of sociology in Britain—especially the contributions by O. H. MacGregor, D. G. MacRae, E. Shils, and myself.

5. A few hours spent with the back files of *The Times* or *The Daily Telegraph* —the newspapers read by the elite—will, in this connection, prove instructive. *The Guardian*, published in Manchester, at times exhibits a certain skepticism; it offers, however, no alternative general view of how things in Britain really get done.

ety has *and* knows its place. Alterations in the distribution of rewards, and even more so in the general balance of forces among the different parts of society, are usually the result of immediate and pragmatic agreements. Indeed, pragmatism is the essence of the British method for dealing with social conflict. It would not be an exaggeration to say that the method consists precisely of having none: Each problem is considered in its own terms, and grandiose attempts at large-scale social reconstruction are eschewed. Of course, Britain has social conflicts; which society does not? In Britain, however, these are settled as they come; in no case do they give rise to those ultimate ideological confrontations which have so troubled less fortunate European societies.

Thus, the *homme moyen intellectuel.* The lower apologetics, further, has a higher counterpart: Some of the most distinguished social philosophers in British universities have advanced universal prescriptions for mankind's ills which read like abstract glosses on this interpretation of British society.[6] The arguments for "empiricism," "piecemeal social engineering," and the like, and against a number of imprecisely defined evils ("positive freedom," "sociological holism" and more) clearly imply that modern Britain is a striking instance of a successful experiment in liberal philosophy. With so much energy expended on ideological self-congratulation, it is not surprising that some of Britain's difficulties have recently had less attention than they merit. This distortion of focus, indeed, may well be due to the painful discrepancy between this simple, almost idyllic, image of Britain and a reality that is more complex and less satisfactory.

Contemporary Britain is, whatever its apologists may say,

6. See I. Berlin, *Two Concepts of Liberty* (Oxford: Clarendon Press, 1958) and K. R. Popper, *The Open Society and Its Enemies,* Vols. 1 and 2 (London: G. Routledge and Sons, Ltd., 1945). M. Oakeshott, *Political Education* (Cambridge: 1951), takes a different tack—and indeed discourages social criticism to a degree (and in a manner) not found in the other works.

a stagnant society.[7] Its citizens are burdened by a miscellany of mutual grievances which seriously affect their morale, many of which are direct derivatives of the peculiarities of the British class system. What sometimes passes for consensus in Britain is rather, the artefact of a tenuous balance of opposing forces. (Where there is so much talk of consensus, we are of course entitled to suspect that it may be defective.)

Far from approaching their problems pragmatically, the British manifest a variety of ideological interpretations of their situation—although those who promulgate contrasting or conflicting ideologies are agreed on the pragmatic value of denying that they do so. In these circumstances, domestic revolt (or, more accurately, dissent) has a curiously strident tone: The rebels sense, rightly, that they have to shout to be heard at all. The British response to the revolution in the outside world, on the other hand, is for the most part a stubborn refusal to acknowledge that it presents an intractable problem. The resultant combination, aggressive protest on the one hand and complacent self-congratulation on the other, produces precisely that paradoxical appearance with which we began. This is the appropriate point, perhaps, at which to begin looking behind appearances. We may turn to the social setting in which these ideological tendencies have developed.

II

The loss of Empire has affected British political attitudes both directly and indirectly. Not alone administrators and businessmen participated in the control of the Empire; during two world wars (and in the more recent conflicts in Ma-

---

7. A careful reading of the weeklies, *The Economist* or *The Spectator* for the past few years will show that a nagging awareness of this condition dogs not a few members of Britain's economic and cultural elite. On the left, *The New Statesman*—until recently, at least—had other concerns.

laya, Kenya, and the Mid-East) hundreds of thousands of ordinary Britons enjoyed what was in effect a colonial situation with respect to Afro-Asian populations. They conveyed their experiences, of course, to their families—a highly effective method of political education. When the Labour Party leadership in 1956 opposed the British government's military intervention in Egypt, it challenged the chauvinistic and imperialistic sentiments of millions of Labour voters in the working class.[8] Many of the latter seemed to intuit, and sympathize with, the psychological components of Sir Anthony Eden's policy. This was conceived not alone as a rational military-political measure, but as a gesture of outraged protest against the seizure of "our" Suez Canal by the "wogs" —a denial of that alteration of forces in the world which was, eventually, to leave the "wogs" in possession of the Canal. The national division over the Suez intervention arrayed, in fact, those still possessed of the middle-class liberal conscience —many of whom were British Socialists—against the majority of the nation.

(To some extent, the racial conflicts that have occurred in Britain in recent years have been encouraged by the transfer of colonialist racial attitudes to the homeland. Hannah Arendt, in her *Origins of Totalitarianism*,[9] argued that the transfer of colonialist attitudes to Europe was itself a precondition of Fascism; this suggestion has, unfortunately, not given rise to a precise program of social research in the two countries where it is presently relevant, Britain and France. The influx of tens of thousands of Africans, Asians, and West Indians—with the resultant pressures on housing and the fear of economic competition—has been, in itself, a sufficient

8. See E. Childers, *The Road to Suez* (London: 1962). The domestic atmosphere in Britain in the late fall and winter of 1956 will not be forgotten by those who experienced it.

9. H. Arendt, *The Origins of Totalitarianism*, 2nd ed. (New York: Harcourt Brace, 1958), Chaps. 6, 7, and 8.

stimulus to conflict.[10] But this particular demonstration of the unity of the Commonwealth has been interpreted by many Britons as something of a reversal of the order of nature, as painfully visible proof that the Empire has become something else.)

The indirect consequences of the end of Empire have been no less effective. Those with liberal consciences could celebrate the liberation of India as a triumph of British statesmanship. The rest acquiesced but viewed the abdication of British power in Asia as part of a steady process of decline that was marked by any number of events: the displacement of Britain by the United States as a major world power; the slow domestic economic recovery after the war (underscored by Germany's economic success and its competitiveness in foreign markets); the rise of Soviet power. The style, the articulateness, the self-consciousness of British reactions to these phenomena vary from class to class. The reactions, however, do have a common tone, in which bewilderment, petulance, and resentment are mixed. This external situation, moreover, has compounded with major changes in domestic social structure to produce a general sense of disorientation which has as yet to be replaced by anything else.

It is common to characterize the alterations in the relationship between the social classes brought about by the Labour government, 1945–51, as triumphs of Socialism. It must be remembered, however, that British Socialism has for nearly forty years, ever since the beginning of the decline of liberalism and the Liberal Party, mobilized the spiritual energies of an important minority of the middle-class intelligentsia. The leadership it gave to the Labour movement was ameliorative and reformist in temper.[11] The gains registered in the area

10. The latest and one of the most interesting studies of this problem is: R. Glass, *The Newcomers: The West Indians in London* (London: 1960).
11. See Beatrice Webb's autobiographical account of her youth: *My Apprenticeship* (London: Longmans, Green and Co., 1926). The recent memoirs

of social policy in 1945–51 were striking, but they hardly constituted (nor were they intended to constitute) a social revolution of a full-scale sort.[12]

The Welfare State, rather, gave the working class a minimal but guaranteed share in the distribution of the national income.[13] The National Health Service, an enlargement of educational provision, the extension of pre-existing welfare services and benefits (which were not always inconsiderable), food subsidies and a rehousing program were the means of redistribution. The continuation of wartime economic controls, the nationalization of the Bank of England, of the mining, power, transport, and steel industries were measures designed to institutionalize a planned economy. (Interestingly enough, there were no experiments with workers' control in industry and the nationalized industries were deliberately insulated from direct parliamentary control.[14]) It was on this latter front that the Conservative counterattack, when it came in 1951, was mounted; the principle of redistribution through a Welfare State was not at first attacked.[15] Instead, social values were propagated which made redistributive no-

---

by the Chancellor of the Exchequer in the 1945 Labour Government, Hugh Dalton, contain much that is useful to an appreciation of the mentality of these middle-class socialists; *Call Back Yesterday*, Vols. 1 and 2 (London: F. Muller, 1953–57). (A third volume, on Labour's postwar governments, is scheduled for publication in 1962.)

12. R. Miliband, *Parliamentary Socialism* (London: 1961) is a critique of Labour's renunciation, explicit and implicit, of the possibilities of revolutionary action. Dr. Miliband is also one of the Labour Left's most prominent theorists; his work is interesting on this as well as many other, counts.

13. R. Titmuss, *Essays on the Welfare State* (London: G. Allen and Unwin, 1957) is the authoritative discussion of these postwar changes and their social effects.

14. See A. Rogow (with the assistance of P. Shore), *The Labour Government and British Industry* (Oxford: B. Blackwell, 1955).

15. The essays by Goldmann and by two Tory ministers, I. MacLeod and E. Powell, in the pamphlet *The Future of the Welfare State* (London: Conservative Political Centre, 1958), are worth reading. They express the

tions seem either inefficient, utopian, or unnecessary, as the ideological context demanded.

The Conservative counterattack, later consolidated in the electoral victories of 1955 and 1959, made very effective use of a number of public discontents with the Labour government. The coincidence of postwar economic difficulties with Labour rule was bad luck. The failure of the government, particularly in its last two years, to develop a positive political appeal was perhaps less accidental. Redistribution had alienated the professional, managerial, and clerical sections of the middle classes. At least initially tolerant of Labour, these groups now tended to view the prospect of a continued Labour government as a threat to their own existence. Redistributive measures, as they affected the tax system, had eliminated some of the differential between themselves and the working class. By 1950 this was interpreted not as a temporary sacrifice but as preliminary to the erosion of their social identity. This anxiety could have been overcome only by a program which appealed to their national sentiments (and activated memories of the 1930's) by emphasizing the need for the modernization of Britain's outmoded social and economic infrastructure. Instead, Labour's program at the beginning of the 50's was curiously bifurcated. The middle-class reformists, tired and without new ideas in domestic policy, demonstrated their sense of "national responsibility" in the sphere of foreign affairs. Rearmament on a very large scale (which, of course, used up the resources that might have been put into a new economic program) was the result. The working-class section of the Labour movement concentrated on the defense of the advantages it had won since 1945. But it was the Conservatives under Churchill who seemed to have unique capacities for "national" leadership, and the defensive

---

view of the younger and more flexible Conservative faction—after seven years of office and while preparing the electoral triumph of 1959.

strategy adopted by the articulate representatives of the working class could not alter, and may indeed have reinforced, the anti-Labour tendency in the middle classes. The marginal constituencies returned Conservative candidates. A much different social experiment began.[16]

The political techniques of the new British Conservativism are not entirely refined, but they have been more or less successful in electoral terms. The new Conservatives have resisted the demands of the more visceral segment of their party, which hoped for an attack on the Labour movement. Instead, the postwar Conservative governments have allowed the working class a certain share in prosperity—if a share that had to be obtained in the market and not by direct political means. The welfare services have, to a certain extent, been allowed to run down, chiefly through the device of not extending them, of increasing welfare expenditure at a rate less than the rate of increase in national income. Frontal assaults on the Welfare State, again, have been conspicuously absent, although there have been two or three guerrilla raids. The essential means adopted by the Conservatives have been two:

1. A generally unplanned and uncontrolled economic expansion has been encouraged. The long-term adequacy of this policy may be doubted, on the basis of Britain's relatively low *average* annual rate of economic growth, but there have been perceptible spurts of increased popular purchasing power.[17]

2. The mass media have been developed as systematic purveyors of the ideology (or lack of one) appropriate to the new

16. See R. B. McCallum and A. Readman, *The British General Election of 1945* (London: Oxford University Press, 1947); H. G. Nicholas, *The British General Election of 1950* (London: Macmillan, 1951); D. E. Butler, *The British General Election of 1951* (London: Macmillan, 1952).
17. A. Shonfield, *British Economic Policy Since the War,* 2nd ed. (London: 1959).

consumer society.[18] As we shall see, this has stimulated protest on the right as well as the left. For the moment, it suffices to observe that the values presented by commercial television and the daily and weekly press, while explicitly apolitical, are implicitly anti-Labour. These include a belief in the propriety and immutability of the prevailing status system, and the endorsement of a style of life which, where it is not centered on personal success, is privatized in the extreme. The mass media seem to be effecting a spiritual homogenization of the British population; awareness of social conflict has been reduced, and a curiously amorphous public ideology has taken its place—as if fewer Britons can identify their own particular interests in a society become ever more opaque.

These techniques are, however, not infallible. The expansive movement of the economy has been checked—as, again, this year—by bouts of restrictionism. The new Conservatives have been unable to mount a coherent economic program. The economic ideology manifested by the more traditional membership of their Party—shopkeepers and small businessmen, small-town professionals, and retired officers—is an obscure conglomerate of instinctive deflationism and self-righteous self-seeking. The pressures exerted on the Conservative leadership in this way are not insuperable, the more so because important sections of British industry regard a rigorous deflationism as absurd.

There are, however, other and equally important economic influences on the Conservatives. The City of London, or more accurately that part of it which deals in international finance, is insistently deflationist. Under these conflicting influences the Conservative Governments have produced an

18. H. H. Wilson, *Pressure Group: The Campaign for Commercial Television in Britain* (London: Secker and Warburg, 1961), shows what importance large sectors of British business (and their allies and spokesmen in the Conservative Party) attached to the introduction of commercial television.

erratic succession of budgets. Tax concessions to the middle classes have been followed by credit restrictions which increased the cost of house purchase; periods of increasing real income for the working class have been interrupted by cuts in the Welfare Services and higher charges for the remaining ones, as well as by substantial patches of unemployment. Briefly put, despite ten years of uninterrupted rule, the Conservatives have not convinced the nation that they are in control of events in the economy, where their successes and failures are most visible.

Similarly, what may be termed the political education undertaken by the mass media has been a considerable, but not an unequivocal, success. However opaque the workings of the new British society, ordinary men and women are able to sense (and not alone in the economic sphere) its impact on their lives. The awareness of social conflict has been reduced, even repressed, but it has not been eliminated. Those brief ten days in the electoral campaign of 1959, when the Labour Party made the running with an attack on what it denounced as "the windfall state," did not overcome the intrinsic advantages enjoyed by the Conservatives. However, they did show that the language of social protest, if spoken with suitable diction, does not find the British entirely deaf.[19] (The coincidence of the election and a sizeable scandal in London property speculation was to Labour's advantage; the discovery by a Conservative newspaper that a rather prominent London Labour politician was an associate of speculative interests was not.)

Despite the mass media's image of Britain as a society of satisfied consumers, the actual and potential discontents of the populace (particularly in the spheres of education and the status system and with respect to their society's general lack

19. D. E. Butler, with R. Rose, *The British General Election of 1959* (London: Macmillan, 1960).

of amenities and dynamism) are very important. They cannot be conjured out of existence. The new British Left at times entertains exaggerated notions of the omnipotence of the mass media which contradict, in interesting fashion, its own belief in the educability of the populace—but this is a point that can be discussed subsequently.[20]

Prosperity has been the chief visible characteristic of Britain for the last half-decade; the uses of prosperity merit examination. For a large section of the working class, the material gains have been very great.[21] Relatively continuous full employment contrasts strikingly with the prewar depression. The National Health Service has broadened the basis of the prewar medical insurance system; a program of re-housing (since stopped, largely, by the Conservatives) has diminished the slum areas, which two decades ago, were among the most pestilential in Europe. Most important, of course, has been the steady amounts of cash which have come to working-class families.

It is true that the workers' market advantages have had to be won and maintained by trade-union pressure, including a number of acrimonious strikes. It is also true that much working-class prosperity is the result of overtime, dual job holding, and multiple family employment. Some claim, indeed, that the working-class share of the national income ceased to increase proportionally early in the current period of Conservative government. Academic economists agree or disagree in terms of their political preferences.

In any case, it is clear that a majority of working-class families have approached or attained some of the material prerogatives of a middle-class existence: reasonable housing, ample

20. The essay by Stuart Hall, "Absolute Beginnings," in *Universities and Left Review*, No. 7 (1959), is a sophisticated instance of this *genre*. See also "TV and Broadcasting," *New Left Review*, No. 7 (1961).
21. Data will be found in Cole and Carr-Saunders et al., *op. cit.*

diet, the possession of durable goods, paid vacations. Security of employment is lacking, of course, and this is one, but only one, reason for the persistence, indeed the reinforcement, of some of the traditional status distinctions between the British social classes. The objective gains of the working class, finally, have not been accompanied by a subjective sense of full incorporation in the national community. Prosperity has eroded but not eliminated its sense of exclusion.

Not everyone in Britain, any more than in America, is prosperous.[22] There are millions living at or below a marginal rate of subsistence: those on state old-age pensions, the chronically or cyclically unemployed, those with large families and small incomes (family allowances have not been increased to match the rise in the cost of living). Moreover, working-class families with adequate incomes for most purposes are frequently stuck in bad housing; public rehousing is no longer available, and their own means are insufficient to purchase or rent alternative private housing. This is particularly true of the colored working-class population, and the resultant crowding into already crowded working-class districts is an obvious source of racial conflict.

Prosperity has affected the middle classes unequally. We may begin by noting that the middle classes have in fact profited from the Welfare State, particularly from the National Health Service and the 1944 Education Act.[23] (The majority of the university students who would not have continued their education in the prewar period are from the middle classes.) This has not, of course, precluded a certain middle-class resentment of the Welfare State, caused by high taxes and the obvious if incomplete closure of the gap between working-class and middle-class incomes. But this resent-

22. See the essay by P. Townsend in: N. Mackenzie (ed.), *Conviction* (London: MacGibbon and Kee, 1958).
23. See R. Titmuss, *op. cit.*

ment is also unequal. It appears to be strongest in certain traditional middle-class occupations, both in the lower middle classes (clerks) and in the middle classes proper (among professionals). These groups, particularly their older members, take seriously the classical ideology of "individual responsibility" and "service." [24] The ideology has, in the past, justified considerable inequality and today is used often to legitimate new inequalities—in which advantages are enjoyed by a managerial elite whose ethic contrasts strikingly with the old professional code. Nonetheless, millions of Britons seem to cling to their old values, although what is striking about their resentment is that it is directed downwards, at the working class, and not upwards at those who, by old standards, are merely earning easy money. There is another segment of the middle classes, shopkeepers at the bottom and some businessmen at the top, whose resentment of the Welfare State is not clothed in an old ideology: They simply want more for themselves and see no way of obtaining this other than leaving less to others.

I have intimated that these attitudes are strongest among older members of the middle classes. It is too early to pronounce on the attitudes of their children, but some interesting changes may be taking place. In a number of occupations, with bank employees, for instance, old resistances to trade unionism are slowly dissolving. There is little or no evidence, however, to suggest that the younger members of the middle classes are moving Left. Their attitudes to the working class, to be sure, are frequently less obscurantist and more calculating. They do not, in large numbers, suppose that the workers

24. Excessively idealized portraits of these groups by two authors who share their ideology will be found in: A. Maude and R. Lewis, *The English Middle Classes* (London: Phoenix House, 1949) and in their *Professional People* (London: Phoenix House, 1952). Both books bespeak much hostility to the Welfare State—and to the working class.

are workers because of "laziness." The working class, they think, is a good class not to be in. There are three reasons for this change; consideration of them brings us to the new middle classes and their response to prosperity.[25]

Changes in occupational structure have greatly expanded the range of technical, semi-professional, and white-collar employment, in both the secondary and tertiary sectors of the economy. Individuals in these posts are usually better educated and less servile than their clerical predecessors in the middle classes. They seem to manifest different attitudes to their work; in any event, the technicians at least evince a certain discrimination between the satisfactions of technical achievement and status gratifications. All the members of this grouping, meanwhile, are openly and unashamedly interested in the things that money can buy; in this respect, they are perhaps among the most "Americanized" elements in British society.

The second factor in this group's response to prosperity is its own somewhat heterogeneous class origins. A sizeable minority in these new middle-class occupations are themselves offspring of working-class families; the rest find themselves in a genuinely ambiguous area, with respect to traditional systems of status allocation, for which neither their parents nor their schools have prepared them. These two factors seem to inhibit the development of hostility to the working class and to promote what appears to be a matter-of-fact attitude to the advantages enjoyed by their own occupations. This relative detachment allows some in the new middle classes to criticize the lack of dynamism of the nation's economic elite, to entertain (vague) suspicions that the society's priorities are wrong. These doubts, however, are confined

25. An excellent analytic and historical treatment of some of the older components of this stratum will be found in D. Lockwood, *The Black-Coated Worker* (London: G. Allen and Unwin, 1957). Something may also be learned from M. Young and P. Willmott, *Family and Class in a London Suburb* (London: Routledge and K. Paul, 1960).

to a small minority. Opposed to them is an *arrivisme* derived from the entire occupational group's ideological dependence upon Britain's new managerial type, the third component in the response of the new middle classes to prosperity.

Never, in the history of the world's first and, for many generations leading, capitalist society, have businessmen been at the top of the status hierarchy.[26] The familiar processes, not unique to Britain, by which industrial and commercial wealth associated itself with antecedent status systems have, in modern Britain, contributed to a certain genteel inefficiency in the British economy.[27] (This inefficiency may well be a national as well as a class phenomenon, of course: The British worker has long since ceased to be the rival of many of his counterparts elsewhere, and the national imperial nostalgia may account for this shared ineptitude.) This is today most visible, perhaps, in certain key positions in the direction of the economy. Some senior civil servants responsible for economic affairs are proud of their lack of academic training in economics and the social sciences. Finance in the City of London works by convention, by gentleman's agree-

26. See R. Clements, *Managers: A Study of Their Careers in British Industry* (London: G. Allen and Unwin, 1958) and the impressionistic but convincing sketch by R. Samuel, "The Boss as Hero," *Universities and Left Review*, No. 7 (1959). The essay by P. Shore ("In the Room at the Top") in *Conviction, op. cit.* is also useful.

27. Among recent British historians, L. E. Woodward and R. C. K. Ensor are not usually thought of either as utilizing a sociological approach or exhibiting much critical detachment toward the British elite. Their volumes in the Oxford History of England series, however, provide data on the development of the elite which are all the more valuable for being presented in so unconscious a fashion. See: L. E. Woodward, *The Age of Reform, 1815–70* (Oxford: 1946) and R. C. K. Ensor, *England, 1870–1914* (Oxford: 1946). Sociological studies of the contemporary elite are practically non-existent. See H. Thomas et al., *The Establishment* (London: A. Blond, 1959) and the special issue of *The Twentieth Century*, "Who Rules Britain?" (October 1957). Biographies are particularly useful sources for the functioning of the British elite. See, for instance, the portrait of the life of a former editor of *The Times*, J. E. Wrench, *Geoffrey Dawson and Our Times* (London: Hutchinson, 1955).

ment, by an implicit set of rules which discourages aggression and innovation. There are other sectors of the economy in which the casualness and inefficiency of managers and staff strike the outsider as slothful. These, of course, are attitudes proper to gentlemen, or those who would be thought such, whatever other causes may be at work.

A new managerial elite, however, has developed in postwar Britain. Its attitudes are different, it works harder, and it values production. It ought not to be thought that Richard Baxter has come to life again: These are new-style entrepreneurs, working through large-scale organizations. It is this group which, through its control of the mass media, is seeking to re-make Britain into a consumer's society something like the managers imagine America to be. There are even persons of this sort in the City of London, although the new managers are generally located elsewhere. Their ostentatious critique of British economic stagnation has combined with certain persistent structural conflicts in the economy (the tension, for instance, between London finance and Midlands industry, which also has a status component).

For immediate purposes, we can say that the diffusion downwards in the society of the new managerial ethic has functioned as a dissolvent of certain ideological rigidities. The new managers do not find it morally reprehensible that working-class families have acquired washing machines; after all, they would like to sell them automobiles. The new economic elite, however, is not able either to assume unquestioned command of the Conservative Party, or to displace more conservative economic interests in the political elite. Its lack of complete success may be due to the ideological resistances the latter have been able to generate, resistances which also blunt the determination of the new managers by inducing many of them to seek recognition by the old ruling class.

I have said that businessmen were never, in Britain, at the very apex of the society; this place was filled by the imperial magnates. The magnates constituted the political-economic directorate of the Empire; they assumed responsibility for the stability of the framework in which ordinary economic activities took place, and they expected and received deference from those concerned only with the latter. In politics, imperial administration, and certain critical economic positions, chiefly in the City and international enterprise, the magnates exercised command of British society.

Amateurs in all but the art of maintaining themselves in power, they were careful not to practice a self-defeating exclusiveness. New men, if they made themselves enough of a nuisance, were admitted to the club. Middle-class servitors in the civil service, the universities and education, the Church, the "responsible" press, were given important responsibilities and rewarded appropriately. (The co-optation of the educated middle class was the easier because the liberal offensive against the ruling class, with time, became attenuated: The latter adopted something of liberalism, and much of the doctrine's substance was taken over and transmuted by the Labour Party, with which many of the intelligentsia were not prepared to make common cause.) In short, the traditional British ruling class managed the Empire with skill and cunning.

What is remarkable is that the entire sequence of events of the last thirty years (depression, the rise of German Fascism, war, the postwar Labour governments, and the loss of Empire and world political power) has not dissolved the group. Its adaptive maneuvers have sometimes been inappropriate and it has exhibited signs of ideological rigidity, which are, in short, the classic symptoms of decay. Yet the imprint it has imposed on all of British culture, perhaps more than the critical economic posts to which it has clung, has enabled it to encapsulate or beat off its divided challengers.

The uniqueness of British society has consisted not least in the fact that it never was a "bourgeois" society of the western European sort. The British fusion of middle-class and upper-class culture is an important component of British political stability. It also, particularly in this century, has tended to empty middle-class culture of its hard and critical elements. Moreover, the combination has effectively excluded the working class from high culture, even through the recent improvement in its material and social fortunes. It is, therefore, to the present situation of British culture that we must turn now.

Much has been written of the "Establishment" in British culture. The "Establishment" takes its name from the Established Church and is commonly supposed to manifest the anti-qualities allegedly associated with the latter: compulsive deference to authority, an unqualified endorsement of the current social order (with an especially hypocritical opprobrium reserved for the latter's critics), and an obsessional revulsion for conflict, change, and new ideas. The recent history of the Established Church, of course, suggests that this is an extremely unfair characterization of it; the description is, perhaps, less inaccurate when applied to some prevalent attitudes in the British cultural elite. What is at issue in recent criticisms of the "Establishment" is the structure of that elite. There is, we are told, a cultural directorate comprising the universities, particularly Oxbridge, the upper reaches of the educational system, the BBC, the "better" newspapers and periodicals, and publishing. Many images of the "Establishment" insist on its political dimensions; it is also supposed to include the senior levels of the Civil Service, the Military, the Conservative Party (some critics of the present Labour Party leadership, indeed, insist that it is too much like a part of the "Establishment"), and the City of London. Nearly all portrayals of the "Establishment" insist that it functions by personal contact; a hint, even a discreet cough, is enough to set in motion the repressive machinery perfected to deal with those who attack the oligarchs. Bound by ties of sympathy and interest, the latter have, in any case, quite definite conventions as to what may and may not be said and done.

It is clear that these images of the "Establishment" are grotesquely simplified; they ignore the conflicts within the British elite. In any case, the term "Establishment" has been used, often, to encompass those aspects of the elite its critics dislike—that is to say, practically all of them. In the sphere of culture, at least, the term "Establishment" can be given a somewhat more limited definition. It applies to all those who defend the moral values, the style of life, and the peculiarly narrow psychological climate of the educated elite in a Britain of defined and enduring class divisions, a fixed world position, and unbroken cultural traditions. Viewed in this way, the "Establishment" is not a power group with an ideology but rather an ideology seeking attachment to a power group: The Britain represented by the values of the "Establishment" no longer exists. The values persist, or rather, their verbal elaboration does. Objectively, this often serves to legitimate interests, practices and groupings alien to the traditional "Establishment." The rhetoric of liberalism accompanies the progress of the British version of the organization man; lessons in the ethic of service are read by tax evaders; the doctrine of public responsibility for mass education justifies a commercial television system of subliminal standards.

The persistence of this set of values which, in its day, put solid ideological ground under the imperial magnates' feet, is an interesting expression of the ambiguity of the present cultural situation in Britain. The fact that these standards have not been forgotten can be interpreted as proof of their educative influence: The new men thrown up by prosperity can claim respectability only in these terms. These values cannot be realized in the actual state of British society. In so far as this is not acknowledged, hypocrisy or cynicism must result from the maintenance of the pretence. The "Establishment," then, is an important negative cultural force: Its promulgation of the values of 1939 hinders a solution to Britain's difficulties in 1961.

The persistence of this ideology has prevented the new men from developing one of their own; it also generates a profound confusion, even malaise, in all sectors of the society. The postwar period has seen a considerable expansion of educational opportunity; offspring of the working class have entered the academic secondary schools in great numbers, and many of them have joined new recruits from the lower and intermediate strata of the middle classes at the universities.[28] Britain never had, and still does not have, a national system of education in the continental manner, nor even in the American one. The universities, the public (that is, private) and the grammar schools were all institutions which provided, rather explicitly, training in a class-specific code of thought and behavior. Now that the universities and grammar schools are heterogeneous in their class composition, their students are (sometimes involuntarily) resistant to this sort of indoctrination. For the moment, however, there seems to be little else to give them.

British higher education has had a marked tendency to produce gentlemen amateurs (the three-year period for a bachelor's degree is short compared to that required for first degree in other European countries). The study of classical languages and literature has had a disproportionate amount of prestige; the natural and social sciences have been relatively neglected.

28. See D. V. Glass, "Education," in M. Ginsberg (ed.), *Law and Opinion in the 20th Century* (London: Stevens, 1959); J. Floud, A. H. Halsey et al., *Social Class and Educational Opportunity* (London: Heinemann, 1956); *New Left Review*, Special Issue on Education, No. 11 (1961); B. Jackson and D. Marsden, *Education and the Working Class* (London: 1962). D. Potter, *The Glittering Coffin* (London: 1960) is *inter alia* an interesting account of a working class boy's response to Oxford.

C. P. Snow's remarks on *The Two Cultures* evoked much discussion recently because they struck home: The traditional British intellectual from the middle classes or the elite is generally not alone ignorant of science but profoundly unaware of his ignorance.[29] The difficulty is not simply one which can be overcome by investing more capital in the science departments of the universities. The dominant national mode of thought is casual; its unsystematic character is defended as "empirical," but it is curiously unable to deal with the complexities of an advanced industrial culture. Historically, it would appear that the great Victorian intellectuals consumed most of the innovating energies available to the British middle classes; their contemporary descendants are unable to add much to their heritage. It is not surprising, in these circumstances, that a new generation of university students sometimes reacts as if its studies were meaningless.

These are problems which, of course, directly affect but a small percentage of the adult population. The others are left to fend for themselves. The schools which the majority of British children attend usually have the outer paraphernalia of the middle-class schools, such as uniforms and a peculiar hierarchical system of authority by which prefects (elder students) discipline their younger peers. In short, they attempt to induct their pupils into that system of consensus which underlies British "individualism." They do so, however, without any discernible cultural content (the contrast with the Continent or even the United States is striking, in this case), culture being reserved for the middle classes. Attendance at one of these schools is generally interpreted by the children as an indication of the occupational and social fate that awaits them—exclusion from a whole range of opportunities and rewards. That the pupils are not, in this

29. C. P. Snow, "The Two Cultures and the Scientific Revolution" (Cambridge: Cambridge University Press, 1959); see the symposium in *Encounter* (August 1959).

event, highly motivated will surprise no one, although of course there are educators who see evidence for the maintenance of the exclusion in this lack of motivation.

The culture of the educated class, then, has become brittle; in a few years, at most, it may relapse into a self-conscious antiquarian nostalgia. The more aggressive claimants of place in the political elite are *parvenus* unable to make a cultural contribution of their own; they have half assimilated, half degraded, the tradition of their predecessors. The working class, its traditional cultural solidarity reduced to an economic defensiveness, has been left to the mass media. This sketch is unduly schematic; it ignores those traces of vitality which, despite the reactive character of protest in Britain, give some of it a certain connection with the more creative aspects of the national tradition. It is to protest itself that we turn now.

PART TWO

I

Protest, of course, must eventually take political forms. Recent protest in Britain has been affected by the inner development of British politics in the last decade. Above, I wrote of the spiritual homogenization of the populace by the mass media and of its limits. We may consider an equivalent phenomenon in the sphere of politics itself. Political homogenization in postwar Britain has this special trait: Sharp conflicts of principle and policy are as likely to divide the two major parties internally as to oppose them to one another. The conflicts between new and old Conservatives, between the moderates of the Labour Party and the Labour Left, have resulted in a largely unintended and generally tacit *rapprochement* between the parties. Unintended and tacit in origins, this *rapprochement* has been reinforced by both parties' leaderships' views of electoral necessity: new Conservatism and moderate socialism have been designed, positively, to attract marginal voters and, negatively, to avoid mobilizing latent class anxieties which might, from each party's standpoint, bring more hostile voters to the polls.

Two principal mechanisms have effected this homogenization. The parties' central organizations have imposed themselves on party congresses and on the local groupings alike. In Parliament, the Cabinet and the Shadow Cabinet (the leadership of the opposition) have imposed themselves on the parliamentarians.[1] It is true that resistance to the parliamentary leadership within Parliament has been much more continuous, overt, and troublesome within the Labour Party; but this resistance has been encapsulated and is now, ten years after the Bevanite revolt, further than ever from assuming command of the Party. Furthermore, the post of Prime Minister has not recently been one of *primus inter pares*. Successive postwar Prime Ministers have exercised extraordinary authority within their own governments. Eden, indeed, with the help of a compliant Foreign Secretary, presented his Cabinet with a *fait accompli* over Suez. The public seems to respond to this concentration and apparent personalization of power. The 1959 election, indeed, had a distinctly "Presidential" atmosphere, with posters of Macmillan and Gaitskell visible everywhere.

The decline of Parliament, the conspicuous absence of striking debate (and the apparent irrelevance of such striking debate as does occur in the course of political decision) have been remarked upon by a host of commentators. What has escaped discussion, in Britain, are the ways in which this

1. See R. T. McKenzie, *British Political Parties* (London: 1955).

phenomenon is a function of a generally intensified process of bureaucratization in British society.[2] The British simply lack a political vocabulary for dealing with this development which has taken place in the economy, among trade unions, and in the mass media as well as in politics. Britain is, of course, peculiarly liable to what may be termed creeping bureaucratization. The highly developed patterns of consensus in the traditional elite have served the new oligarchs as models; power is exerted discreetly, often hidden from public awareness by an ideology which denies that anything of public concern is in fact happening. Liberalism in Britain, by insisting on the distinction that ought to prevail between the state and society has, by a sort of compulsive irrealism, allowed the fusion of state and society to proceed apace.

In these curious circumstances, three general reactions may be noted:

1. A considerable amount of political disorientation exists. Large numbers of Britons do not seem to know how their present political system works. Where they sense their own ignorance, they do not quite know how to overcome it, but this is, in any event, the minority case. That ignorance, in most instances, is overlaid by another source of disorientation: Many Britons are without consistent standards of political judgment. Much of this stems from political withdrawal; not having any explicit political ends, they are disinterested in political means.

2. The prevalent political withdrawal often takes the form, noted in a number of countries, of privatization. Prosperity, of course, facilitates this response: A sphere has apparently (and, in some cases, actually) emerged in which individuals can do things for themselves and can renounce self-conscious collective action. But privatization has also

2. With his usual perspicacity, R. H. S. Crossman has seen something of the problem. See his Fabian Tract, *Socialism and the New Despotism* (London: 1956).

been observed in non-prosperous societies (as in the Soviet Union). What is at issue, perhaps, is a long-term tendency of modern politics from which Britain is not exempt.

3. The resultant depoliticization of the populace is a political fact of the first importance. It reinforces that popular passivity which is in any case a correlate of bureaucratization, and, despite the persistence of a liberal ideology, increasingly assimilates elections to plebiscites. Those who point to the continued existence of conflicts, or who criticize Britain's social institutions in this atmosphere, threaten not only the civic, but the psychic peace of their fellow citizens. In these circumstances, depoliticization is implicitly but emphatically conservative; a commitment to politics has become either the mark of the political professional or the rebel.[3] It remains, now, to examine Britain's rebels, near-rebels, and pseudo-rebels.

The British Communists, unlike their counterparts in France, Weimar Germany, Italy, and Republican Spain, never attracted a massive working-class following.[4] The Party was, instead, an alliance of working-class militants and members of the intelligentsia. The former worked through the trade unions (in some cases, as members of the shop stewards' movement, against the official trade-union leaders). The latter, in the professions, education, journalism or the arts, were most influential, as we might have expected, in the 1930's; in that period British Communism attracted many of the well-born, and many more of the well-educated, in a revolt against a ruling class which seemed both powerful and callous. Where in Western societies a Marxist party wins the allegiance of the intelligentsia, we may suppose that the

3. The reactions of a younger group of Leftist thinkers have been set down in E. P. Thompson (ed.), *Out of Apathy* (London: Stevens, 1959).

4. See H. Pelling, *The British Communist Party* (London: A. and C. Black, 1958) and N. Wood, *Communism and the British Intellectuals* (New York: Columbia University Press, 1959).

privileged are ambivalent about their own privileges. In Britain, this source of middle-class support for the Communists was all the more effective because of the class-specific character of middle-class culture. Joining the Communist Party (or accepting its leadership or collaboration on a range of issues) appealed to many as a mode of enlarging their experience. Furthermore, British Communists often fused a peculiar form of nationalism with revolutionary doctrine: The coming elimination of class antagonisms was to be an act of national self-discovery and re-integration. This theme, in a number of variants, continually recurs in the ideology of the British Left. Socialist internationalism and a devotion to little England (or Welsh or Scots' or Irish nationalism) have coexisted for decades. Working-class recruits often joined the Communist Party because it seemed unrestrainedly militant in its strategic doctrine; whatever tactical concessions it made to the Labour Party, it insisted on the political value of industrial action. Hopes in and illusions about the Soviet Union, for a long time, were approximately equivalent in both sectors of the Party.

The purges of the 30's and the consolidation of Stalinism had the usual effects on some of the intellectuals. This was countered, in the United Kingdom, by the especially intense concern of the intellectuals with the fate of the Spanish Republic (as well as the rise of Fascism in general.) Were the Spanish Communists not defending the Republic and, in these circumstances, was not criticism of the Communist movement a gratuitous contribution to the Right? (It was only much later that Orwell's critique of Stalinism struck home.)

It must also be remembered that, in contradistinction to Franklin Roosevelt's government, the Conservative governments of the 30's were viewed as, until 1939, bent on encouraging European Fascism. Even among those who entertained doubts, therefore, as to whether the 1936 Soviet Constitution had been applied to the letter in the Soviet Union, there were effective inhibitions on a break with the Communist Party. The German-Soviet Non-Aggression Pact of 1939, for many, overcame those inhibitions. But these were difficulties more or less peculiar to the intellectuals, and to other middle class recruits either to the Party itself or to its orbit; the working class militants, by and large, were either less squeamish about Stalinism or treated accounts of it as inventions. (The response of the working class rank and file in France and Italy to the crisis of 1956 was not dissimilar.)

The end of the 30's, then, saw a serious decline in the numbers and influence of the British Communist Party. The Soviet Union's entry into the war, however, reversed this trend. The hard-core militants remained in the Party; the more sensitive of them hoped that the postwar period would bring a relaxation of Stalinist repression. They prepared themselves, however, for their eventual acceptance of Zhdanovism by viewing the German attack on the Soviet Union as a justification of the Stalinist terror that had preceded it. Meanwhile, newer and younger recruits joined the party from the middle classes. Their social and occupational origins were discernibly different from those of their predecessors in the 30's: They were from the intermediate and lower ranges of the middle classes, and they tended to be technicians, scientists, and administrators rather than intellectuals with humanistic interests. They were attracted by an image of Communism as a system which, transferred to Britain, would pulverize its traditional inertia and inefficiencies and give it a newer and higher national unity. In this respect, they were ideologically closer to the working class militants in the Party than their predecessors. This explains something of the Party's cohesion in the postwar years.

The Labour victory of 1945 compelled the British Communists to adopt a policy of critical support of the Labour Government. The number of Communist M.P.'s elected in

1945 was but two; a small group of Labour M.P.'s suspected of being Communists were subsequently dropped by the Labour Party as candidates. The pronounced moderation of the Labour Government's domestic policy gradually altered the policy of critical support to one in which criticism became predominant; the foreign policy decisions which aligned the Labour Government with the United States at the beginnings of the Cold War completed this process.

From the late 40's onwards, the Communist Party was reduced, with respect to the Labour Party, to fishing in its often troubled waters. The domestic effects of the Cold War in Britain were not as striking as they were in the United States. Nothing like McCarthyism developed, although it need not be imagined that known Communists were entirely without occupational difficulties. The chief effect of the Cold War (compounded with the Labour Government's loss of momentum) was to discourage critical political thought. The British Communist Party, therefore, was forced back into a defensive ideological position; new recruits to it were few, although it did attract some who were psychologically repelled by the generally restrictive social climate.

The Twentieth Congress of the CPSU, and the crisis of the Communist movement in 1956 had profound effects on the British Communists. Following Khrushchev's speech, a number of Communist intellectuals began to publish, in opposition to the Central Committee, a journal, *The Reasoner*. Its editors were Edward Thompson and John Saville. Thompson and Saville were never Stalinists; they had, rather, suffered in silence throughout the Stalinist period. Their attack on the leadership of the British Communist Party was interesting particularly for the discrepancy between its objectives and its actual results. Its objectives were nothing less than the conversion of the Party into an independent and critical group of British socialists, exerting pressure from the Left on the

Labour Party. *The Reasoner* attracted the support of a number of Communist intellectuals, but in the end, the Party leadership beat off the challenge with little difficulty. The dissidents were either expelled or forced to resign.

The crisis in Poland, in October 1956, and the Hungarian Revolution strengthened the resolution of the intellectuals; the singular conclusion to the period of the "Hundred Flowers" in China in 1957 finished the process. Dozens of intellectuals left the Party, including some very respectable scholars in the universities. This time, the scientists and technicians were not unaffected. Another loss to the Party, however, was that of a group of working-class activists who went over to the hitherto minuscule British Trotskyite group. It is difficult to say why these men, not numbering more than a few hundred but highly experienced and influential in factory agitation, chose the crisis of 1956 as an occasion for leaving the Party. It can be supposed that they were long restive under Party discipline, and that they had begun to suspect that the Soviet Union was not an unequivocally revolutionary force. The Hungarian repression, and the ideological justification for a break with the Communists supplied by the Party's own intellectuals, allowed them to shift to a pure agitational culture. This, and other losses in the working class and the trade union movement, was apparently evaluated by the Party leadership as more severe than the defection of the intellectuals.

The Trotskyite movement, which received new impetus from the difficulties of the Communists, had always exhibited those centrifugal tendencies which characterize the life of Leftist sects. The new infusion of personnel in 1956 and 1957 allowed some surprised Trotskyite leaders to imagine that, for them, a new period of ideological prosperity was at hand. The adherence to Trotskyism of two or three intellectuals may have contributed to their euphoria. In fact, the intrinsic sectarianism of the movement by 1959 had produced new splits. The ultimate beneficiary of the crisis in the Communist Party was the Labour Party.

Enough has been said in the preceding sections of this essay to suggest that the Labour Party is not now, and in the discernible future will not be, a revolutionary force in British society.[5] Quite apart from the rather obvious difficulty that Britain is not a nation with a revolutionary potential, the Labour Party is and has been a coalition of exceedingly different elements. The (occasional) near-revolutionary impulses manifested by the minority have always been cancelled out by the (persistent) reformism of the majority. On the one occasion when a pre-revolutionary mood swept over the Party and millions of its voters (during the 1926 General Strike),[6] the leadership was ideologically unprepared to give expression to it; in any case, the weight of that particular struggle was borne by the trade-union movement. Despite some legacies of syndicalism, the unions were unable, and unwilling, to develop the struggle in a revolutionary direction.

The chief elements in the Labour coalition are the trade unions and a group of middle-class intellectuals. Whereas middle-class voters constitute, in ordinary circumstances, a relatively low proportion of the Labour vote (1945 was something of an exception), the influence of middle-class leaders in the Party, and particularly in the Parliamentary Party, is very great. Attlee and Gaitskell are of upper middle-class origins; despite their alliance with working-class politicians they have retained the personal *habitus* and style of thought of the educated middle class. Their undeviating refusal of an ideological critique of the social structure (disguised as ideological pragmatism), their extreme respect for the rules of

5. See G. D. H. Cole, *British Working-Class Politics, 1832–1914* (London: G. Routledge and Sons, Ltd., 1941), and *A History of the Labour Party from 1914* (London: 1948).

6. J. Symons, *The General Strike* (London: Cresset Press, 1957).

the Parliamentary and political game (which the Conservatives, sure of their status as the party of gentlemen, have more consistently violated), and above all, their implicit assumption that a new British social policy could be derived from a middle-class ethic, are evidence of the tenacity of their heritage. This last point requires emphasis: At times it has seemed that the Labour Party's vision of the egalitarian "New Jerusalem" in Britain was one in which all were to be elevated to middle-class standards. In another version of what a socialist Britain might look like, to be sure, a more organic theory predominates: The place provided for the working class is to be made worthier of human beings, access to the elite and intermediate levels of the class structure is to be thrown open, but the class structure, however modified, is to continue.

It well may be asked why the working-class segment of the Labour Party accepts middle-class leadership. The answer is that its attitude is not entirely unambiguous.[7] The trade-union leaders are often, of course, recruited from the sections of the working class most receptive to the cultural pressures of the larger society. The incorporation in the British class struggle of the British class system strikes them as not alone part of the nature of things social but as a positive asset. In fact, the middle class does have the education, the techniques of command and compromise, and the experience lacking to all but the most exceptional of working class leaders. Underlying the trade unionists' acceptance of middle-class political leadership, additionally, is their definition of the market struggle as a limited one. Having renounced syndicalism, they are only logical to seek a political alliance with the more sympathetic sections of the middle classes. There is, however, a powerful, if presently suppressed, counter-

7. M. Harrison, *Trade Unions and the Labour Party Since 1945* (London: Allen and Unwin, 1960) and F. Zweig, *The Worker in the Affluent Society* (London: 1961).

current. The British working class has long been encapsulated in its own peculiar culture, one which emphasized familiar, neighborhood, and class loyalties and which was drastically separated from the higher national culture by idiom, perspective, and a certain bluntness of style. Working-class and middle-class Labour politicians are no less marked by these differences than the rest of their countrymen. The important role in the Parliamentary Party of articulate and sophisticated journalists, lawyers, and university teachers has at times irritated working-class sensitivities.[8]

It is striking, however, that the present intense ideological conflict within the Labour Party can on no account be derived from these differences. The positions taken by the middle-class leadership under Gaitskell are supported by a majority of the trade unionists in the Party. (The most able and important trade-union leaders, incidentally, now exercise their influence outside the Parliamentary Labour Party; the trade-union M.P.'s are not a conspicuously distinguished group.) The leader of the Party's Left, Michael Foot, is from a noted middle-class family. It is true that Frank Cousins, the General Secretary of the Transport and General Workers' Union, supports the Party's Left: but his predecessors in that post supported the Right.

Gaitskell's general line is reasonably coherent, and its major elements may be stated as follows:[9] Capitalism has had

8. On working-class culture, see R. Hoggart, *The Uses of Literacy* (London: Chatto and Windus, 1957); A. Bullock's biography of the late Ernest Bevin [*Life and Times of Ernest Bevin*], Vol. 1 (London: Heinemann, 1960) tells us a good deal about these conflicts within the Labour Party.

9. The recent debate on the future of the Labour Party is compounded of a number of elements: differing interpretations of recent changes in British social structure and their political consequences, conflicting views of the sources of popular electoral decision, and divergent conceptions of socialism. The earlier anthology edited by R. H. S. Crossman, *New Fabian Essays* (London: Turnstile Press, 1952), reflects the views of many in the Labour Party at the beginning of a prolonged and unanticipated period of political drought for British Socialism. Many of the tendencies expressed in the sub-

its teeth pulled; Democratic Socialists have to deal with opponents vastly different than those of a generation, or even two decades, ago. The outlines of the Welfare State have been accepted by most parties to political debate; the question really is the extent to which the welfare function is to be extended. Wholesale nationalization is very likely to prove inefficient (and in any case is an electoral liability). The workers themselves seem, through their trade unions, to abjure anything like workers' control of industry. Government direction of a mixed economy, and generous expenditure on the Welfare Services (and on national necessities like education, as well as on national amenities like the arts) are to be the mechanisms of socialist politics. The gradual elimination of painful discrepancies in material rewards between the social classes and, above all, the provision of adequate educational opportunity to open careers to talent from all of them will, in time, erode that exaggerated snobbism which still disfigures Britain.

This interpretation of contemporary British society dictates a particular approach to electoral politics. Gaitskell's opponents in the Labour Party, quite unfairly, hold that the reverse order applies, and that the Party leadership's ideological justification of its tactics and strategy is simply intel-

---

sequent debate can be found, however, *in nuce* in this text. C. A. R. Crosland's *The Future of Socialism* (London: J. Cape, 1956) opened the current phase of the discussion. Two recent contributions represent antithetical views: Crosland's *Can Labour Win?* and Crossman's *Labour in the Affluent Society*, both Fabian tracts published in London in 1960. The reflections on the election written by M. Abrams, R. Rose, and R. Hinden, *Must Labour Lose?* (Harmondsworth: Penguin Books, 1960) appear to be consonant with what a large majority of the Parliamentary Labour Party thinks. See the critique by R. Samuel, "Dr. Abrams and the End of Politics," *New Left Review*, No. 5 (1960). Abrams originally published his views on the 1959 election in *Socialist Commentary*, and from August 1960 a number of issues carried an interesting discussion of the problems he raised. It is interesting that in this debate, John Strachey's very serious text, *Contemporary Capitalism* (London: V. Gollancz, 1956), has gone largely unremarked.

lectual opportunism. If it were simply that, it might well prove less resistant to their attacks on it. In fact, these views constitute a perfectly plausible response to a situation of objectively limited possibilities; it is their adaptation to the situation which makes them so effective. The working class, or important sections of it, is undergoing a process of partial assimilation to a middle-class style of life; an aggressive class emphasis in Labour politics in these circumstances would be inappropriate. Moreover, it would alienate precisely those middle-class voters, in a period of expansion in the tertiary sector of the economy, without whose votes no Labour government is possible.

Precisely the most self-conscious and articulate elements in the working class are affected by the new prosperity; previously they have been traditional Labour voters. Approximately one-third of the working class usually votes Conservative; pending the conclusion of a number of current inquiries into "The Tory Worker," we can guess that they are among the most economically, intellectually, and psychologically restricted manual workers. Their Toryism well may be a classical case of what Engels termed "false consciousness"—insofar as it is conscious at all. The threat to Labour's traditional working-class vote, clearly, is of a different kind. What, during the 1959 election campaign, Gaitskell termed "a modest programme of social reform" is clearly designed to meet the ideological requirements of those seeking group and individual advancment within the present social structure. That is what the Labour Party's battered Left cannot forgive Gaitskell.

The Left of the Labour Party draws upon a number of traditions: Christian Socialism and pacificism, the militancy of the old Independent Labour Party, the blunt and atheoretic British Marxism of the old Social Democratic Federation. Mostly, however, it seems to draw upon nostalgia—for a period in which all lines were sharply drawn, the enemy was clearly identifiable, and the need for immediate and drastic action was clear.[10] It rejects the recent analysis of British society propagated by the Labour leadership (which found its most cogent expression in Anthony Crosland's *The Future of Socialism*). Behind the newer public-relations techniques of a reformed British capitalism it detects an ancient and unrepentant beast. The burden of its charge against the leadership is that it allows the Conservatives to define the limits of Labour politics; the Labour Left, for instance, does not share Gaitskell's doubts about the constitutional propriety and political efficacy of industrial action for political purposes. The Left enjoys considerable, practically massive, support in the local party organizations. There, the intellectuals (often school teachers and technicians) and trade-union militants to whom an unambiguous vision of political conflict appeals, are relatively independent of those groupings which dominate the Parliamentary Labour Party—in which the Left is a small minority. Once led by the gifted Aneurin Bevan, then deserted by him, this minority is in continual conflict with the Party leadership.

The Party's Left did, recently, twice score on the leadership. After the Party's defeat in 1959, Gaitskell proposed to amend that clause in the Party's Constitution which called for the "common ownership of the means of production, distribution and exchange." The storm that followed in the Party, aligning with the Left many who customarily supported Gaitskell (a certain element of working-class resentment against the middle-class intellectuals in Gaitskell's *entourage* played some part in this), may best be characterized by recalling Kautsky's injunction to Bernstein during an ideological crisis in the German Social Democratic Party: "One doesn't say things like that; one simply does them!"

The Party's present continuity with its socialist traditions having been reaffirmed, Gaitskell was again free in fact to

10. See the weekly, *Tribune*.

revise them. In 1960, an even more striking success occurred when the Party's annual conference approved a policy of unilateral nuclear disarmament for Britain. The fiction that the Party's parliamentary leadership, or even its executive committee, was subordinate to the conference had publicly to be discarded, but a year later the decision was reversed. The Left, which had temporarily won trade-union support on this issue, lost it when trade-union officialdom reimposed its authority.

In general, however, the Labour Left can claim a considerable, if negative, sort of success. Some members of the Party who rationally agree with the leadership appear, at times, to accept the Left's claims to be sole custodians of the Party's Socialist Conscience. The Left has an embarrassing competence in discovering just those issues on which the leadership's tendency to moderation pushes it either into tacit acceptance of the government's policies or into a somewhat half-hearted opposition. The Left is not so incurably sectarian as to suppose that a Labour government under the present leadership would not differ from a Conservative one. What it does is to create an intra-party atmosphere in which the leadership has been forced onto the ideological defensive; that some element of drive and inner resolution is missing in the party is a proposition with which it is difficult to disagree. (The more intelligent opponents of the Left do not take seriously their own stated view that the Left is responsible for most of the Party's present electoral difficulties.)

The Left's success is, however, strictly negative; neither its parliamentarians, nor those who support it elsewhere in the Party, have been able to develop a political program to oppose Gaitskell's. The Left's demand that the total working-class vote be mobilized by a militant Socialist politics is unrealistic; quite apart from the Tory worker, the remainder of the working class is not at the moment responsive to the political appeals of the 1930's. The Left despite the fact that many of its personnel come from the new middle classes is even more incapable of making contact with this stratum at this stage of its development. It takes such consolation as it can from the fact that Gaitskell himself does not appear to be very effective in this respect either. Given this condition of mutual *stasis,* indeed of frustration, it is not surprising that in a sphere where the differences between party factions do seem more meaningful—foreign affairs—they are intense and bitter.

The Attlee government, from the very beginnings of the Cold War, accepted America's intiatives in policy toward the Soviet Union. The stationing of American nuclear strike forces in the United Kingdom dates from 1950, and the Labour Party leadership has more or less consistently followed the logic of both its decisions to make available the bases and to develop an independent British atomic and thermonuclear arsenal. German rearmament, NATO, the entire chain of alliances and pacts thrown up about the borders of the Soviet Union, have all had official Labour support. The Labour Party opposed the Suez intervention (not least, on grounds that it had no American sanction), but in 1958 it gave only cautious expression to its doubts about the American-British intervention in the Lebanon and Jordan. It is true that the Labour Party has taken a rather different line on the recognition of the Chinese People's Republic, and that it has urged "flexibility" in the approach to the Soviet Union, particularly in the period when Dulles appeared not to have read Stalin's death notice; but in these respects Labour policy has not differed appreciably from that of the Conservatives.

Indeed, the bipartisanship of official Labour foreign policy has at times seemed to constitute a major source of irritation to the Labour Left; the roots of its opposition, however, lie rather deeper. Firstly, the Labour Left finds it exceedingly difficult to participate in the ideological defense of the West.

This strikes many in the Labour Party as the extension into foreign policy of that alleged acceptance of the capitalist social system they find so repugnant in the Party's domestic program. The obvious deficiencies in the West's ideological position (the alliance with a number of regimes of dubious democratic credentials, the ambiguous nature of Western Germany's recent conversion to democratic values, and the more unreasoning sorts of anti-Communism manifest in the United States) have been less causes of this attitude than not entirely unwelcome justifications of it. Secondly, the Labour Left is ideologically incapable of a pure form of anti-Soviet politics; many of its supporters conceive of the Soviet Union as an errant socialist state, but a socialist state nonetheless; this attitude, difficult to justify during the rigors of Stalin's last years, has been greatly reinforced by recent developments inside the Soviet Union and the Communist bloc generally. Other attitudes, exhibited by perhaps more members of the Left, constitute a third and more complex source of opposition on foreign policy; these may be imperfectly summarized as the conception of an independent British mission in the world.[11]

For the Labour Left, it is clear, this mission would take the form of some kind of neutralism; Britain would either leave NATO or assume a highly independent role within it. (The closure of, or the imposition of very severe controls upon, American bases is a *sine qua non* of this policy.) Equally important, Britain would strengthen its ties with the Commonwealth nations, not least, those in Africa and Asia. Free to resume social democratic experimentation at home—it is one of the least implausible theses of the Labour Left that the material and psychological requirements of Britain's adherence to NATO have severely restricted opportunities for a Socialist politics in Britain—and linked to the Commonwealth

11. See the pamphlet by J. Rex, *Britain Without the Bomb, New Left Review* (1960).

nations by ties both economic and ideological, Britain would once again emerge as an independent force in the world. What is at issue, now, is not the degree of realism or irrealism this conception entails, but the fact that it is a socialist version of what may be termed imperial nostalgia. Britain's neutralist-socialist mission in the world, upon closer examination, appears to have interesting similarities with the Labour doctrine to which it is opposed: the Party leadership's conception of "responsible" foreign policy. Both, briefly, are derived from the liberal conscience's strenuous notion of the duty of the educated and the privileged in the world, Britain being cast for international purposes not incorrectly as an educated and privileged nation. (We shall see, subsequently, that the ideological similarities between those who would, at any price, renounce British nuclear weapons and some of those who would risk the suicidal implications of retaining them, in so exposed a country, are equally striking.)

On one set of issues, both factions of the Labour Party seem to agree—those connected with the process of decolonization. Important differences on specific questions of tactics and timing (the Party's leadership as we might expect, tends to take a more administrative attitude to some of these questions, that is, it is not instinctively suspicious of the police) are discernible. By and large, however, the entire Labour Party favors an accelerated process of decolonization and tends to sympathize with the liberation movements in colonial territories. This has not always been an unequivocal way to win votes: Some years ago Gaitskell found it necessary to repudiate Barbara Castle, a prominent Left M.P., who had publicly intimated that the behavior of British troops in Cyprus was not beyond reproach. On the critical issue of Suez, however, the Party was largely united.

What is striking about the attitude of the Labour Party is not so much its morality as its peculiar moral temper: Much emphasis is placed upon Britain's responsibility for colonial peoples, even though this is a responsibility the colonial peoples would often be pleased to have the British shed. Often enough, and particularly on the Party's Left, a curious idealization of colonial liberation leaders and movements may be noted; it seems extraordinarily difficult, for instance, for any number of Labourites to deal with the fact that in Ghana the opposition finds itself not merely outnumbered in Parliament but in jail. Perhaps this is connected with the fact that the recognition of the omnipresence of one-party regimes in ex-colonial countries might lead to a critical examination of the proposition that Britain has unique ideological goods for export.

The possibility of a new British contribution to socialism has also been a preoccupation of that group known as the British New Left.[12] The European New Left, as a whole, emerged in the late 50's in a fusion of two streams of discontent. Communists, or Communist sympathizers, began to express their criticisms of Stalinism and bureaucracy in Communist society and in the Western Communist parties. This led, quickly enough, to a search for a principled basis of criticism and, often, to a break with the Communist movement.

Some Social Democrats, meanwhile, were mounting an attack on the particular forms of reformism found in the Western European parties; this frequently led them to a reconsideration of Marxism. These two tendencies met, ideologically, in a revival of the problem of *alienation* discussed in Marx's early manuscripts. The revisionist Communists and revolutionary Social Democrats engaged on this intellectual terrain were somewhat surprised to find a good deal of it already occupied by Catholic and Protestant social thinkers

12. See the journals *Universities and Left Review* and *The New Reasoner* which merged at the end of 1959 in *New Left Review*. The essay by G. Lichtheim on the British new Left in *Soviet Survey*, No. 32 (1960), is a reasonable assessment.

seeking to humanize (and socialize) their ethics; the European New Left has in fact been strengthened by the participation of socialists with religious commitments.

This deviation from the socialist traditions, rigidified in the second half of the nineteenth century, is significant; the New Left is a movement which has attracted a new generation, indifferent where not hostile to ossified concepts of socialism. The particular concatenation of events which has produced the New Left has varied from country to country. Everywhere, the crisis of Communism was important. In Italy, it was the major event; there, the movement includes many not only in Nenni's Socialist Party and some Socialist Democrats, but some who have remained in the PCI. In France, the coincidence of the Hungarian Revolution and the Suez intervention affected both the PCF and the SFIO and the new PSU was the eventual result—a party which has also gained a notable convert to socialism in Pierre Mendès-France. In Great Britain, the crisis of the Communist Party was an important but not the dominant event. Rather, the Suez intervention awakened the political interests of a younger generation—anticolonialism fusing almost immediately with the campaign against nuclear weapons. The younger generation, many of its members "scholarship boys," was also critical of the cultural traditions it was supposed to assimilate in the universities; a concern with cultural questions is a special characteristic of the British New Left.

I have spoken of the New Left as a movement; it would be more accurate to characterize it as a mood—particularly in Britain, where it has not assumed any definite organizational form. Those in the New Left consider it their duty to work inside the Labour Party, where they have effected a tactical alliance with the Bevanite rump led by Michael Foot; the boundaries between the old and new left are sometimes obscure. Indeed, in Britain, all the boundaries are fluid. The work of Richard Titmuss and his associates, a sustained and careful critique of the Welfare State, is generally associated with the New Left; but the Titmuss group were the authors of the Labour Party's new pension plans. The fluidity of the boundaries may well be another instance of the curious absorptive capacities by which British society and culture seem able to encapsulate and assimilate, while degutting, new ideas. The New Left did become fashionable for a while, and has subsequently lost much of its drive and originality; the phenomena are connected.

The publication of two journals, subsequently merged (1959) in the *New Left Review,* constituted the beginning of the New Left in Britain. *The Reasoner,* which became *The New Reasoner* when it changed from mimeographed to printed form and its editors were expelled from the Communist Party, has been mentioned. Its editors, readers, and contributors were generally in their late 30's, at least; it was produced in the industrial north of England, and its editors did have contact with the Labour movement, which is so important in that part of the country; it was, finally, marked by an obsessive insistence on finding new content for Marxist forms of thought. The *Universities and Left Review,* begun by a group of recent Oxford graduates, was much livelier; its readers were younger; it attacked a number of themes not hitherto central to discussion within the Labour Party; and, finally, it was an instant success.

The success of *Universities and Left Review* (edited and distributed in a manner which may charitably be termed improvised, some 8000 of each issue were sold, and its contents were often publicly discussed elsewhere) is not entirely easy to explain. The idiom of the younger generation, of course, was fresh; the concentration on problems of mass and high culture, of the quality of daily life, and the search for a new socialist ethic seemed both new and revelant. What was remarkable about much of this was that it represented an effort, mainly unintended, to admix British socialist thought with

American and Continental elements. The emphasis on mass culture owed much to *Dissent*, even if the British problem was set in the context of the prosperity of the British working class. The discussion of a new socialist morality was imported from Paris. The image of British society developed in *ULR* bore a striking resemblance to Wright Mills' portrait of America. This intellectual internationalism, rather exceptional in recent British socialism, may be explained by the cosmopolitan identities of the four original editors of *ULR*— a West Indian, a Canadian Catholic, and two offspring of the Eastern European Jewish immigration of the turn of the century. It is also explained, in part, as a reaction to the provincialism of much instruction in the social sciences in British universities. The simultaneous renewal of certain characteristically British socialist concerns (Titmuss' inquiries into the material conditions of the nation and the discussion of the working class and national culture by Richard Hoggart and Raymond Williams)[13] seemed to promise a genuine renewal of British socialist thought. The promise has not been fulfilled; it remains to ask why.

The merger of *ULR* with *The New Reasoner* in *New Left Review* in 1959 marked an implicit renunciation of the program of *ULR*. The new journal turned, increasingly, to the daily stuff of politics. The editors and contributors of *The New Reasoner*, liberated from the Communist Party, gradually lost their ideological identity in the old Labour Left. It is rather more surprising that much the same thing happened to the younger *ULR* group. On the colonial problem, foreign policy (the New Left is, of course, neutralist and in favor of British nuclear disarmament), and on domestic social policy the New Left appears to have little to say that is not being said by the old. Its very real intellectual break-through in the sphere of culture (and the related area of education) has not

13. Titmuss, *op. cit.;* Hoggart, *op. cit;* R. Williams, *Culture and Society* (London: 1957) and *The Long Revolution* (London: 1960).

been followed by the development of a program for a new socialist politics.

The *ULR* began, in effect, by asking if a new socialist politics was possible; its lack of success suggests that the question was painfully relevant. The *ULR* and the *New Left Review* have both published interesting inquiries, to be sure, into the structure of the new British capitalism; these have not given answers to the problem of inducing a socially critical, much less revolutionary, consciousness in an electorate only too eager to cooperate with its masters. The New Left insists on the manipulability of public opinion, but occasionally drops this theme in favor of an impassioned defense of popular capacities for spiritual growth, despite indoctrination. The contradiction has not been resolved in any practical way. Neither has the promising fusion of continental socialist theory and American social criticism which British Labourism developed. In these circumstances, the energies of the journal's young readers (and of nearly every other homeless member of the British Left) have gone into a movement ostensibly apolitical; the Campaign for Nuclear Disarmament.

The Campaign for Nuclear Disarmament was founded in 1957 by a group of senior London intellectuals, the most prominent of them being Bertrand Russell. The leaders' original conception of the campaign was significantly different from its eventual course. Press statements signed by lists of notables; occasional public meetings to be addressed by the same notables; the gradual enlightenment of the public; the gradual conversion of the politicians. In short, what we may, with some justice, term the Left-Wing of the elite supposed that the usual methods of elite persuasion were appropriate. They reckoned without the fact that their attack on the manufacture and stockpiling of British nuclear weapons was interpreted by the government and the custodians of "responsible" opinion, including the Labour Party leadership, as beyond the limits of acceptable political debate. The notables of the Campaign were surprised, then, to find that their pronouncements were very largely ignored by the press and the other media of information; insofar as the Campaign was mentioned—not often—it was derided. The politicians and the editors who refused to play the game in the conventional British way did, in fact, sense more about the Campaign than its founders.

The latter insisted on its moral and non-political character. The manufacture and stockpiling of nuclear weapons with a view toward their eventual use was simply evil; the theory of the deterrent, moreover, entailed suicide for Great Britain. To these propositions were joined no political proposals. Some in the campaign initially thought their position compatible with the retention of American nuclear strike bases in Britain; others denied that it entailed a break with NATO; still others talked of a "British example to the world," to be echoed much later in Gaitskell's "non-nuclear club." No particular effort was made to enlist the support of the Labour Left; the trade unions (whose members, after all, produced British nuclear weapons and built nuclear bases) were ignored; a generalized critique of British foreign policy was simply lacking. The appeal to the public was based on conscience and self-interest: The apolitical formulation was supposed to mobilize the reserves of humanitarianism and common sense to be found in all parties. Contrary to the intentions of most of its initiators, however, the Campaign did assume an increasingly political character. It threatened and still threatens the leadership of the Labour Party, and it has introduced into contemporary British politics an ethic and tactics which almost merit the designation, revolutionary.

The initiators of the Campaign made only cursory provision for local organization. They were rather surprised when local groups not only developed at a rapid rate, but demanded a voice in the formulation and execution of Campaign policy. The Campaign, at its local levels, attracted three sorts of support:

1. A good many young people (many of them in their teens, in universities or schools), chiefly from all strata of the middle classes, seemed to find in the Campaign an occasion for expressing the usual discontents with their elders. The peculiar atmosphere of complacency with which the political elite dealt with the problem of nuclear weapons added to their irritation: Many of the young were and are far from complacent about the future of their nation, and complacency on this score struck them as symptomatic of the general incapacities of their parents, teachers, and rulers.[14] It must be emphasized that this youthful recruitment for the Campaign was by no means limited to the politically conscious, although participation in the Campaign for many served as a form of political education. Most of the young were apolitical, concerned expressly only with nuclear weapons; their general discontents were by and large unarticulated. Of the politically engaged, Liberals and even a scattering of Conservatives were outnumbered by those with Labour sympathies, but they were not overwhelmingly outnumbered.

2. The Campaign, along with the short-lived Suez protest that preceded it and the continuing movement against colonialism (a formal Anti-Apartheid Campaign has also been organized), mobilized the remnants of the bearers of the liberal conscience among those who cannot be described as young. Many of these Campaigners, as Christians, brought to the Campaign a moral fervor matched only by their consistent refusal to think in political terms. It is this group which means what it says when it proposes a British moral example to the world. It is as convinced of the political efficacy of

14. See Potter, *op. cit,* for a reasonably typical statement of the views of the younger intellectuals.

direct moral utterance as it is of Britain's unique capacity to deliver such utterance.

3. Somewhat later, the Labour Left began to appreciate the potentialities of the campaign. Although many on the Left of the Party endorsed the Campaign from its inception, they tended to think of it as an utopian or unrealistic instrument of politics. The Campaign's activists, most of them exceedingly uninterested in conventional Labour politics, convinced them that they were wrong.

The activists had, first, to convince the leaders of the Campaign itself. Against the latter's premonitions of disaster they pushed through, in 1958, a project for a four day demonstrative march from London to Aldermaston, the British nuclear weapons factory in Berkshire. The march, begun in Trafalgar Square, was mainly composed of the young. Their blue jeans, beards, jazz band and songs attracted derisive comment from the press,—but comment had been attracted. Next year's march, from Aldermaston to London, increased geometrically in size; the one in 1960 was larger, and by 1961 the march had to be split into two divisions, converging upon Trafalgar Squire from Aldermaston and from an American NATO air-base in Essex. (This last point is of some interest because, by 1961, the Campaign had begun to formulate a political program.) The marches themselves attracted so much publicity that the CND was able, increasingly, to gain a kind of hearing in the mass media; at any rate, the ability of CND to put nearly 100,000 demonstrators into Trafalgar Square is a measure of the size and determination of the movement.

The activists did not stop with the marches. Sit-downs at rocket bases and in front of government buildings precipitated a split over tactics in CND. Most recently, Bertrand Russell formed his Committee of One Hundred to pursue a policy of civil disobedience; H.M. Government obliged with a massive opportunity for further propaganda by jailing

Russell for a week. The "civil disobedience" in question has consisted mainly of deliberate violations of minor police regulations during sit-downs in Trafalgar Square or in front of the Ministry of Defense and the American and Soviet Embassies. There have been efforts, however, to board the American submarine tender and the rocket-equipped submarines based not far from Glasgow. The general public regards these demonstrations with astonishment rather than with hostility or sympathy. There is little doubt, however, that they have enlarged the range of debate about British foreign policy; despite the obvious absence of public sympathy for the demonstrations, these have contributed to a national mood in which the government is unable to take an authentically "strong" line in the current East-West crisis.

During these developments, the Labour Left has seized upon the CND and used it as a very effective weapon of intra-party warfare. The Left has claimed that the youthful and moral energies mobilized by CND can be captured by the Labour Party only if it renounces its current bipartisan foreign policy. The leadership has executed a number of maneuvers under this pressure, one of the last of them being the proposal for a "non-nuclear club." In 1960, however, the Left was able to defeat the leadership and the Party Conference passed a resolution favoring unilateral British nuclear disarmament; the leadership's triumph on this issue in 1961 was accompanied by its defeat on another resolution, which demanded an end to the American nuclear submarine bases in the United Kingdom. Despite the fact that the Labour Party today is not committed by its Conference to unilateral nuclear disarmament for Britain, nuclear disarmament remains an effective focus of many sorts of intra-party discontent.

Moreover, the Labour Left has given CND an increasingly political complexion; it has also been used as a recruiting ground for younger socialists, through the curious argument that only by joining the Labour Party (and campaigning against its leadership) can the young turn it into the kind of movement they now find it not to be. The demonstrations and the recent tactics adopted by the Russell group, in particular, also appeal to the Labour Left. These help, after all, to relieve its electoral and parliamentary frustrations and to create that atmosphere of simple moral struggle which it finds psychologically necessary. For the moment, despite a number of prominent converts among trade union officialdom, the movement against nuclear weapons has made little headway in the working class. It remains an expression of middle-class social protests. In a society organized like Great Britain, this is important enough: Elite and sub-elite recruits disaffected on so critical an issue can be an embarrassment to those in power. As yet, however, the nuclear protest movement in all of its variant forms has not encompassed enough people to pose an immediate threat of political disruption. Its ultimate potentialities (of which its leaders are now more aware) for something approaching revolutionary action ought not to be underestimated.

Finally, it may be well to add a word on the Communist Party's relationship to the nuclear disarmament movement—on which a certain confusion persists in the United States. The Communists at first regarded CND with contempt; this changed to embarrassment as the movement registered its initial successes. Precisely in a situation in which only the broadest and most flexible of tactics could allow it to make contact with any movement outside its own, the leadership of the British C.P. could not transcend its own incurable sectarianism. The psychology of the membership of CND and the movement's loose and haphazard structure made efforts at Communist penetration seem peculiarly unpromising. More important, CND and, more recently, the Committee of One Hundred have failed to distinguish between "imperialist" and "socialist" megatons and have condemned all nuclear weapons with equal energy. The C.P. has been reduced to ambiguous endorsement of the Aldermaston marches and to deploring the nuclear disarmers' tendency to criticize the Soviet Union. There are no Communists in the CND leadership and there is not much evidence of Communist participation at the local level. That the movement, with its attack on Britain's present foreign policy, cannot be entirely unwelcome to the Soviet Government is obvious.

This essay has often, too often, referred to the liberal conscience as surviving in contemporary Britain; what can be said about the recent revival of the Liberal Party itself? The fact that in the 1959 General Election, the total Liberal vote rose appreciably, and that in some constituencies the Liberals displaced Labour in second place on the ballot, suggests that the revival merits attention. The Liberals freely criticize both major parties and have doubtless profited, not least from among the young, from a certain revulsion for the recent political climate. A new generation of Liberal politicians has assumed command of what was a party in an advanced stage of spiritual arteriosclerosis; it is difficult to see what positive policies they will develop in their effort to attain major party status.[15]

For the moment, the Liberals have struck a number of attitudes, and in this respect they are not unlike the New Left—if rather more respectable. The Liberals have criticized the psychological restrictionism and the obsessive inability to innovate which characterizes much of British society. Not being bound to the Labour movement, they have also intimated that it affects the working class and its organizations as well. (Only a very few in the Labour movement, mainly intellectuals like Richard Crossman, Anthony Crosland, and Raymond Williams, have dared to do this.)

But the Liberals seem to lack a total picture of what has

15. The leader of the Liberal Party has recently published a tract which is a remarkable exercise in generality. See J. Grimond, *The Liberal Future* (London: 1959).

brought British society to this condition; furthermore, their image of a changed Britain is expressed in vocabulary which emphasizes its psychological consequences for individuals but says little or nothing about its institutions. The Liberals have drawn heavily upon the new middle class at its lower and intermediate levels; the negative components in the ideology of its supporters have been emphasized. They do not wish to be identified with the working class; they do not accept at face value the Conservatives' claim to be the only possible governors of Britain.

It is a striking indication of the potential disdain for conventional judgments to be found in the new Liberal Party that it very nearly approved a policy of unilateral nuclear disarmament for Britain. Unless concretized in rather a more substantial fashion, however, the potential independence of judgment of the Liberals is likely to evaporate; the social groups it represents are unable to alter British politics by themselves and must seek alliance with the strata above or below. There is no indication that the Liberal Party will be able to enlist either substantial sectors of the working class or, as it might have hoped, the managerial elite. If the liberal conscience is to find a modernized political expression, those interested in the effort are likely to throw their energies into the intra-party disputes of either the Conservative or Labour coalitions.

The tendencies described above range from Left through center, insofar as the traditional alignment applies to British politics. We may now examine, briefly, the extreme and eccentric Right. These are groups in pseudo-revolt; what interests them is not the defense of fixed interests and positions but the destruction of a world they never made.

The traditional Right-Wing of the Conservative Party does not appear to have grasped what has happened to British and world society; indeed, it may be doubted whether it quite understands its own fate within the Conservative organization. It has a leader with impeccable credentials, Lord Salisbury—but Salisbury, after helping Macmillan to power, became a nuisance and was induced to resign from the Cabinet. He resigned precisely on an issue which troubles the Tory Right greatly: the nature of Britain's relations to its colonies and ex-colonies.

On balance, the hesitant, but final liquidation of Empire by a Conservative government is incomprehensible to the Party's old guard.[16] It seems to them part of a process which includes inflation, working class prosperity, juvenile delinquency, colored immigration to Britain, American domination, and a general dissolution of all received expectations and standards. To these manifold ills, the Conservative Right cannot even oppose a coherent theory. (The one intellectual in Britain who consistently speaks for it, T. E. Utley, sees fit to spend his time denouncing not Communism or the Welfare State, but the French Revolution. This demonstrable capacity for going to the root of things has at times embarrassed the party of his choice; it is interesting that Utley is no longer an editorialist for *The Times*.)

The Tory Right would like, of course, an attack on the Trade Unions and the working class; it has a *rentier* mentality. Its pleasure at measures of economic restriction has been somewhat diminished by the fact that these tend to affect Conservative voters as well. The government's latest economic policy does indeed call for a restriction in wage increases; it also proposes some form of economic planning. In this, and a number of other questions, the Tory Right has been able to hinder but not block its own party leadership.

The analogy with the Labour Party Left has often been drawn, but it is not entirely satisfactory. It is true that, by and large, the parliamentary representatives of each oppositional faction are older and more inflexible than their party

16. The Party's *avant-garde,* however, understands very well what is happening. See the Bow Group pamphlet, *The New Africa* (London: 1962).

leaders. But the Labour Left is, at least, allied with the younger intellectuals of the Labour movement while the Conservative right is particularly disturbed at the views of those younger Conservative intellectuals who are in the "Bow Group." [17] They fear that these ideologues of the new Conservatism are covert socialists. Insofar as the Tory Right rests on a *rentier* base (retired officers and respectable ladies are very prominent in traditional local Conservative politics), and the Labour Left on an eroding working-class base, the analogy may be maintained. Both seem to speak for declining social strata.

There is this additional and important difference between the two extremes: The Labour Left's ideology is elaborated by intellectuals not directly recruited from the traditional working class. This gives the Labour Left the objective possibility, which it may or may not take, of constructing a political theory which can account for the transformation of that class. The Tory Right has almost no intellectuals; its spokesmen are members of the groups which respond instinctively to its appeal, and their capacity for articulating an appeal to other groups is extremely limited. They can, and do, speak the language of chauvinism and of "little England," which is not peculiar to themselves. (Obsessed by the belief that Britain itself is in immediate danger of internal Bolshevization, they are also resentful of the alliance with a powerful America.) But it is not, by itself, a vocabulary with which an entire election can be fought.

What the Tory Right feels about its own government, a curious and enterprising group known as the League of Empire Loyalists says—and does. The League supposes that a monstrous conspiracy to denude Britain not only of its Empire, but of its very national substance is at work and has no hesitation in pronouncing the present Conservative Gov-

17. See the Bow Group essays edited by D. Howell and T. Raison, *Principles in Practise* (London: 1961).

ernment party to the conspiracy. The forcible maintenance of the colonies and the exclusion of colored immigrants from the United Kingdom seem to be the main, if not the only, planks in its platform. The League is a very small group, but it has attracted a certain notoriety by its demonstrative attacks on the government. Its most notable feat, recently, has been the smuggling of two pseudo-bishops into an Anglican Ecumenical conference to protest an invitation to Archbishop Makarios, then leader of the Greek Cypriot campaign for independence. It has also sent commandoes into battle during the numerous recent London street demonstrations against Apartheid and colonialism.

These last battles, few but sharp, also have been joined by the British Fascists, who still exist. Mosley, their aging but brilliant leader, now takes the line that his only fault was "premature anti-Communism." [18] His journal, significantly, is entitled *The European*. Mosley propagates a doctrine of national renaissance through a new-style authoritarian state; he does not appear to have anything to say that he did not offer (on German and Italian Fascist models) twenty-five years ago. The racialism and anti-Semitism of the movement attract, of course, a number of recruits from the *lumpenproletariat;* the Fascists do carry on agitation in districts where racial conflict is latent. They are, equally, few in number; their few parliamentary candidates recently invariably have done very badly. Although the Fascists may well express the latent racialism and xenophobia of a good many people who ordinarily vote either Conservative or Labour, it is difficult to envisage circumstances in which many will be prepared to follow Mosley onto the secrets or vote for him. In this respect he must envy the nuclear disarmers.

This survey of the situation in Britain can conclude with some remarks on what may be termed cultural revolt, or cul-

18. See C. Cross, *The Fascists in Britain* (London: 1961).

tural dissent. Much has been heard about Britain's "angry young men," a group of dramatists and novelists who dominated discussion, at least, on the London literary scene during the second half of the recent decade.[19] In fact, the "angry young men" by no means constitute a unified movement with a single aesthetic or social doctrine. Rather, their works, like John Osborne's "Look Back in Anger," or Kingsley Amis' earlier "Lucky Jim," are conspicuous for their negative aspects. They represent a break with the genteel tradition in British literature (a break attempted many times before, it will be recalled) and an attack on the culture of the upper middle class. This last they depict as utterly lacking in vitality, at best empty and at worst a façade behind which brutality and egoism are at work. Some have insisted on a connection between the new literary mood and the alteration in the social composition of the educated brought about by the 1944 Education Act; the hypothesis is plausible. The *dramatis personae* of the new literature are provincials, *parvenus,* gypsies, workers, even Jews from the East End of London; there has emerged a British Jewish theatre which resembles nothing so much as the New York Group Theatre of the early '30's. What has occurred is a certain widening of perspective; the self-depiction of British society has become complicated and more differentiated. Some of this has a socially critical or a socialist content, if a rather vague one; the rest, like the surveys of British life projected on television, does not. It is difficult to avoid the impression, however, that much of the new realism is really a new version of British provincialism.

Certainly, the most profoundly "anti-bourgeois" novels produced recently in Britain have been written by the Oxford

19. See the symposium edited by T. Maschler, *Declaration* (London: MacGibbon and Kee, 1957). See also the recent study by J. Mander, *The Writer and Commitment* (London: Secker and Warburg, 1961). A particularly effective statement on the class character of British high culture has come recently from a young Briton who, like many, prefers the United States. See M. B. Green, *A Mirror for Anglo-Saxons* (New York: Harper, 1960).

philosopher, Iris Murdoch,[20] whose debt to French existentialism is very great. Iris Murdoch's novels lack all direct political or even social commentary; her subjects come from the more esoteric reaches of middle-class society itself. But her message, that all is not as it seems, is profoundly corrosive of British middle-class culture.

Cultural corrosion in the arts, of course, must have some kind of correlate in society itself. Particularly among the young, something has been happening to the British style of life. London is the center of these developments, and they radiate to the provinces at an unequal rate.[21] For the young in the entire range of strata constituting the middle class, the predominant influence has been Continental: Interest in good food, a certain ease of manner lacking in the older generation, and an open interest in sexuality have crossed the Channel.

For working-class youth, the models are American: Mass entertainment has transmitted a spectrum of conceptions and values strange to the older working-class generation, with its tight-knit familistic culture and its extremely limited sensuality. Although traditional Dixieland jazz may or may not still be found in New Orleans, it is exceedingly hard to avoid hearing it in the Midlands. These influences have been gladly, even generously, received by the young; what is striking is that they have not been assimilated with indigenous cultural elements, and that these seem to be declining by default.

Here, too, the passive and reactive character of the contemporary British response to social change is evident. Among certain intellectuals, particularly but not exclusively from

20. Miss Murdoch's latest novel, *The Severed Head* (London: Chatto and Windus, 1961) is rather far from Socialist realism.
21. Colin MacInness fictionalized account of the London race riots of 1958, *Absolute Beginners* (London: MacGibbon and Kee, 1959), provides a colorful and accurate *montage* of the new culture of central London and of the eagerness of working-class youth to adopt it.

working-class families, the response has been a curious senti-
mentalization of the old working-class culture; its traditional
solidarity and human solidity have been portrayed as the only
possible basis for the development of a future national culture. The pronounced negative components in working-class
culture have been ignored (its philistinism and narrowness,
for instance); the difficult problem of transcending a middle-
class culture, to the external accoutrements of which some of
the working class now aspire, has not even been faced.[22]

Although the young experiment in this fashion, and the intellectuals speculate as to how the pieces of a fragmented national culture may be fused, a considerable part of the traditionally cultivated middle class insists that nothing is really
wrong. The recent and absurd trial over the publication of an
unexpurgated version of Lawrence's *Lady Chatterley's Lover*
is a case in point.[23] The prosecution asked the jury if this was
fit literature to be placed in the hands of shop girls. The defense paraded an impressive set of witnesses, including a
bishop who defended the portrayal of sexual intercourse as
sacramental and a large number of university teachers of English who declared that Lawrence's openness about sexuality
was puritan in inspiration. The point is not whether these
experts were correct, but that they were forced to fight on
alien terrain. The maintenance of the fiction that Britain is a
Christian country, neatly divided into classes, all of which accept that middle-class moral authority preserved especially in
the ancient universities, may be regarded as an historical
curiosity. It is also an interesting example of a defense mechanism, of a refusal to come to terms with historical change,
which does not allow an optimistic prognosis as to Britain's
future.

22. A recent Fabian pamphlet by R. Wollheim has the merit of raising some
of these problems: *Socialism and Culture* (London: 1961).
23. C. H. Rolph (ed.), *The Trial of Lady Chatterley* (London: Penguin Books,
1961).

II

In conclusion, something may be said about the possible effects of the social and cultural situation sketched above on Britain's foreign policy. In one respect, this is very difficult: Britain is an opaque society, even when undergoing changes which might be expected to render its basic structures more visible. In another respect, nothing is easier: The balance of social and cultural forces in contemporary Britain is so exquisite that, barring catastrophe, we can suppose that things will continue as they are.

Internally, a major alteration in political forces can be produced only by prolonged economic crisis accompanied by a material and persistent drop in the national standard of living. (Some of the most radical of British socialists now say that, contrary to their normal image of capitalism, the working class will not be the only class to suffer from a crisis, even if it is the first one to do so.) A depression of this sort will presumably put another Labour Government in office; it will also so reduce its scope for experimentation as to limit it to emergency measures. These measures will be drastic, but they will not necessarily constitute preliminary steps toward a social revolution in Britain. If we may extrapolate from the recent past, a Labour Government elected in these circumstances under the present Labour leadership will be careful to establish working relations with important segments of the economic elite. It is probable that a government of this type can institutionalize in Britain the sort of economic planning now found in France, and this with the cooperation of some from the managerial elite. No profound innovations in Britain's international commitments need be looked for from such a regime; the economic crisis will *not* provide incentives to considerable displays of British independence of NATO.

There is, however, a further possibility about which we can only speculate; it lies in the realm of national psychology. A severe economic crisis of this sort must deal a further blow to the self-esteem of the nation, as sensed by millions of ordinary Britons. It is possible that this will accentuate the current British inversion, and that a bout of chauvinism and xenophobia will result, with direct consequences for the position of the colored minority in Britain and indirect consequences for Britain's foreign relationships in general. A certain withdrawal may take place; it is even possible (but not very probable, to be sure) that a domestic swing to the Right may be accompanied by an external *rapprochement* with the Communist bloc.

Britain's entry into the Common Market, at this writing by no means certain, may precipitate just this sort of psychological crisis. It is significant that membership in the Common Market is opposed by the Labour Left and the Tory Right with equal indignation, if with somewhat different arguments. The Labour Left entertains chilling visions of an international capitalist conspiracy to extirpate (hypothetical) advances toward British socialism; it appears to have overlooked the existence of large and militant working-class parties in Belgium, France, and Italy—not to mention German Social Democracy.[24] The Tory Right fears the political implications of a European economic union; Britain's sovereignty is allegedly threatened. Both insist that joining the Market must entail the sacrifice of Britain's unique mission in the world, a mission which it can exercise only through those Commonwealth ties which the Common Market would supposedly weaken. If Britain does enter the Market, the pound will be almost certainly devalued; Continental competition will have painful effects on the entire British economy. The new Conservatives and the Liberals think that only

24. See the pamphlet by M. Barratt-Brown and J. Hughes published by *New Left Review*, "Britain's Crisis and the Common Market" (1961). The Labour center and Right, however, also have their doubts on the Common Market—both Harold Wilson and Douglas Jay are opposed to Britain's entry.

this shock will revivify Britain; many industrialists and econo-mists, more crudely, anticipate lower wages. The experiment will be just that; its success is not certain, and its failure would have incalculable consequences.

An undercurrent of resentment at the United States, which has urged Britain to enter the Market, is discernible in some recent public discussion in Britain. Indeed, the conception of an independent world role for Britain (in the context of the Commonwealth) is often intended to make Britain inde-pendent of the United States. It is at this point, finally, that we may examine the peculiar strains which affect Britain's membership in the anti-Communist alliance led by the United States.

The present British political elite is aware that it rules a small country, extremely vulnerable to nuclear attack. It has long since decided (Suez was both an aberration and a con-vincing lesson) that it can at best fight delaying actions in colonial areas. The decision to allow South Africa to leave the Commonwealth, and Britain's recent tacit support for the Katanga regime, are not as contradictory as may appear; both are part of a policy of cutting losses. The elite, further, senses that the population of the United Kingdom is tired of war and the threat of war.

The process of depoliticization discussed in this essay also has contributed to a massive public indifference to the more militant forms of anti-Communism; to this must be added a surprising residue of wartime pro-Russian sentiment[25] and the fact that, untroubled by a domestic Communist movement of any importance, the British do not consider themselves ideologically threatened by Communism. The American at-titude on this score is held by millions of Britons to be a sign of either political immaturity or political pathology. Further,

25. The extremely enthusiastic reception given the first Soviet space pilot, Major Gagarin, when he visited Britain in 1961, was partly a response to the Berlin crisis.

the elite aspires (or pretends) to a higher form of political wisdom and supposes that it can transmit this to its American allies; this almost invariably takes the form of urging patience and restraint in situations of crisis. Briefly put, the British commitment to the anti-Communist alliance is more ambiguous than is commonly supposed. It is true that Britain has placed nuclear strike bases at America's disposal; it is increasingly clear that the British elite assumes that the Americans can always be persuaded not to force matters to the point where they must be used.

So much for the Conservatives; what about the Labour movement? The strength of Gaitskell's own commitment to the American alliance need not be doubted. At times, it has seemed somewhat stronger than that of H.M. Foreign Office. It may be suggested, however, that the vehemence of Gaitskell's view, and that of the Party faction he represents, is directly proportional to their awareness of the unreliability, on this issue, of the Labour movement as a whole. In general we may suppose that the more acute the international crisis, the more likely are the centrifugal tendencies in the Labour movement to be activated.

The specific circumstances of particular crises will, of course, vary. The frankness with which almost the entire range of British opinion has declared that Britain is unwilling to fight on Berlin suggests that no foreseeable confrontation of the two super-powers will result in the sort of partisan consensus that would allow a British government to take the country to war. It can be urged that, with American bases in Britain, British assent is not indispensable. To this it must be said that between five minutes to midnight and midnight even, or especially, Conservative Government may prove capable of very decisive action on this score.

There is one final reason for accepting this line of argument. It is that the movement for nuclear disarmament does not do so. Its leaders and followers are convinced that the

Conservative Government and the present Labour leadership would in fact, to use the official phrase, "honour their commitments." In these circumstances, pressure from this movement not to participate in American military moves can only increase. Labour official policy is not immune from yet another and perhaps more enduring reversal.

The movement for nuclear disarmament, despite its inner confusion, hesitations, and consummate amateurishness (perhaps because of the latter) has succeeded where all other postwar social protest in Britain has failed. It has focussed a variety of discontents on one issue and fused an heterogeneous set of supporters into a body which refuses to accept the British political consensus. Many members of the movement believe that nuclear weapons symbolize the ultimate pathology of a society to which they are opposed; many find nothing wrong with the society that the elimination of nuclear weapons cannot cure.

The coexistence in the same movement of these divergent types of motivation may be an indication of a potential weakness; for the moment, it is effectively a strength. The capacity of the movement to put thousands onto the London streets, a capacity which in a moment of acute crisis will surely be exploited, is the most astonishing feature of the current British political scene. This quasi-revolutionary development is, in the last analysis, also a reaction to the nation's changed position in the world. A moralizing politics of conscience originally enabled the British middle class to master the imperial and industrial power at the nation's disposal. It is not the least of ironies that with that power drastically reduced, the politics of conscience now emerges as a radical critique of conventional politics. The revolt, however, remains a reactive one.[26]

26. See the very perceptive account of Britain's current *malaise* by George Lichtheim, "The British Way of Life and the Common Market," *Commentary* (October 1961). See also, the valuable essay by S. M. Lipset, "The British Voter," published in two parts in *The New Leader* (November 7 and 21, 1960).

A Journey to Eastern
Europe (1965)

"Have you ever been abroad?" I asked the taxi driver in
Budapest. "No," he replied, "only in Vienna." The answer
was not, apparently, intended as a joke. It reflected something
essential in the new East European atmosphere: the recrudescence of national peculiarities. Hungary was, after all, part
of the Hapsburg empire; Budapest and Vienna are less than
an hour apart by air, four hours by road. (The Austrians take
their heritage seriously: they seem to have found or made a
vocation as a spiritual and economic meeting place for the nations that were once in the empire, the Czechs, Hungarians,
and Poles especially.) What I have termed the recrudescence
of national peculiarities in the case of Hungary, and the other
East European nations, has led to a new internationalism in
Eastern Europe. Old traditions, among the intellectuals, of
contact with Western Europe have been renewed—and this
at a period when the intellectuals and the intelligentsia as a
whole have gained more importance than they previously had
in the Communist societies, and constitute a much larger social grouping than they did even 15 years ago.

What I have termed the new nationalism cannot be narrowly circumscribed. It may well entail phenomena like distinctive national patterns of Communist economic development, although experiments in areas like economic planning

343

seem to be crossing frontiers. Perhaps the simplest statement of the case is also the most accurate one: the new nationalism is part of a general emergence of spontaneous, often unexpected, sometimes not entirely pleasant social developments as a consequence of the relaxation of rigid Party controls, the abandonment of dogmatically derived attempts to impose a detailed map upon reality. A noble intellectual critique of Communist reality and strong popular currents which reject any collective aspirations whatsoever, courageous political dissent and a totally cynical careerism, a new internationalism and old nationalisms—these are the results. During my travels in Eastern Europe in 1965 and 1966, I was able to glimpse some of these forces at work. I visited Hungary, Poland, and the German Democratic Republic—as well as Yugoslavia which, politically, is in a class by itself.

During my visits, I saw friends and colleagues with whom I (and no doubt many of my readers) share much: a certain skepticism about authority, in particular the authorities under which we have to live—each in our parts of the world; a certain hope for a world changed for the better, not unmixed with despair that this will ever come about; a persistent interest in Marxism as a doctrine, at once of social analysis and human liberation.

I visited Hungary in October of 1965, nine years after the revolution and its tragic aftermath. Let it be said that the revolution's long-term consequences have not been entirely tragic, despite the bloodletting, repression, and moral savagery attendant upon its defeat. At this moment, Hungary is a relatively porous society: the border with Austria is easily crossed, travel to the West is not difficult, and the limits of intellectual freedom within the country have been steadily widened. An increase in intellectual freedom is not, of course, automatically productive of similar developments with respect to political freedom—but it can lead to the latter. At any rate, I found no oppressiveness in the Hungarian atmosphere. It is quite true that the foreign newspapers sold on the newsstands are *Unita* or *l'Humanité,* but those who wish to do so can subscribe to Western periodicals. (Lukacs himself has a subscription to the *Frankfurter Allgemeine Zeitung,* the extremely mediocre daily which in Western Germany is an object of contempt for every right-thinking leftist.) Most of the intellectuals have traveled to the West, frequently on official grants.

The persons I saw were, indeed, not very close to the Party; they were critical Marxists. The breadth and openness of their culture was quite impressive—they were in this respect no different from the intellectuals of Paris, London, Frankfurt, or Milan. What did make them different (and at the same time curiously like some socialists in Western Europe) was their sense of obligation to what we may term the unfinished revolution. They felt that it had indeed begun, with the expropriation of the means of production—but that nearly everything else needed to be commenced again. In particular, they thought that popular education or re-education for socialism was exceedingly defective, that the entire quality of life in Hungary was questionable. They were deeply critical of what is known as goulash communism—despite no visible aversion to that excellent national dish. Their revulsion for the construction of a society organized primarily around material progress and material emulation seemed as great as that of the British New Left as I knew it in the late fifties—and their rhetoric was not all that different.

Here, perhaps, are some of the psychological sources of that discussion of alienation which is now beginning in Eastern Europe. It is a remarkable fact about the entire discussion of alienation, East and West, that it reflects the response of the intellectuals to their society—their condition generalized. It would be the most arrant philistinism, however, to suppose that this exhausts the problem. The discussion of alienation in Eastern Europe is also exactly what it is in the West—a response to a generalized condition of unfulfillment by those whose privileged position in society enables them to think and feel. The powerlessness and lack of autonomy of important parts of the population, their recourse to available substitutes for genuine participation in their society, seem to mock the hopes of mankind for a better life. On this view, the intellectuals' concern with alienation entails an assumption of moral responsibility toward others.

Discussions of alienation in Eastern Europe have had to proceed elliptically. There was a time when discussions of the theme of alienation in Marx's early writings were denounced as "revisionism," "bourgeois falsifications," and the like. We have now reached a phase in which philosophical considerations of Marx's early writings are acknowledged to be legitimate. (It is a sign of the total degradation of official intellectual life under Stalinism that we should have to treat this as progress.) There is evidence, also, that the next phase has begun: the effort to apply the notion of alienation in concrete analyses of the Communist societies. When I visited Hungary, the discussion was still generally on a fairly theoretic and abstract note. A conference had been held, under more or less official auspices, at which a number of views had been expressed.

Some took the view that alienation had in principle been overcome with the establishment of state socialist regimes. Any remaining difficulties had to be understood as transitional phenomena, or as due to political mismanagement, but not to essential aspects of the structure of the new society. Still others held that alienation in a socialist form was present but that in principle it was eradicable, a position of course compatible with the view that a good deal of alienation (however defined) could be found in socialist society. I was told of no one who held that alienation or some form of it was inevitable, due either to certain social arrangements in socialist society (for instance, a single party's monopoly of power) or to perennial features of any society's existence.

346

Lukacs himself, if I have correctly understood his views, thinks that alienation was a necessary phase in the development of socialist consciousness in capitalist society, and that in the same society the crushing weight of direct exploitation has been replaced by the more subtle forms of domination associated with the integration of the working class into an economic system which requires high levels of consumption expenditure. He was not reported as having expressed a view on alienation in socialist society, directly, although he has said that the problem has changed within the past 50 years.

This was all fairly abstract, but I gathered that there were a good many tensions just beneath the surface. The Sociological Research Group of the Hungarian Academy of Sciences had in effect begun a concrete series of inquiries into occupational attitudes. They had shown that the larger the sphere of autonomy and command in the exercise of an occupation, the more identification with the task on the part of the worker: a finding not all that specific to socialist society, and interesting on that account. The director of the Group, incidentally, is the man who was prime minister at the time of the revolution in 1956, András Hegedüs. He left politics thereafter for socio-economic research, took a doctorate in economics (in Moscow), worked in the Central Statistical Bureau of the government, and has now turned to sociology. I have read a number of his essays and also talked with him: I have the impression that he uses sociological research in the pursuit of new political ends which I shall describe as a form of technological humanism. He is skeptical of formulas and clichés, East and West, had noted that "optimization" (of efficiency and production) often conflicts with "humanization" in all management systems, and holds that no real progress toward this goal in socialism can be made until socialist elites and their decision-making processes are subject to the most rigorous public criticism. He seems much closer to the followers of

Lukacs, who are very much on the fringes of the Party, than to his old associates in the Party itself.

How far can the discussion of alienation go, if concretized in this fashion? The intimation that alienation exists in socialist society opens the way not alone to a thoroughgoing critique of Hungarian social life under the new regime, but by implication challenges one of its moral fundamentals. A thorough critique can be contained, however distasteful to those in power: abuses could be attributed to a set of circumstances which did not necessarily cast doubt on socialist principles. But the admission that alienation was not necessarily terminated by socialization of the means of production could desacralize the regime. It would have to be judged by its capacity to meet human needs rather than by imputed final ends. Some aspects of the current ideological crisis in Eastern Europe are reminiscent of the crisis of liberalism (resolved in nearly every country but our own); when it became clear that a large measure of civil liberty combined with parliamentary rule were insufficient to attain liberalism's ideal ends, socialism gained adherents among those previously liberal. In the event it was a democratic socialism which incorporated elements from liberalism. Expropriation and centralized planning have not been sufficient to attain the ends of Marxism as a political philosophy: the right *praxis* has as yet to be found. When it is, it will clearly incorporate much of today's Marxism—certainly it will be more Marxist than today's democratic socialism or neo-capitalism is liberal. But it will also have new elements, the outlines of which we can hardly discern at present.

In the meantime, my friends in Budapest seemed to live the same busy lives as the rest of us. No discussion of persons ignored the political views of those being discussed, nor did they ignore their strengths and weaknesses of character. In one thing I noticed a certain similarity between Budapest, London, Paris, and New York: weakness of character always seemed to be a more prominent feature of the moral profiles of those absent than of those present. Life is crowded in Budapest, in a literal sense: apartments are small and many persons live in extremely cramped quarters. Money as such seems not to be very much of a problem for the Budapest intellectuals, but currency for foreign travel is scarce; obtaining it depends upon the often arbitrary decisions of obscure bureaucrats. The penalties for deviation have changed: those who ten years ago faced jail are now irritated by the denial of travel subsidies, or by being confined to less attractive posts, or by exclusion from the activities which lend influence, money, and prestige. But if Budapest intellectual society lacks the openly parallel and competing networks of intellectual activity we are used to, it does offer any number of interstices in which persons of a critical disposition can work. And, it should be said, these are often protected and patronized by those with rather more adequate political connections.

One evening, some of my friends took me to supper with Lukacs—an excellent central European cold supper. I found Lukacs at eighty astonishingly young; he gave the impression of a very spry sixty. He was of course quite in touch with events in France and Germany, less so with the English-speaking world—although he did not complain of an absence of visitors. He questioned me about the New Left in America; did it have contact with the trade unions and the working class? If I understood him correctly, he seemed to think that in the U.S. the politics of coalition is the only possible socialist politics. He talked freely of his own work, a complete edition of which is being published in West Germany. He was busy on a treatise entitled *The Ontology of Social Existence,* which may well constitute a later version (forty-five years later) of his celebrated *History and Class Consciousness.* He has withdrawn from the critique of daily political existence and is free to work quite unhindered pursuing his major theoretic interests. He pronounced himself as more optimistic than ever on the future of the socialist societies, although his optimism seems to concern the distant rather than the near future. One remark did astonish me: if he had to relive his life, he said, he might well choose to study political economy rather than philosophy and literature. Perhaps it was one of those offhand remarks which require no deep analysis.

I left Lukacs bearing one indelible impression: the decor of his apartment, his manner, the intensity and discipline of his application to his work, all mark him as a representative of that cultivated Central European *Bürgertum* which recent history has either destroyed or overtaken and to which Karl Marx himself belonged. After having met Lukacs, I understand his esthetic doctrines better, including his lack of sympathy for many of the modern movements in art. There is a sense in which Marxist humanism is a very direct successor to *bourgeois* ethics (in the historical and not the pejorative sense of *bourgeois*); the most distinguished of the Communist Marxist thinkers attests the link.

A day later, on a café terrace, I met a Hungarian social scientist who is distinctly post-bourgeois. Z has suffered horribly in the past, had been imprisoned under Rakosi for "espionage," and was now enjoying a quite different sort of life. He has dropped Marxism. He had spent a good deal of time flying between Siberia and California in connection with some gigantic research project, and he was especially proud of his connections with the American universities. [He seemed to have an infallible gift for selecting those most immune to any social ideas whatsoever.] He assured me that there was little difference between socialist and other economies: we had General Motors and they had the national planning boards, in which they too were shareholders. I observed that I was not myself a GM shareholder but that in any case I doubted the analogy. It was clear that Z could be used by the regime in a way in which Lukacs (and some of those he had influenced in an empirical direction) could not. The regime required, not critical Marxism but technical specialists and Z was prepared to be as technical and specialized as possible. He justified this in precisely the same terms as his counterparts in the West: the collaboration of men of science with existing regimes served to increase the rationality of the latter. Perhaps so, but even Marx's greatest opponent in German thought, Max Weber, held that scientific rationality could not in itself provide men with goals. These had to come from without the scientific process, narrowly defined. As I understood it, Z seemed to think that he had escaped what some of us still feel to be a dilemma, connected with our doubts about the moral uses of such knowledge as we have. Z supposed that the regime (or regimes) he served were intrinsically moral, or at least no less moral than other historical regimes and capable of being educated to do better. He also supposed that he was a pure scientist: insofar as his technical services to men in power caused him doubts, he could view them simply as an exercise in technique and refuse responsibility for the uses to which his services were put. I felt half envious of his complacency, as I left Budapest and went on to Warsaw.

The atmosphere in Warsaw was much different. Hungary is a country of ten million; Poland is four times as large. I sensed (and perhaps this was simply one of those idiosyncratic judgments which travelers make) a larger view, a less cramped and parochial feeling in Warsaw—but then I saw more people. At any rate, the Polish intellectuals had an acute sense of the importance of the conflicts within their own society: in particular, they had the conviction that their problem was less to make contact with movements of ideas outside of Poland than to make a distinctive Polish contribution to those movements. This, perhaps, accounted for the despair of some who took the view that the Polish ruling party was ineradicably narrow and frequently inept, as well as for the relative satisfaction of others who had concluded that they had won enough scope for the exercise of a certain amount of influence. Again, the distinction I had observed in Budapest seemed important in Warsaw as well: there were humanistic Marxists who were made to feel rather like utopian socialists, and there were those who wished to lend the regime more intelligence. The latter, it should be said, seemed more downcast in Warsaw than in Budapest; more of them seemed to wonder how much intelligence the regime could absorb.

When I arrived, the acute question was how much critical thought the regime could stand. Adam Schaff was then Director of the Institute of Philosophy and Sociology at the Academy of Science, a member of the Central Committee of the Communist party, and a prominent representative of Poland and official Marxism generally at international conferences; he had just published a sensational book. The sensation consisted in the fact that among his assertions were the following: The conception of alienation found in Marx's early writings was a central element in all of Marx's thought and gave it a humanistic component the ignorance or suppression of which deformed Marx's thought and intentions. Alienation had not disappeared with the expropriation of the means of production since, above all, the state in socialist society continued to function in a manner which was frequently oppressive. The Communist party, which could not entirely renounce its educational aims, would do well nonetheless to end its arbitrary and rigid attempt to control art and science. Meanwhile, if responsible and socially conscious behaviour was expected of the populace, then perhaps the new socialist elite could begin to set a good example to ordinary persons by improving its own conduct. Finally, no useful purpose was served by denying that chauvinism, xenophobia, and anti-Semitism were still found in socialist society and even among Communists.

Schaff's book has been published in German (in Austria and Western Germany but not in the German Democratic

Republic). The bluntness of the assertions I have listed is attenuated only slightly by Schaff's insistence that the distortions of socialism could be explained by the historical circumstances of the seizure of power in countries lacking a bourgeois democratic tradition: indeed, the explanation was in itself a highly unorthodox one. Schaff, it should be emphasized, was not simply writing a retrospective critique of Stalinism but analyzing the present situation of Marxist humanism in the countries ruled by Communist regimes.

He begins with an account of the present crisis in ideology and cites Roger Garaudy: all philosophy today is in some way the philosophy of existence, since values are everywhere in question. In the West, the principal question seems to be: how can man live with dignity? In the East, "the wish for a better and happier life shows itself to be stronger than theoretic problems." His own work then (under the title *Marxism and the Human Individual*) is intended as a contribution to the attainment of an improved life for those under socialism. Its focus is on the individual's possibilities of fulfillment in present historical circumstances. He continues: a disciplined revolutionary movement can be as effective in repression as the exploitative system it overthrew. A new Marxist theory of the individual, based on old Marxist conceptions but not in contradiction with the findings of the empirical sciences, can help overcome that sort of repression.

Schaff's discussion of Marx's conception of man owes much to the recent discussion in the West—and he does not hesitate to acknowledge his debt to those Western Marxists and Marxologists who have often been abused in Communist writings. Marx distinguished between real man as he is known to us and true man—as he can become. Real man, according to Schaff, still has to contend with alienation:

> In all forms of socialist society known to us until now various forms of alienation have appeared. This implies that no automatic mechanism exists which can introduce the abolition of

alienation along with the abolition of the private ownership of the means of production. And that for the simple reason that the state continues to exist, just as before, as a power apparatus.

Even an optimum of democratization, far from attained yet in socialist societies, will leave men confronting a state apparatus which in the nature of the case will not wither away. Two real forms of alienation continue in socialist society: the monopolization of power by a privileged group and the necessity of work in an economic organization characterized by the division of labor. The resultant difficulties and oppressiveness can be reduced—but only if the problems are recognized and not if their very existence is denied. A new view of the relationship between the socialist citizen and the state is necessary, and there are circumstances in which the welfare of the collectivity demands a "wise disobedience" from individuals opposed to authority.

It is not surprising that this text, well documented with appropriate citations from Marx, did not please all of its readers. I was told that Gomulka himself was enraged, and that he complained that Schaff had found words to justify his (Gomulka's) imprisonment in the Stalinist period; now that things were improved, the philosopher had nothing better to do than to discover alienation in Poland. The anecdote is probably apocryphal, but if Gomulka complained in these terms, I can understand his feelings. I was shown article after article attacking Schaff in the press, in reviews, in journals. One particularly lengthy attack (to judge by the translation made on the spot for me by a Polish friend, a particularly vituperative one) was made by someone described to me as "a great thinker." "Really great?" I inquired. "Yes, he thinks all the time." "About what?" "He thinks about how he can keep his job as head of the state radio system. . . ." The Party convened a special meeting of intellectuals to discuss Schaff's book. They met in great secrecy while I was in Warsaw: that very afternoon, I had several accounts of the meeting. Some, apparently, said that Schaff was "one-sided." Few said he was entirely wrong. Schaff (whom I saw) was very pleased with the controversy; whatever may have been said to him, he continues in his official and public functions.

I also had the privilege of spending some time with the philosopher Leszek Kolakowski. Kolakowski has been celebrated in the West as a spiritual hero of the Polish October of 1956 and is best known for his critical studies of the crisis in Marxist political philosophy. It is less well known that he is an immensely distinguished technical philosopher, the author of a significant book on Spinoza, a student of the philosophy of the Counter-Reformation, and a writer fully identified with the national tradition in Polish literature. We did not talk about politics, but about his most recent work. He has written a series of parables on biblical themes and is much occupied with phenomenological philosophy's search for the essence of man and culture. I interpreted this as a withdrawal from the Marxist notion of the realization of philosophy. Marx held that the revolution would make philosophy and metaphysical reflection (including religion) redundant: philosophy developed to its highest point would become life itself, in the form of revolutionary activity. Kolakowski's interest in other aspects of the classical tradition in philosophy seemed to me to be an implicit commentary on the immediate possibilities of realizing philosophy: history still made philosophy necessary. A year after I saw him, he was expelled from the Party—allegedly for remarks made at a political discussion at the University of Warsaw, where he teaches.

A visit to the University was also on my program, and I was invited to talk to sociology teachers and students. The recent achievements of Polish sociology have been considerable: important, lucid, and penetrating studies of Polish society have been made, and some general contributions to our larger understanding of all societies. (The immediate past president of the International Sociological Association is, indeed, a Polish colleague, Jan Szcepanzski, and his election was clearly intended as a tribute to Polish sociology.) There is an important Polish positivist tradition of sociological thought and moral inquiry; this has combined with the regime's obvious need for social accounting to encourage Polish sociologists to work in a rather empirical temper. Ten years ago, this in itself had political implications: to produce responses to a questionnaire which showed workers less than overcome with enthusiasm at socialist management required some courage in the immediate post-Stalin period. Today, the emphasis on empirical work may well have a meaning not dissimilar to that which often attaches to this sort of work elsewhere: it is a mode of keeping a certain distance from larger social criticism. I do not really know what the situation in Poland may be in all its complexity. I can simply report that, when I finished my talk, some students told me: "At last, someone who takes Marxism seriously."

After having visited Poland, I went to the German Democratic Republic. I was struck by the German characteristics everywhere evident in the German Communist state: efficiency, orderliness, and the inevitable bureaucratic pedantry (a characteristic much less visible in the other Germany). Here, too, national feeling was not entirely lacking—and where previously it had taken the form of resentment against a regime imposed by military force on a reluctant population, it now expressed itself in identification with the regime's visible economic progress. While I was there, the Communist leader Walter Ulbricht declared that the East German state was not only the legitimate guardian of the national interest, in its policy of alliance with the Soviet Union, but the legitimate heir to Bismarck's foreign policy: I could not imagine that this was received with enthusiasm in Poland.

My visit to Germany brought me to a conference center of

the Protestant Church, where I took part in a discussion of "Technology and Humanism" (exactly the sort of theme favored for such discussions in West Germany, too). The participants were mainly Protestant technicians: computer specialists, technologists, agronomists, officials from the various ministries, physicians. It became clear to me rather quickly that they were more technician than Protestant. They were quite delighted with my remarks to the effect that in the new Western class system a technological elite was gaining in importance. Their view was that their own regime was being transformed from one based on dogmatic Marxism to one based on what for want of a better term I shall call technological Marxism. They complained about the slowness of the transformation, announced their willingess—verging on enthusiasm—to collaborate with a Communist party directed by technicians like themselves. Perhaps the most significant of their remarks was made by a younger physicist who declared that the historically privileged class of the future, privileged in the sense of having a historical mission which it alone could fulfill, was not the proletariat but the technical intelligentsia. Certainly, some elements in the Communist party believe in something like this: their newest slogan is "Die gebildete Nation" ("the educated nation") and their economic planning seems predicated on their not giving up the advantage they now possess over the other Communist countries—they have the best educated labor force of any of them. What did come rather short in the discussion were both Protestantism and Marxism.

My trip had begun, in effect, in Yugoslavia—at the 1965 summer school convened by the *Praxis* group. These philosophers and sociologists, from the universities of Zagreb and Belgrade, worked on the premise that philosophy consists in the relentless criticism of everything that exists. Since they find themselves in a Marxist state with a Marxist official doctrine, they criticize it, much to the displeasure of the more dogmatic elements in the League of Communists. The 1965 summer school, and the two that preceded it, served as a meeting place for critical spirits from both power blocs; the 1966 one, for reasons unclear to me, was cancelled. From the 1965 session I took away some striking memories of the intellectual vivacity and political forthrightness of many in the Yugoslav intellectual elite. I also recalled what had been said by Rudi Supek, a Zagreb professor who is one of the editors of *Praxis,* about the fundamental division which occurs within rather than between the two world power blocs. The real conflict, he declared, was between the libertarian humanists and the bureaucratic technicians; he was later to repeat these views, in a way which was much appreciated by his public, at the World Congress of Sociology in Evian, in 1966.

A considerable over-simplification, no doubt: but one which can focus thought. The Communist societies now proclaim, and their political and economic elites are beginning to practice, a new doctrine of efficacy. Increased production, skillful administration, even a consciously pursued (and publicized) policy of facilitating social ascent are on the new agenda of Communist politics. Domination of a soft-tempered kind, however, remains domination. Wage workers are subject to managerial discipline even in the absence of factory owners; criticisms of "bureaucracy" are aimed at the clumsiness of certain bureaucrats and not at the principle of hierarchial organization. The utopian goals of Marxism have receded from view, or rather, have been replaced by a certain amount of discussion about the "creative" use of leisure time —a discussion which could just as well occur (and frequently has) under a capitalist regime. It is quite true that some of the more noxious aspects of the commercialization of culture are missing in Communist Europe; my own impression is that this may be a European trait rather than a specifically Communist one. In these circumstances, and precisely at the moment when a new type of Communist political and economic technician is emerging to begin the replacement of an older and more dogmatic generation in the leaderships of the several parties, the intellectuals have had occasion to refer again to the early Marxist texts on alienation.

The terrible experience of Stalinism is now past. (Where once the East German regime put down a revolution with the aid of the Soviet Army, it now wrings its hands in embarrassed helplessness when attacked by its own Bob Dylan, Wolf Biermann.) The content of routine, as well as its pervasiveness, has encouraged the East European intellectuals to conclude that whatever else they may live in, it is neither utopia nor likely to become so. Their philosophical reflections on this have, for the moment, only limited political implications. But Marx himself proceeded from the elaboration of the doctrine of alienation to devise a new social theory and to prescribe a new politics. Some intellectual processes have their own momentum: it remains to be seen where the recent interest in primitive aspects of Marxism will lead the embattled humanists of Eastern Europe.

Note: Adam Schaff's book was published in 1965 by the State Scientific Publishers in Warsaw under the title *Marksize a jednostka ludzka*. A German translation was published in the same year by the Europa Verlag, Vienna, under the title *Marxismus und das menschliche Individuum*. An essay on Schaff's book by Z. A. Jordan, "Socialism, Alienation and Political Power," appeared in *Survey*, July, 1966. As I edit, an English translation has appeared, *Marxism and the Human Individual*, McGraw-Hill, New York, 1970. Schaff lost his post in the Polish wave of anti-semitism of 1967–68 and is "on mission" in Vienna. Kolakowski has chosen exile and teaches at Oxford. The Yugoslav *Praxis* group encountered difficulties as a result of its support for the Yugoslav student revolt of 1968, but is far from silent. The Soviet invasion of Czechoslovakia in 1968 has, of course, cast a pall on all of eastern Europe: it is to be hoped, however, that a new Soviet intellectual generation will assume its critical responsibilities.

The Making of

a Counter-Culture

Our historical period evokes total re-evaluations of the human condition as a matter of routine—at increasingly frequent intervals. I began serious reading in 1939 and I can recollect, in very approximate sequence: the relative moral strenuousness of old left politics; the willed secularization of the philosophic humanism of the 1930's; the application to culture of the several varieties of psychoanalysis, pessimistic, optimistic, Apollonian and Dionysiac; the tenured professoriat's search for a "tragic" view of life, accompanied by its installation in a capitalism declared to embody the achieved social revolution; adumbrations of existentialist despair, and joyous promulgations of the news of God's death; the conviction of the American intellectuals that we alone defended culture in a philistine society and the more recent view, that society having become less philistine, it is our duty to defend it against the new barbarians, its critics and our students. Art itself has had to assume tasks extending from the depiction of our history to those more proper to a religion of salvation: our aesthetics have been influenced by masters as diverse as Lionel Trilling and the Living Theatre; where Jackson Pollock once spoke for us as well as to us, it is now Philip Roth to whom we look. I can remember the celebrated attack on the "liberal fifth column" in *Partisan Review*—as well as the *New York Review of Books'* instructions on the making of firebombs. In this extraordinary montage, names tumble about, not quite at random: Albert Camus and Max Lerner, Hannah Arendt and Paul Goodman, John Kenneth Galbraith and Norman Brown, Reinhold Niebuhr and Susan Sontag. With so much innovation, such shifts of fashion, it is not surprising that many of us suffer from weariness. Too many communications are directed at us, too many sensations excite us, competing visions of the world make it difficult for us to see at all, and we are made irate by the suspicion that ideas we once abandoned as exhausted may shortly turn out to be (*horribile dictu*) relevant. Our sense of vocation prevents us from declaring our own fatuity, inutility or worse but, nevertheless, we feel as if we were on a treadmill. Meanwhile, the decomposition of the American polity constitutes a dreadful backdrop for our spiritual playlets.

In this situation, we ought not to deny to Theodore Roszak a considerable measure of gratitude. This younger historian has brought enthusiasm, indeed elan, to a job we cannot do. Our surfeit and weariness, he tells us, constitute the least of our troubles: our entire enterprise is false. Some of us still seek to make sense of the modern tradition, others ask if anything at all remains of bourgeois culture, yet others suppose that a new culture must await a new politics. In the book before us,[1] a talented and perceptive critic proposes to put us out of our miseries. In a total repudiation of both western intellectuals and the traditions that sustain us, he declares that we have become—wittingly in some cases, unwittingly in others—subjects of a fiendish mechanism. In an eschatology not quite new, he describes a new fall. The new Adam, erring in a loveless and mechanical world, can be saved: by a return to those instinctive sources of vision, those primitive modes

---

1. *The Making of a Counter-Culture: Reflections on the Technocratic Society and Its Youthful Opposition.* By Theodore Roszak. Garden City, N.Y., 1969. $1.95.

of knowledge, we had arrogantly supposed we had outgrown. Roszak's primary intent is to declare futile, because resting on a pervasive misreading of the human situation, the present terms of aesthetic, intellectual and moral-political discourse.

The author considers that we are ruled by a technocracy. It is difficult for anyone, indeed, to suppose otherwise. Roszak, however, refuses the usual terms of the current discussion. He declares that technocracy is incapable of transformation; indeed, all industrial regimes must eventuate in technocratic domination—welfare capitalism, democratic socialism, or authoritarian Communism are but transient political forms with the same material content. This consists not of the institutions of power but of a far more profound mode of rule: the systematic deformation of the human psyche by industrial culture. We are being exploited, not by the extraction of surplus value nor by the several types of cooptation and corruption (insofar as these can be distinguished in contemporary practice and verbal usage), but by the systematic eradication of the very depths of our souls.

Much is covered in the text: the conflict of generations and the revolt of youth, the recourse to drugs and to psychedelic experience generally, the thought of figures as diverse as Watts, Ginsberg, Marcuse, Brown, Goodman and Leary; descriptions of the visionary experiences of primitive shamans and modern poets. Its critical argument, however, resides in the analysis of "the myth of objective consciousness." Roszak's description of this entity is not fundamentally new: the analysis may be found, *inter alia,* in Max Weber's analysis of "rationalization," and in the neo-Marxist critique of "reification." Protests at the process may be traced to the mystical revolt, in the middle ages, against scholasticism. In their early modern form, these protests were of course embodied in romanticism. Roszak manifests a rather general awareness of the origins of his critique of the "objective consciousness"— but he tends to extract precedents from spiritual history without considering the problem of alternation in the modes of experience as a problem with serious implications for his own position. In any event, he adds a psychological patina to the usual portrait of a dessicated humankind. A rigidified and imprisoned "I" confronts an inert and mechanical external-ized reality: "In Here," in his words, is opposed to an "Out-There." The secularization of the western spirit and the rise of science have led man to think that the only permissible relationship to reality is intellectual, the ordering one of scientific thought and its derivative, technological manipula-tion. All awe and reverence, all delight, all possibility of com-munion with nature and with our fellow man, have gone. It is not alone a matter of our having been denied access to the riches of the human personality: we have been forced to live with but a fraction of our being, in such a way that even this has become distorted and deformed. Roszak proposes, in effect, a new religion of the heart, and insists that men begin now out of their inner selves "to proclaim a new heaven and a new earth, so vast, so marvelous, that the inordinate claims of technical expertise must of necessity withdraw to a sub-ordinate and marginal status in the lives of men."

The children's crusade constituted by the youth and stu-dent movement is in his view significant not for its politics but for its culture—more precisely, it is this movement, in all of its ramifications, which constitutes the counter-culture of which he writes. The counter-culture, as Roszak describes it, is in fact an anti-politics. What is needed is not the familiar re-ordering of social priorities but, in effect, their abandon-ment. The long march of the spirit through western political history has led nowhere: the youthful demonstrators who in 1967 attempted to levitate the Pentagon were expressing a just rejection of a futile politics. "If violence and injustice could be eliminated from our society by heavy intellectual research and ideological analysis, by impassioned oratory and sober street rallies, by the organization of bigger unions or lobbies or third parties or intricate coalitions . . . then we should long since have been living in the New Jerusalem."

363

Roszak expresses a skepticism, clearly intended to be withering, about the French May revolt of 1968 and its demands for a participatory democracy ("auto-gestion" in the French version): "The social composition of the technocracy would alter but the change would amount to nothing more than broadening the base on which the technocratic imperative rests." He criticizes Cohn-Bendit, the French-German student leader, for his attempt to initiate a democratization of knowledge, and proposes a "more subversive strategy . . . to show people that 'knowledge is theirs,' not for the asking but for the debunking."

Roszak's argument wanders, entertainingly and occasionally persuasively, over a good deal of contemporary terrain. Much of what he writes is hortatory (some of it is condemnatory); the rest is often mythopeic, if at times unavowedly so. He does convince us of the truth for himself of inner experience, of a pantheistic openness to nature. Yet he seems to suppose that the experience can be generalized by a systematic refusal of our history. In this sense, he is an authentic spokesman for the young whom he so praises and his very style expresses his generational affinities. The intellectual framework of the book is neither concealed nor entirely spindly. It is, instead, concentrated in not too many pages and then diffused—or suffused—throughout the rest of the text. He writes, in other words, rather like some of our students—if with a good deal more elegance and learning—not sequentially, or with much attention to the structure of the argument, but vividly and with feeling, as the mood strikes him and carries him.

Roszak's book was written to capture a moment. Has he situated that moment in history with any degree of accuracy? As I write, the youth movement seems to be searching for a new understanding of itself. Abbie Hoffman, on trial at Chicago, has encountered a reality not to be conjured away by pot or visions. Roszak spends much energy portraying Marx as a bewhiskered old fogey, a romantic in his youth and a tiresome bore in maturity, with his arid statistics, interminable lessons in political economy, and ascetic devotion to revolution—after which, Roszak mockingly suggests, life could begin. Marcuse, that most contemporary of Marxists, fares little better. Roszak is quite consistent: the Marxist notion of a mankind freed by revolution (and of course by advanced industrialization) from economic constraint and able to enter a new realm of freedom strikes him as worse than illusionary, as a capitulation to the machine rather than defiance of it. Roszak at one point seems to prefer psychoanalysis, with its insistence on psychic reality, to Marxism. In the end, however, he asks—Freud or Marx, and answers: William Blake. His praise of primitive shamanism as a mode of experience is of a piece with these views. How can we, with our jobs, our machines, our organizations, accede to the realm of experience opened by shamanism? Roszak seems to say that we must learn to think of life without these things, that we must flee our history and start another one. In the guise of an analysis of this historical moment, he has written a profoundly ahistorical book, a confessional and a homily—but not a serious prescription for meeting, or even defining, our agonizing historical problems.

Two matters seem fundamentally wrong in Roszak's thought. There can be no doubt that the characteristics of industrialization as such are implicated in the absence of human emotive freedom which he so bitterly deplores. Yet, consider the hardness of American life: is there not some connection between our emotional constriction and that sort of capitalistic social organization—unto its more modern bureaucratic forms—in which Americans live? Those who have lived in Europe will have noticed the difference between variants of industrialization—and it is too simple to declare that Europe is becoming "Americanized." The abandonment or reversal of industrialization, as a project, is impossible. Its humanization is incredibly difficult, and we hardly know where to begin—but if we do not strive for this, we become resigned accomplices in our own degradation.

The second error in Roszak, then, pertains to politics. He hails the revolt of youth as a revolt against industrialism (his concept of technocracy is rather undifferentiated, and is of not much use, analytically and politically). American youth since the early years of this decade have not attacked industrialism as such, but have attacked particular facets of its current organization of power: in racial oppression and exploitation, in the educational bureaucracies, in imperialist wars against overseas peoples, and—increasingly—in its criminal assault on nature. Roszak's disdain for politics is a disdain for the Promethean side of human nature—but only the activation of this can give us a chance, once again, to feel. Finally, the revolt of youth is on Roszak's own testimony, evidence that feeling is seeking a politics which will make possible that expansion of consciousness he demands.

It may well be that a certain stoicism, indeed a certain renunciation, may have to accompany the process. In this sense, Marx may have more to tell us than Roszak seems to believe. Let us recall this: "A man cannot again become a child, or he becomes infantile. But doesn't the naivete of the child delight him, and must he not strive to reproduce again at a higher level its truth? In every epoch, does not the nature of the child express the natural truth of its own character? Why should not the historical childhood of mankind, as it developed so beautifully, exert an eternal attraction as a phase which will never return? There are bad children and precocious children. Many of the developed peoples belong in these categories. The Greeks were normal children. The charm of their art for us does not exist in contradiction with the undeveloped social period in which it grew. It is rather its result, and is inextricably tied to the fact that the immature social conditions, under which it originated, and under which alone it could originate, will never return." (Karl Marx, *Grundrisse der Kritik der Politischen Okonomie*, Dietz, Berlin, 1953, p. 31.)

Late Capitalism

in the United States

The problem of applying Marxist categories to an analysis of the late capitalist social order in the United States has now begun to attract a considerable amount of attention. After a hiatus of some twenty years (1945–65)—years, to be sure, marked by some honorable exceptions, represented by C. Wright Mills, Paul Sweezy, and William Appleman Williams—a growing number of scholars and, most encouragingly, younger scholars, have begun to ask if there is still something in the Marxist tradition which may, if properly employed, prove illuminating with respect to our own social and historical situation. I have employed the term "Marxist tradition" quite deliberately. A mechanical application of Marxist categories derived from a body of work developed to deal with the peculiarities of the nineteenth century to contemporary society is not likely to prove very penetrating. We might just as well attempt to analyze the military-industrial complex in terms borrowed from Marx's portrait of Napoleon III—although there may be more in that analogy than some might think. In any event, our task is a dual one—to seize the movement of contemporary society in its essentials, and in so doing, not alone to apply Marxist categories but to revise them in such a way that they can be employed in further intellectual work.

It is quite true that in this respect our colleagues and contemporaries in Europe are appreciably in advance of us. The works of Perry Anderson, Lelio Basso, Jürgen Habermas, Eric Hobsbawm, Henri Lefebvre, Serget Mallet, Ernest Mandel, Rudi Supek, and Alain Touraine bespeak a penetration, a willingness to take intellectual risks, and a historical finality difficult to find in work on America by Americans. Nevertheless, the current situation is rather different from what it was even a half-decade ago, thanks to Eugene Genovese, S. M. Miller, Gabriel Kolko, Herbert Gintis, Herbert Guttman, Christopher Lasch, Harry Magdoff, Barrington Moore, James O'Connor, James Weinstein, and a number of scholars at first grouped around *Studies on the Left* and later extending from the *New York Review of Books* to *Radical America* and *Monthly Review*. The present paper attempts to apply ideas developed in the Western European discussion to American problems.

MARX AND ENGELS ON AMERICA

Marx and Engels devoted most of their theoretical and practical work, of course, to Western Europe. Engels did make a trip to the United States and both Marx and Engels maintained a considerable correspondence with former comrades in the German radical democratic movement who after 1848 took refuge in America. Marx's work (not entirely unaided by Engels) as a European correspondent for the *New York Herald* is well known. In the circumstances, they did give a certain amount of attention to the United States and some of their broad conclusions may be worth repeating in this context. In the first place, they tended to accept theses now quite familiar to us about the peculiarity of the American social system. They adduced the availability and cheapness of land, in other words the open frontier, as an explanation for the capacity of American capitalism both to expand and to master severe discontent. They adduced the ethnic fragmentation of the American working class as a source of its disunity. They noted that the Anglo-Saxon migrant group, amongst the first to arrive and often highly skilled by contrast with others, developed the status of a labor aristocracy in the American setting. They argued that as long as American capitalism continued in its expansive phase, little could be looked for by way of revolutionary socialism from a divided American working class, which in any case prospered in relative fashion from American capitalism. They depicted the atheoreticism of the American working-class movement as both positive and negative. It was positive insofar as the Americans (here Engels in particular who was not above using ethnic analogies with Northern Europe) could learn from experience and would, in fact, only learn from experience. In this respect, Engels and Marx mocked the sectarian European and above all German refugees who imported to the United States their own quarrels as to the revolution. If atheoreticism, in the eyes of Marx and Engels was a potentially positive factor in the emergence of a distinctively American socialism, it was also, in their view, a hindrance to the emergence of a long-term perspective on the part of American working-class leaders.

It is interesting, also, to see that Marx and Engels favored for the American working class something that we would today term a politics of coalition. They held that the working class would have to unite with the smaller farmers against large-scale capitalism. The smaller farmers have by now, of course, virtually disappeared as a powerful and enduring political force in the United States, to be replaced by agricultural entrepreneurs. The notion, however, that the working class in a differentiated social system must seek allies outside of its own boundaries is one which may be applied in the

American situation today, even if it is characterized by a different alignment of social forces. They insisted on the strength of the tradition of democracy and representative government in the United States and asserted that the working-class movement as it grew to maturity in America would have to build on this tradition if it was to develop at all. In this connection, it is remarkable that they were the authors of a eulogy to Abraham Lincoln sent by the first International Working Men's Association in 1864. On the whole, Marx and Engels were, if anything, rather too optimistic about the chances for radical discontinuity in America's economic development which could radicalize the working class. They thought that the absence of feudal and aristocratic traditions and the newness of American capitalism would ultimately make the conflict of antagonistic forces in American capitalism that much more profound. They under-estimated, in other words, American capitalism's intrinsic capacity for self-renewal and continued expansion. However, they were shrewd enough to see that there were distinctive elements in the American historical experience, and in particular in the American cultural situation, which rendered the tasks of socialist organization and the development of socialist consciousness rather different from those confronted by Europeans. I propose, later, to return to this problem in its modern form.

The New American Class Structure

The problem of the new American class structure is specifically an American version of a general problem: how may we conceptualize a class system in which the division between the propertied and the propertyless expresses itself in antagonisms different from those envisaged by Marx? Much of the recent discussion of the "new" working class has been addressed to this question and new political possibilities have been seen in the propertyless status of groups ostensibly remote from the dreadful bottom of modern industrial societies. What is called for is an analysis of the emergent forms of antagonism, a consideration of new mechanisms of the integration of the social classes, in short, an account of the present situation which deals with its extreme differentiation, complexity, and obscurity.

To begin, it is difficult to recognize in the contemporary working-class and the white-collar salariat a classical proletariat. We do have a proletariat, in the sense of a group living at the margins of existence, at the mercy of the most minute alterations and cyclical rhythms of capital investment, and suffering from not alone a sense but the reality of exclusion from the general processes of accumulation which characterize the system as a whole. This proletariat in our country is made up of a diversity of groups, commonly designated as the impoverished. This category includes a considerable segment, but by no means the totality of the black population, some, although not all of the aged, the chronically ill without economic support from those relatively well placed in the socioeconomic system, the unskilled—in both urban and rural sectors of the economy. It should be pointed out that a not inconsiderable portion of this proletariat can under certain conditions be integrated into the regular labor force of the economy but that this depends upon cyclical movements and social control of the rate of unemployment. No economic policy devised by any American government has been able to bring that rate down permanently and barring changes in our market mechanisms, it does seem that a large proletariat of this sort is a permanent feature of the present American economy. It is clear, of course, that the economic position of this proletariat merges with its racial and cultural attributes. A considerable segment of the black population is incorporated in the proletariat, both in urban and rural areas, and is not yet equipped culturally to enter the industrial labor market on terms of equality with most of the white population. Moreover, it has hitherto lacked incentives to do so in view of the absence of opportunities. Cultural defects of this kind on the part of the blacks is matched by equivalent phenomena on the part of some whites like those who have migrated to the cities from areas of rural poverty and economic decline. A considerable argument has taken place as to whether cultural or economic factors are primary, but from the viewpoint of a structural analysis the argument has a certain remoteness about it. If the black population were culturally equipped to enter the labor force at higher levels, it would not at present find the corresponding employment. (This is quite apart from its encounter with a continuation of the gross prejudice and hatred which is the fate of blacks in America.) On the other hand, if economic opportunities were suddenly made available, the legacy of the system's defects in the past would incapacitate large numbers of those ostensibly eligible and make it impossible for them to seize these opportunities. This last possibility, however, does seem to be an exercise in fantasy for the moment.

We may conclude that modern America does have a proletariat, that it is a minority, if a substantial minority of the labor force, and that its prospects of integration in that labor force, at the moment, appear to be rather low. This by no means entails the assertion that this proletariat is directly and totally exploited by all the other elements in the class structure—even if elements of exploitation are present insofar as cheap services supplied by those recruited from this proletariat keep the general cost of living down, even for the members of the regular working class. Transfer payments for welfare serve to foist the burden for keeping part of this proletariat alive not necessarily on the most advantaged elements in the class structure, but on the working-class group, in itself hard put to maintain a minimal standard of living. Below, I will consider the revolutionary and the general political potential of this proletariat but I wish now to proceed to discuss the manual working class itself.

Much has been made of the recent relative decrease in the size of the manual working group in the labor force. Attention has been given to certain changes in its own inner structure and conditions of work. We may observe, to begin with, that if the manual workers as a category have declined in numbers relative to the newly expanding white-collar sector of the labor force, in absolute terms the manual labor force has indeed expanded in recent decades. Moreover, certain important internal transformations merit attention—notably a decline in the number of unskilled workers relative to an increase in the number of skilled operatives, an increase as well in the number of supervisory manual workers in foreman or supervisory posts. Changes in industrial technology and organization, American capitalism's relentless drive for higher productivity, have clearly accounted for these changes. They have brought with them ostensibly higher wage rates, but also difficult and often exhausting conditions in the workplace. The trade unions have recently purchased higher wages, and in some cases shorter hours and a variety of fringe benefits, at the cost of "productivity." Productivity agreements have made the unions themselves enforce a more relentless work discipline.

As the technical capacity of the manual labor force has increased, in other words, it has been subjected to increasing supervision and a certain blockage of what might be termed autonomy on the job. This has been accompanied, in certain key industries where the trade unions are strong, by rather different kinds of advantages with respect to medical and retirement benefits, seniority rights in times of economic constriction, in short, an attempt by the unions to turn job rights into a simulacrum of property rights. It may be pointed out in this connection that the tendency of unions to invest their pension funds in stocks, not infrequently the stocks of the corporations for which their members are working, constitutes another link between the manual labor force and the maintenance of the present set of economic relationships.

Meanwhile, it may be of interest to consider for a moment the alleged "embourgeoisement" of the American manual work force. It is interesting that this is supposed to have taken place mainly in the private sphere—that is to say, in the acquisition of owner-occupied dwellings, the purchase of consumer-durable goods, the lengthening of vacation periods, and the transmission of certain economic gains to children in the form of expanded educational opportunities which would allow them to move out of the manual working class. No allegation has been made of "embourgeoisement" in terms of career progression on the job, increased autonomy at work, or greatly enlarged cultural perspectives and opportunities for the manual workers themselves. The "embourgeoisment" is an "embourgeoisment" almost solely of consumption, and not of the productive function itself. It obviously represents a relatively tenuous acquisition by the working class which will certainly prove ephemeral in times of economic constriction —as recent recessions have shown. The political consequences of this "embourgeoisement" are multiple and will be dealt with below in the section on consciousness. The burden of recent critical work on income (especially that of S. M. Miller) is that income must be defined in terms not alone of gross personal revenue but in terms of the capacity to earn (sometimes in kind or fringe benefits) over a lifetime. High levels of disposable wage income for the working class at a given moment in the business cycle do not necessarily continue. The kind of income constituted by the earning capacity attached to a college degree is a more convincing characteristic of a real "embourgeoisement." Here, however, we may note in passing that the notion of "embourgeoisement" may entail a re-definition of property itself.

The future position of the manual working class in the

class structure depends upon two factors. The first concerns its technical function, the second entails larger questions of consciousness and politics which will be dealt with subsequently. With respect to its technical function, the increasing technicalization of industrial work, and the introduction of automation and computerization, would appear to entail higher skill qualifications for the manual labor force. A debate between those who argue that this will result in an increase in the number of unskilled operatives or indeed unemployment, and those who argue that this will result in a general elevation of the level of the industrial labor force's qualifications with no necessary diminution of employment, is as yet unresolved. It can be said, however, that the prospect of an increase in the proportion of unskilled operatives with marginal or cyclical employment possibilities does not necessarily represent a "proletarianization" of the working class— much depends upon the political response to this putative development. Equally, an increase in general skilled qualification, in productivity and presumably wage rates, does not necessarily entail a total "embourgeoisement" of the working class. A development of this sort would depend upon the total system of class relations into which an altered working class would be inserted. An extrapolation from present tendencies would suggest that an increase in skilled qualifications by no means will end the gross, more disguised forms of exploitation of the labor force by corporate capitalism and its social system. We touch again upon problems of political consciousness in the United States, which have proved so intractable from a socialist perspective.

Much of the recent discussion of a "new working class" has referred to the fastest growing sector of the American labor force, those types of employment which require educational qualifications; civil servants, school teachers, semi-professionals and professionals. In brief, those who service the administrative processes of an advanced capitalist society have been increasing in number relative to the manual workers. This greatly expanded white-collar grouping has given rise to a considerable literature (consider C. Wright Mills in 1951). At first considered a social grouping of an extremely labile kind politically, the group has more recently been seen as a new avant-garde, indeed, as having the potential of replacing the manual working class as a revolutionary agency. Surely, not both of these views can be correct. It remains to examine the dimensions of this grouping before analyzing its consciousness, real and potential.

A majority of the recruits to the newly expanded sectors of employment are integrated into one or another form of bureaucratic hierarchy. That is to say, in contrast to the professionals of previous epochs, they must place their educational qualifications at the disposition of those with economic and social power. An orderly career progression in bureaucratic systems for members of this group depends upon a minimum compliance with the imperatives and ideology of the system. The very fact, however, of bureaucratic integration has converted offices, the civil services of federal, state, and local government, and other areas of work into something like modern versions of the nineteenth-century factory. The workplace is cleaner, the mode of discipline is usually far more subtle, the level of autonomy exercised by the individual worker may be greater. Nevertheless, this newly expanded work force in great numbers confronts a small group of controllers or supervisors. The span of control exercised by those in command of the bureaucratic hierarchies has accordingly been widened. John Kenneth Galbraith has written of an "educational and scientific estate." If, in fact, all or most of those in the newly expanded white-collar sector who have educational qualifications are to be included in this estate, we can only say that it resembles the third estate well before the French Revolution. It is not yet ready to assert itself, and its power, vis-à-vis the other and older estates, is limited. Nevertheless, we may point to some sources of contradiction and tension in the occupational existence of those in this grouping. They do exercise a certain autonomy on the job, but that autonomy is severely restricted by commands from above and by the imposition of purposes generated by the organizational imperatives of the capitalist social system as a whole.

In short, those with knowledge may not be able to apply it in terms of their own conception of the social good, but are obliged to take orders from those following narrower and more partial social interests. This is a transposition of the classical case of alienation through the vending of wage labor to a somewhat more spiritualized plane, but it remains a case of alienation. Those with knowledge and competence do not necessarily have the power to apply it. Further, the very imperatives of bureaucratic coordination and of work discipline can produce, and in some cases have already produced, a counter-reaction in the form of the trade unionization of certain occupations within this general grouping. Trade unionization does not necessarily entail a demand for total control of the work process, but it may well entail a demand for regulation of some of its more arduous aspects, in addition to the usual trade-union insistence on improved gross conditions of work in terms of salary, fringe benefits, and hours. The conditions of trade unionization are, clearly, the emergence of a critical mass of new salaried workers, such that an individualistic approach to a career has seemed for many unrealistic and inappropriate. The concentration of these new workers in certain sectors of the economy gives promise of a further progression of trade unionism. However, it should be pointed out that trade unionism can go very far without leading to a qualitative change in class relations; indeed, it can formalize relationships between the classes and act as a regulatory and indeed stabilizing factor. It must be said in conclusion, that insofar as this group has expanded, it represents, in terms of improved status, relatively agreeable conditions of work, and higher and more consistent levels of remuneration, a decided channel of upward social mobility for the offspring of the working class. This group cannot be ascribed *a priori* a revolutionary or even a very reformist role. Hitherto, many in this social category have accepted their integration in society and the benefits this brought them. In certain countries this group has traditionally been politically on the right. A certain openness on the edges in contemporary America should not lead us to expect its immediate or its total transformation. Much depends upon the total social context in which this group, like the manual working class, has to function.

I have previously referred to Galbraith's use of the concept of an "educational and scientific estate." If this estate does exist, the term can only refer to a relatively small group of persons—appreciably smaller than the census category "professional and technical workers"—who exercise indispensable command or knowledge-producing functions for the society. This elite, which we may refer to as technocratic, would consist of educated managers, higher civil servants, those in effective daily command of the media of communication, those at the top of the knowledge industry. Viewed from this perspective, the "educational and scientific estate," whatever its recent restiveness, is an appendage of the system of power. Insofar as men of knowledge are elevated to power by virtue of their knowledge, they cease to function exclusively as men of knowledge, but function as men of power. If we take account of the fact that there are no purely technical or cognitive criteria for political decisions, if we recall that such decisions always involve choices of political values, that is to say, they alter the balance of power in one or another way (if only by maintaining it), then we can see that the technocrats do not rule in a vacuum. Their exercise of technical capacity in the interests of power follows the present division of power in the society. The existent institutional framework has been modified somewhat by the great importance of knowledge in administration and production, but it has not collapsed before the onslaught of an avant-garde of Ph.D's. Rather, when the Ph.D's have been given a function and rewarded for the performance of services indispensable to the system, a change in the mode of rule from entrepreneurial domination to technocratic manipulation does not alter the locus of rule. The great corporate structures dominate the economy and the state, which in turn exercises the indispensable function of the political coordination of the social order as a whole. That International Business Machines Corporation, for instance, is able to offer its senior personnel conditions of work as agreeable as those found in a university, does not mean that I.B.M. functions according to the ethic of the university. Indeed, we may say that more and more universities have come to function according to the ethic of I.B.M. —or at least, have become increasingly integrated with the sorts of corporate power in the society represented by I.B.M. Many of the assertions made, therefore, about the existence of an autonomous American technocratic elite require severe emendation.

The question of property and of property-owners in American capitalism must now concern us. It is clear that most large-scale industrial property is impersonally owned—by large corporations, by holding companies, by insurance companies, and the like. It is equally clear that those who manage and manipulate this sort of industrial property, do not necessarily own very much of it. (We should not, however, underestimate the proprietary role of managers who benefit from stock options.) A complicating factor is introduced by what we might term administrative property—the capacity to render those administrative and coordinating services without which industrial production and distribution could not proceed. Much of what I have termed administrative property in this country, as in any other, is in the hands of the state, which has become an element in the productive system itself and not outside it. In this complex state of affairs, it is obviously impossible to suppose that *rentiers* actually control the economy (however much they may benefit from it) and we seem to be forced back toward a hypothesis verging on the notion of the direction of the economy and the society by a technocratic or managerial elite—precisely the hypothesis I so strongly criticized some lines above.

Can this dilemma be resolved? We may begin to resolve it by noting that concentrations of impersonal property remain property. Now, even more than in Marx's day, industrial and administrative property organized into large-scale units has assumed something very like a life of its own. Corporations are entities which seem to make midgets or to some extent puppets of the men who direct them. The enormous powers of the state apparatus are such that a John F. Kennedy could respond to the demand for an alteration of federal policy, that he was willing to alter it, but he did not know if the government would agree with him. The concept of bureaucracy gives us the mode of organization of these powers, but not quite its substance or essence. Years of painstaking work by economists, both Marxist and other colleagues with different methodological assumptions, have shown us that the intrinsic or immanent tendencies of the system (occasionally modified by the exercise of political will) do constitute the driving forces which determine the decisions of those in command of large-scale property. In these circumstances, the question of the identity or personification of the owners of property is for immediate analytical purposes less important than the question of control (understood in a short-term sense of control). We may understand control as exercised in such a way that its span of prevision which attaches to it is strictly limited. Decisions are frequently taken with a view to short-term interests in accumulation or in profitability—even if these occasionally add up to long-term developmental tendencies.

Nothing I have asserted is meant to deny, indeed nothing in it can deny, the existence of something like a "power elite." That large-scale *rentiers,* and those who manage large-scale property, are dominant elements in this elite cannot be denied. It does not follow that the power elite, however we describe its composition, reigns sovereign over the workings of the economy and polity with few opposing forces to stay its hand. Quite apart from the amount of direct political opposition its dominant position may generate or evoke, this grouping must reckon with impersonal and structural elements of the situation which shape both the mode and content of its rule. Perhaps we can best deal with these questions if we turn to the next theme, namely, the political integration of late capitalism in America.

Political Integration of Capitalism

Employing the term "integration," I by no means imply that all societies are or can be integrated. I do not wish to propound a consensual theory of politics for any society, much less contemporary America. I do wish to begin with the rather obvious proposition that a considerable amount of political integration is a pre-condition for the functioning of a complex system like capitalism. It does not follow that political integration requires consensus; it may require widespread and structural ignorance, apathy, or privatization on the part of its citizenry. Many of these problems were anticipated by Engels in his remarkable conception of "false consciousness"—which has proven rather more of a political force in advanced capitalist societies than the revolutionary consciousness he and Marx so confidently expected to develop. In any event, the political integration of American capitalism must be understood as a general tendency of the system and not as an absolute and fixed state. The extremely large role of government in the function of the economy makes of politics a factor inseparable from the analysis of the control of property.

I have previously introduced the notion of "administrative property." The bureaucratic apparatus which is the modern mode of social integration and of organizational function may be understood as "administrative property" in both its private and state forms. The large industrial organizations and the state do function according to remarkably similar patterns: a formal and legal circumscription of office, a career progression for officials, the application of criteria of efficiency to the workings of the units of the system. It is quite true that the larger corporations measure themselves by their profitability, and that criteria of political profitability for the operations of government agencies are in fact less susceptible of quantitative evaluation. If we consider, however, that most of the functions of government consist in providing an infrastructure for the operations of industrial enterprise, we do find that increasingly explicit notions of social profitability do serve as criteria for governmental decisions.

Much has been made of the oppressiveness and remoteness of bureaucratic forms of organization. There have been demands for "community control" through which a part of the American left has reaffirmed—however unwittingly—some of the traditional American revulsion for impersonality and bigness. Let us be clear: a frontal onslaught on bureaucracy as a social form is not necessarily equivalent to a creative transformation of bureaucratic control, and may indeed represent a desperate rear-guard action. (The American right also claims an anti-bureaucratic ethos.) The remoteness and oppressiveness of bureaucracy in this society is in large measure a function of the remoteness and oppressiveness of political and economic decision in general. That is to say, it is a product of the ends which bureaucracy serves and not of the mere existence of bureaucracy itself. In this connection, efforts to assimilate late capitalism to the state socialist social order prevailing in the Soviet Union are exercises in the avoidance of historical analysis rather than anything else.

What has characterized American capitalism most recently is the enormous growth of a public sector. This public sector has two principal functions. The first is to coordinate the workings of the capitalist system—budgetary and fiscal policy, the control of the level of social investment, above all the tax mechanisms, have been the chosen instruments of control. We have seen symbiotic relationships between government regulatory agencies and the "private" industries they are supposed to regulate. The second function of the expansion of the public sector has been already mentioned—the provision of an infra-structure without which capitalist accumulation could not continue. This includes the provision of essential services like transport, more recently a great expansion of education and health services, and of course the development of an empire to provide a suitably safe world market for American capitalism. We may include the defense industry in the public sector: certainly a remarkable instance of the socialization of loss and the privatization of profit.

What is clear is that the boundaries between "private" and "public" are frequently difficult to establish. The intervention of the state in the sphere of production is so very great as to make dubious the very term intervention. We have to develop new concepts to deal with new historical tendencies and it is here that our conceptual apparatus has fallen rather seriously behind the progression of our empirical knowledge and our political experience. The recent work of James O'Connor, in particular, seems to offer some hope that this deficiency may be made good. At any rate, the deficiencies of critical social analysis in America in this respect seem to parody a more widespread general defect in the society and its political system: our popular and conventional political reflection, and political practice, are not at all adequate to confront the problems of late capitalism. Our society operates with retrograde concepts in a historically advanced situation. It is at this point that we touch the problems of American political and social consciousness to which I now turn.

Problems of Social Consciousness in America

If there is one basic American disorder, it certainly entails our inadequate and distorted social consciousness. The sources of defect and distortion are many. Perhaps these go back to the very roots of our culture. It is historically false to argue that the Puritans in New England were without a social ethic: the Mayflower Compact was an exercise in social theology. However, the importation to this country of early bourgeois notions of community and polity combined with the development of a market unrestrained by pre-capitalist institutions and traditions. It eventually resulted in the society's continuing inability to find a social ethic adapted to its real situation. Our social ethic has always evinced a serious lag with respect to the social contradictions it has to master. It is quite true that no one any longer will promulgate imbecilities like the assertion that the family farm is the backbone of America; the struggle in 1970 over welfare-state institutions which hardly represent an advance over Bismarck's nineteenth-century social policies does suggest that there are still serious historical discrepancies in our public vision.

The first source of these defects must be found in the strange fate of high culture in America. By high culture I mean that tradition of systematic reflection on man, society, and nature developed in the medieval church and the medieval universities and continued at times within and at times without the universities by those intellectuals who assumed the responsibility for the custody of tradition. America has had groups which have manifested a high culture but they were rarely like the European elite and its community of discourse with their society's intellectual and cultural elite. (Marx's own cultural attitudes would no doubt horrify many dues-paying members of our own New University Conference.) The history of immigration to the United States has been the history of a constant infusion of groups cut off from European high culture. This has been particularly, although not exclusively, true of much of the American working class. The market, therefore, and life goals and life styles derived from the working of market forces, have imposed themselves on most of the American population as an institutional context which could not be imagined away. Critical notions based on other perspectives for human life, as developed by intellectuals who were instinctually anti-capitalist, have met incomprehension, hostility, and even murderous hatred. The secularization of American Protestantism (and of the other American religions) has been so profound that not alone a flattening but a virtual eradication of the metaphysical horizon has reduced most of the American population to the point at which it cannot imagine a concrete transcendence of its conditions of existence. Revising Marx, we may say that precisely the absence of religion has contributed to a state of political quietism in America.

The social classes in America have generally lacked the cultural resources to develop self-conscious and articulated images of their own interests. The southern slaveholders and the New England merchants did for a period develop coherent ideologies. These were not generalized, indeed they could not be generalized, to cover any substantial section of an expanding society—even if they were consonant with the culture, life style, and interests of the groups at issue. It is significant that American liberalism has been a curious fusion of entrepreneurial materialism on the one hand and vulgar egoism on the other—whatever its ideal or more civilizing elements. These last have frequently remained in the realm of moral pronouncement and moral criticism, a realm to which the intellectuals were confined until the emergence, at the beginning of this century, of a true technical intelligentsia. Briefly put, the fragmentation of class struggle in America, the ethnic diversity of the population, have contributed to the prevention of a true cultural homogenization of the population. The homogenization which has now taken place is rather an imposed one and not necessarily an entirely profound one.

Another way of looking at this is to assert that America has developed no political conception of a general will, no genuine notion of a polity and political life. C. Wright Mills in *The Power Elite* called our attention to Aristotle's definition of an "idiot" as private man with no communal or general interests. The reduction of a considerable section of the American population to this sort of idiocy can be seen as due to the interaction of two factors: long-term cultural values (or their absence) and the heavy pressure of a manufactured mass culture. In the circumstances, the wonder is not that America has never had a full-scale or enduring movement of social criticism expressed in political terms, but that so much social criticism and so much radical politics have emerged in our history.

American society, then, lacks the ideological resources to make a correct estimate of its historical situation. Popular notions of social causality remain relatively primitive however much suspicions and intimations of exploitation move large groups. The targets of popular hostility are frequently displaced. The intellectuals do speak to a larger group—but a good deal of the intellectuals' public is so bound to white-collar or technocratic occupational routine that its perceptions of social contradiction remain, for the moment at least, without serious political consequences. In the circumstances, attacking policemen with lead pipe does not seem to be an entirely appropriate response to the problems of mass political education. I propose in the final section of this essay to turn to questions of contemporary politics and in particular to the question of the possibilities of a development of a new socialist avant-garde.

POLITICAL POSSIBILITIES IN AMERICAN CAPITALISM

The search for a new socialist avant-garde has pre-empted so much of the recent discussion that one might think that we were agreed on the major outlines of our social analysis. The notion of an avant-garde, however, is closely connected with the results of that analysis and, as I have attempted to show, our analysis remains sketchy and far from complete. Let us consider, however, some of the candidacies advanced for the role of political avant-garde.

The first, of course, is youth as a new social category. A general approach insists on the totality of the young as subjected to the vicissitudes and contradictions of late capitalism. The college educated, and those funneled into college, are victims of manpower channeling. Those excluded from college are thrown onto the labor market and excluded from many of the major benefits of the system as presently constituted. All, or so runs the argument, are extremely restive under work discipline and its educational concomitant. The appeal of the new youth culture, of rock music, of drugs and of a certain hedonism in life style, is precisely the appeal of a counter-culture—a form of political protest which ranges from open to covert but which must inevitably bring youth into conflict with the dominant ideologies and agencies of power in the society. These general notions underlie, variously, certain theories of the student revolt and the general doctrine of the existence of a counter-nation argued with such pathos by Abbie Hoffmann in his *Woodstock Nation.*

The trouble with the young, however, is that they will have to grow up. Growing up must mean, inevitably, their assuming roles in the occupational system. It may well be that a permanent minority of the young will be encapsulated in counter-cultures or counter-communities. These will either live parasitically off the larger technical-bureaucratic system or entail an increasing reversion to some parody of American pastoral ideals; an implicit dismantlement of not alone capitalism, but of industrialism as a whole. Others may fall permanently under the domination of drugs. Whatever the moral revulsion felt by the Agnewites for this sort of thing, it is indeed a political factor of some importance. Yet it is important to see that the counter-culture movement does not constitute a substitute for a socialist politics in America. If the young are indeed to grow up in the larger sense of the term, perhaps we may be able to characterize what has been happening recently in the universities and elsewhere as an anticipatory strike by the labor force of tomorrow. We have had an inchoate demand for a more humane society; by those who will be called upon to live in it as adults shortly. This, however, will require that they develop political consciousness and political skills, above all the ability to effect short-term and long-term coalitions with other groupings for the sake of comon political goals.

The most obvious of these groupings recently has been constituted by the dispossessed—in particular the blacks and the other ethnic minorities excluded from the mainstream of the productive and administrative system. This is not the place to rehearse the familiar debate over black power and black culture. It is difficult for me to see how a black culture compounded of the agrarian experience of the blacks in rural poverty in the south and their experience in the northern ghettos can provide the basis for the emergence of the blacks as a separate power group in a technically advanced society. In any event, a revolutionary strategy based exclusively on the dispossessed must inevitably entail the shifting of revolutionary responsibility from the "mother country" to other external agencies—like the (exceedingly fragmented and disunited) movement of liberation from colonialism and imperialism in the Third World. It may be necessary and honorable for American socialist intellectuals to proclaim their own impotence in this way, but there is nothing in the record of recent history to sugest that the imperial metropolis can be brought down by a tactic of this sort. Unless a socialist politics can enter the main stream of American political life, deflect it from its previous course and give it a new structure, faddism and sectarianism of the most varied kind will lead to an interminable series of defeats.

We have, finally, to consider the political potential of the so-called "new" working class—particularly in its white-collar and technocratic sectors. I have covered this ground before and can be brief. It is quite true that this grouping experiences the contradictions of capitalism in several ways. It does not exercise autonomy at work despite its high educational and skilled qualifications. The products of its labor are systematically distorted for social purposes other than those which would benefit the collectivity. The fragmentation of existence which distinguishes those members of this somewhat amorphous stratum in their capacities as citizens, as workers, and private persons, seems to continue apace. It is the revulsion for this fragmentation which does seem to motivate their offspring. This grouping canot be induced to confront the real sources of its own condition and to take the beginnings of action to remedy it without a prolonged process of political education and political organization. The unionization of important occupations in this group may be a beginning in this direction, but the history of trade unionism in America again imposes a certain caution upon us. Trade unionism, as we know, may also become a factor which tends to integrate the political system rather than the reverse.

Given the relatively developed general consciousness of the white-collar and technocratic grouping, it may be liable to critical political thought about its situation. As citizens, members of this grouping suffer from the distortion of social priorities entailed in the military-industrial complex and the general unresponsiveness of our electoral and congressional system to changed national requirements. As private persons, they respond already (perhaps too much so, and in exceedingly simple terms) to the issues of environmental degradation. As private persons, as well, they are responsive to the pressures of their children. Finally, as workers, they are both integrated with the system and able to develop critical views of its functioning. The notion of a campaign for the equivalent of "Workers' Councils" at IBM is indeed fantastic—but given the general movement of discontent and criticism in American society, the chances for institutional transformations of this sort do seem higher today than they have been for forty years. Here, a heavy responsibility is incumbent upon the left to devise institutional critiques of advanced capitalism which carry some pragmatic weight: a utilization of some of the propensities of the middle class (admittedly, in its educated sectors) to political organization in conventional terms ought not to be excluded. Finally, given the cultural stratification of American society, the beginnings of radicalization amongst adult members of the middle class may have some influence upon the working class—particularly if the trade unions can be persuaded to take a more radical course.

The contradictions remain. What is lacking are the political mechanisms and a political will to translate these into a coherent and long-term strategy for either revolution or reform. A good many self-designated revolutionary theorists in the United States are unable to distinguish between a revolutionary situation and a situation of simple social decomposition. They do not underestimate the repressive power of the state and of the society, but they certainly underestimate the recuperative power of advanced capitalism. It is entirely possible, after all, that new welfare-state institutions may be developed by the much despised theorists of "corporate liberalism" and that these may well have a stabilizing and integrating effect on the social totality.

What we face is a situation of genuine historical indeterminacy. Analyses of the contradictions of late capitalism predicated on a mechanical or quasi-automatic generation of revolution simply repeat the mistakes of the vulgar Marxism of the late nineteenth century. Our situation is, rather, not unlike that of the first generation of Marxists in the face of new historical forces. A new phase in the existence of bourgeois society calls for new modes of analysis, and above all, new forms of political organization. We do not, however, commence entirely anew. Our harsh judgments on the American political tradition should not lead us to overlook the positive democratic elements within it. A fusion of that tradition with socialism is long overdue. It is striking in this connection that while denunciations of "electoral politics" from radicals rend the air, as reformist a thinker as John Kenneth Galbraith has just called for an explicit socialist program for the Democratic Party. In a society generally affluent, whatever its social impoverishment, old revolutionary rhetoric will not do. Indeed, the dilemma of revolution versus reform may well be out of date. (That has been seen by the Italian Communist Party, whose Marxist credentials can hardly be challenged.) The task before us is not alone to deepen our analysis of the workings and fatalities of late American capitalism, but to develop a realistic politics based on its inner contradictions. If men make their history, they do so because they possess sufficient political will and political vision to alter their circumstances. The difficulties of American historical consciousness can only be met by a changed consciousness. In this respect, a heavy burden falls upon those intellectuals and not least those intellectuals who have recently renounced critical analysis in favor of a stereotyped recourse to unreflected doctrines about the efficacy of the "counter-culture."

Is There a

Post-Industrial Revolution?

The recent literature of social and cultural analysis and political commentary stresses the changes induced in advanced industrial societies by what is termed a "post-industrial revolution." The purpose of this essay is to analyze the components—sometimes discordant ones—of this very general notion, to see what bases in historical fact they possess and to inquire into their political implications. These last are important: those who describe the supposed revolution not only assert that profound structural changes in our societies have important consequences for politics; they frequently use these changes to justify one or another course of political action. In presenting my argument in abbreviated form, I may be doing injustice to the complexity of thought of some contemporaries—and I am attempting to bring under one rubric a rather disparate body of material from a number of countries. However, the effort may prove rewarding if it occasions renewed thought about our general historical context.

The components of the supposed post-industrial revolution are various. One component, presumably responsible for the very term "post-industrial," has to do with changes in production technology. The increasing utilization of automated and computerized means of production and administration, it is argued, has transformed the conditions of production as dramatically as did the first industrial revolution two centuries ago. Society now faces unprecedented problems of choice in the regulation of its production but—so the argument runs—does not have to struggle for material existence.

Another component of the theory has to do with the changed composition of the labor force. Education, indeed higher education, is increasingly a qualification for remunerative employment in the labor force of advanced societies. The general role of white collar workers—of the tertiary sector, as it is called—and of intelligence-intensive and knowledge-producing industries has expanded to the point at which the traditional working class has been replaced. Some describe the new working class in terms not so long ago reserved for the so-called new middle class. These are not merely disputes as to terminology, but have to do with divergent judgments as to the political and social functions and possibilities of this grouping. Most theorists of the post-industrial revolution, however, agree on the importance of this change, and it is clearly a major component in other aspects of the argument.

Still another element in this very general idea of a new revolution is the notion of a new elite structure. Control of industry and, indeed, of the state, it is argued, has shifted from capitalists and entrepreneurs to technocrats. Opinions differ as to whether or not these constitute a self-contained grouping, but most theorists do argue that technical expertise has become indispensable to both economic exploitation and political domination. Some see in this a mode of enlightenment, others simply a continuing form of power. All agree that elite structure has changed.

Paradoxically, notions of a new elite structure in these arguments are admixed with notions of new political possibilities. It is argued that changes in the social composition of the labor force and of the educational level, combined with the effects of greater affluence, have led to heightened demands for citizens' participation in politics (in the industrial countries with democratic regimes). These demands are seen as likely to be satisfied, variously by the so-called new politics associated with Senator McCarthy and the late Senator Kennedy and—more radically—by the proposals for participatory democracy developed by the New Left. Others argue that the rise of the technocratic elite has led to a diminution of ideological politics in favor of a more rational and balanced pragmatic kind. The French May revolt and the recent explosions of bombs in American cities have tended to make this argument less audible, but this ought not detract from its intrinsic persuasiveness.

Finally, a whole range of arguments has to do with cultural change, indeed, with a "cultural revolution." They assert, with differing degrees of regard for the relationships of primacy and derivation, that these social changes have been accompanied by cultural changes no less profound. These include, but are not exhausted by, changes in communications technology; a decline of the work ethic associated with previous phases of industrial production; new attitudes toward sensuality and sexuality; briefly, a new sense of cultural possibilities. Much of the argument about a cultural revolution assumes the avant-garde role of youth as a social force or category—or rather, as a category having political force. Unbound to the past, youth is free to experience the new historical epoch in all its concreteness and directness. Not yet tied to occupational routine, youth is free to demand a better world. The student revolt, and the larger conflict of generations, are here viewed as motor forces for historical change.

The argument at this stage is still exceedingly imprecise. We will try to render it more specific by considering each of the components in turn and then proceeding to another view of the whole. In so doing, I shall not hesitate to join philosophical or political criticism to what might otherwise be thought of as straightforward sociological analysis—the more so as I do not believe that the one is separable from the other.

The basis of the post-industrial revolution has been found by many to reside in changes in production technology. These entail the systematic and ever more rationalized application of science to the production process and to the ancillary processes of administration. The changes also account for a higher gross productivity for the entire system, if we measure productivity in quantitative terms. That is to say, fewer men working with more efficient machines produce more goods. Similarly, fewer administrative and clerical workers, equally equipped with machines, can handle more administration. These workers are growing in number, to be sure, but so are their tasks. The resulting changes in the composition of the labor force, however, have not been converted immediately into unprecedented affluence—and our problems are not those of the dignified consumption of an enormous productive surplus.

Only certain large corporate entities are capable of employing the new highly productive technology, because its costs can only be met by economic and political concentration. These may be gigantic firms in the private sector, state industries (as in the neocapitalist regimes of Western Europe), or some combination of the two (as in the American defense industry, that curious instance of a socialized private industry). Politically, these concentrations exercise more power than their more diversified and fragmented predecessors in the sphere of production. Administratively, the same may be true: think of the political difficulties and threats to freedom posed by so-called data banks. That these concentrations of economic and political power may, under certain circumstances, call forth countervailing power of various kinds does not alter the fact that the initial concentration is in the hands of those who control the new technology. It remains to be seen whether the post-industrial revolution leads to a wider distribution of economic and political power, but at first sight it would appear to entail a narrower distribution. If this is the case, it is difficult to see why it is called a "revolution" at all: it simply follows a general tendency of modern economy and politics, one long since predicted for capitalist society by thinkers as divergent as Marx and Weber.

Let us now consider affluence. It is quite true that the higher productivity of the system would appear to create objective conditions under which more affluence could be generated. However, the system requires heavier and heavier investments if it is to be kept going. Much of the generated affluence, in other words, has to be put back into newer forms of production technology. More importantly, perhaps, the affluence created by the system is spread in a most unequal fashion throughout society. It is unclear whether the wage and salary rates of the newer sections of the labor force have risen in proportion to their productivity. Moreover, in societies that are conspicuous for the absence of any generalized planning mechanism (and even in some in which planning of a kind takes place), economic affluence in one sector has been accompanied by social impoverishment in another. The decline in environmental quality suggests that an affluent society can also drown in its own effluence. Further, psychologically and culturally, the heightened productivity of the system may give rise to a generalized status anxiety in the society, with unpleasant consequences for the transmission of high culture, with a degradation of all values to monetary or careerist common denominators, and with feelings of extreme resentment on the part of those who do not fare well in the status competition. If these are the effects of affluence, it is difficult to see again why they should be characterized as "revolutionary" when they seem to reproduce at a "higher" level the inanities, crudities, and horrors of early capitalism.

This is not the place to repeat what is known about poverty in America (a condition that has parallels elsewhere, as in the case of the foreign workers in Western Europe, or socially "superfluous" categories everywhere). Additionally, the present curve of inflation in the United States and continuing wage struggles in Europe suggest that even unionized workers are continually menaced by cuts in their hard-won standard of living. Briefly, the affluence of the affluent society is greatly exaggerated—and no more so than in the United States, where the provision of social and public services is so defective.

As for the composition of the labor force, the quantitative dimensions of the change are well known: everywhere, white collar workers of many categories are growing in number faster than blue collar workers, while the agricultural sector is in decline. Within the blue collar sector, certain phenomena of polarization are visible, such as that more training is required for the skilled posts which, indeed, are often difficult to distinguish from those of white collar technicians. That these developments are long-term trends, that they are concentrated in certain critical industries or sectors (in this country, the public sector, for instance, has recently witnessed the most rapid growth), does not seriously affect the argument. Those on the American Left who call for a "working-class strategy" ignore these developments.

Some time ago it was common enough to speak of the new white collar grouping as politically extremely labile, as often quite passive as well as dependent in status upon the older and more established middle-class and elite groupings, and, indeed, as prone under certain historical circumstances to reactionary politics. Yet today we are told that these groups have a great potential for citizens' participation in the democratic process or that they may constitute a revolutionary vanguard for a new kind of socialism. Surely, not all of these things can be correct. Where does the truth reside?

In the first place, we would do well to pay attention to the extreme internal differentiation of this group. The rates of growth have been fastest in its subordinate categories: clerical and minor public officials, schoolteachers, technicians, professional auxiliaries and the like. These persons work, generally, in large bureaucratic hierarchies, and their new-found numerical prominence in the labor force by no means points to a phenomenon of de-hierarchization. It is true that under certain circumstances they may be liable to trade unionization (as with the American schoolteachers and public service workers generally), but trade unionization and revolutionary politics are rather different matters. Indeed, the integration of this group in occupational hierarchies commanded by elites can to some degree counteract the effects of solidarity and group consciousness generated by their subordinate occupational position; they may feel that a certain community of social and cultural interest unites them with those who actually dominate them. This is the familiar pattern of the so-called *embourgeoisement* of the lower middle class, and it is a phenomenon which empirical social research has pointed to in a great many societies—not least in societies like Poland. Where, as in France and to some extent in Italy, these new white collar groupings are politically radical, this appears to depend upon the existence of a general tradition of bourgeois radicalism as much as upon the strictly objective conditions of work in which the group finds itself. At any rate, we may say that the new white collar masses may well be the old white collar group writ large. Its own propensities to trade unionization may, however, exhibit significant differences from certain traditional patterns of trade unionism in the United States.

Before turning to these, we had best deal with the skilled sector of the blue collar labor force under conditions of new production technology. These groupings may come to resemble, in income and status prerogatives on the job, the white collar labor force. They may also, however, experience a certain contradiction between their technical capacity and their limited autonomy on the job—not unlike the professionals and semi-professionals in the new white collar labor force. In these cases, we may expect trade union concern not alone with hours, wages, and the like, but with conditions of operation and control of the administrative and productive units in question. There is some evidence that the white collar and public service unions in the United States in particular are tending in that direction—schoolteachers being the most prominent but by no means the only example. Tendencies in this direction are visible in other countries, most notably in France but also in Italy, Germany and elsewhere in Western Europe. The Czech experiment of 1967 and 1968 included a large component of workers' control in factories and in administrative hierarchies, and this was no small cause for the eventual Soviet repression of the experiment.

What we can say here for both the blue collar and white collar sections of the work force clustered about the new technology is that their technical skills may, but need not necessarily, give rise to demands for more control of work operations. In the French May revolt of 1968 and in the Czech experience, these tendencies were quite visible; other tendencies have been visible elsewhere. In the recent Italian metal industry wage conflicts and the strike movement at Fiat, there were demands for a greater egalitarianism in wage payments; that is to say, on the level of wages, a movement against differentiation. This was accompanied by a movement for greater worker control of the work process itself through revivified shop steward arrangements. It is interesting to note that all of these developments may eventually lead to something like profound structural changes, even revolutionary ones in our societies, but that they begin on the job itself. Now, most of the literature about a post-industrial revolution deals with the effects of these changes in production technology, off the job, on persons not so much as workers but as consumers, citizens, members of the public and the like. I am at a loss to account for this discrepancy, except to say that some of the advocates of the view that socialism is no longer relevant seem to think it is not necessary to pay close attention to work and occupational, productive, and administrative process as such, but concentrate instead on the effects of these in the larger society. This is a severe oversight.

There is another aspect of the recent change in the composition of the labor force which cannot go unremarked. I have said that the expansion in the lower reaches of the new white collar labor force or in the skilled sections of the blue collar labor force has been greatest. There is another way of looking at this: the same number of people are now commanding larger and larger operations; the span of control exercised by elites has been extended. If, in fact, on the day-by-day job operations the newer recruits to the white collar labor force are expected to exercise a certain amount of autonomy, others integrate their occupational activities in some larger whole. These others, controllers and members of various elites, emerge from this process with heightened and not lessened powers. This is a phenomenon of implicit polarization, which (again the French and Czech phenomena apart) does not seem as yet to have produced very many direct and persistent confrontations. Indeed, one acute observer, Alain Touraine, argues that confrontation thus far in what he calls the "programmed society" has opposed general social and political elites to those subjected to various forms of general manipulation and control. This is a result of large-scale political-economic planning—and not of direct confrontation at the workplace itself. This, however, would appear to be a matter for examination in our general consideration of new elites and new politics.

The question of the existence of a "new" elite structure, or power structure, is clearly of great importance to assertions about the post-industrial revolution. These assertions vary from those which claim a severe limitation on the power of previous elites, almost to the point of a new and widespread diffusion of power in our society, to those which simply argue for the replacement of an older elite by a new one. Clearly, definitions are central to the matter, but we do not confront what is only a definitional exercise. Real questions of power, property and control intrude. There can be no doubt that the mode of exercising power has, to some extent, shifted in advanced societies—from (under normal circumstances) co-ercion to manipulation; from entrepreneurs to managers; from politicians to bureaucrats. This is a shift in mode and is therefore clearly insufficient in and of itself to justify the assertion that we have entered a technocratic epoch in which political and economic technicians make decisions on purely technical criteria, while the population, subject to manifold political and economic pressures that reflect these decisions, follows suit.

In the first place, there are no purely technical criteria for political and economic decisions: decisions are made with respect to adequate means for attaining new ends and the setting of ends is always a political question. The search for means is also a political question, since the selection of means entails resource reallocation, employment for some and un-employment for others, and at least a partial and segmental redistribution of advantage. It follows that so-called technocrats, whether in the private or public sector—it is difficult to see why a General Motors executive should be thought to be in the private sector—are deeply involved in the day-by-day stuff of politics. A more interesting question, and more fundamental, is the extent to which these persons with technical competence or expertise are integrated in command hierarchies. If they are so integrated, who is at the top of the hierarchies? It is at these points that allegations of some grave structural change in our society appear to break down. Those who command concentrations of power and property are able to employ technical experts—for good or for ill. That expertise is bought, either in the form of bureaucratic organizations producing knowledge, or in the services of individual technical experts. When technicians do rise to actual command positions, they cease to function solely as technicians but function as men in command, men with power.

What has happened, in effect, is that our society has integrated knowledge with the command process to a far greater degree than has been the case heretofore. This is true particularly of technical and administrative knowledge and very obviously much less true of what might be termed moral or esthetic knowledge (which is not of the same kind). The integration of knowledge in the command structure has effected a change in the modalities of command but not in the fact of the exercise of power. Whether a background in the intermediate, knowledge-producing and knowledge-administering, technical hierarchies of the command structure is increasingly indispensable for admission to the upper reaches of the command structure is an interesting question about the recruitment of new elites. It does not, however, point to a diffusion of power but rather again to new modes for its exercise.

It is argued that we live in societies which are increasingly "programmed." No society, however, has as yet put all of its ordinary requirements onto a single computerized system. Even if it were to do so, some specific group of persons would have to follow specific guidelines in constructing the program. The ancient question *cui bono?* still holds. In whose name is society programmed, for what ends, and with what effects— intended or unintended? That remote and impersonal hier- archies of a bureaucratic kind increasingly push large masses of the population around is something we know. That this should be thought to be a higher form of political rationality precisely because the modes of manipulation are more tech- nical is perhaps an astonishing proof of the capacity of aca- demic men for self-delusion, but it is not a serious political argument.

Moreover, none of the evidence adduced for the existence, real or imaginary, of a technocratic elite has been able to ex- plain away the continuing existence of large concentrations of power and property in industrial societies. In the Soviet Union, the party reigns supreme over the managers; indeed the party has made it its business to recruit and control managers. In the United States, federal regulatory agencies exist in an interesting form of political symbiosis with the industries they are supposed to regulate. In France, with its great centralized state tradition, the state technocrats work closely with a private sector into which in the end many of them are recruited and, in any case, these technocrats work at the direction of governments whose major policies are set by broader political and economic considerations. There is in no society a general social programming; programming re- mains segmental and contested. Insofar as programming exists, it is imposed upon subject populations whose passive wishes may, from time to time, be consulted and who, from time to time, may rise in protest or electoral revulsion, but whose day-by-day influence upon the controllers is minimal. The alleged diffusion of power attendant upon a high-tech- nology society, with or without affluence, is nonexistent.

The notion of a post-industrial revolution really implies that the changes so far considered—new production technology, affluence and its social distribution, the composition of the labor force, the composition and mode of action of elites—result in changes in the structure of our political life, or that they will do so shortly. The arguments for the kinds of changes we may look for differ. One view is that we are entering a new epoch in which new forms of political participation are objectively possible and likely to spread. Just as the distribution of affluence is by no means egalitarian, so the new modes of administration and production by no means have egalitarian consequences. It is difficult to see, therefore, why those enmeshed in a highly complex and bureaucratic society should suddenly develop new political capacities; they may by a process of revulsion gradually develop new political desires, but desires and capacities are quite distinct, the one from the other. We can say that a number of phenomena in many societies have recently pointed to a widespread conviction, on the part of even those in relatively well situated positions in the social structure, that they are powerless to alter the major political direction of their societies. This has been true across a good many ideological boundaries. At any rate, it is difficult to see any new forms or institutions for formal political participation developing. What we have witnessed, instead, is an end to the pervasive period of de-politicization that characterized the late Forties and Fifties.

The end of this depoliticization, most conspicuous among the young, does entail a search for new forms of political control—but these remain to be invented. If it is true, as some assert, that our formal political mechanisms are incapable of coping with the functioning of the system on its own terms—how much more must this be true for those who seek to give the system newer, more humane goals. The French heretical Communist, Roger Garaudy, has recently promulgated the notion of a computerization of political choice, such that consoles at the disposition of individuals and groups could be used for a newer and higher rationality in political decision-making. This seems to be a curious return, if I have understood him correctly, to a free market notion of political choice. The recourse of so sober and intelligent a thinker to such a fantasy is a sign of the desperate emptiness to which the present situation has reduced us.

Meanwhile, the argument about the new politics is pursued by those content to allow the system to function within its present boundaries. Here it is argued that politics has become less general, that it has become segmentalized, that the competition of a plurality of interest groups has replaced the general confrontation of social classes. This is not on the face of it to be denied, but what is striking, if this is indeed a product of post-industrial revolution, is that the "revolution" has served further to denude society of a conception of its own general interest. In other words, the alleged revolution will have contributed to a further breakdown in our polity and to the increasing consolidation of a kind of Hobbesian political condition. The recent decomposition of the American polity is an extreme case in point; similar phenomena are observable elsewhere.

To the view that new possibilities of affluence and new changes requiring a more highly educated labor force bring great possibilities for democratization, the Left has been able to reply only in very general ways. That is to say, the search for specific institutional forms of participation, the search for specific modes of control of giant bureaucracies, the search for alternatives of an institutional sort to a numerical electoral politics, the search for counter-institutions in a very broad sense, have resulted in no very coherent political program. In this country, much of the critique has taken the form of a flight into clichés, or into the privatization of the movement into communes. In France and Italy, and even more among the oppositional communists in Eastern Europe, the question has been one of devising tactics for the mobilization of the working class and sectors of the middle classes for an onslaught on the system. The devising of counter-institutions there also has been rather defective. It is interesting in this connection that the Right, or the technocratic middle, seems content, in general, to retain electoral politics to serve as a kind of plebiscitarian validation of technocratic or allegedly technocratic decisions.

Finally, I turn to the notion of a cultural revolution as part of the larger process of social change we are experiencing. A cultural revolution may be understood in two senses. The first is that of a purposive revolution, a self-conscious and directed attack on previous values, as a mode of establishing the primacy of new beliefs, new patterns of feeling, new modes of life. Cultural revolutions of this sort are usually the work of an avant-garde working with new historical possibilities, but appealing to a public, however inchoate, larger than itself. The second sort of cultural revolution is more diffuse. This, too, would involve changes in belief, feeling and action, but the entire process of change would be more in the nature of a discontinuous drift, with its full import realized by few participants and its major outlines obscure even to contemporaries. Much of the discussion of contemporary cultural change moves from one type of "revolution" to another and a certain precision is in order.

Perhaps the most striking, if not simplistic, version of a doctrine of an objective cultural revolution has been supplied by those who, with Marshall McLuhan, insist that changes in communications technology have altered consciousness. The ubiquity and psychic reality of television, the striking ascendancy of film as a medium of expression, the rise of mixed media works of all kinds, and above all the easy and instant accessibility of these media, are the objective conditions for this supposed change in consciousness. Much has been made, especially by McLuhan and his school, of the supposed substitution of simultaneity as a principle of the organization of experience for linearity based on the transmission of experience by print. Whether McLuhan may be mistaking a technical form taken by a historical development for the cause of the development itself is an open question. My own view is that the changes in consciousness described by McLuhan (not without a certain degree of accuracy) are due to radical historical discontinuities in social experience and not to changes in communications technology alone. Further, the doctrine of the "global village" advanced by McLuhan to explain contemporary perceptions of politics does not seem to deal realistically with the extraordinary and central residue of provincialism and naked egoism that still lies at the heart of much contemporary politics, even in advanced societies, as well as with the fact that political experience for each participant in group or nation is mediated by an objective structure of social relationships—a structure of domination and exploitation, and not merely a structure of easy communication or ideological permeability.

A more convincing case for profound cultural change has been made by those who, with accents as varied as Erik Erikson, Kenneth Keniston, and Margaret Mead, have argued the importance of youth as a social and psychological category in our society. The argument has a number of components: early biological maturation combined with delayed social maturation do produce strains; so does the problem of defining an identity in a society which seems to offer a multiplicity of psychological possibilities but, in fact, is rather strenuous in its delimitation of possibility for those entering its bureaucratic hierarchy. Yet another component of the argument is that the young, who have grown up in the shadow of universal nuclear destruction, have at once a heightened sense of dreadful and benign historical possibility, having known in our own societies a high degree of affluence but also the threat of instant and total extirpation.

408

This, it is supposed, has led to a demand for instant experience, to a restiveness with the restraints and the usual canons of apprenticeship, whether psychological or occupational, and to impatience with cultural codes designed for earlier modes of existence. These modes, it should be noted, were at once more continuous, less threatened, and more restrictive.

Above all, one point is common to the views that insist upon the distinctive youthful contribution to the current cultural ferment: the changing composition of the labor force has resulted in a great expansion of education, not least higher education, and therefore the educational system has become, in effect, a prolongation of the system of production and administration. I myself have in another context referred to the student revolt—no doubt too simply—as an "anticipatory strike by the labor force of tomorrow." It is difficult to see why this heightened occupational utilization of education should result in a general cultural revolution by the young, and perhaps the two phenomena are connected contextually rather than directly. This is to say, the young experience as a contradiction the heightened sense of human possibility and the increased demands imposed upon them for earlier forms of occupational or pre-occupational socialization. Perhaps this contradiction accounts for the frenzy of the youth revolt, in particular of the student revolt, in a country like our own which lacks a viable socialist tradition. It may be said, however, that frenzied and guerrilla-like actions, the seeking of role models in figures like Ché Guevara, the extraordinary cult of Mao and Maoism (which seems to be strongest in inverse proportion to real knowledge of China) are not entirely missing in Western Europe.

There is a notion of youth as a new historical agency, of youth replacing as a force for social change the proletariat of classical socialist theory. These tendencies are most prominent in the thought of the Yippies, Abbie Hoffman and Jerry Rubin, although even as sagacious a student of political science as Tom Hayden speaks in a similar vein. Stated in its pure form, by the Yippies, the revolt of youth is almost entirely a cultural phenomenon—and minor matters like the new organization of production and distribution are simply dismissed in cavalier fashion. One is reminded after reading Rubin's *Do It!* of the disdain for matters of mere economic organization voiced by Charles de Gaulle: *"l'intendance suivra"*—"housekeeping arrangements will follow in due course."

The cultural revolt is principally borne by youth. It is obviously something rather deeper than wearing long sideburns or beads. In this country it takes the form of an attack on the Protestant ethic, on certain narrowly defined conceptions of psychological and behavioral normality, on certain notions of limitation of impulse expression and the expression of feeling, and in that sense may be thought of as an enlargement of human freedom. But is it really that? The Protestant ethic may be an outdated cultural form, but it is or was a cultural form. Many involved in the cultural revolution seem to exist in a general formlessness. There is a certain amount of talk of the search for new forms of existence, and experimentation in communes and the like, but I cannot avoid the impression that a good deal of the "revolution" consists of a negative attack on cultural form as such, a slothful disinclination to engage in the hard work of cultural apprenticeship and an almost barbarian disregard for what is positive in the legacy of the past. We may remind ourselves that Marx and Freud, to mention but two of the great destroyers of bourgeois self-confidence, were in many respects cultural traditionalists.

Much of the attack on high culture, particularly in the universities, is justified by the argument (difficult to refute at first sight) that high culture serves as a vehicle of elite domination. Access to a university has been, and is certainly increasingly, defined as access to the upper reaches of the occupational hierarchy. The universities are therefore hopelessly enmeshed in the power system, even if we abstract from them their direct services to the agencies of power (defense research, consultancy and the like). On this argument the authority claimed by those who possess high culture is simply an extension of the authority, illegitimate because it is rooted in the relations of property, of those who command the larger society. The argument overlooks the fact that cultural forms are never the *direct* result of social process, but mediate social processes in a different, symbolic way. That mediation may well contain notions which are critical of those social processes, which express their inner contradictions, and which point the way to future social forms of a nobler, more humane kind.

Certain demands being made upon the universities are ambiguous. The demand for open admissions is an attack upon the class society, or rather the university's incorporation in the class society. If applied unreflectively, however, it can overwhelm the universities with narrowly occupational and implicitly conformist goals. This could cripple the capacity of the universities to develop critical modes of thought. The demand for total democratization of the learning process can cater to the ahistorical illusions of the offspring of a culture afraid to confront its own history. The notion that requirements and grades are exploitative rests on a facile identification of the university with the workplace. In the long run, the democratization of the university will require considerable commitment and experimentation.

It is a fact that the American universities, for all their servitude to the agencies of power, have also served as a protected space in which a critical culture could develop. Radicals in the university faculties have been few; they have been fewer in the larger law firms or on the staffs of important media of communication. Moreover, in addition to

411

this pragmatic argument for the continuation of high culture, the cultivation of the depths and resources of the human spirit is indeed a classical end of socialism in its democratic variant, and it is impossible to see why an American socialism should begin with an onslaught on high culture—the more so as militant philistinism has long been the prerogative of the American Right. Insofar as the cultural revolution has these negative characteristics, it reflects the decomposition of society in its bureaucratic form, but is not a contribution to the emergence of a new and more just or humanly satisfying social order.

During the Paris May revolt, a number of psychiatrists observed striking personality changes in their patients. In a much earlier and much more circumscribed episode, the American lay analyst and psychologist Nevitt Sanford observed that during the Berkeley loyalty oath controversy affecting the faculty in 1948–49, the external crisis seemed to touch the deepest levels of the personalities of his colleagues and in some cases provoked changes. It is clear that the present period of social disruption, of radical discontinuity, challenges us again to think anew about our notions of the stability and continuity of personality as such. We have tended to think of personality as an organization of psychobiological forces in a social and cultural milieu. Now we can see how changes in milieu activate some of these forces and enable their entire organization and function to alter. Human nature appears rather less fixed than we thought. This is not the least cause of that generalized nervosity, and the psychological and moral uncertainty of our current cultural situation is an important contributing factor to the general impression that we live in a "revolutionary" period. It must be remembered, however, that a cultural revolution so diffuse, so multiple in its forms, and so contradictory and retrograde in many of its aims, is not necessarily productive of political progress. It can be tied to a political program, but only with great difficulty and over a period of time. For the moment, all that we can say is that possibilities, some very good ones and some very disheartening ones, for radical change in our culture do exist—but that these do not constitute a purposive cultural revolution. Where they do, as in the case of the program—if it can be called that—of the Yippies, the political results thus far attained are not entirely positive. I would not underestimate the profound political uses of satire, indeed of derision, nor would I wish to denigrate the moral position that frequently attaches to the critique of routine made by some advocates of youth culture. I would point out that these alone do not suffice to generate a coherent politics. Suppose that the present power system proves perfectly capable of encapsulating and indeed of commercializing this form of dissent? Evidence that this may be so is not entirely lacking.

Much has been made of the fact that the major effort of social scientists, and indeed of social critics, has been concentrated on the description of existing institutions and on programs that take their immutability as given. It is perhaps interesting to recall in this connection that the term "post-industrial" was given wide currency by two essays in *The Public Interest* in 1967 by Daniel Bell under the title "Notes on the Post-Industrial Society." Professor Bell is an able and interesting thinker, the thrust of whose work and political message has been to deny the possibilities for a political and social revolution in advanced societies. His analysis, and the analysis of other thinkers, cannot be refuted simply by pointing to its political purposes; the analysis has to be met on its own terms. Equally, analyses motivated by a desire to find revolutionary possibilities in the situation must stand the test of analytic rigor; we cannot accept these simply because we agree with their proponents' political purposes. A precise analysis of aspects of our social structure can, in certain circumstances, provide a framework for political reflection; a successful analysis can present us with an image of the balance of political forces, and of hitherto untapped political potential in situations of material contradiction or ideological discontinuity.

I hope that this survey, despite its fusion of great scope and brevity, has shown that the notion of a post-industrial revolution cannot be used in serious discussion unless those utilizing it are prepared to do the rigorous work of specifying precisely the social forces at work, their direction, and their consequences for the future of industrial societies. We *are* living through a period of extremely rapid and convulsive social change, but the elements of a purposive revolution are few, and confined to an avant-garde (mainly students) which cannot claim to speak for large groups of the discontented who lack, as yet, a revolutionary ideology. At the same time, the objective elements of social change, such as change in the production system, have not been directly transmuted into political and social innovations—this would require a *general* political will that is conspicuous by its absence.

Not the least source of the current confusion, and the surprising mixture of dismay and optimism with which some greet the situation, is its openness. A good many historical possibilities appear to be congealing or crystallizing just out of our reach, somewhere in the near future. With the passage of time, however, it may appear that they are out of reach in another sense: those of us who wish to introduce social innovations may lack access to the levers of social command, and may indeed lack an adequate knowledge of where these levers are to be found, and how they are to be seized. The notion that the struggle will in itself generate a sufficient theory seems to me adequately disproven by a hundred and fifty years of history: struggle there has been, yet bewilderment and defeat are not smaller now than they have been, whatever the concrete historical gains achieved.

The onslaught on high culture mounted by certain elements in the New Left seems particularly disastrous. Traditionally, not the demand for the destruction of high culture but the demand that it be humanized and generalized has been characteristic of socialist movements. Without a disciplined view of our social condition, without a reflective and developed sense of history and of the implementation of human values, the Left is likely to imitate the Right in philistinism and vacuity. Since the Right has the power, a Left devoid of thought is likely to blunder into self-destruction.

There are times when politics is a leap into the future; there are also times when politics is a matter of simple decency and morality. None of these qualifications can serve as an excuse for theoretic slovenliness on the part of those who would change society. The crisis calls for more and not less rigorous intellectual work.

The Problem of

a Knowledge Elite

The governance of modern societies has become both more obscure and more oppressive. Movements of dissent seem to have a sectarian character: no sooner battle engaged with one enemy, the struggle assumes exemplary or pseudo-mythic dimensions—precisely because attacking one enemy requires moral energies disproportionate to the results of any single campaign. Those in power need not respond with a total counter-offensive against dissent. The inextricable elements of contemporary social regulation entail patterns of defense which contain, encapsulate, and trivialize opposition. It is not surprising, in our circumstances, that a convulsive reaction to modern society among the young—profound in its sentiments if shallow in its thought—should strike at interlocutors both immediate and visible. The student movement may not be a revolt of intellectuals: it is a campaign directed against an intellectual élite.

What may be termed the political theory of the student revolt assigns an important, indeed indispensable, function to the university—and by extension, to the groups and activities it houses and generates. The university has abandoned or de-emphasized its task of mediating a high culture, in favor of the preparation of educated manpower for the ad-

416

ministrative and productive apparatus of a technically complex society. Further, that manpower is indispensable to the effective governance of the society: it monopolizes the knowledge, whether abstract or applied, employed in the coordination and direction of the whole. The university, as the primary location for an élite of knowers, is therefore integrated in the system of power. Indeed, in giving or withholding degrees, demanding and sanctioning performances, it reflects the contemporary forces of domination and manipulation. The applications of its researches (frequently by the professoriat itself) constitute—if anything—a more direct exercise of power. The attack on the university is, therefore, an attack on an ancillary agency of power.[1] By extension, the educated as a group or a stratum constitute a new class—or a new mandarinate—at the service of the other and primary agencies of power.[2] Moreover, there are some (not alone in the student movement) who see the university and the research center as, increasingly, a primary agency of power itself.[3]

What I have called the political theory of the student revolt is by no means exclusively the work of students. Some of its elements will be found in thinkers as diverse in beginning point and political inclination as Bell, Chomsky, and Habermas: the analysis of the social functions of the university may be found in Kerr.[4] The theory connects with those

1. Perry Anderson and Alexander Cockburn, editors, *Student Power* (London: Penguin, 1969). Julien Nagel, editor, *Student Power* (London: Merlin Press, 1969). *L'Homme et la Société*, No. 16, 1970.

2. Noam Chomsky, *The New Mandarins and American Power* (New York: Pantheon, 1969).

3. Daniel Bell, "Notes on the Post-Industrial Society," *The Public Interest*, Nos. 6 and 7, 1966–67. Daniel Bell, "The Measurement of Knowledge and Technology," in Eleanor Bernert Sheldon and Wilbert E. Moore, editors, *Indicators of Social Change* (New York: Russell Sage, 1968).

4. Jürgen Habermas, *Protestbewegung und Hochschulreform* (Frankfurt: Suhrkamp, 1969). Jürgen Habermas, *Towards a More Rational Society* (Boston: Beacon, 1970). Clark Kerr, *The Uses of the University* (Cambridge: Harvard, 1963).

417

asserting the emergence of a new social group, understood variously as a technocratic élite or an educational and scientific estate with social functions so important, with a qualitative political role so essential, that our previous models of industrial social organization require severe emendation. In Europe, Lichtheim and Touraine, in the United States, Galbraith, have promulgated models of this sort.[5] Clearly, we are experiencing a reconsideration of an ancient problem, the relationship of knowledge to power. It may be suggested that the recent spate of works on the anarchist tradition and its contemporary relevance is an antagonistic response to the notion of social dominance by those who possess a monopoly of knowledge.[6] It is supposed—or hoped—that new institutions of a decentralized kind may enable men to rule themselves in a situation in which the historic promise of democracy has encountered new obstacles, power exercised outside formal political institutions by manipulative means. From a rather different perspective, a revivified sociology of science has touched—if often unreflectively—on another version of a familiar philosophical theme: the possibility of the institutionalization of reason.[7]

Contemporary reason is, however, fragmented. The disassociation of what was once a unified sensibility (or one, at

5. John Kenneth Galbraith, *The New Industrial State* (Boston: Houghton Mifflin, 1967). George Lichtheim, "The New Social Order," in *Europe and America* (London: Thames and Hudson, 1963). Alain Touraine, *La Société Post-Industrielle* (Paris: Denoel, 1969). (Translation forthcoming.)

6. Kingsley Widmer discusses this literature in "Anarchism in Revival," *The Nation,* Vol. 211, Nov. 16, 1970.

7. Donald Price, *The Scientific Estate* (Cambridge: Harvard, 1965, New York: Oxford, 1968), is a good introduction to these problems. See also the interesting report, which concretizes the problems of science and politics, "Technical Information for Congress," Subcommittee on Science Research and Development of the Committee on Science and Astronautics, U.S. House of Representatives, 91st Congress, April 25, 1969. Further, Bertram Gross, editor, *Social Intelligence for America's Future* (Boston: Allyn and Bacon, 1969). Stimulating and distinctive perspectives on these problems are found in the following: from Czechoslovakia, Radovan Richta, *La*

any rate, less divided than our own) and the instrumentaliza-
tion of reason are, clearly, related. Compelling interpretations of modern culture which rest on these tendencies are
not new: Max Weber and Lukacs, once a member of his circle in Heidelberg, have developed these in antithetical political directions.[8] We may, indeed, understand the work of
the Frankfurt School (Adorno, Benjamin, Habermas, and
Horkheimer) as an effort to determine the dimensions of new
forms of alienation which rest on the division of cultural
labor.[9] It is clear that much of the modern debate on education, its content and uses, implies positions with respect to
the political possibilities of a modern cultural sensibility.
This paper is an attempt to clarify the terms of the debate, by
making more precise some of its dimensions. I shall sketch
these, briefly, and then analyze each in turn.

1. Perhaps the first issue to be considered is whether a
knowledge élite has displaced other élites in important command and co-ordination functions at the top of industrial
societies.[10] We shall have to consider the educational and
intellectual composition of contemporary élites, but above all
we shall have to ask whether knowledge gives power directly,

Civilisation au Carrefour (Paris: Anthropos, 1969); from France, J. J.
Salomon, *La Science et la Politique* (Paris: Seuill, 1970); and from Germany,
Jürgen Habermas, *Technik und Wissenschaft als "Ideologie"* (Frankfurt:
Suhrkamp, 1969).

8. George Lukacs, *Geschichte und Klassenbewusstsein* (Berlin: Malik, 1923).
George Lukacs, *History and Class Consciousness* (Cambridge: Technology
Press, 1970). George Lukacs, *Die Zerstörung der Vernunft* (Berlin: Aufbau,
1954). See George Lichtheim, *George Lukacs* (New York: Viking, 1970).
On Weber, see the discussion in Otto Stammer, editor, *Max Weber und
die Soziologie Heute* (Tübingen: Mohr [Siebeck]), 1965.

9. On introduction to the Frankfurt School, with bibliography, is given in
Goeran Therborn, "Frankfurt Marxism: A Critique," *New Left Review*,
No. 65, 1970. Therborn's critique strikes me as wrong, but the essay is
useful, nevertheless.

10. Thomas Bottomore, *Elites and Society* (London: Watts, 1964), is a good
introduction to élite studies. See also Suzanne Keller, *Beyond the Ruling
Class* (New York: Random House, 1963).

or whether we have to confront its institutional utilization. Put in another way, do men of knowledge exercise power by virtue of their intellectual capacities and educational attainments, or are these ancillary to other aspects of their roles when they do occupy posts of power? Viewed differently, we may ask whether power accrues to institutions primarily concerned with producing knowledge, or whether other institutions use knowledge acquired from other sources.

2. Undoubtedly, a knowledge élite exists. We may conceive of it as composed of those in charge of the process of acquiring and diffusing knowledge: administrators of universities and research institutions, senior professors, heads of foundations, and a range of persons in those institutions diffusing knowledge: the educational system generally, the media, the professions. The very enumeration of these roles and agencies suggests two obvious and related facts about them. The first is that those who command knowledge hierarchies are élites in a specialized sector of society. Nothing follows mechanically for their élite position in other sectors. The second is that the complicated modes which relate knowledge hierarchies, and their products, to other institutions do not allow us to conclude that there is a relationship of domination—in principle—between the sectors directly producing knowledge and those using it. Further, I have introduced the notion of knowledge as a product.[11] This requires stringent reflection: in what sense is a laboratory experiment, a social theory, a work of artistic and literary criticism, a product? We may recall that the intellectual marketplace is confused, that sellers and buyers—if such there be—do not invariably employ the same pricing criteria. Additionally, the bureaucratization of knowledge—a theme I shall discuss in greater detail—has been accompanied by very great diffi-

11. Fritz Machlup, *The Production and Distribution of Knowledge in the United States* (Princeton: Princeton, 1962), is an indispensable analysis of some of these problems.

culty in the establishment of valid criteria for treating knowledge production as a bureaucratic performance, as some of the recent difficulties of universities show. Our problem, briefly, is not to demonstrate the existence of a knowledge élite, but rather to describe its mode of operation and its relationship to other élites.

3. I have mentioned the difficulties of treating the production of knowledge by either market or bureaucratic criteria. Indeed, the idea of the production of knowledge implies an economic dimension to the process, an artisanal or industrial one, which may or may not hold in some important instances. Here, our essay touches questions fundamental to the self-definition of modern culture. This is not an exercise in the taxonomy of intellectual life, but we do well to consider differences in the types of knowledge at issue. The work of a biophysicist and that of a historian differ in inner structure, object, and possible social consequences; in the synthetic realms of philosophy and value systems, or the symbolic areas of art, the differences are, if anything, greater. The recent discussion of the problem described by Snow as that of "the two cultures," science and the humanistic fields, has important components which bear on the institutionalization of different sorts of intellectual activity and their consequences.[12] Once, theologians promulgated images of the universe and of society which were morally binding on entire communities. Their secular successors, the philosophers, attempted the same task until a world which had outgrown thought reduced their operations to those of technical commentary on thought (and despairing reflection on the world). Scientific inquiry presents us with problems of a moral sort, but does not directly provide us with evaluative criteria. The problem is complicated when, as in the pure and applied social sciences, implicit evaluative criteria attach to empiri-

12. C. P. Snow, *The Two Cultures and the Scientific Revolution* (Cambridge: Cambridge University Press, 1959).

cal findings. The knowledge élite, upon examination, appears to be the custodian of a remarkably diversified, often contradictory, intellectual and moral legacy.

4. Great utopias and great anti-utopias have this in common: both insist on the institutionalization of reason in society, on the uses of mind and spirit to direct its activities. Notions of the diffusion of knowledge in the populace at large animate democratic utopias. Ideas of the impossibility of this process, whether adopted with enthusiasm or resignation, infuse the familiar prescriptions for hierarchical societies. In our own situation, the political claims of knowledge have led to a recrudescence of the debate on technocratic rule. Saint-Simon has come to be regarded as having been more prophetic than John Stuart Mill or Karl Marx.[13] To what extent we are actually ruled by technocrats, to what extent technocrats can actually exercise power, and the possible limits or alterations that may be imposed on this process by a citizenry jealous of its sovereignty are themes which shall concern us.

5. A direct line of descent in modern cultural criticism links both contemporary radicals and their opponents. Marx first elaborated notions of the alienation of a human essence in a labor-divided society. Tönnies academicized those notions in his analysis of the antithesis between community and society. Weber wrote of "rationalization" as a general cultural process but he also gave the idea precise modern form in his treatment of bureaucracy as the institution mediating knowledge, and in the sharp separation between fact and value which was central to his epistemology. (By insisting that evaluations as to the choice of objects for study guided factual inquiry, he provided a link between bureaucratic utilization of knowledge and the process of knowing.) Building on these foundations, a host of thinkers have developed

13. Frank Manual, *The New World of Henri de Saint-Simon* (Cambridge: Harvard, 1956).

notions which point, variously, to "rationalization" and "alienation" as central aspects of modern society. The contributions vary, but most insist that the partial derivatives of reason have escaped the control of a totalizing reason, that the social organization of knowledge distorts man's rationality in ways quite like the process attributed by Marx to the division of labor as a whole. Clearly, not the least of the problems of a knowledge élite is its role in this process. Can the knowledge élite recapture, for society as a whole, control of man's rational powers? Or does its very existence and activity confirm a fatal fragmentation in our existence, possibly never to be made whole? There is little point to sociological inquiry if it cannot, at the least, attack such philosophical problems—by converting them, insofar as possible, into categories connected with empirical inquiry.[14]

KNOWLEDGE AND POWER IN MODERN SOCIETY: PROSPECT AND RETROSPECT

1. A critical aspect of the relationship of knowledge and power in modern society is in the recent change in the educational qualification of political élites.[15] By political élites, in societies like our own, I mean those who exercise power—whether directly, in the governmental apparatus, or by exerting irresistible pressure on the state generally from the economic sphere. Indeed, in modern political economies

14. Robert Nisbet, *The Sociological Tradition* (New York: Basic Books, 1967), is a serious attempt to deal with this legacy in sociology. See also Henri Lefebvre, *Positions: Contre les Technocrates* (Paris: Gonthier, 1967).

15. From the considerable range of literature available, I cite the following: Jacques Billy, *Les Techniciens et le Pouvoir* (Paris: P.U.F., 1963); George Fischer, *The Soviet System and Modern Society* (New York: Atherton, 1968); R. K. Kelsall, *Higher Civil Servants in Great Britain* (London: Routledge, 1955); Jean Meynaud, *La Technocratie* (Paris: Payot, 1964); W. Lloyd Warner *et al.*, *The American Federal Executive* (New Haven: Yale, 1963); Wolfgang Zapf *et al.*, *Beiträge zur Analyse der Deutschen Oberschicht* (Tuebingen, 1964).

(whether in the state socialist regimes or in advanced capitalist ones), state and economy are very difficult to distinguish from one another. Those in power now have generally higher educational attainments than their predecessors, and this in turn reflects the increased importance of knowledge in the complex contemporary structures of administration and production. It is important to see, however, that the possession of an educational qualification does not mean that the exercise of power depends directly upon the utilization of knowledge. The capacity to evaluate knowledge, or to use it in a situation of political choice, may be a reserve capacity, a latent one. Power consists, as it always has, in the capacity to give effective commands. Moreover, there is no intellectual calculus which can give the powerful complete indications for a political decision: as always, these must be made from among competing value alternatives. Recent efforts to introduce "systems analysis" in political decision serve, perhaps, to frame and narrow certain alternatives for the decision-makers. The decisions that come out, however, do depend directly upon the range of choice put into the programmed system.

The shift in the control of economic enterprise, from entrepreneurs to managers, has been the subject of a voluminous literature.[16] It should be clear that property administered impersonally remains property, and that it is access to property which confers power upon the managers as it once did upon entrepreneurs. However, one difference between early and late capitalism in the exercise of power does call into play the resources of knowledge at the disposal of both the industrial managers and the state technicians with

16. Paul Baran and Paul Sweezy, *Monopoly Capital* (New York: Monthly Review, 1966). Adolph A. Berle, *Power Without Property* (New York: Harcourt, Brace, 1959). Andrew Shonfield, *Modern Capitalism* (New York and London: Oxford, 1965). Maurice Zeitlin, editor, *American Society, Inc.* (Chicago: Markham, 1970).

whom they work so closely. The sheer span and complexity of the activities which they direct, of the processes they seek to steer, requires the exercise of manipulative modes of power. Prevision and innovation have become, therefore, indispensable elements of the control function in modern societies. Where the managers and state technicians do not themselves dispose of the capacities for prediction, they must be able to command these. The provision of an adequate supply of scientific services (or in the worst case, of pseudo-scientific ones)—"science polity"—is, therefore, not the least of the responsibilities of today's rulers.[17] The nature of the modern situation, and the prospect before us, may become more clear by contrast with the relationships of power and knowledge in previous historical epochs.

The development of the relationships of knowledge to power has been accompanied by a progressive fragmentation of the institutions and roles bearing knowledge. The medieval universities were guardians of a theological tradition and of a highly abstract kind of knowledge (while many of the activities we think of as in the purview of technology and technical education were treated in purely practical terms, by artisans trained in the guild system.) They did offer professional education, in law (statecraft) and medicine.[18] The post-medieval universities educated jurists for the absolutistic state, and later still, civil servants for the bourgeois state. With the advent of modern machine production, higher technical education fell within their scope. Today, the universities educate both administrators for the welfare state and technicians and managers for the private sector. Their formal mode of functioning, in one respect, has changed little. The

17. Valuable sources for this process are the reports of the Organization for Economic Cooperation and Development on national science policies. See, for instance, *France* (Paris: OECD, 1966), *The United Kingdom, Germany* (Paris: OECD, 1967), and *The United States* (Paris: OECD, 1968).
18. Jacques LeGoff, *Les Intellectuels au Moyen Age* (Paris: Seuil, 1957).

universities transmitted a culture (as time went on, an increasingly partial one) taken into practical activity in the minds of its graduates. The practical and ideological significance of the universities' activities were certainly recognized as such: popes used their theological verdicts against resistant bishops and secular rulers alike, and Napoleon enjoined silence upon an Academy of Moral Sciences too enthusiastic about the principles of the Revolution he had inherited.[19] The universities, however, had primarily an educative function: a certain insulation from the daily conduct of affairs was possible. This is not, let it be said, a way of declaring them to have been either politically quiescent or neutral in the great conflicts which ravaged their societies. Rather, their mode of intervention was usually indirect or ideological. Moreover, the artisanal organization of teaching and scholarship in the universities, the very notion of a considerable or rounded segment of culture in one head, was adopted to one phase in the development of bourgeois society. Paradoxically, the modern emphasis on research teams, on communities of students and teachers, may remind us in its formal dimensions of aspects of the medieval universities—with their emphasis on the sharing of a divine science.

The organization of secular knowledge now knows no one center, and the ways in which society and its élites are linked to institutions specialized in knowledge are many. Élites can no longer depend upon the routine acquisition of sufficient competence by their staffs at early stages of their careers; the slower rhythms of ideological exchange with the universities have given way, additionally, to an accelerated relay system. Among the many casualties of the process are two of some considerable interest: the notion of a generally educated man, and the idea of an educated citizenry. In their place have come the technical specialist and an entire population

19. Hans Barth, *Wahrheit und Ideologie* (Zuerich: Manesse, 1945).

426

reduced to a form of plebiscitarian approval of such decisions as technocratic élites care to submit to public scrutiny.

The components of this process are several. The enormous quantitative growth in knowledge, and its qualitative differentiation among the many fields of learning, have of course made the notion of a general education extremely difficult to sustain. The educated bourgeois of the nineteenth and early twentieth centuries, and his professional or technological counterpart, were supposed to share (and largely did) a common core of knowledge. Perhaps what they shared was, more importantly, a common set of assumptions about the uses of knowledge—in effect, a definition of their social roles as actualizing the combined operations of the capitalist market and the bureaucratic state. In this setting, it was easy enough to depict certain areas of knowledge as "pure," as isolated from routine social processes. The not quite inextricable contemporary links of knowledge to ordinary administrative and productive process have rendered these assumptions obsolete. Highly specialized knowledge of an administrative or technical kind may be applied by those who know relatively little about it: the educated, in effect, renouncing such autonomy as they once had in the utilization of their education.

The universities, and specialized agencies of research (often attached to specific enterprises or to governmental bodies), now have in addition to an educative function one of preparing and at times supplying cadres for the application of specialized knowledge. Government, and the command posts in the private economic sector, may be thought of as an instrument of mobilization of knowledge resources—provided, of course, that we understand that the decisions as to resource utilization fall not to the knowers but to their employers.[20] All the material available to us from the state

20. Richard Barnet, *Intervention and Revolution* (New York: New American Library, 1968). Harold Wilensky, *Organizational Intelligence* (New York: Basic Books, 1967).

socialist regimes suggest that the same process is at work there.

Enough has been said, perhaps, to make plausible the assertion that we have to deal with the problem not of a knowledge élite replacing other élites, but of political élites of various kinds (political élites may also be found at the top of the economy) employing knowledge élites for purposes different than those of the latter. It remains to examine the inner structure of the knowledge élite.

THE KNOWLEDGE ÉLITE: INNER STRUCTURE AND PROCESS

The gradual decomposition of a unitary world view has had as its vehicle the development of a stratified, if only loosely coherent, sector of society specializing in the acquisition, production, and distribution of knowledge.[21] I use these terms in full awareness of their obvious imperfections: qualitative differences in the types of knowledge at issue render an economic model of knowledge activities questionable—but the very defects of the model may eventually illuminate the theme.

The medieval church and the medieval university promulgated a unitary world view, but even in medieval society, heresies and specialized groupings provided for considerable internal conflict and variety in the stuff and social consequences of knowledge. Theological disputation was often a symbolic mode of political conflict; heresies were modalities of total social dissent; the language of permitted discourse in the universities allowed an enormous range of intellectual

21. The literature is, again, considerable. See Lewis Coser, *Men of Ideas* (New York, 1965), for an excellent treatment of the evolution of this development. See also, Louis Bodin, *Les Intellectuels* (Paris: P.U.F., 1962), Frederic Bon and Michel-Antoine Burnier, *Les Nouveaux Intellectuels* (Paris: Cujas, 1966), and Philip Rieff, editor, *On Intellectuals* (New York: Doubleday, 1969).

conflict. It is familiar enough to conceive of the Protestant Reformation as a spiritual expression of changes in European society which heightened the power and self-consciousness of the bourgeoisie. It is no less important to see in it a consequence of the bitter and entirely theoretic controversy between realists and nominalists which had shaken the world of learning. The Reformers, in their attack on the idea of the Church as an institution constituted by Grace, drew the ecclesiastical consequences of the nominalist attack on metaphysical ideas of indwelling qualities in objects.

The Reformation continued a process of the gradual emancipation of the mind from strict theological control which had, indeed, begun in the medieval universities themselves. The great triumphs of the seventeenth century in the study of nature occurred partly inside, partly outside, conventional academic institutions. Academies and societies developed to take up the burden of thought, and depended for support and energy on the beginnings of what we should think of as an educated public.[22] This was composed of gentry, courtiers, civil servants, professionals, and merchants. At the same time, an inverse movement began the formation of those circles and coteries we know of today as "the intellectuals," groups sharing an esoteric set of cultural concerns—united, often enough, with the bourgeoisie socially but differing from them in their single-minded concentration on problems of culture. Upon examination, the rise of a public depended upon a contrapuntal movement: the emergence of a set of intellectuals to supply the public with ideas, whether for immediate social consumption in daily life or for entertainment. This last, upon examination, was often another

---

22. Jürgen Habermas, *Strukturwandel der Öffentlichkeit* (Neuwied: Luchterhand, 1962). Christopher Hill, *The Intellectual Origins of the English Revolution* (Oxford: Clarendon, 1965). Daniel Mornet, *Les Origines Intellectuelles de la Révolution Française* (Paris: Colin, 1933). Ian Watt, *The Rise of the Novel* (Berkeley: California, 1957).

form of social consumption: everything we know about the sociology of aesthetic experience points in this direction.

At the same time, others in possession of knowledge crystallized into professional groupings—vending specialized services to the public, or rather to clients, at a price. Lawyers and notaries, doctors and architects, began that process of specialization which links important aspects of contemporary intellectual activity to the work and practices of the medieval guilds. Yet others employed their knowledge in the state service, and subsequently, in the employ of new bureaucracies in the private sector. With these developments, the lineaments of the modern situation of knowledge were consolidated.

The contemporary diffusion of knowledge may be thought of as addressed to three groups. A generalizing set of intellectuals speak to a public or—given the fragmentation of modern society—to increasingly specialized publics. The very notion of a public, however, carries a connotation of generality. Intellectuals dealing with the public conceptualize general issues: the social role of intellectuals as critics, as the conscience of societies, often reflects a moral task which in an increasingly specialized and bureaucratized society, falls to them by default. Recent adumbrations of the decline of the intellectuals are also expressions of regret about the attenuation or extirpation of viable notions of a public good.[23]

Yet others work for clients. The enormous recent increase in professional services has been accompanied by monopolistic or oligopolistic phenomena among knowers, attempts by promulgating standards of professionalization to attain or retain a privileged market and social position. Perceptibly, however, the professional diffusion of knowledge has been joined to another type, which we may term bureaucratic. The state and the private sector require expertise: this may

23. Christopher Lasch, *The New Radicalism in America* (New York: Knopf, 1965). Karl Markus Michel, *Die Sprachlose Intelligenz* (Frankfurt: Suhrkamp, 1968).

be acquired in two ways—either by purchasing on limited time contracts the services of professionals, or by the direct employment of knowers (in whatever fields) in the framework of daily bureaucratic operations.

These operations surely now consume most of what we may think of as intellectual production. Bureaucracies not alone employ knowers, they employ those who know where to find knowers. The characteristic of the bureaucratic utilization of knowledge is its remoteness from direct public control, from immediate inspection by those (frequently, the intellectuals) responsible for the critique of knowledge and its uses. Bureaucratic knowledge is not arcane in its origins, but may well be so in its utilization. Whether the process of filterage, by which knowledge is passed upward in a bureaucratic hierarchy for political decision, results in a crudification of it, is an open question. Much of what knowers think of as crudification may be, instead, a selective utilization by bureaucrats—who frequently can take only that knowledge consonant with their political ends.[24]

Limits on the communicability and communication of knowledge must now concern us. One of these is set by the esoteric or specialized nature of the knowledge itself. Another is set by the social organization of the process of communication, by prior rights to knowledge—either formally, in a legal sense, or effectively by virtue of differential access —exercised to keep it arcane. One of the paradoxes of what has been termed a knowledge-based society is how much of the communication of knowledge falls to specialized agencies and channels outside any general social control or visibility.

We may, for the sake of convenience, categorize the channels of communication as (1) communication among know-

24. Good instances of the present state of the discussion on bureaucracy are the politically contrasting texts of Michel Crozier, *The Bureaucratic Phenomenon* (Chicago: Chicago, 1964), and Theodore Lowi, *The End of Liberalism* (New York: Norton, 1969).

ers, (2) communication to users, (3) communication to the
public, taken in a general sense. It may be hypothesized that
these communications occur in decreasing order of fre-
quency. Of more importance, however, is precisely what is
communicated. Let us distinguish (1) abstract knowledge,
(2) applied knowledge, (3) aesthetic or moral knowledge. It
will be seen that these seem to correlate with the three channels of communication. What follows for our general discussion?

The fragmentation of the types of knowledge gives us yet
another indication of the dubiousness of claims about the
existence of a knowledge élite which rules by virtue of its
knowledge. Abstract knowledge is communicated among and
between specialists, who may indeed hardly speak the same
language across the borders of the several fields. Applied
knowledge is communicated by specialist knowers to those
able and willing—distinct considerations—to put it into
effect. Moral and aesthetic knowledge, which might generate
judgments as to the application of abstract knowledge, is communicated to a general public—or to a fraction of it—not
necessarily close to the centers of decision about the application of knowledge of an abstract kind. We may now turn to
the problem of the institutionalization of reason.

THE INSTITUTIONALIZATION OF REASON

A politics which treats the polity as a device for the allocation
of desired objects is a parody of the market economy. It also
represents a degradation of political thought, which in a
tradition not quite yet dead has treated of the public good.
The social philosophical (and later sociological) discussion
of the institutionalization of reason is a derivative of political
philosophy. The reason men have sought to integrate (or
master) in state and society is not simply accumulated intelligence or codified knowledge. It is, rather, these last at-

tached to a determinate notion of the public good, a conception of reason as regulated by a social morality itself subject to a perpetual critique by reason.

The fragmentation and differentiation of modern societies has led to opposing ideas of the institutionalization of reason. The liberal tradition located reason in the individual mind, in the citizen. A variant of this doctrine (for obvious reasons, highly developed in America) placed it in groups of citizens, giving us a pluralistic liberalism. In either case, reason born by individuals or groups could determine the shape of the polity, as a vector of their negotiations. There was, in other words, no social reason. Conservativism envisaged conflicts as un-negotiable, as irreconcilable. Reason consisted, therefore, in the insight into the essential arationality of politics: Weber's doctrine, in this respect, has been depicted as leading to authoritarianism.[25] Reason, briefly, could be imposed upon society—but never could emerge from it. Marx, following Hegel (and before him, Aristotle), saw society as potentially rational—on the condition that it synthesized the individual's highest needs with a conception of self and activity consonant with, indeed constitutive of, community. The Marxist doctrine of ideology, as found in the original texts, does not simply oppose a true image of the world to false ones, much less speak of a competing series of world images.[26] Rather, the pre-condition for the elimination of ideology is the attainment by men of a true version of their highest selves, the actualization of what had previously been only a potential. Reason, on this view, was historical reason—the institutions which would realize human capacity.

It is clear that this extremely brief excursus has dealt with

25. See the extremely vigorous discussion at the German Sociological Association's 1964 observance of the centenary of Max Weber's birth: Stammer, *op cit.*
26. George Lichtheim, *The Concept of Ideology and Other Essays* (New York: Random House, 1968).

reason as a quality expressive not of mind alone, in the cognitive sense, but of spirit, in a meaning compounded of psychological and social existence. Reason in this interpretation has, or could have, a behavioral significance: it means the right mode of conduct. Is this impossibly remote from our concern with the social uses of knowledge, the institutionalization of reason? Obviously, I have dealt in summary fashion with reason as codified knowledge, reason as moral and aesthetic reflection on man and society, reason as providing models of behavior. The inter-relation of factual and evaluative judgments, the differences in the structure of knowledge among and between the fields of learning, the modes in which these can and do influence behavior: all are involved in the question of the institutionalization of reason. I have preferred to indicate difficult problems where the scope of the essay does not permit efforts to solve these—the better to situate the initial problem.

Suppose, to give the discussion a bit more precision, we distinguish between knowledge-generating and knowledge-using institutions, and add to this enumeration a set of publics and persons applying knowledge in their daily contexts. As highly organized as the system is, we find no institutions charged with allocating different uses to different sorts of knowledge in the light of some general calculus of the public good. We do find, to be sure, certain implicit calculi in the allocation of funds for education and scholarship (under the general rubric, science policy). We find calculi in the allocation of resources, insofar as one is made, for a national research and development effort. In the latter two cases, however, society as a whole purchases knowledge in certain categories. It is not quite a blind market mechanism, but it is far from a situation of a purposeful social decision on the application of knowledge to specific social processes. No blind market mechanism may be at work directly in science policy and research and development, but we may certainly say that market mechanisms set the context for social decision in these cases, as the most effective component in the formation of choice by those powerful enough to exercise it.

We find ourselves at an earlier theme. There is no principle or mechanism of cultural stratification in our societies which is superior to political stratification. Moreover, the stratification of culture is consonant—although not perfectly so—with the organization of power in modern society. Those aspects of cultural complexity which lead to hierarchies in the organization of knowledge, indeed, often facilitate the working of the political system. Knowledge élites, by their very existence, are visible and available for integration with, and subordination to, political élites. These élites may act in the name of the social whole, but the social reason they represent is at best partial, at worst (the usual case) a self-serving distortion. The institutionalization of reason, insofar as it has occurred in our societies, appears to be the work of a technocratic élite using reason for its own purposes.[27]

Does the intellectual division of labor preclude the development of a social reason of the sort (however dimly) apprehended by Marx? If so, the use of reason by enlightened technocracy appears to be the most we may hope for—if for no other reason than promising the most reasonable possible organization of a fundamentally arational society. The imposition of order on society by a technocracy—whether by the direct exercise of political commands or by the manipulation of social processes—is indeed a late version of an ancient conservative tradition. Conservative doctrines, usually, have a good deal of empirical utility: they describe a reality whose existence it is pointless to deny. Their historical durability,

27. The literature on technocracy grows daily. Good introductions will be found, in addition to works cited above, in Viktor Ferkiss, *Technological Man* (New York. Brazillier, 1969), André Gorz, *Réforme et Révolution* (Paris: Seuil, 1969), and Claus Koch and Dieter Senghaas, editors, *Texte zur Technokratie-Diskussion* (Frankfurt: Europäische Verlagsanstalt, 1970).

however, is often matched by a certain foreshortening of perspective. By insisting on perennial aspects of social reality, they not infrequently obscure our vision of the possibilities intrinsic to the movement of history. The question about a contemporary technocracy, then, is not alone its existence and mode of function—but whether it may be replaced by other institutions capable of mobilizing knowledge.

Technocratic rule, in a customary model of it derived from Saint-Simon, has a number of elements. The technocrats enjoy a virtual monopoly of knowledge. Insofar as they obtain knowledge from pure scientists, they (the technocrats) function as immovable gatekeepers: pure knowledge can be applied only through their intervention and assent. Their decisions are opaque, at times invisible, to subject populations. These strike a bargain with the technocrats, legitimating their reign in return for some participation in its benefits—income and order. Legitimation does not rest upon performance alone, however, but upon the population's insight into the necessity of rule by those with knowledge—a limited attribution of the characteristics of a citizenry to those who otherwise remain subjects.

The propositions at issue require examination. The technocrats do not seem to be identical with scientists, since they are concerned with the application of knowledge rather than its acquisition. Whatever concrete political goals or long-term programs may attach to their decisions—these seem to be taken on criteria other than those derived directly from knowledge. Brifly, there are no technocratic criteria for political decisions, only political ones, having to do with the maintenance or alteration of the balance of power in society. That, in the circumstances, technocrats invariably take decisions which will maintain or maximize their power is not surprising: what is surprising is that the claims by which they seek to justify this should be widely believed. Technocratic rule may entail new modes—especially manipulative ones—of exercising power: it does not constitute a qualitative alteration of the fact of domination.

Current mechanisms for the institutionalization of reason will be found in the relationships of the knowledge élite (or élites) to those who mobilize and utilize their knowledge. The predominantly bureaucratic form for the organization of vendable knowledge facilitates these relationships: knowledge bureaucrats trade with their counterparts, really their superiors, in other hierarchies. The higher we mount in organized systems for the acquisition of knowledge, the more we depart from the study, the laboratory, the library, the experimental or empirical field of inquiry.[28] At the heights, we meet persons who have, of course, careers at these levels behind them, but their present function lies precisely in the co-ordination and command of the dispersed activities of their colleagues. The qualitative differences which mark the acquisition of knowledge, by contrast with the production of goods and services in other bureaucratic settings, renders delicate the activity of co-ordination and command. Delicacy, however, does not quite conceal its omnipresence. It is striking that those activities which call for a (relative) minimum of facilities are those which are ostensibly most free of bureaucratic command: inquiry in the humanities and the artisanal sectors of the social sciences. If we look more closely, however, we note that a molecular biologist may require more expensive facilities than a historian or a moral philosopher, but that he is as independent in his work of direct commands as his colleagues. The bureaucrats at the top of knowledge hierarchies, therefore, have the difficult task of rewarding (on behalf of the larger society) performances they cannot directly control. This has often led to adumbrations of the democratic or egalitarian status of intellectual activity,

28. Alvin Weinberg, *Reflections on Big Science* (Cambridge: Technology Press, 1967). Harriet Zuckerman, "Stratification in American Science," *Sociological Inquiry*, Vol. 40, No. 2, 1970.

when this is viewed as performed in a relatively closed community.[29] Perhaps this is a potential point of conflict with a larger society ordered in terms of other types of relationship. It is equally true that the knowledge hierarchs negotiate or buy protection for knowledge communities by minimizing conflict and maximizing what has been termed "service."

We are back, or very nearly so, to the student movement's critique of the university as hopelessly bureaucratized, as a modern factory. The analogy does not quite hold. Students are not productive workers but, if the imagery is useful, trainees—higher students are apprentices. The manpower recruiting and channeling functions of the higher educational system, on the other hand, are obvious. These have become especially important with the change in the composition of the labor force, and the consequent predominance of white-collar posts. The universities are the training sites for the technical intelligentsia. The training they receive is a curious and ambiguous fusion of traditional induction into a high culture and utilitarian preparation for specialized tasks. Not the least of the sources of the crisis of the universities is this duality—to which is added the burden of the universities having to add simultaneously to our accumulation of pure knowledge and to supply useful knowledge to the society's agencies of power.

Spirits are divided over the question of whether the universities have ever served as a source of social criticism, have ever generated those utopias which have infused new models of society. This has occurred, from time to time, but we may also note that much critical and utopian thinking has taken place outside the formal realm of the academy. We can point to a contradiction which may affect the politics of the knowledge élite. The society requires trained personnel. There is

29. Edward Shils, *The Torment of Secrecy* (New York: Free Press, 1956), and in particular the excerpt reprinted in Bernard Barber and Walter Hirsch, editors, *The Sociology of Science* (New York: Free Press, 1962).

no way to train these, however, given the rapid obsolescence of the knowledge which can be imparted in universities, than by giving students a general education. Teaching them to think in conceptual or abstract terms, however useful as a preparation for their eventual mastery of the changing occupational tasks which will confront them, may well awaken their critical faculties. Once awakened, these may be directed against the institutions of the society—or at the least, probe its weaknesses in a way damaging to the élites in control of it. Fragmented reason, in other words, may be institutionalized; it may also have an immanent tendency to make itself whole again.

PERSPECTIVES ON THE FUTURE

Reason's tendency to make itself whole may be termed immanent, but men are the bearers of reason. They are also assigned by society to roles which limit their perspectives, shape or suppress their hopes, canalize their energies.[30] The fragmentation of reason is not alone a consequence of the cumulative and quantitative development of knowledge, but of its social organization. Specialized knowledge is assimilable by the society; general knowledge may be subjected to discipline only with difficulty.

Previous epochs limited access to knowledge on the basis of society's organization for the reproduction of privilege. The diffusion of learning, in one or another form, attendant upon the stage of total bureaucratization reached by the industrial administrative and productive apparatus now may have had consequences unanticipated by those who planned educational expansion. An educated public may demand a

30. The classical references are not out of place. As well as Mannheim, however (*Ideology and Utopia,* translated by Edward Shils and Louis Wirth [New York: Harcourt, Brace, 1936]), see Max Scheler, *Die Wissensformen und die Gesellschaft* (Leipzig: Neuer Geist, 1926).

modification of bureaucratic organization, a share in its administration. The incapacity of the uneducated, the immersion in routine of those with education, were formerly defenses against this intrinsic critique of power. The highly educated, additionally, have generally been given enough rewards to be able to appreciate the necessities of a power from which they profited, if in which they did not share.

We here encounter a paradox. The modern form of alienation may reside, not least, in the division of cultural labor, in the fragmentation of such reason as the society possesses, in the blockage of its capacity to mobilize reason for total social ends. Yet those who have been least alienated, who have had the most knowledge, have lent themselves not infrequently to the consolidation of this state of affairs. Moreover, those without knowledge have either denied its value, or focused on its instrumental or most obviously utilitarian aspects: envious of others' ability to use it as an instrument of domination, and unable to envisage it as a means of liberation.

The spread of knowledge may increase, under present circumstances, the demand that knowledge be converted into a social reason. The spread of knowledge, its diffusion to strata hitherto untouched by it (and their consequent transformation) is not, however, identical with the diffusion or distribution of power. It may be a pre-condition of it, particularly if the newly educated gain some insight into the modes in which knowledge has been used for social domination. That insight will have to consist, for the moment, in the ambiguous and not entirely heartening conclusion that the historical process of rationalization can be mastered by élites more easily than it can be democratized. There seems to be no area or sector of knowledge entirely immune to exploitation for the purposes of power—and critical moral and social reflection, rare enough, is not all that difficult to encapsulate and neutralize.

We may take some consolation from one aspect of the functioning of the knowledge élite itself. Integrated with other élites, or subordinate to these, it may be. The condition of its usefulness, however, is that it continue to produce knowledge—and the conditions of this escape the control or specification, to some extent, of other élites. One of these is the predominance of the capacity for inter-subjective judgments, the intellectual egalitarianism of the community of knowers. Out of their own social existence, the knowers may draw a moral model applicable to wider areas of society—or so succumb to spiritual exploitation that their own community disintegrates. It is in the face of threats like these that moral heroism sometimes develops: we should be well served if our own knowledge élite could be induced by its spiritually precarious position to engage in systematic moral reflection.

Name Index

442

Name Index

Name Index

Levi-Strauss, C., 4–5, 17, 30–31, 53, 125–26
Lewis, R., 293 n
Ley, R., 146 n
Lichtheim, G., 320 n, 342 n, 418, 419 n, 433 n
Lincoln, A., 370
Lipset, S. M., 36, 193–94, 342 n
Little, F., 146 n, 155 n
Lockwood, D., 36
Loewenthal, R., 25
Lortz, J., 133 n
Lovejoy, A., 83
Low, D., 73
Lowi, T., 431 n
Löwith, K., 117
Lukács, G., 7, 9, 27, 33, 98, 115, 117, 166, 235, 345, 347–50, 419
Lukács, J., 173
Luther, M., 21, 134, 143–46, 148, 156, 160 n
Lutz, B., 222
Lynd, R., 39
Lynd, S., 278 n

Maccoby, M., 278 n
MacDonald, D., 262 n
MacGregor, O. H., 281 n
Machiavelli, N., 11
MacInness, C., 336 n
MacKenzie, N., 292 n
MacLeod, I., 286 n
Machlup, F., 420 n
Macmillan, H., 332
MacRae, D. G., 281 n
Magdoff, H., 368
Makarios, Archbishop, 334
Maliniak, J., 138 n
Malinowski, B., 207
Mallet, S., 368
Mandel, E., 368
Mander, J., 335 n
Mannheim, K., 4, 10, 18, 28, 53, 98, 117, 188, 207–8, 439 n
Manson, C., 246
Manual, F., 422 n
Mao Tse-tung, 43, 409
Marcuse, H., 13, 117, 119, 362, 365
Marr, N. Y., 46
Marsden, D., 300 n

Marx, K., 6, 8, 9, 28, 40, 83, 87–88, 90, 98, 101–2, 109, 112, 114, 117, 119–21, 123, 164, 166, 170, 172, 176, 191–92, 195–96, 199, 201, 205, 210, 212, 217, 221–22, 264, 278 n, 346, 350–54, 364–70, 385, 397, 410, 422–23, 433, 435
Maschler, T., 335 n
Maude, A., 293 n
Mauss, M., 16, 32, 40
McCallum, R. B., 288 n
McCarthy, E., 395
McKenzie, R. T., 303 n
McLuhan, M., 407–8
McNamara, R., 170
McNeil, J., 134 n
Mead, G. H., 222, 408
Mead, M., 15, 20
Meillet, A., 16–17
Melbourne, Lord, 65
Merleau-Ponty, M., 23
Merton, R., 21, 25–26, 216
Meyer, P., 146 n, 156 n, 158 n
Mill, J. S., 83, 98, 208, 216, 217 n, 218 n, 278 n, 422
Millar, J., 207, 217
Miller, D., 21
Miller, S. M., 228 n, 368, 374
Mills, C. W., 13, 36, 39–40, 202–3, 222, 276, 323, 367, 376, 386
Mitrani, N., 37
Molnar, E., 187, 194, 196
Moore, B., 368
Morin, E., 226 n
Mornet, D., 429 n
Moser, C. A., 281 n
Mosley, O., 334
Mounier, E., 76
Mowat, C. L., 279 n
Moynihan, D. P., 227 n, 228 n, 229 n
Mozart, W. A., 166
Muhamed, E., 208
Murdock, I., 336

Nabholz, H., 156 n
Naess, A., 33
Nagel, J., 417 n
Nagy, I., 200
Napoleon I, 426
Napoleon III, 367
Nathan the Prophet, 72

Subject Index

448

Subject Index

Technical intelligentsia, 41–42, 102–3, 357, 416–41
  in America, 375 ff.
Technocracy, 243–44, 379 ff., 402–5, 416–41
Third World, 106–8
Totalitarianism, 260–61
"Two cultures," 421 ff.

Universities, 411 ff., 416–41
  British, 201–13

Universities and Left Review, 322 ff.

Welfare State
  American, 383 ff.
  British, 207–8, 286, 288
Work, 120–21

Youth, 387 ff., 409 ff.
Youth-culture, 360–66

Zürich, 133–61